Politics in Western European Democracies: Patterns and Problems

Politics in Western European Democracies: Patterns and Problems

GARY C. BYRNE
San Diego State College

KENNETH S. PEDERSEN
San Diego State College

JOHN WILEY & SONS, INC.
New York   London   Sydney   Toronto

Library of Congress Catalog Card Number: 77-162421
ISBN 0-471-12900-3 (Cloth)   ISBN 0-471-12901-1 (Paper)

Printed in the United States of America

10   9   8   7   6   5   4   3   2   1

Preface

In the field of comparative politics much of the postwar period has been a time of infatuation with the so-called developing or nonwestern areas. While individual scholars continued their inquiries into the political problems and processes of the Western European nations, their contributions were frequently overshadowed by the encompassing concern given to what were once regions of peripheral interest to the discipline.

There are, however, indications that a growing number of political scientists are again turning their attentions to the political life of Western Europe. The result has been the production of a number of high quality articles and books.

We have attempted in this volume to bring together the best of these scholarly contributions. As with all endeavors of this sort, some limitations proved necessary. Thus, we have chosen to concentrate on the "big four" democracies of Western Europe: Great Britain, France, West Germany, and Italy. We have rejected, in other words, the scatter-gun approach, which all too frequently permits the objective of including a piece on each country, no matter how small or peripheral, to get in the way of concerns for quality or coherency. In our view, whatever sacrifices in comprehensiveness are entailed in our approach are more than compensated for by the gains in depth and direction.

The selected pieces focus on the general problem of balancing stability and change. They are organized in such a way that the student is systematically exposed to the competing forces at work in Western Europe as the nations of that area seek to adapt time-honored political forms to a host of new demands and challenges.

We are particularly grateful to Nekita Hobson and Veva Link for their assistance at every stage of this project.

Gary C. Byrne
Kenneth S. Pedersen

June, 1971

Contents

Politics in Western European Democracies: Patterns and Problems

Western Europe in Transition

It is an acknowledged fact that social change is a constant feature of human existence. At the same time, it is clear that some historical periods are marked by great stability in values and institutions while others are characterized by flurries of restructuring activity. Insofar as Western Europe is concerned, benchmarks such as the Renaissance, the Reformation, and the Industrial Revolution appear as eras when traditional social formulations were successfully challenged by forces aimed at fundamental modification of the status quo. Whatever the stimuli may be that cause such times of dynamic confrontation, they are unquestionably periods of particular interest to the student.

The organizational focus for this volume is provided by the belief that much of Western Europe is today caught up in an important moment of transition. Behind it is a long and often glorious history of world leadership. Within the confines of the continent are countries whose dominions, a few decades ago, extended around the globe and whose wealth and influence placed them at the cutting edge of Western Civilization's advance. It is understandable that the years spent at the summit of international supremacy fostered in the minds of many Europeans a sense of superiority directed not only at themselves but toward the institutions and practices associated with their dominant status.

1

This self-assurance was shaken by the interwar collapse of the world's economy and by the German and Italian experiments with dictatorial rule—events that touched off speculation concerning the enduring validity of prevailing socioeconomic practices and shattered the sanguine faith of Europeans in their own political sophistication. The Second World War, which left all the major continental nations razed and broken, was one of those historical turning points which signal the certain end of one era and usher in periods of introspection and adjustment.

For Britain, France, and Germany, accommodation with the postwar world meant accepting the unfamiliar status of second-rank powers. The final orgy of internecine conflict had momentarily depleted their resources and energies, allowing the political and economic initiative to pass westward across the Atlantic into the domain of their American ally. Western Europe's demotion from pacesetter status to a more subordinate, emulative role has been accompanied by the inevitable efforts at self-examination and prescription. As is common to periods of transformation, the diagnoses are varied and incorporate a broad range of emotions. Thus the author of one recent work writes of the "surrender" of Europe to American colonization;[1] J.-J. Servan-Schreiber sees "Europe in Confusion";[2] others speak of a "New Europe";[3] and Carl J. Friedrich asks whether Europe is not "an emergent nation?"[4]

In his article, which is included in Section I, Stanley Hoffmann suggests the current restiveness resembles the repercussions of an "identity crisis." Professor Hoffmann employs the phrase "between the past and America" to describe and explain Western Europe's state of indetermination. On one hand, the leaders of the major continental nations are keenly aware of their debt to and continued reliance upon American contributions and leadership. Moreover, the citizens of Western Europe are drawn toward the manifold material and social benefits associated with the mass-consumption-based postindustrial age, whose symbol and pattern is the United States. At the same time, there is a reluctance, slightly noticeable in some instances but strongly marked in others, to acknowledge American pre-eminence and to relinquish familiar and indigenous facets of European existence. The vested interests of well-entrenched groups combine with the resistance of custom to produce an apprehensiveness toward change. The result is an ambiguity of character and purpose, punctuated by charges of foot-dragging and denunciations of the Continent's capitulation to "Americanization."

The reliance on such shorthand expressions as "Americanization" or "Old Europe vs. New Europe" should not be allowed to obscure the complexity of the situation. The conflict between tradition and change involves engagements on a number of fronts. At a minimum, the final shape of the Western Europeans' efforts to cope with their general task of identity building will be determined by the manner in which the following subconflicts are resolved:

(1) The struggle between a social order characterized by stratification, privilege, and restricted mobility and a more fluid order of expanded access and increased opportunities for upward (and downward) movement.

(2) The conflict between historically divisive ideological politics, epitomized by the activities of dogmatic, inflexible political parties, and a pattern characterized by a moderate, pragmatic political style.

(3) An uncertainty regarding the form that basic decision-making processes should assume. Advocates of classical parliamentary liberalism vie with proponents of experiments in "heroic leadership" and both confront tendencies toward bureaucratized systems of planned and directed policy formulation.

(4) The confrontation between the generalist-humanist orientations of many European elites and the challenges loosed in an era fascinated and captivated by the fruits of corporate technology.

(5) The clash between the enduring concern with national perspectives and benefits and attempts to promote transnational and supernational solutions to Western European needs.

These problems, then, are the nuclei around which the reading selections are grouped, and these are the problems which pose the central issues to which the selections respond.

The excerpt from Daniel Lerner and Morton Gorden's work and the article by Stanley Hoffmann are stage-setting pieces. The two selections sketch in broad, insightful strokes the array of forces that have converged on postwar Western Europe and tell something of the efforts by the Continental nations to evolve self-images and practices which are both comfortable and timely.

Lerner and Gorden focus their attention on the shifting attitudes of Western Europeans toward the various features of "Americanization." They speak of a series of phases. Thus an initial period of anxiety was supplanted by a period of acceptance. This has been followed by a phase of ambivalence when the pull of new aspirations is in active competition with the hold of old constraints. This latter condition sounds much like the one that inspired Hoffmann's "between the past and America" formulation.

For his part, Hoffmann decries both the nondiscriminatory, helter-skelter adoption of American practices by Europeans and the retreat to anti-Americanism that he brands as "merely an evasion of Europe's own responsibilities." Arguing that the nations of Europe are captives neither of their past nor of the American syndrome, Hoffmann calls for an effort on the part of awakened Europeans to create a new profile that blends the best of the past with the promise of a democratic and industrial age. It is a demanding challenge and a fitting note on which to launch an investigation into the ideas and issues that currently engulf Western Europe and make it a fascinating subject for study.

FOOTNOTES

1.   John Ney, *The European Surrender: A Descriptive Study of the American Social and Economic Conquest* (Boston: Little, Brown and Company, 1970).

2.   J.-J. Servan-Schreiber, *The American Challenge* (New York: Atheneum, 1968).

3.   See, for example, the essays in Stephen R. Graubard, ed., *A New Europe?* (Boston: Houghton Mifflin, 1964).

4.   Carl J. Friedrich, *Europe: An Emergent Nation?* (New York: Harper and Row, 1969).

1

DANIEL LERNER and MORTON GORDEN

Europa and Atlantica: The American Nexus

"Americanization" is an epithet that evokes strong feelings in the contemporary world. It indicates a widespread anxiety among peoples living in societies that have not achieved the unique adaptive capacity of the United States, the capacity to absorb innovation routinely and to maintain dynamic equilibrium. These peoples are concerned about their own society's absorptive capacity: Can it really incorporate the bewildering diversity of American perspectives and practices? They also are worried about the American impact on personal and conventional morality: Are American ways feasible ways, or even proper ways, for themselves—and especially for their children? Despite their anxieties, however, people everywhere perceive that American lifeways are penetrating and pervading their traditional ways of thinking and acting.

Nowhere has the concern over "Americanization" been more acute than in the relatively diminished nations of postwar Europe. And nowhere in Europe has the anxiety about America's "cultural imperialism" been more poignantly articulated, or more transparently fearful, than in France. There is a long tradition of French ambivalence—of admiration transfused with anxiety, of awesome envy—going back over a century to Tocqueville's classic analysis of the American democracy.

Its modern French expression was formulated in the aftermath of World War I by André Siegfried, revered scholar of the *Académie Française,* who wrote: "The United States is presiding at a general reorganization of the ways of living throughout the entire world." This prescient perception of "Americanization" as a global process was shared by other European intellectuals observing the collapse of their dynastic monarchies at home and the disruption of their colonial empires around the world. Everywhere the impact of the American Model—its lifeways as well as its ideas of the Good Life—was great and growing. But it was in the highly developed countries of Europe, with their larger capacity for absorption and adaptation, that "Americanization" proceeded fastest and furthest. While the smart set of Cairo were learning to smoke Lucky Strikes, the Europeans of London-Paris-Berlin were teaching their provincial compatriots to absorb and adapt jazz, to experiment with mass production, and to demand direct universal suffrage.

By the same token, European observers of the "Americanization" process were the first to interpret its inexorable impact upon their familiar world—often admiring its promise for their democracy, often deploring its vulgarization of their culture, only occasionally (since Tocqueville) penetrating to the source of America's special potency for promoting multifarious goods and ills. This deeper source was thematized in the peculiarly American commitment to the "pursuit of happiness"—the right of Everyman to the richest and fullest life he could win for himself. When wedded to the political ideas of respect for "life, liberty, equality, fraternity" (which America shared with France and other democratizing Western societies over the past two centuries), the "pursuit of happiness" augured a social revolution of unprecedented dimensions. Its myth became known in more recent decades as The American Dream—an inspiring dream for some Europeans and for others a nightmare.[1]

It remained for an American sociologist, Daniel Bell, to identify the psychosocial source of Europe's acute postwar *malaise* about "Americanization" in the *equalization* of Everyman's expectations and demands from the pursuit of happiness. With modesty and delicious irony, Bell formulated a "Tocqueville's Law" capable of universal application in postwar Europe as earlier in prewar America: "In a society pledged to the idea of equality, what the few have today, the many will demand tomorrow." Perceptive Europeans have, as we shall see in the last section of this chapter, formed a just—if often reluctant— appreciation of this aphorism. "Americanization," now conjoined with the existential superpower of America, is recognized as the common condition for the two major options through which postwar Europeans seek to build the good life. These options, which are the central subject of this book, we designate as Europa and Atlantica. We postulate that recognition of America's crucial role in the achievement of either or both of these presumably compatible goals—European integration and Atlantic partnership—has permeated the thinking of enlightened Europeans.

To gauge the psychic distance many Europeans have traveled to reach this perspective, and to appreciate the continuing appeal of such political counter-formations as Poujadism, Gaullism, Little Englandism, it is useful to sort out the attitudinal components of European ambivalence toward "Americanization." We examine first the sources of fearfulness among the European elites, both in their perception of American lifeways and their projection of these lifeways in their own countries. We then conclude with a summary evaluation of European-American relations in the present phase of acceptance.

THE PHASE OF ANXIETY

Traditional ambivalence about America has been heightened in postwar Europe by its dependence upon American superpower. The acute and utter dependence of the first postwar decade, when Europe lay devastated and distraught in a world bipolarized between the dictates of Moscow and Washington, has lessened considerably. By the second postwar decade, which is the historical period covered by this study, most of the West European nations (in the "American camp") had recovered a fair measure of economic prosperity and political equanimity. Relaxation of the Cold War between Russia and America also had loosened the bipolar vise. But Europe's dependence on American power and purpose, though now less extreme and obvious, was no less fundamental to its well-being. It was certain that Europe could not guarantee its own military security and likely that it could not promote its own long-term economic prosperity. Under these conditions, what assurance could there be for political autonomy and stability?

These conditions are defined by the key issues of protection, prosperity, and prestige, which we shall later examine in empirical detail. They represented national needs which, in the majority opinion of European leaders, could no longer be satisfied by national means. Needed were transnational modes of collective action—Europa and Atlantica—that could be achieved only with the active cooperation of America. This became postwar America's "vocation in Europe" and its reciprocal form was postwar Europe's "American vocation."

The interpenetration of collective action required a massive "American presence" in every country of Europe—military and diplomatic establishments, Marshall men and businessmen, supplemented by task forces of technical advisers and research specialists. American people brought with them American ways along with American films, radio, picture magazines, and news media. Fearful Europeans began to speak of the "American invasion"; hostile ones derided America's "Coca-Cola culture" and "bathroom civilization." Among the graffiti on European walls, "Kilroy was here" was replaced by "Yankee go home!"

These were the vocalisms of the politically organized and emotionally overwrought "protesters" of postwar Europe. There was much occasion for anxiety and hostility in their lot, and rich America was a convenient object-symbol for its displacement. But what motivated the more sophisticated and responsible European leaders who are the subject of our study? We trace their anxiety and ambivalence to the fear of three trends that were widely identified in Europe as "Americanization": (1) mass culture; (2) mass consumption; and (3) mass politics.

Each of these, which we describe in this chapter, derives from the common concern of the European elites that their own inherited emblem of equality, activated by the new American "pursuit of happiness," would undermine the foundations upon which European civilization had been built: ". . . what the few have today, the many will demand tomorrow." Considering the scarcity of material resources in postwar Europe, responsible leaders could infer that such an acceleration of popular demand would rapidly outrun the available supply of satisfactions. Unsatisfied demands, spiritual as well as material, would magnify existing frustrations, undermine social equilibrium, and subvert political stability. In general, they feared the disruption caused by an intolerable gap between what people want and what they get. The stimulus of "Americanization," they feared, would produce the scourge of every traditional social order: an excessively imbalanced Want:Get Ratio. As Whitehead put it: "The major advances in civilization are processes that all but wreck the societies in which they occur."

Fear of Mass Culture

The association of mass culture with American society has been sufficiently publicized, in this country and abroad, to need no elaboration here. Our interest is not to argue the pros and cons of mass culture as an American phenomenon but rather to diagnose its alleged role in the "Americanization" of Europe. It is well to note that this discussion has concerned mainly the intelligentsia of the two continents, and to note further that intellectuals historically have occupied a more prestigious and influential place in European than in American society. European intellectuals have had a more important set of vested interests to defend—and for many of them the attack on mass culture has been, at least in part, a defense of those "class interests."

This is not to imply that there has been no genuine issue of intellectual standards and aesthetic judgment. On the contrary, mass culture has produced definite and often deliberate depredations upon the high standards of traditional elite culture. As custodians and beneficiaries of this tradition, European intellectuals have felt themselves threatened by these depredations and increasingly powerless to prevent or remedy them. It was indeed the set of constraints imposed by their tradition of high culture that inhibited European intellectuals from absorbing and adapting the new skills needed to shape and share the great potential of mass culture.

The rapid rise of the mass media, particularly the audiovisual media operated by electronic instruments, is a case in point. Quite a different order and organization of skills is required to produce a television show than a play, opera, or ballet, as television often requires elements of all three traditional forms plus some others. An oral newscast needs different talents than does a printed *feuilleton*. Commercial art, industrial design, and broadcast commercials are simply a different world of cultural experience than the *beaux arts*.

The routinized artists and intellectuals who served and conserved the traditional high culture of Europe had neither the skills nor the talents required by the new media of mass culture. In defense of their own interests, they counterattacked with fine contempt and resonant phrases. As the historically anointed and ego-involved curators of high culture, they proclaimed that mass culture was the beachhead through which would march the menacing armies of mass consumption and mass politics. Their fears were justified, but their warnings fell on deaf ears. For mass consumption and mass politics, it soon became clear, were exactly what the peoples of Europe—just as peoples everywhere in the world—wanted.

Fear of Mass Consumption

In sounding the alarm against mass consumption, European intellectuals were appealing to the bourgeoisie of their own society, the relatively small (by American standards) middle class from which they mainly derived and by whose implicit values they mainly operated. The concern was that the standards and amenities of bourgeois society would be degraded and cheapened by "vulgarization" (the symbolically appropriate term which Europeans use instead of the Americanism "popularization"). Just as mass culture threatened the intelligentsia as intellectual and aesthetic arbiters, so ran the argument, mass consumption threatened the bourgeoisie as arbiters of manners and morals. But the counterattack on mass consumption—as so much else in Europe during the first half of the twentieth century—was too little and too late.

The inexorability of mass consumption and its linkage to the spreading mass media were more quickly and clearly perceived by the elites of the ex-colonial, newly independent "emerging nations" seeking development. While these elites often had acquired their higher education in Europe, it was much easier for them to slough off the routinized habits of European ideas and tastes as they faced the accelerating imbalance in the Want:Get Ratio among the peoples they were to lead into new ways of life. To them Bell's formulation— "what the few have today, the many will demand tomorrow"—was readily apparent and acceptable as a guide to public policy. Thus Sukarno, a charismatic leader of the *tiers monde,* made the essential connection between the spread of mass culture and its sequel in mass consumption and even mass politics:

> The motion picture industry has provided a window on the world, and the colonized nations have looked through that window and have seen the things of which they have been deprived. It is perhaps not generally realized that a refrigerator can be a revolutionary symbol—to a people who have no refrigerators. A motor car owned by a worker in one country can be a symbol of revolt to a people deprived of even the necessities of life. . . . [Hollywood] helped to build up the sense of deprivation of man's birthright, and that sense of deprivation has played a large part in the national revolutions of postwar Asia.

Readers who reflect on Sukarno's words will perceive their relevance to the peoples of postwar Europe. While Lerner's 1950 lectures at the University of Paris were picketed with student placards reading "Coca-Cola Professor, go back to your refrigerator!" villagers in Lorraine were still piling dung heaps at their doors to provide winter fuel and spring fertilizer, and peasant women in Alsace were still pitching hay onto horse-drawn wagons where their husbands sat in the driver's seat. But this centuries-old social order was to change abruptly as Europeans recognized among themselves the Want:Get dictum pronounced by Sukarno: "a refrigerator can be a revolutionary symbol—to a people who have no refrigerators. A motor car owned by a worker in one country can be a symbol of revolt to a people deprived of even the necessities of life. . . ."

Fear of Mass Politics

Just as mass culture stimulated the demand for mass consumption, so both together accelerated the expectation of mass politics. Clearly, when the refrigerators and motor cars portrayed by motion pictures become "revolutionary symbols," then the political life of a society must be deeply involved. The postwar return to "politics as usual" in the great nations of Europe was only a routinized reaction to the pronouncement of international peace. But it soon became apparent to Europe's leaders that republican "politics as usual" was as surely a casualty of World War II as dynastic monarchies had been a casualty of World War I. Willy-nilly, and in one way or another, they had to face the immanence of mass politics.

Recognition was forced upon them in the immediate postwar years by the demand for self-determination among the subject peoples in their colonies and dominions around the world. In 1947, a full year before the Marshall Plan focused attention upon its own domestic growth, Britain symbolized the new political order by declaring the independence of India. Once again, it was among the elites of these emerging nations that perception of a mass political process was most acute. Nasser, among the most durable of the postwar generation of charismatic leaders, stated the case in these terms:

> It is true that most of our people are still illiterate. But politically that counts far less than it did twenty years ago. . . . Radio has changed everything. . . . Today people in the most remote villages hear of what is happening everywhere and form their opinions. Leaders cannot govern as they once did. We live in a new world.

Fear of mass politics was a long-established tradition among European leaders, whom successive generations of Jacobins, *communards,* and anarcho-syndicalists kept in a state of chronic anxiety throughout the nineteenth century. The anxiety became acute between the two world wars, even among the democratic intelligentsia of Europe, as they watched mass politics sweep their countries under the direction of totalitarian ideologues. These totalitarians used the mass media to promise mass consumption in order to enlist mass participation in their political campaigns. None who lived through the 1930's can readily forget the radio oratory of a Hitler, who promised the German people oranges for their children and *Volkswagen* ("Peoples' Autos") for themselves. Intellectuals from every European land sounded the alarm against this version of mass politics. A Russian, Serge Chakotin, exposed its dependence upon mass media propaganda in *The Rape of the Masses* (1940). José Ortega y Gasset, the Spanish republican exiled in France, foresaw the rising demand for mass culture and mass consumption in *The Revolt of the Masses* (1932). Emil Lederer, the German professor exiled from Hitler's Reich, gloomily appraised the future of mass politics in *The State of the Masses* (1967). The interwar era of "coercive ideological movements"—the Bolsheviks, Fascists, Nazis, Falangists who took power; the Vichy, Quisling, and other puppets who were dominated by them—left a strong distaste and distrust of mass politics among the postwar elites of Europe.

Small wonder, then, that even as late as 1956 the European elites we interviewed pronounced a resoundingly negative judgment on the idea of mass participation in the formation of public policy—and especially foreign policy. We asked each of our panels some variant of the question whether "the public should have more influence on foreign policy," prefaced by the rather leading preamble: "Since war and peace concern ordinary people as well as their leaders, would you say that . . . ?" Nevertheless, the elite panels remained firmly opposed—negative responses amounting to about half in France, two thirds in Britain, and three fourths in Germany.

Mass politics, like mass culture and mass consumption, remained intellectually *non grata* to the elites—but behaviorally they were already reshaping the ways of living among the peoples of Europe. "Americanization," upon which the fearful elites projected their anxieties and hostilities, was accelerating at an unprecedented tempo. We turn next to a cursory review of these accelerated changes in the structure of European societies. We consider these changes "structural" in the sense that they modified the behavior of many or most individuals, that they codified new interpersonal modes in institutions which routinize and regulate behavior, and that they altered the international relations of Europeans—elite and mass—*across* as well as *within* countries. . . .

Accelerating Europe: New Questions and Answers

What has happened in France is visible as well in Britain and Germany, and indeed throughout Western Europe. Everywhere the new mobility has unbound European peasants from their native soil (though it comes as a shock to many Americans when they learn that there were many, and still are some, real peasants in postwar Europe). Urbanization has mobilized the regions and urban regions have incorporated the parishes. Men have been liberated from ancient bonds by every form of mobility—notably *job mobility,* an aspect of "Americanization" that has impressed Europeans ever since the perspicacious Karl Marx, a century ago, publicized a letter written home by a young Frenchman who had emigrated to San Francisco in the wake of the gold rush:

> I was firmly convinced that I was fit for nothing but letterpress printing. . . . Once in the midst of this world of adventurers who change their occupation as often as they do their shirt, egad, I did as the others. As mining did not turn out remunerative enough, I left for the town where in succession I became a typographer, slater, plumber, etc. In consequence of thus finding out that I am fit for any sort of work I feel less of a mollusk and more of a man."

Mobility has liberated the women of postwar Europe as well. In traditional European society, woman's primordial role as a sex-object was supplemented mainly by her function as a work-horse (if poor) or a clothes-horse (if rich). Postwar women have acquired a great number of new roles in the professional, clerical, and industrial sectors of the economy. When the women of provincial France "go to town" nowadays, they are garbed in multicolored frocks rather than the black shrouds which over long centuries certified their custodianship of the dead (*culte des morts*).

The mobilization of youth in postwar Europe was sped by the newly available, cheap technology of motorization—whose early seed, the Vespa of Italy, has fertilized multiple progeny of motorbikes and motor scooters in every European land. The modernization of postwar youth is a dazzling exhibition of this phase of acceleration.[2] Although the process was labeled "Americanization" in the early postwar years, when the "zoot-suiters" of this country were paralleled by the "zasus" of France and the "teddy-boys" of Britain, its indigenous sources have since become evident. It was in Britain that the "mods" invented long-haired boys and mini-skirted girls—along with the innovative music so brilliantly exemplified by the Beatles. And it is among French youth, despite De Gaulle's parochial judgment that Britain is not sufficiently European, that these "mod" ways have come to represent *le standing* (a nice example of the *franglais* that Gaullism rejects as anti-liturgical).[3] A Berlin student, recently on trial for throwing a rock at the visiting Shah of Iran, declared himself in terms that would by now sound familiar in virtually every major city of the Western world:

> Teufel, who is pleased that his name means "Devil," eagerly pleads guilty to despising contemporary German society and to practicing nonviolent rebellion against it, particularly with active ridicule.

Although this was reported in a front-page survey by *The New York Times* under the headline "European Youth Is Found Mutinous Against The Establishment," it is noteworthy that The Establishment takes a relatively tolerant, and even sympathetic, view of its mobilized youth—especially in a country where parental authority and disciplined children were long regarded as the cornerstone of the social order.[4]

For it is likely that such exhibitionistic behavior is perceived by the European elites as only a transitory symptom of an accelerated process of social change that is transforming the lifeways of all their peoples. Tolerance by the elites is expressed in active programs to absorb the accelerating changes among youth by adapting traditional institutions to meet their demands. The *Times* survey concludes: "However amorphous younger Europeans may be as a group, they are now regarded by the Governments in power as an important element on the national scene." An instance of the process at work is the accelerated growth of public education in every country of postwar Europe. None has moved more vigorously in this direction than France, where the population of university students has multiplied manyfold in the postwar years. Yet the 1968 winter semester at the Sorbonne began with a massive and violent demonstration because even its greatly expanded (and overcrowded) facilities could accommodate only 130,000 students—whereas 160,000 applicants demanded admission.[5]

This is a deeper and more serious matter for the European elites than the length of boys' hair and girls' skirts. For this phase of acceleration has brought the European economies to a level of unprecedented prosperity and continuing growth. As each country passed through its own "economic miracle," beginning with the German *Wirtschaftswunder* in 1950, its psychocultural traditions and sociopolitical institutions became obsolescent. By the start of the second postwar decade, when our study was initiated, it was apparent to many European leaders that a "cultural gap" of major proportions was already in being. Projected growth rates showed that a comprehensive program of social change had to be activated promptly and accelerated rapidly. For guidance in shaping public policy that would provide new answers to these new questions, European leaders turned from their inherited ideologies to the American Model.

THE PHASE OF ACCEPTANCE

We have seen that Europe moved from a phase of anxiety in the first postwar decade, under the impact of "Americanization," into a phase of accelerated growth. Our survey shows that by 1961, as the visible benefits became apparent midway through the second decade, the European elites entered a phase of acceptance. American tutelage was sought and welcomed. An appreciation of American practices was consolidated which led to an unprecedented acceptance of American policies among the opinion leaders and decision makers of postwar Europe. This entailed a reversal of inherited roles which, as we shall see in the next section, appears to have become a permanent feature of Euratlantic relations. This we call the "American Nexus."

It is essential to observe that while acceptance of the Euratlantic relationship is durable, it is also partial. The reversal of roles, given the postwar acceleration of social change on both sides of the Atlantic, means that Europe and America have bypassed each other in the historical process. The American Model has been only partially incorporated by Europeans—and partial incorporation, as Harold D. Lasswell has shown, is one way of restricting external influence.[6] That part of the American Model which has been most fully absorbed and adapted is its allegedly technological component. Not so the psychocultural and sociopolitical components—nor even, fully, the economic component. The fear of mass consumption, we have seen, interacts among anxious Europeans with the fears of mass culture and mass politics. They have incorporated only slowly and partially the lessons taught by the American Model on the shaping and sharing of all values in a social system that is continuously expanding its scope while accelerating its tempo. This is not surprising when one considers that America has been developing its lifeways for nearly two centuries, while the living generation of European leaders has confronted the contemporary configuration (as represented by the American Model) only over the past two decades.

Rather more surprising to Americans is the reversal of world perspectives entailed by the reversal of world roles in the postwar period. While America has been enlarging its new commitments to every continent of the world, Europe has been retrenching its old imperial commitments by decolonizing its global domains. These role reversals, to which the European elites have been more acutely sensitive than most Americans, have altered traditional American notions of European "sophistication." The matter is well summarized by a scholar who studied the responses of American management personnel to sustained working experience in Europe:

... thoughtful Americans discussing life in Europe sooner or later mention their shock at discovering how provincial in outlook many Europeans are. This is a reversal of old roles. Moved to Europe, where their businesses and outlook tend to be as wide as the Western world, these Americans find well-educated men and women in many capitals who are influential members of an elite, who speak several languages, but who hardly think in terms beyond those of their own social group, much less the continent on which they live or the world beyond. Such Europeans confuse social sophistication with knowledge of the world.

The parochialization of European perspectives was manifest in the attitudes of Europeans not only toward the wider world but even with regard to their own country and continent. This has been apparent, even among the Europeanizers, since the defeat of EDC in the French National Assembly. It was a French parliamentarian who, in that Great Debate, warned his colleagues against merely "raising parochialism to the European scale." The subsequent analysis of this major setback of postwar Europe's effort to enlarge its national perspectives concluded:

> One type of oversimplification that strikes a foreign observer is the French tendency toward explanations that are wholly contained in the universe of internal events.

That strong traces of parochialism still exist in Europe, and not only among the French, is reported by a researcher among scientists of different nationalities at CERN—Europe's international center for nuclear research—and several other transnational science centers. They often complained to him of "a characteristically American tendency to speak of Europe as an entity in places where a European probably would not have done so. If Americans sometimes lose nuance by gazing at the whole forest, Europeans often lose perspective by staring at a few trees. The difference helps to clarify the process of "partial incorporation" whereby postwar Europeans have sought to absorb and adapt the American Model to their own perceived needs.

The American Model: Apprenticeship and Achievement

The perceived needs of postwar Europe may be ranged under three broad heads: protection, prosperity, and prestige. The three P's are a shorthand expression, used for expository convenience, which subsume the major values operative in every modern society organized as a polity. It was to satisfy these needs that postwar Europe, receding from world power, turned for help to the acceding superpower of America. There was great poignancy, of course, in this historic reversal of roles. While America was long decolonized from Europe, Americans in large numbers retained, at the level of popular culture as of high society, a sense of filiopietism toward the European lands of their origin. Such sentiments did not inhibit the even stronger sense that America was superior in every form of power—certainly material and probably moral—to the folks who had been left behind on the Old Continent.

It was with the conviction of beneficent power and purpose, having twice accomplished the rescue of Europe from self-immolation in flames ignited by the incendiary Huns, that America now turned its "know-how" to accomplish the recovery of Europe. These were the men of the Marshall Plan. The success of the Marshall Plan and its sequence of agencies—ECA, OEEC, OECD—are writ large in the conspicuous achievement of European Recovery. Be it noted as well that rarely, if ever, in the annals of proconsulship has role-reversal between great nations been accomplished as rapidly, effectively, and even graciously as by the men of the Marshall Plan.

From Paul Hoffman down, the Marshall Men diffused among Europeans from their headquarters in the Palais Talleyrand a new image of contemporary Americans in action. They supplanted the older stereotypes associated with bohemians self-exiled on the Left Bank or tourists dressed in loud neckties and expensive cameras or the hurly-burly G.I.'s of an improvised civilian army. They provided Europeans of diverse social standing, but particularly those elites and subelites with managerial and operational responsibilities, a vivid example of "know-how" as a behavioral mode rather than a self-congratulatory slogan. The great psychological lesson taught by their example was the reality of goal-oriented effort. The Marshall Men knew what they wanted to do, how to try to find the best available way of doing it, and when to go on to the next task. Europeans absorbed this lesson fast. When the Americans mounted their amazing Berlin Airlift a year or so after the Marshall Men went to work, awed and admiring Europeans readily recognized this as another instance of the "know-how syndrome" in operation.

A second major lesson taught by the Marshall Men was the efficacy of *pluralist task-force institutions.* The Marshall Men included industrialists and bankers, officials and academicians, professional specialists and labor leaders, administrators and publicists. Moreover, these teams from the society where "private enterprise" was alleged to be the official religion were exercising their combined know-how under the blessing of American public policy in behalf of European public welfare. To the compartmentalized sectors of European society, the very existence of such a "multidisciplinary task-force" appeared miraculous. As these radiated out from the Palais Talleyrand to the cities and towns of Europe in task-oriented "productivity teams," their message was writ plain for all to see by their behavior. It was by rapidly absorbing and adapting this message that Europeans recovered and, as productivity took command, prospered.

Europe was "ready" to receive the message and to act on it. Wartime devastation had deprived many millions of the basic needs of life: food, clothing, shelter. Such needs had to be satisfied without delay. Europe was also relatively well-advanced in the techniques of mass production and distribution. In Britain such firms as "The Fifty Shilling Tailors" were experienced in the large-scale merchandising of clothes. Even the finicky French had been prepared by such gastronomic "chain stores" as *Cercle Bleu* and *Nicolas* for the second postwar decade's explosion of *supermarchés* (supermarkets) in the American style and very nearly on the American scale. The German prewar effort to produce motor cars for mass consumption, Hitler's publicized *Volkswagen,* rapidly became a postwar reality. With such breakthroughs into heavy industrial production for mass consumption, the dikes of traditional European economy were rapidly flooded. Not only the fundamental human needs of food and clothing but also the mass production of amenities expected in developed societies were accelerated by Europeans apprenticed to the American modes of industrial production.

Before long Americans conveying advanced technologies to their opposite numbers in Europe noted that their apt apprentices had passed to the stage of independent achievement. Indeed, before much longer, they further noted that the European apprentices had begun to overtake and surpass their American tutors in some advanced sectors of modern technology. The same observer who reported the shockingly "provincial outlook" of many Europeans also evaluated their accelerated technological progress in these terms:

> Before and after World War II, America was known as the land of mass production, the Mecca of advanced tooling and design. This is no longer the case—at least not to the same degree. The Renault assembly line in France is the envy of the industry. Germany's Volkswagen trundles out over one million cars per year from an effective and continuously improving plant. Ignis, the Italian refrigerator manufacturer, has conveyerized production equipment that is modeled from, and an improvement upon, older U.S. systems. An American industrial consultant, recently back from a trip through a number of Italian plants, was dazed to discover that investment-happy engineers were writing off and replacing major items of equipment in three years. There have been changes. The best equipment in Europe today is as good as, or better than, much of the best U.S. equipment.

Partial Incorporation: A Psychosocial Note

This, then, is the current state of the "great leap forward" that China has dreamed of but Europe has accomplished. It was an accelerated leap into the world of modern technology based on a willing acceptance of the American Model. Given the widespread aspiration for prosperity and aptitude for technological change among Europeans, they were able to pass rapidly from apprenticeship to achievement. "Takeoff" has led Europeans, in apparent accord with the Rostovian model, toward the stage of "high mass consumption." As Europeans moved from poverty to recovery, their demands for the good things of life accelerated, thus illustrating the wisdom of the old French aphorism that *"l'appétit vient en mangeant"* (appetite comes with eating).

But "partial incorporation" has its limits. To absorb and adapt the technological component of the American Model was a giant step forward in the direction Europeans wished to take. The promotion of mass consumption was another important, if as yet insufficient, step in the same direction. These forward strides stirred among the peoples of Europe new demands that are generally associated with rising mass consumption—namely, demands for the media of mass culture. These, as Nasser and Sukarno have reported from underdeveloped societies where mass consumption is still but a gleam in some eyes, incorporate deeper demands for mass participation in public affairs and political life. As the European elites confronted these new popular aspirations in the prospering societies of the second postwar decade covered by our study, their need shifted. Having passed through the phase of anxiety about "Americanization" into a phase of acceptance of the American Model, they now faced the consequences of their own accelerated success. Partial incorporation, we recall, signifies *restriction* by partial incorporation. The Europeans had traveled a considerable distance along the American route to modernization. Could they, should they, now seek to go all the way? As they pondered the pros and cons of this profound issue for their own future, the European leaders entered a new phase of ambivalence.

THE PHASE OF AMBIVALENCE

Ambivalence differs qualitatively from either anxiety or acceptance, although it combines properties of both in a kind of anxious acceptance with reservations. For the ambivalent person, full acceptance is not possible; the object of desire has some competitor and full rejection of the competitor is not possible. While the object of desire is highly valued, so is its competitor. Ambivalence results. This is the most difficult situation in the theory of decision-making; it is much harder, for example, than the classic political choice of the "lesser evil," for it faces its victim with two "almost-equal goods." Where the goods appear to be truly equal, the ambivalent person suffers from paralysis of will and immobilization of action; where the valued goals are "almost equal," he usually exhibits vacillation in choice and oscillation in decision. On many key issues that now confront the European elites, as we shall see in the findings of this study, vacillation and oscillation are fairly characteristic responses in the present period.

Reach and Grasp: New Aspirations and Old Constraints

The issues that evoke European ambivalence are both internal and external: They concern the evolution of their domestic society and the place of that society in the new world environment. Precisely this interaction between what one is at home and what one is abroad remains difficult for European leaders to grasp. This may be a residue of their traditional imperial perspective, now obsolete, which allowed Great Britain to develop a political democracy in its home islands while managing the world's largest empire by political fiat. It may account for the posturing of De Gaulle, in a world of continental superpowers, *as if* his now relatively prosperous "hexagon" of fifty million Frenchmen were an adequate base for world leadership.

We are dealing here with an extension of the French tendency, noted above, "toward explanations that are wholly contained in the universe of internal events." This is the tendency that led some Frenchmen to misinterpret the real options available to them in rejecting EDC and as a consequence to beat a hasty and humiliating retreat, four months later, when they were obliged by American insistence to ratify WEU (West European Union), which included Britain. Since WEU did what the French rejection of EDC tried to prevent (Germany's accession to NATO), but without the measure of French control that EDC had conferred, this was a costly error of perspective. It was an error committed after four arduous years of vacillation and oscillation.

De Gaulle has simply reversed this erroneous perspective by his effort to act in the world arena as if external policy today could operate without any reference to "the universe of internal events." His severe setback in the French elections of 1967 has shown that the lessons of EDC still apply—even to De Gaulle. The most poignant lesson is that one cannot be "great" outside, in the postimperial age, without being "great" inside. As our post-mortem on EDC put it:

> The effort to comprehend foreign policy decisions in *any* country requires a context in which "internal" and "international" events endlessly interact and reciprocally influence each other. It is no less true in France than elsewhere that national sovereignty has been compromised by the facts of life in a bipolar arena of world politics. The current arena of world politics requires many "international decisions" to activate policies that exceed the independent capacity of any single nation.

The interaction of internal and external policy is operative today in all nations that bear any responsibility for world order, including *a fortiori* the United States and Russia. As this book will deal mainly with the external relations of the great European nations, we focus on internal issues in the concluding section of this chapter on the domestic evolution of European society. In particular, we are concerned with the efforts to bring mass culture and politics into an equilibrium ratio with the accelerated growth of mass consumption.

We have seen that France has been not only highly ambivalent but laggard in the postwar acceleration of mass culture. Its per capita growth of television, for example, is among the lowest in Europe. As compared with Britain and Germany, radio as well as television remain under exclusive and rather rigid government control—a source of severe and growing complaint among Frenchmen who seek to promote the mass media as the vehicle for mass politics. Again turning to the American Model for guidance, opposition candidates in the 1967 elections accused the Gaullists of government monopoly over information and opinion—and demanded the American rule of "equal time."[7]

A rather different picture is presented by postwar Germany, where the mass media developed rapidly during the past decade. As a result, current German debates about mass culture are well in advance of those in France. Be it noted that the postwar German media were initiated and shaped largely by Americans who manned the Information Control Division of the military government. If the press and radio have been "tame" on some issues—fewer and farther between with the passing years as the affair of *Der Spiegel* and the resignation of Strauss dramatically demonstrate—they have generally honored their commitment to be "free and responsible." Television, which developed after Allied Information Control lapsed, has followed suit. Postwar Germans have been well served by their mass media. This was shown, as early as 1956 in our surveys, by the elite responses to our question: "Is it possible for people who are interested to keep well informed on international politics?" The great majority of German panelists saying yes (77 per cent) was only slightly smaller than in Britain (81 per cent), where the long and rich history of media development had not been deformed by a Goebbels ministry under a Nazi regime. The German panel, moreover, was more than half again as positive as the French panel (50 per cent).

This appears to account for the relatively high level of discussion among German opinion leaders about the future development of their mass media, which they see as the dynamic component in the further evolution of mass participation in culture and politics. The point is illustrated by a thoughtful feature article in the prestigious *Frankfurter Allgemeine*, November 11, 1967, which started from the thesis "that in small and medium-sized towns there is a growing demand for things cultural." It cites a series of cases where specific towns have "rejuvenated the traditional and the modern" by creating new institutions of enlightenment: Regensburg by a university (due to which "the decline that set in during the nineteenth century has been reversed"); Ulm by a secondary school; Wolfenbüttel by a library; Ingelheim by new industry; Höchst by a theater; Oberhausen by a film club. The concern with extending the perspectives and participation of the hinterland illustrates what Karl Deutsch and Stein Rokkan have aptly called "the mobilization of the periphery."

For, says the *Allgemeine,* "any one of these can widen the horizons of the people in a town by making them aware of current movements in 20th century life." And this development of mass culture among provincial Germans is required not only by its interactive function with mass consumption and mass politics but as the psychological condition for a satisfying life in a modern, democratic, participant society. The *Allgemeine* concludes:

> The cliché that small town life is quiet and restful no longer applies. Mass media such as the cinema and television have introduced into medium-sized towns a noticeable tendency to imitate large towns and cities, outstripping them in modernity. Nowadays the large town or city is often quieter, more serious and generally less hectic than many a market town. In outward appearances and in the general pace of life in a small town it would seem that the community was suffering from nervous strain. There would be reasons to deduce that inner development in the small town was not keeping up with the outside tempo of life.

German concern to follow social diagnosis with therapeutic action stimulated the formation of the Michel Commission on the mass media. Modeled on the American and British Commissions of a decade earlier, its 242-page report is a document worth reading for its judicious and detailed concern with "free and responsible" institutions of public enlightenment. Issued in October 1967, the report "concluded that press and radio, in contrast with various sectors of the film [and television] industry, have developed favorably." Within a month, on November 6, 1967, the Munich Film and Television College was opened. Press commentary was enthusiastic: "This special college will combine scientific, technical, and artistic studies. Plans for a college of this kind were made ten years ago, and actual preparations have taken three years. At last the Federal Republic has its 'directors' factory'!" Within days thereafter, the appropriate Bundestag committee unanimously approved a Film Promotion Bill designed to give financial help to film makers who help themselves—on condition that they reinvest earnings in new films, particularly films for young people and documentaries (which are eligible for special grants). The stated objectives include "raising the standard of films, encouraging cooperation between film and television corporations, and an equitable market-oriented evaluation of the films promoted."

This rapid and reasoned policy response to felt social needs demonstrates that Europeans have achieved an absorptive and adaptive capacity appropriate to highly developed societies. The mobilization of mass participation in culture, consumption, and political life is no easy matter for any country, however developed it may be, but Europeans have been moving in this direction rapidly and, by and large, effectively. . . .

FOOTNOTES

1.   For an exposition of how The American Dream has been routinized over the past two centuries, see Daniel Lerner, "Comfort and Fun: Morality in a Nice Society," *The American Scholar,* Vol. 27, No. 2 (Spring 1958), pp. 153-165.
2.   The leadership of European youth in accelerating social change is now being seriously studied by Roy Macridis and others.
3.   The Sorbonne "happening" of May 1968 bears witness.
4.   That the youth mobilization has spread beyond the three "great powers" of Europe is illustrated by the Dutch "Provos" (from the word provocation) and their comparable numbers in Belgium and Sweden. Even in Franco's Spain the youth today engage in psychocultural exhibitions and sociopolitical demonstrations. The process is operative as well in the Communist countries of East Europe, notably the "tamed" regimes of Poland and Czechoslovakia.
5.   Note that this passage was written in January 1968. The Sorbonne eruption, which brought a reported ten million Frenchmen out on strike, occurred in May 1968.
6.   The concept of "restriction by partial incorporation" was developed by H. D. Lasswell in *World Politics and Personal Insecurity* (New York: Free Press, 1935; 2nd ed., 1965), a truly seminal work which built theoretical foundations for this and many other subsequent studies.
7.   The ironic outcome was that telecast time was divided "equally"—half to the Gaullist Party (UNR) and half to all other parties combined. (To this we add the May 1968 nationwide strike demand for liberation of radio-TV.)

2 STANLEY HOFFMANN

Europe's Identity Crisis: Between the Past and America

"AMERICANIZATION" WITH A DIFFERENCE

The "Americanization" of Western Europe is not a mere cliché. It is a fact recently documented by *Dædalus*. Economic expansion, higher wages, a peasantry whose numbers dwindle and whose production grows, classes that are less different from and feel less hostile to each other, a "service class" on the rise, a drive for mass education, the "end of ideology" in political life, intellectuals reconverted from tragedy to expertise, collective bargaining with the participation of "technocrats" instead of deliberations by a political class of leisurely generalists: all of this does indeed make Europe much more like the United States. Had *Dædalus* included in its issue studies of the new public role of the Catholic Church, the transformation of the family, the phenomenal progress of "mass culture," it would have become even more obvious that Tocqueville's prophecy of the democratic age has come true at last. What Tocqueville did not realize was that egalitarian society would triumph in Europe only after the spread of material prosperity. Nor did he see that those voluntary associations without

Reprinted by permission of *Dædalus*, Journal of the American Academy of Arts and Sciences, Boston, Massachusetts, Volume 93, Number 4, Fall, 1964. Text abridged and footnotes omitted by the editors.

23

which he thought liberalism would perish from the twin dangers of social conformity and political centralization would in fact grow out of an industrialization that proceeds in the framework of liberal democracy.

And yet industrial society in Europe may remain quite different from America's, for a reason Tocqueville would have well understood. He knew that a single type of society can be ruled by opposite types of regimes. He knew that the face of the polity in the democratic age is shaped by the relations between classes and the state in the predemocratic age. He would have realized that Europe's current emancipation from its past cannot help being shaped by that past—a past entirely different from America's. There are three areas of significant differences. First, there is the problem of the *polity*: America's industrial democracy was a creation; Europe's industrial society involves a conversion of the previous order. Second, there is the problem of *historical conscience*: the United States, on the whole, is at peace with itself; Europe's transformation entails a catharsis. In each of these areas, America's originality is double; not only does the American experience diverge from Europe's as a whole, but America's is single, whereas Europe's is fragmented into separate national experiences. Finally, and as a result, there is the problem of *beliefs*. America's growth is rooted in a creed; Europe's revolution unfolds amidst the repudiation of past creeds.

Creation vs. Conversion

Tocqueville saw the United States long before the age of mass consumption. Yet much in his description remains valid. Obviously, industrial society in America has been affected by the network of pre-existing institutions, laws, customs and values more than it has affected this network. The ideal type of advanced industrial society or that of capitalism tells us little. They are liquids which take the shape of whatever vase they are poured into, although they give their color to the vase. What matters in America's case—it has become a cliché to say so—is that industrialization proceeded in a society already democratic, freed by its revolution not from a previous aristocratic phase but from outside tutelage, and constantly confirmed in its essence by new waves of immigrants. Moreover, industrialization expanded in and benefited from a single national framework, which survived the great test of secession. In both respects Europe's past has been different. It plagues the present and mortgages the future. The industrialization of nations deeply marked, socially and politically, by their "predemocratic" stage and by their rivalries means the laborious breaking down of class barriers and borders. Consequently, on the one hand they are not "like America" *yet*, for the task of conversion still entails both much destruction of the old and the tough resistance of major residues. On the other hand, the new Europe might not be "like America" *ever*, for the task involves innovations which either confirm old differences or create new contrasts with the United States.

What is being destroyed in Europe's social structure would not deserve being mentioned in a study that focuses on what is likely to keep Europe lastingly distinct from the United States, were it not for three reasons. One has to do with the difference in social structure and values; the elimination of various groups whose economic or political function has disappeared has left a residue of bitterness not only among the victims but also among other groups who shared the values if not the social position of those victims. The second reason has to do both with the difference in social structure and with Europe's fragmentation into separate states; the process of elimination has put new strains on already fragile political systems, for it is much more troublesome to deal with angry farmers, displaced miners or depressed areas when they represent a large fraction of the population or of the space of a country than when they occur in the "wide open spaces" of a sparsely settled continent. The last reason has to do with national differences in Western Europe; the destructions and dislocations brought about by economic change have affected these nations unevenly, depending on the degree of development they had reached at the start of the process. Thus Germany, despite the influx of refugees, has suffered least; France has had serious troubles with shopkeepers, peasants and workers made jobless by progress; Italy is the country in which change has entailed not only "the disintegration of agriculture and of traditional rural communities" through a huge rural exodus, but also a problem of regional imbalance of enormous proportions. Despite the common movement toward industrialization and the efforts made by European communities to ease the journey, the fact that each nation has had to deal with its own incidents and its own casualties of progress has strengthened separateness just as it was being undermined.[1]

It is not only Europe's social structure that is affected by destructions. Partly as a result of those just mentioned the load which Europe's political institutions have had to carry has crushed one vital organ: parliament. The decline of a body that symbolized one important difference between Europe's and America's political systems has, however, not made for any rapprochement. In Europe's cabinet system, parliament was supposedly the fount of all effective and responsible power in contrast with the United States Congress, handicapped by the separation of powers. Today, parliament's share in decision-making and its role in supervising the execution of decisions are far smaller than the share and role of Congress. The dispossession of parliament not only by the civil service and interest groups but also by the executive has been much greater. Congress is now protected by the strict separation of powers, by the fragmentation of the bureaucracy, and by the very looseness of American parties. Whenever the party system worked, parliament's decline has occurred because of the control exerted over the majority by the cabinet or by the majority party's ruling organs; where the party system has failed (i.e., in France), parliament has been demoted to a position legally much narrower than that of the United States Congress. Here again, differences among the Europeans compound the difference with the United States. Outside France, parliament, having lost its role, at least preserves its "myth"—that of the body that speaks for the people and that can overthrow the cabinet. In France's hybrid political system, the president plays the part of the people's voice and combines the advantages of a chief executive in a presidential system with those of a cabinet leader in a parliamentary regime—at the expense not only of parliament's position but also of its reputation. Outside France, it is the strength of the parties that has weakened parliament in parliamentary regimes. In France it is the very weakness of the parties which has brought the demise of the parliamentary regime altogether and which is being perpetuated by the practice of so-called "direct democracy." . . .

The resilience of old patterns of behavior is also visible in the whole area of class relations. The way in which social groups face each other in the new society remains deeply marked by the past history of social and political contests. To be sure, recent European writings show a longing for the "American model" of group politics, democratic authority, face-to-face discussions and compromises. But the model is not really relevant. Whereas America is a fluid society, Europe remains a set of sticky societies. Mobility within each and between them is less practiced and less highly valued. Such viscosity preserves past obstacles to social harmony and even to further economic development (for instance, in keeping the size of enterprise much below the "American model"). Moreover, despite growing prosperity, inequality remains a major social and political issue: first, because everywhere in Europe the differences in living conditions between the rich and the poor are still huge (the access of the latter to higher education and power is far from assured); second, because the underprivileged groups' attitudes toward inequality remain shaped by the European tradition of global protest against and challenge of the "established disorder"; third, because the discontent and the expectations of the underprivileged are far more focused on the state than in the United States; finally, because of considerable variations from nation to nation. Thus, although one can rightly speak of a moderation of the class struggle and of a decline in revolutionary messianism, the long record of contests between the workers and the upper classes and the constant role of the state as a stake and a force in the struggle introduce a lasting distinction between the American and the European cases. In every European country the workers' organizations—unions or parties— are more concerned with the global economic development of society and with the role of the workers in the management of enterprises than are those in the United States. It may well be that this concern now expresses itself in requests for "participation" instead of the old demands for revolution, but even this points to a difference in scope and temper between America's well-established reformism—more fragmentary and more placid—and Europe's new one.

If one examines not merely the political expression of social grievances in the "new Europe" but political behavior in general, one reaches the same conclusion: despite real changes, old reflexes resist. Ideology in politics (and in the writings of intellectuals on politics) may be declining, in part because of the moderation of the class struggle, in part because of a reaction against the ideological excesses of "secular religions," in part because of the increasing irrelevance of "isms" that grew out of the conditions of preindustrial society. But proneness to ideology (in the sense in which a weak body is prone to diseases) and attachment to old ideological symbols persist, even if the symbols have lost much of their "objective" content. Thus in France and in Italy neither the rise in the standard of living within societies still marked by grave injustice nor the relative decline of groups that provided the bulk of the support of the Communist party (proletarian workers, landless farmers) have seriously reduced the electoral strength of the Communist parties. For where ideology was strong it was never exclusively related to the stage of economic development. There simple discontent still expresses itself in ideological terms, and events unconnected with either the old class struggles or the old stable constellations of political doctrines still provoke ideological reactions. Thus in France the divisions created by the new postwar issues—the Cold War, decolonization, European integration—have been anything but moderate, and the attitudes of the opposed factions anything but pragmatic.

The resilience of old forms of political behavior and traditional styles of political argument explains in large part why the European political problem continues to differ from that of the United States. The American issue is the efficiency of institutions that are stable and legitimate. The issue in the three largest countries of Western Europe is the stability and legitimacy of their institutions. Neither in France nor in Italy nor in Germany are they so secure that they could survive a prolonged period of inefficacy. In none of those three countries could allegiance to the Constitution be the symbol of national integration. Before their alleged death, the ideologies of yesterday left deep scars on the institutions.

Finally, the weakness of representative government, the residues of ideology and the persistence of old habits in class relations all contribute to the preservation of two important differences between Europe's and America's political life. Divided polities in which the state has played a major part in class conflicts and in which a core of efficiency and continuity has been indispensable have produced professional civil services with traditions of their own and also with a natural tendency to persist even if the conditions of their earlier rise and role have changed. The bureaucracy of the European state has preceded the age of democracy; its power and centralization create a problem of control far more acute than in the United States, with its mixture of often rather low-grade professionals and temporary recruits from business or the universities, and its fragmentation of bureaucracy into countless agencies and services. Moreover, the strength and staying power of the civil service continues to limit the scope of representative government, that is, to curtail the chances of what one now calls "participation." Tocqueville is again the more relevant reference: Europe's politics still suffer from that radical distinction between "us" and "them," the subjects and the rulers, the citizens and the state, which has been perpetuated by centuries of absolutism, authoritarianism, and even liberal politics that entrusted the polity to men of knowledge and order only, and thus served the interests of some classes alone.[2]

Indeed, this is a difference which has been confirmed by one of the major innovations of the new Europe. There has been an increase in the scope of the state. The Europeans' conception of public functions has radically expanded in this century, whereas the Americans' has changed but little—there is a gap between the practices in the two areas, and an even greater one in their "public philosophies." In part because of the differences in the background—greater poverty, the ruins of the war, the need both for reconstruction and for regulation of the sudden boom—Europe has allowed more overt intervention of the state in economic and social affairs, has shown greater concern for welfare and balanced growth, has repudiated uncontrolled laissez faire and has tried to avoid the scandal of public squalor in the midst of private opulence. Although the private virtues have been practiced in Europe so much more fervently than the civic ones, by contrast with the United States, the hold of the state on the individual and the subordination of private gratification to collective require-ments have been strengthened. Both the bureaucracy and the interest groups (what the French call les forces vives) have received a role in the preparation and execution of state decisions that is both greater and more readily recognized than in the United States. This innovation has not only created a new difference between the United States and Europe; it has also consolidated two old ones. On the one hand, the role and prestige of European parliamentarians has declined even further, whereas United States congressmen cling (and sometimes behave according) to a theory of representation that crowds all public concern within the charmed but occasionally vicious circle of Capitol and White House, and makes of the member of Congress the only legitimate spokesman for his constituents. On the other hand, the expansion of state functions has benefited the public "technocrats" and provoked a renewed demand, often utopian in its scope, for "participation," symbol of a growing gap between "us" and "them." Thus the basic relationship of the American citizen to his officials may well be one of apathy, based both on trust or a sense of identity, and on rather modest expec-tations; the European's relationship is often a mixture of apathy based on distance or distrust, and hostility due to heavy dependence as well as fear of arbitrariness.

Another area where innovations have both confirmed and added to the contrasts between Europe and America is that of class relations. Both in France and in Germany the structure and the behavior of labor unions have been molded by the past attitudes of the upper classes and the earlier role of the state, as indicated above. Today the circumstances which shaped these French and German unions have disappeared. And yet, on the one hand, the traditional behavior and organization of the workers have been confirmed by the new events. The French workers' pattern of protest and blackmail of the state developed at a time when the bourgeois, who had adopted many features of the French aristocracy in their fight against it, resisted proletarian demands and slowed down economic growth. Today, despite the change in business attitudes, the new and leading part played by the French state in development has perpetuated what Michel Crozier calls the unions' fascination with Power, and has made blackmail even more useful as a way of affecting the distribution of the national income. Moreover, Communist preponderance among the workers provides a new force of protest against inequities in this distribution and a new focus for business and labor hostility to face-to-face discussions. In pre-Weimar Germany, labor unions were more cohesive and less rebellious than in France because of faster economic development promoted by the aristocratic class and by a "Gnaden-bourgeoisie." Today, the influx of refugee labor has contributed both to the numerical strength and to the cautious behavior of the unions. On the other hand, the innovations have sharpened the difference between Europe and America insofar as they have broadened previous differences among the Europeans, thus offsetting the unifying impact of industrialization. The divisions of French unions and the fact that the biggest one is under Communist control oblige the labor movement to concentrate its efforts on the central level—that of Power. German unions are wholly without Communist influence, and their strength allows them to concentrate on the control of the workers in the factory and on relations with business. Moreover, each European nation has created its own network of procedures—ranging from ineffective to quite effective in the Dutch case—for the settlement of social conflicts.

In one area, old differences have been confirmed and a new one has been created not merely by European innovations but by a combination of destructions, resistance and novelties: I refer to the attitude of social groups and nations toward the new industrial society. What is being destroyed is the former bourgeois "sobriety" which once kept the European way of life far below America's splashes of conspicuous consumption, as well as the former reluctance of bourgeois and aristocrats alike to mass production, which meant dependence on the market. What is, however, resilient is the concern of even hard-working Europeans (businessmen or industrial workers) for "whatever . . . is beyond work": "distraction, pleasure, evasion." There is a desire to put limits on work; there is a determination to preserve "elite cultures" that coexist with but are not submerged by the progress of mass culture and that continue to set standards in the arts. Both show the imprint of the "aristocratic age" in which work was a disgrace for a few, a curse for most, for others a means to rise but not an end in itself, for some a tunnel through which one had to pass before one could culti- vate one's inner freedom and fulfill one's deepest aspirations. What is new is the possibility for many more Europeans than in the past to enjoy what is "beyond work"—holidays or paperbacks. As a result an old difference from the United States has been deepened: despite, and even to some extent thanks to, the progress of mass consumption and mass production, Europeans keep "asking more from life" both in terms of an "insatiable demand" for material goods and "in terms of fulfillment" than the Americans, whose society "remains oriented toward and by work."

Moreover, the contrast between America's rather uniform orientation and Europe's has been increased by new differences among the Europeans. The more European societies become alike in their social structures and economic makeup, the more each national society seems to heighten its idiosyncrasies. Recent surveys among young Frenchmen and Germans who have visited each other's country fail to reveal any "homogenization." Clichés about national character live on, and national disparities get stronger: the spectrum extends from Italy, in which the task of economic and social change is least advanced and where the Communists have a powerful intellectual and political hold, to France, whose economic and social transformation has so far made no constructive impact on the party system, and to West Germany, whose values and politics remind observers far more of the United States, for federalism divides its bureaucracy, the disasters brought by past ideologies have singed all who have not been charred, and the ideal of the *Marktwirtschaft* (although it is *Sozial!*) has more than a few illusions in common with American free enterprise. To be sure, there are regional differences in the United States as well, but how pale they look by comparison! The national state, exorcised daily by the prosecutors of its obso- lescence, continues to make a difference. Each European country adjusts its "national character" to the new age in its own style, and particularly in its own style of authority. . . .

Values vs. Void

Although in the depth of its memories each European nation remains unique, and although the color of its memories makes of the European family an heir to the Atrides, the surface appears much more rosy, more homogeneous and more like that of the United States. The memories, being evaded, do not loom large by daylight. Then too, Americans and Europeans alike celebrate the progress of European pragmatism. Tolerance replaces the clash of ideologies; a concern for concrete issues and practical solutions inspires the politicians and the voters alike. Intellectuals try to contribute to the national discussion and settlement of those issues instead of indulging either in global justification or in a total *mise en cause*. The Europe of "carnivorous idols" has become *l'Europe du dossier*; it celebrates technology and compromise, expertise and empirical research. Does not all this show that American values are sweeping the Old Continent?

In my opinion, it shows nothing of the kind. Europe is converting itself to the functional necessities of a new type of social order—it has not converted itself to a new set of values. Europe flees from its past because it cannot look at it honestly—not because of a deliberate and mature repudiation. America's pragmatism, pluralism and "engineering approach" rest on a solid bed of beliefs, those of classical liberalism, which the Declaration of Independence and the Bill of Rights embody and a common loyalty to the Constitution symbolizes. Pluralism can be harmonious or cacophonic. America's is harmonious because of a basic consensus: what is never questioned because it is not merely accepted but cherished is always larger and deeper than what is contested. The engineering approach is that of men concerned with the means because the ends are not in doubt. Empirical research is guided by a formidable body of theory, much of which (despite its value-free pretense) conceals or sublimates a firm conviction in the superiority of America's way of political and social life. The school system produces—consciously and enthusiastically—Americans, that is, men and women capable of cooperating because of a common respect for the values of liberal democracy and a common faith in America's purpose. In no society is conflict more universal, and yet its social theory takes consensus, not conflict, as its conceptual framework. There is logic, not paradox, in this apparent contradiction, for conflict flourishes at all levels precisely because it is contained within well-accepted limits and channelled through procedures and institutions to which loyalty is assured. The role of those devices is not to turn conflict into consensus; it is to find for limited conflicts solutions that are inspired by the procedural and substantive consensus which keeps the system going, and which such solutions strengthen in turn. In support of this proposition, we find both the silence of social theory (and the lack of effective procedures) in the one area where consensus was missing—race relations—and the gradual progress of theory and procedures as consensus begins to grow.

None of this is true of postwar Europe. Here there is no agreement on fundamentals. What works in America works because Americans believe in it; what Europeans believe in today is what works. The European consensus is negative: like culture, which a Frenchman defined as "what is left when everything has been forgotten," today's consensus is around "what is left after everything has been discarded." The French who have discovered the virtues of a presidential system, the Germans or Italians who praise liberal democracy often do so not because of any conviction but because everything else has been tried and has failed. The same is true of the intellectuals who repudiate the past tradition of "totalism"; often they do so not because of a deep belief in the intellectuals's responsibility as an expert but because of the obvious failure of Grand Intellectuals to bridge the gap between thought and action. There is all the difference in the world between an affirmation and an auto-da-fé. America's intellectual stand has been on the plateau of a democratic *juste milieu*; Europe's road has gone from a mountain range of disparate ideologies to the present naked plain. Intellectuals who believed too fervently and too long that the polity was a battlefield of rival conceptions of good and evil, the *locus sacrus* for saving one's soul, have now fallen into a state of nihilism. It is not a nihilism of despair;[3] this phase is over. It is a happy nihilism, to be sipped in prosperity after all the great nectars of the past have turned sour. It has, of course, its reassuring charms. But it also brings with it three dangers that can be summed up in two words: Europe's silence.

The first danger is a lack of imagination. The old questions were too big, too vague, too murderous. Today there are no questions. In the past European intellectuals seemed to assume either that the worst was certain or that everything had to be subordinated to the triumph of the best. Today they act as if the worst was certain not to happen, and the best required no choice at all. Not long ago Raymond Aron denounced the ideological opinions which sacrificed the present to the future. Today he wants to investigate how the desire to calculate where one is going has come to replace the desire to ask where one ought to go; his and Camus's plea for modesty, against fanaticism, seems to have been interpreted as an appeal against intellectual probing, for the sacrifice of the future to the present. The accumulation of facts and figures, the extrapolation of trends, the discussion of forecasting and planning as if they involved no fundamental choices but only technical problems—better instruments of detection as it were, or better statistics—as if only the point at which the ball will stop rolling along the slope remained to be discovered, all of this betrays an intellectual fatigue that is excusable, given the past, but hardly encouraging. The fact that in a world *où l'action n'est pas la soeur du rêve* attempts at realizing utopian dreams turned life into a nightmare is no reason for chasing all dreams away. Past questions may have led to the wrong answers, but the avoidance of questions is not likely to prove any better. The man who drives himself into a ditch may get killed; so may the sleepwalker.

The European intellectual who today either borrows American theories, often without questioning their relevance, or else assumes that the questions have been already formulated and answered gives up a role which has been both his glory and the only clean feather in Europe's dirty cap: that of raising the fundamental problems about society—its direction, the ethical validity of its actions, the relative worth of the choices open to it. A society without some judge who frets over its behavior, admonishes, advises, at times indicts and at other times approves, tends all too easily to fall into complacency. America is often charged with it; and yet both in domestic and in foreign affairs the issues are more sharply discussed, the choices more clearly spelled out and more hotly embraced than in present-day Europe. The reader of *Dædalus*'s "A New Europe?" cannot find a single European answer to such questions as: What political institutions would be most capable of protecting the individual altogether from excessive bureaucracy, from special interests and from arbitrary executive power? Should Europe's industrial society keep trying to regulate demand so as to give precedence to collective equipments (if not cathedrals) and to preserve some realm for quality? Should intellectuals accept as good and final the demise not only of verbal efforts to "change the world" but also of their role of overall social critics?

Here lies the second danger. The refusal to ask such questions means the implicit or explicit acceptance of unquestioned illusions. There are three which are quite common. The first is the technological illusion, according to which the progress of the sciences, material expansion and the spread of specialized knowledge will gradually eliminate that residual category, politics. Authoritative answers will at last be given to social problems that have remained unsolved (that is, political, if one accepts Jouvenel's notion that the political is what is insoluble) only because the material and intellectual elements of a solution were missing. Aron once wrote that the day when intellectuals, having discovered the limits of politics, would become indifferent to it was not yet threatening. He may well have been wrong—or rather, having discovered that politics was not all, many intellectuals seem to assert that it could somehow be reduced to nothing. Alas, there are only too many social problems which cannot be erased either through a welfare calculus or through the tidal rise of the learning process, for instance, all those of political philosophy.

A second illusion is the procedural one. It consists in believing that the method for solving problems is to put around a table all the interested parties, informed of course by the spirit of compromise; participation and goodwill shall provide the answers. This is merely a new version of Europe's traditional attitude toward conflict. The recognition of deep-seated cleavages has always been at the core of Europe's social theory, but the practices of European polities—in part because of the prevalence of nondemocratic styles of authority, in part because of the role of state bureaucracies—have always tended toward the settlement of conflicts not through compromise but by acts of authority. Today the old practices are increasingly discredited (although they still abound), but the same desire to eliminate conflict as one removes a spot on a suit shows in the proliferation of suggestions for orderly procedures of settlement, based on the hope that the procedure would transmute conflicts of values and interests into harmony, painlessly and without friction. A kind of *escamotage* at the bottom has replaced the *escamotage* from the top. Once again the parallel with American beliefs is strong, but once again one has to say that there is no *escamotage* where the conflicts are marginal, often technical, and steeped in a culture that values agreement for agreement's sake. Where social groups remain divided by memories, suspicions and insecurity, where citizens do not recognize themselves in their public authorities, where interest clashes are made more rather than less ferocious by a dearth of ideological beliefs that lends interests a vicarious fierceness, the situation is not auspicious for procedural solutions. There would be less discussion of "democratic planning" in France if one would at last realize that what is involved in a so-called "income policy" in nothing less than a philosophy of social goals. A coherent policy has little or no chance of resulting from interest compromises and conciliation procedures, for the simple reason that groups and parties disagree drastically on ends and means—the real choice remains (once again) between a decision by fiat and the pluralism of cacophony.

There is a third illusion: believing that Europe's undeniable progress since the twenties in the difficult art of making a society aware of its problems and of its collective responsibility for solving them means an increased capacity to identify the problems of the future or a greater relevance to the concerns of less developed nations. It is true that in the areas of social security, planning, and regulation of the economy, European postwar reforms have carried collective consciousness beyond what exists in the United States. The long battle over medicare seems incomprehensible to many Europeans. But nothing yet shows that the techniques developed in order to solve the problems and allay the fears born out of the thirties will prove equally capable of dealing with the next phase. When it comes to automation and the problems of leisure, to the fate of the aged and to juvenile delinquency, all "societies of plenty" find themselves in the same wasteland. If Europe has been more inventive in battling the scourge of poverty, it is because the pressure was so much greater there. But applied Keynesianism is of little help in the new situation.

What is striking in those areas and in many others as well is the third danger of the void: the absence of a European *projet*—that is, of a European social and cultural design. It is easy to argue that there has never been a European design or that those we find in the past are *ex post facto* intellectual reconstructions. But this is not the way in which Europe appeared to non-Europeans; moreover, whoever reads Europe's doctrines of the past century discovers two sets of convictions. One was the conviction of an over-all movement of mankind. This faith was symbolized by all those philosophies of history that our superior "scientific" knowledge ridicules (but that are still represented in much of America's more sophisticated grand theory of today—*vide* Walt Rostow); the movement was marked not merely by the unfolding of material progress but by political progress as well: the drive toward parliamentarism or imperialism, those summits of human ascent, or at least so they seemed at the time. The other was the conviction of a national purpose, carried at times to incredible chauvinistic lengths but nevertheless of value in unifying national elites often deeply divided on other issues. There is little of either left in today's Europe; smart debunking has replaced rash belief. We should not be surprised; the development of a *projet* requires a sense of stability, a belief in man's capacity to set the course of the journey and to get to the destination through his own means. What prospers instead is either the belief that technological forces will drive one to the end of the road or that the best one can do is hold high the lamp so as to illuminate the next steps. . . .

At this point the tired reader may well inquire: "Granted that today's Europe is not like America in its institutions, in its past and in its values, so what? The differences so laboriously listed are mainly marks of transition: Europe is like a huge disposal that must incinerate its habits and beliefs of yesterday before it can create new creeds and customs, or else those differences will be eliminated as soon as the United States moves in the direction already taken by Europe in the realm of public welfare, and as soon as European integration unites the European nations. At the end, there will be two largely identical industrial societies."

This may well be the case. But it is not at all certain. There comes a moment when the most "agnostic," critical and cautious social scientist must do what Kelsen does with his pure theory of law: he reaches a *Grundnorm* which is a mere hypothesis. We are faced here with a choice of *Grundnormen*. On one side there is the belief in a kind of economic and social determinism—a belief which runs through writings on both sides of the Atlantic, from Marx or Comte to Lipset or Duverger. On the other side there is the belief in a broad and complicated autonomy of the polity: the whole area of man's relation to the overall community and of the relations between the communities is seen certainly not as one where pure chance rules, but as one which is shaped *both* by the economic and social order and by the memories, the cultures, the political institutions and calculations, the ideas and the passions which are so largely independent of the underlying order. The former *Grundnorm* has the merit of simplicity. The latter strikes me as more fertile. As a disciple of Montesquieu, Tocqueville and Aron, I choose the second. It is the one that leaves most room for collective creation and statesmanship. For it shows that there are many forces at work—often at cross-purposes; that none of them determines all the others; and thus that there is room for using them, blending them, shaping them and building a future out of the very contradictions of the present.

There is a first implication from this choice. If the similarity of economic and social orders does not guarantee the similarity of polities, if a certain type of social order does not breed the desired values or obliterate the past all by itself, then the Europeans, supposing they *wanted* to take the United States as the over-all model, would still have to make a special effort of imagination and action. They would still have to overcome residues and resistances the

United States never faced; they would have to face their past instead of fleeing it; they would have to adopt American values consciously; they would have to unify Europe less sluggishly and haltingly. They cannot adequately analyze their affairs in American terms, or accept American explanations of Europe in American terms. What is *sui generis* in Europe has to be accounted for; the optimism of various American theories makes sense in and for the United States, but no sense at all if transplanted in Europe. Elections may be the democratic form of the class struggle on this side of the ocean; on the other side both elections and the class struggle remain rather more complicated undertakings. Leaders of private and public bureaucracies who share the values of their subordinates and who rule according to a democratic style of authority may not be dangerous, but when the style and the values of the elites have traditionally not been democratic there is less room for complacency. Even if optimism were justified, Europeans would still have to discriminate. Otherwise the light by which one chooses to be guided could happen to be that of a dead star. The presidential system many Frenchmen admire is that of the Hundred Days, not that of the trench-and-guerilla warfare of recent years; the mass education system which impatient European reformers envy is busy trying to introduce some of the very methods and institutions which those reformers decry. Thus there is a risk of the two cultures crossing each other without ever really meeting or merging.

But there is another and more important implication. If, on the one hand, nothing determines that Europe will be a replica of the United States; if, on the other hand, the past institutions and history of Europe's polities are just as likely to affect Europe's future as the new social order, then the Europeans have no excuse for silence, passivity or complacency. For they are still free to analyze critically America's own experience and to sort the good from the bad so that Europe may be spared the latter. They are still free to make of tomorrow's Europe an industrial society that will have its own profile, not simply because many of the old features will not have been erased by the plastic surgery of industrialization but also because of a deliberate effort to preserve Europe's originality. Nor do the Europeans have any excuse for anti-Americanism. For if they understand that "Americanization" is really just the passage to industrial society, that it has come out of European developments (although the United States encouraged it), that many of the "American" features the process has developed are due either to an almost gleeful European imitation of what is worst in America's industrial society or to the impact of the world's dominant power on a weakened and fragmented continent, but in neither case to any permanent fatality, then they will realize that anti-Americanism is merely an evasion of Europe's own responsibilities. America should be neither imitated nor blamed blindly. Some Europeans are anti-American because they do not want to accept the fact that industrial society has come of age. Denouncing the United States saves them from the difficult task of trying to make a virtue of necessity. Others are anti-American because it is easier to blame the United States for the blemishes of Europe's new society than to trace them back to Europe and to admit how difficult to remove they are. These men are like atheists who, while denying God's existence, never stop making God responsible for man's own plight.

In other words, what is required is Europe's return to a normative attitude. The situation permits it, and moreover *noblesse oblige.* This means, first, that Europeans ought not to act as if all of their social and national past deserved oblivion. Long after Tocqueville, Domenach and Crozier have observed how much the Europeans' concern for the defense of the individual against social pressures and care for the preservation of the intellectual's prestige were linked to the aristocratic age. This is no reason for giving up either. On the contrary, it is a reason for trying to adapt both to the age of democracy. All individuals, not just an elite, ought to be shown how to escape from the alienation of labor, from enslavement to technology, and from the shrill demands of the mass media, of the neighbors or of all sorts of groups. The distance which the intellectual liked to keep between himself and the mass, the irresponsibility to which he often laid claim ought to be abolished, but not his right and inclination to question. *Noblesse oblige* means also that Europeans have no justification for dropping what made Europe great—it was the continent of the examined life. Its spiritual silence of today is as deafening and disheartening as its earlier clamor of despair.

FOOTNOTES

1.   The difficulties encountered in trying to define a common policy on energy for the Six are partly explainable thereby.
2.   Alain Clément ("Vers l'Amérique," *La Caravelle,* No. 17 [Spring, 1964], p. 6) shrewdly attributes the Europeans' distrust of the official American version of President Kennedy's assassination, and the Americans' almost universal acceptance of this version, to this radical difference in the attitudes of the citizens toward public officials.
3.   Except in a few cases, like Sartre's—of all people; he who taught that there are no absolutes has turned politics into the "short change of the absolute."

Western European Publics in a Changing Environment: Integration and Alienation

Politics, Professor Harold Lasswell once wrote, is concerned with determining "who gets what, when, how." Although many efforts at further delineating the scope of the political realm have been made since these words were written, the questions posed by Lasswell continue to structure and guide the inquiries of political scientists. In seeking answers, students of governmental affairs, at least those investigating modern democratic societies, have frequently turned to the notion of group interest as a primary unit of analysis. Today, few political scientists would subscribe to the philosophy of "interest group determinism," according to which the policy outputs of a political system are simply the end products of an indiscriminate clash of self-serving interests. Fewer still, however, would deny that groups are important elements in the politics of Western democracies.

An observer of European politics cannot help but be impressed by the growing number of groups seeking access to the policy-making system. The signs of what Samuel Beer has called the "collectivist age" are abundant. In London, Paris, Bonn, and Rome,

39

governmental officials find themselves confronted by a proliferation of organized and semiorganized interests demanding attention, protection, and in some instances, structural revolution.

To a great extent this stepped-up pace of interaction between the political systems of Western Europe and their constituent elements is an outgrowth of a second development: the increasingly activist role governments have come to play in shaping and ordering the various facets of domestic life. This expansion of governmental involvement has placed a high premium on political organization. Quite simply, the potential rewards for effective group action, as well as the possible losses arising from complacency, have climbed enormously as a larger share of the national product is subjected to governmental control. The political arena has, as a result, become the site where the wide variety of interests indigenous to complex industrialized societies converge in search of satisfaction.

In an effort to accommodate the array of interested parties and at the same time to increase their own regulatory effectiveness, Western European governments have increasingly drawn organizational spokesmen for the major economic sectors into a network of formalized and semiformalized relationships. It is the rare European democracy, for example, which does not possess hundreds of advisory councils where public officials meet on a regular basis with representatives from specialized areas of the business, labor, and agricultural worlds. These institutionalized confrontations are supplemented by even more numerous informal contacts. It is this system of "functional representation" which is scrutinized by Michael J. Brenner in the article which leads off this section. Though Brenner's piece is directed at British practice, his efforts to relate the emergence of the functional mode of interest group representation to politico-economic changes of a type occurring in many Western societies give the article a timeliness which transcends the boundaries of a single nation.

Just who is normally benefited and who is deprived by this emergent system of democratic corporatism is a matter of some scholarly debate. According to one point of view, the ascendancy of functional representation as a political *modus operandi* in the democracies of Western Europe represents the successful penetration of the governmental machinery by special interests who obtain thereby near dictatorial powers over the shape and substance of policy outcomes. It is the pressure group tail—which S. E. Finer once called in Britain "the anonymous empire"—that is seen to be wagging the government dog.

There is, however, another possibility—namely, that functional representation will tend to compromise the autonomy of major interest groupings, draining them in practice of any meaningful influence. In his contribution to this volume, J. P. Nettl argues that British business, long held to be an interest sector with substantial political clout, has in fact been "colonized" by the occupants of Whitehall. According to Nettl, the concern for reaching and demonstrating consensus, a concern toward which functional representation is particularly aimed, has resulted in the British captains of industry becoming captives of the bureaucratic apparatus.

In addition to the question of *how* inputs are to be channeled into the political system there is the matter of *who* is to be found rapping on the governmental door. A dilemma facing any society caught up in a moment of change is the clash between historically dominant interests and newly vitalized groups seeking to establish or expand their political influence.

One actor with a long heritage of active participation in Western European political life is the Roman Catholic Church. And nowhere among the major continental democracies is the impact of the Church greater and more pervasive than in Italy. The intimate linkage between the Vatican and the Italian political system is revealed in that nation's Constitution which, through the incorporation of the Lateran Pacts of 1929, reaffirms the Church's special position. Yet, at the same time, Italy is caught in the throes of transition from a traditional agrarian economy to a modern urban industrial society. And one more or less universal aspect of the modernization process is a push toward greater secularization, a development which cannot help but threaten the power position of the Church.

The two most visible political allies of the Church in Italy are the Christian Democratic Party and Catholic Action. The latter is primarily a layman's organization with a broad membership base. The selection by Joseph LaPalombara, excerpted from his book on Italian interest groups, represents one of the few attempts to probe the political philosophy and strategy of Catholic Action. As LaPalombara notes, it is an organization regarded throughout Italy as "the single most powerful interest group operating in the political system . . ." Without question, a major share of the effort to defend and preserve the Church's privileged status against the encroachment of more secular interests will fall to the leaders of Catholic Action.

Another bulwark of tradition being buffeted by the winds of change blowing across Western Europe is the peasantry. In many European minds, the farmer living out his life in a small village is a familiar symbol of the area's cultural continuity and idyllic virtue. In France, particularly, the preservation of small marginal farms and the protection of their occupants assumed the stature of a near political cult in the first half of the twentieth century. Ensconced snugly behind sheltering tariff walls, the French farmer was driven neither into the city nor toward a program of agricultural modernization.

For decades, the peasant sector served as a drag on France's efforts to industrialize, leaving the nation economically enfeebled and militarily vulnerable. Following the debacle of the Second World War, it was apparent that a large and highly splintered agricultural sector was a time-honored commitment which France could now ill-afford to support. At few other points are the practical elements of Western Europe's identity crisis so clearly visible as in the efforts of the French peasantry to adjust themselves to the demands of an industrial, mass-consumption age. It has been a process fraught with violence and unrest. The selection authored by John Ardagh conveys some of the details and much of the spirit of this struggle for survival and adaptation.

The subsequent piece by Val R. Lorwin also focuses on the group consequences of economic change. This time, however, the subject is the European working class. In most Western European nations the forces of the industrial revolution combined with feudal and aristocratic traditions to produce stratified societies, marked by serious inequities in the distribution of the mounting economic wealth. Even allowing for national differences, the typical European laborer was set apart from his American counterpart by a lower relative income, limited mobility opportunities, and deeply rooted feelings of class animosity. The resultant frustrations were manifested through protest and in the emergence of organized working class movements, often espousing revolutionary notions of political and economic change.

Much has occurred in recent years, to bring into question the continuing validity of the stereotyped European worker as a disadvantaged, alienated being. "Economic miracles" in most of the major Western European nations have produced levels of blue collar prosperity which have noticeably eclipsed the former discrepancies between working-class and middle-class standards of living. In addition, the technological and managerial emphasis of modern industrialization has fostered a proliferation of white collar positions, greatly increasing the chances for upward occupational advances by manual workers or their offspring. As the objective distance between social classes has narrowed, it is likely that the subjective dimension has undergone a mellowing process. The worker is less apt to perceive society in terms of a class struggle and less likely to feel himself part of a deprived class community.

Although Professor Lorwin utilizes a time perspective of approximately 150 years, his inquiries into the political implications of shifts in working class conditions remain timely and pertinent. Lorwin's remarks regarding the mitigating effects which continued economic growth may have on proletarian protest and radicalism touch points of interest to many observers of contemporary European politics, especially students of French and Italian government.

While many political scientists would agree that blue collar prosperity is making European workers into less fervent political participants, there is uncertainty as to how far this moderation is likely to extend. In particular, will material "embourgeoisement" of large sectors of a nation's working class produce a corresponding tendency to desert the traditional parties of labor and adopt middle class patterns of partisan behavior? It is specifically to this question that J. H. Goldthorpe, *et al.* address themselves, utilizing modern sampling and interviewing techniques to probe the attitudes and habits of a collection of relatively affluent British factory workers. Their findings serve as a valuable warning against underestimating the forces of tradition and over-extending the explanatory power of economic factors.

European workers have a long tradition of sustained political activism. In contrast, the involvement of students on a broad front has had a more sporadic history. After more than a decade of relative lethargy, youthful Europeans have re-emerged as forceful participants in the political process. In good measure, the student uprisings which have appeared in cities all across Europe are part of a worldwide pattern of youthful discontent. Yet, as Renate Mayntz and Michel Crozier point out in their contributions, European students are also reacting to a variety of more parochial irritants.

Student leaders in Western Europe are prone to argue that like the classic proletariat they and their colleagues constitute a repressed social group, laboring under difficult study conditions, archaic procedures, and insensitive instructors. Indeed, appeals for common-front campaigns linking activist youths with workers' groups have been a frequent feature of student demonstrations. For the most part, these overtures have met with disinterest or even antipathy on the part of laborers, who, despite the general validity of many of the students' grievances, tend to consider them spoiled, middle-class ingrates.

The student reaction in Western Europe has not been limited to attempts at remedying educational deficiencies. Motivated by a strain of youthful idealism and a variety of specific ideologies, the students have also turned their attentions toward broader social and political questions. The "sterility" of German consensus politics, the stifling "bureaucratism" of French existence, and the gross economic inequalities of Italian life have all been the targets of student condemnation. This determination to reshape their environment makes European students appropriate symbols of their age. Though their visions are frequently Utopian, they leave little doubt that, should their efforts bear fruit, yesterday's Europe—a set of more or less closed, stratified, and privileged societies—will not likely survive the present period of introspection with much of its image intact.

3 MICHAEL J. BRENNER

Functional Representation and Interest Group Theory: Some Notes on British Practice

ECONOMIC POLICY-MAKING AND INTEREST POLITICS

In his seminal study of economic policy in Western societies, *Modern Capitalism*, Andrew Shonfield notes five outstanding features of postwar politico-economic conditions. In an abbreviated form they are:

1. "There is the vastly increased influence of the public authorities on the management of the economic system.

2. "The preoccupation with social welfare leads to the use of public funds on a rising scale.

3. "In the private sector the violence of the market has been tamed.

4. "It has now come to be taken for granted, both by governments and by the average person in the Western capitalist

Reprinted from *Comparative Politics*, II, No. 1 (October 1969), pp. 116-134, by permission of the author and publisher. Footnotes omitted by the editors.

countries, that each year should bring a noticeable increase in the real income per head of population.

5. "The characteristic attitude in large-scale economic management, both inside government and in the private sector, which has made itself increasingly felt during the postwar period, is the pursuit of intellectual coherence. Its most obvious manifestation is in long-range economic planning."

In making these five points, Shonfield is calling attention to the significant increase in the use of public power to remedy two chronic conditions of industrial life: (a) the instability of the market-based economy which, liable to periodic and sharp fluctuations caused by seemingly uncontrollable forces, increased social tensions and caused great personal distress; and (b) wide disagreement over the extent of public obligation to guarantee the well-being of a citizenry less and less able to rely upon its own resources for its economic security. One dimension of the issue involved a technical debate (naturally strongly overlaid with political bias) as to the capacity of public authorities to resolve the problem with the available theoretical knowledge and administrative tools. The other engendered a more general debate as to the virtue and desirability of the government's assuming responsibility for economic direction and/or welfare. Each of these questions could be dealt with only in the light of suggested answers to the other. The problem of welfare was made all the more acute by society's inability to domesticate the market, accentuating the individual insecurity which is a concomitant of industrial organization. An effective welfare program that sought to rationalize public aid as part of a coherent national policy, rather than simply serving as an elaborate dole, required that intelligent coordination of the economy which governments were unwilling or unable to establish. And a concerted government effort to master the market was not forthcoming until a political consensus had crystallized in favor of it. For once a government undertook to assure the minimal well-being of its citizens, it was compelled to arrogate to itself powers necessary for the distribution of the national product, redirecting portions of that product into those areas which otherwise would be starved for resources—a radical policy departure on which there was no general agreement. If it were to act on the confident expectation that it would not be crimped by economic recession, government had to concern itself with making prosperity routine, through establishing that element of control and taking those steps which would enable it to prevent any serious relapse. This commitment, once made, inevitably would lead to some form of planning—an initiative which political conditions and the state of economic learning did not allow.

For a nation like Britain the exigencies of World War II accomplished what peacetime politics could not do. Bearing witness to the fact that a modern government enjoyed the administrative acumen and economic expertise necessary for effective economic management, wartime experience pointed the way to a number of innovations in public policy in the years after 1945. Measures that would never have been envisaged in normal circumstances were employed. The crisis government saw to it that investments were effectively coordinated, the movement of labor was directed, relations between management and trade unions were made an explicit state responsibility, prices and wages were fixed, and even physical allocation of scarce resources was undertaken when necessary. Not only was the practical question of planning in large part answered by wartime experience, but also a consensus on the welfare issue had grown up. A new sense of national unity combined with the demands for social justice produced by the agony of the depression to lay the basis for expanded welfare activity. The 1930's had attuned society to the magnitude of the problem. Common sacrifices established the principle that the community should be responsible for guaranteeing its citizens a minimum standard of living. Willingness to accept these obligations dovetailed with the confident expectation that it would now be possible for the government (following the rules of financial and monetary regulation) to bend the economy to its will.

The economic component of the new attitude is neatly outlined for us by Shonfield. The question remains, however, as to the manner in which political practices have been affected by the requirements for policy-making in these areas. Let us try to specify and delineate some of these effects.

The first, and most obvious, consequence is the expansion of government activity in these fields to the point where issues of economic and social organization have become the major preoccupation of public officials, at all levels, in terms of the time and energy expended on them. Government has the distinct function of overseeing the mechanisms of the economy as a whole. It is the only agency that can "see the forest for the trees"—performing a vital task of coordination among groups, organizations, and industrial enterprises each of which has only a partial vision of the productive system. The *de facto* division of labor among these institutions, which creates of the entire society an implicitly cooperative enterprise, has come under the charge of the state in its role of political arm of the community. Governments' powers of technical synchronization, which include welfare policies, are a logical expression of this unique role.

The second political effect of a successful welfare society is a lessening of the scope and intensity of economic strife. The potential of an affluent industrial society to reduce conflict to nuanced differences over income distribution and mobility opportunities has been realized to an appreciable extent. The confrontation between self-conscious classes of "proletariat" and "bourgeoisie," the source of most industrial strife, has given way to a looser system of social differentiation that blurs the lines between strata. It is the occupational group, whether union, trade or professional association, that has increasingly become the focus of loyalty—society tending toward a pluralism of groups whereby material interest, productive function, and communal identity all coincide. Through acknowledgement of a common dependence on a stable industrial order for their individual gain, groups limit their competition to secondary issues. Rather than fight over the recipe to be used in baking the economic pie and over who should be invited to the feast, they limit debate to practical questions of how to make the pastry bigger and bigger. Politics increasingly centers on alternative means for reconciling and coordinating diverse interests, while maintaining unity and equilibrium by compromise and consultation within a broad consensual framework. Government thus tends to become the regulator of particular interests, registering the demands of groups while fulfilling its foremost obligation of maximizing welfare.

The third aspect of economics-focused postwar politics is the rise in influence—although rarely prominence—of administrative managers in the national civil service. As the attention of governments is directed increasingly toward the arduous and demanding task of promulgating and administering carefully drawn plans to regulate the financial and industrial infrastructure of society, the status and policy responsibilities of high-level bureaucrats have been raised. In effect, the personnel of the state have come to perform many economic functions which were previously the responsibility of private citizens. The French sociologist Raymond Aron describes the situation thus, "The three vital propensities of industrialism for which an entrepreneurial group has served as cynosure now pervade all sectors of society; the spirit of science and technology, the spirit of economic calculation, and the spirit of progress." They have become routinized. Now the ethic of the whole society, it is logical that the state should have moved to affirm, develop, and direct these propensities. The state's assumption of this task quite naturally has entailed some shift in the accent of government leadership. Specialists in technical fields, expert executors of the myriad legislative acts and administrative decrees that make up economic policy, and manipulators of the industrial power constellation have grown in number and importance. Their *forte* is their managerial skills; their attributes usually include a high level of practical competence and a predilection for situations amenable to technical calculation; their performance is characteristically evaluated according to standards of tangible accomplishment. These "technocrats," as they are loosely referred to, are a distinct feature of postwar government.

The movement of organized interests into the heart of the governmental process is equally a feature of postwar politics. It has been one of the generally unforeseen by-products of innovations in planning and welfare to give economic interests an essential role in making and implementing policy in these two fields. For economic management to be effective in a democratic society, organized representatives of the various productive forces are necessarily in regular consultation with those government authorities responsible for economic policy. As Shonfield states it, "All planning of the modern capitalist type implies the acceptance of some measure of cooperatism in political organization: that follows from basing the conduct of economic affairs on the deliberate decisions of organized groups of producers, instead of leaving the outcome to the clash between individual competitors in the market." One implication of limited, indirect planning, as found in virtually all Western societies, is that administrators and politicians concerned with matters of economic steering cannot base policy on a purely objective calculation of those measures most likely to expand national production. Policy-making is not a simple academic exercise, nor can they implement their policy without regard for the character of the economic organizations that are ultimately responsible for translating government programs into concrete productive actions. Government officials are obliged to engage in regular exchanges with organized interests in an effort to secure their cooperation, and, if possible, their approval. The actual processes of economic management are thus more flexible and introduce many more "nonobjective" factors into the decisions of policy-makers than would be the case if society were organized as one highly centralized, administrative unit *cum* workshop, à la Saint-Simon.

The welfare component of economic policy reinforces this tendency to moderate standards of technical efficiency with concern for the desires of economic associations and their organizational personalities. As both public authorities and the public at large have come to define social rights in group terms, the welfare concept has been broadened to encompass programs intended to minimize the dislocation and material loss caused by changes in the technology of production and the decline of certain industrial sectors. Welfare thus connotes a community obligation to protect the material well-being of significant economic groupings as represented in organized associations, and to consider carefully the effects of any given policy on all interests concerned.

"FUNCTIONAL REPRESENTATION" AND ADMINISTRATION

"Functional representation" in the administrative realm refers to the semi-institutionalized pattern of contact and consultation between permanent officials of economic ministries and the officers of economic associations. As a concept, it also reflects the important place both parties now hold in the policy-making process. For this relationship to be made intelligible, it is necessary to revise the conventional interpretation of bureaucratic function, the activities of interest groups, and their mode of interaction. Such a revision is offered herein.

The classical definition of bureaucracy as developed by Max Weber underscored the impersonality of its operation. As an instrument for the execution of laws it was understood to be totally impartial, avoiding all particularisms in applying universally valid rules to individual cases. However appropriate this concept might be in civil administration, it has proved difficult to sustain this principle when government enters into the field of economic management. The rapidly expanding contact between formal authority and private persons in this area is of a radically different nature. Interchange is not characteristically between official as rule-making automaton and individual citizen as legal entity. It is between the administrator using his discretionary powers to achieve more general goals and a well-organized association representing appreciable economic interests whose cooperation is often necessary for the realization of these ends. Administrative responsibility has increased commensurately with growth in the complexity and differentiation of industrial society. It today represents the manifest need for mechanisms of coordination, since government has assumed an unprecedented set of functions tangential to the classical problem of bureaucratic authority. Permanent civil servants are influential public actors in their own right. They are active collaborators with ministers in the formation of policy within their spheres of departmental authority as well as participants in regular exchanges with economic associations. In Great Britain they are the source for virtually all the technical information and advice essential to development of economic programs.

A distinction must therefore be made between "formal rationality" and "substantive rationality" in public administration. The former derives from a concept of bureaucratic authority which endows citizens with individual civil rights. The legal status accorded persons denotes rights and duties which, by their codification in formal rules, make possible "the abstract application of authority." Public authority, so defined, as in Weber's "law-community," is insulated from all outside influences, creates self-contained spheres of administration, and acknowledges no intermediary groups between individual and state. In practice, the concept of "formal rationality" has now been modified by the principle of functional representation that points to "group specific" rights. Where social rights are understood in group terms, there is a progressive tendency for bureaucratic insulation to be replaced by a wide range of organized and informal contacts between state agencies and corporate groups. In the present industrial context, they stand as the institutional symbols of the public obligation to protect, and engage in a dialogue with the significant economic and social interests as represented by organized groups. Thus, a form of industrial corporatism has appeared—unplanned, and almost by inadvertence.

The practical reasons for growing functional representation are most obvious. Trade associations and trade unions possess technical knowledge and expertise that are very useful to government agencies. No one can deny that the implementation of any economic program is improved by enlisting their cooperation. Their control over one functional area of public life necessitates some connection with government. And, in any event, political realities demand that they be given a voice in the determination of policy. The extensive network of interchanges between official departments and private organizations has become part of the routine of government.

There are, however, reasons for favoring and nurturing corporate ties that derive, in the British context, from a broader conception of the group's place in society. The concept of corporate representation is a very old one that never entirely lost its influence on public thinking. Liberalism might have been the dominant philosophy for over a century, yet it never succeeded in completely destroying pre-industrial attitudes.

As a constituent component of society, it is felt that organized interests, in Professor Beer's words, "deserve(s) a share of power to protect and promote . . . (their) just needs." Unity depends upon having all segments of the nation work together, at once properly concerned for their own interests and integrity, and cognizant of what is required for the good of the whole. In this circumstance, the basis of group recognition is less some precise notion of performance than a general understanding that each group is a building-block of society. Group rights, in turn, are contingent less upon meeting practical standards of economic function than upon the continued recognition of groups as organizational representatives of the sector with which they are identified. Their contribution is, therefore, not always tangible and their right to participate in government decisions is not predicated on a prior agreement as to practical achievement.

THE MODE OF INTER-ACTION

We shall center the discussion of functional representation in Great Britain around three main questions, the answers to which hopefully will clarify the nature of the relationship of interests to administrative departments.

Question I.   What areas of policy-making are viewed by private and public actors as properly those for interest group involvement?

Our foregoing discussion suggests that the vestiges of pre-modern, i.e., pre-individualist, political culture in Britain have combined with the several impulses of industrial life to produce a distinctive style of corporate politics. One of its clearest expressions is in the careful delimitation of governmental and private spheres of authority and obligation. There exists: (a) a recognition of the substantial rights enjoyed by organized groups to be primarily responsible for their internal affairs and to be protected from outside pressures which might necessitate changes in their organizational structures; and (b) a common acceptance by corporate groups of an autonomous sphere of decision-making which is the responsibility of national leaders and which centers on matters of "high policy"—especially foreign affairs—in which those corporate groups refrain from interfering.

It is within this frame of reference that we can better understand the single-minded attention paid to the maintenance of jurisdictional boundaries, especially by trade unions, a factor that is often bewildering to the outsider. For it is a matter of history that corporate groups have been as concerned with safeguarding their independence against the possible encroachment of government as with availing themselves of the privilege to make demands and influence policy. This is manifestly the case with labor unions which could never be certain whether the state was presenting itself as friend or foe. (Evidence of this fear of ensnarlment is the skepticism with which large segments of the business community, as well as the Trades Union Congress, reacted to the creation of the National Economic Development Councils, and then the Department of Economic Affairs, which sought to institutionalize procedures for coordinating public policy with the decisions of private groups.) This conception of interest group rights has been a real impediment to the development of new techniques for economic management. An activist philosophy of economic direction requires a willingness to use a modicum of persuasion, often backed by coercive sanctions, to secure the tacit support and optimally the active collaboration, of private interests in the launching of new policies. To put it another way, a prime pre-condition for planning is that government have at its disposal discretionary powers to influence the flow of capital and skilled human resources. To do so, however, necessitates making choices as to which enterprise or sector of the economy should expand and which should be restricted or allowed to contract. British commitment to a principle of formal equality among groups makes preferential economic treatment extremely difficult if not impossible. For it entails encroaching upon the organizational rights of corporate groups, with the use of weapons powerful enough to call their very existence into question. For example, the series of measures needed to meet Britain's chronic balance-of-payments problem—an income policy, coordinated investment decisions, monetary reforms—requires a concerted effort on the part of government to convince, cajole, and even, where necessary, command the groups affected. Such an attempt runs up against the obstacle political actors run to preserve traditional practices that sanctify jurisdictional preserves. The implication is, in Professor Shonfield's words, that the "British allow effective power to slide into the hands of the corporations without subjecting them to public control of it." Among industrial associations, jurisdictional sensitivity has been given practical meaning by the movement toward planning techniques that seem to threaten the associations' freedom of action and freedom for profits. The opposition of both business and labor to inroads upon the principle of a limited government role in economic direction and their rejection of a French-style indicative planning can be understood in this light. Imbued with these beliefs—at once liberal and traditional in origin—organized groups have sought to preserve their essential autonomy while looking askance at any radical attempts to bind them more closely to officialdom—whether the latter's overtures be threatening or benevolent in intention. Their success in avoiding the embrace of state agencies owes much to the absence of an administrative ideology of positive government among bureaucrats. Civil servants have largely shared these views about the impropriety of infringing upon the preserves of corporate groups. Thinking in terms of quasi-independent jurisdictions, they, like the heads of private groups, cannot help but see the type of embrace offered by comprehensive planning, for example, as fatal to the rights of economic organizations as presently constituted.

The counterpart to this anxiety about improper intrusions of the state is a willingness to accord a significant freedom of action to national leaders in their "rightful" areas of responsibility. A vague, tacitly agreed upon, yet very real line is drawn between government's proper decision-making prerogatives and interest organizations' right to be self-determining. However subtle and complicated the relations between government agencies and corporate groups have become, neither side has demonstrated a desire to blur completely the distinction between formal political authority and private economic interest. By reserving for itself a carefully delineated realm of initiative in policy formulation, the government secures its own powers even as influence is extended to nongovernmental groups. The latter are primarily concerned that they be kept reasonably well informed about events, that their views be given a sympathetic hearing, that their established rights be preserved, and their basic interests guaranteed. Otherwise, their leaders do not usually seek a direct voice in the process of policy formulation in areas affecting the national interest—such as foreign policy—in their capacity as officers of an interest organization.

Question II.   What is the characteristic mode of exchange between government and private interests?

Our discussion up to this point has proceeded abstractly and has dealt in generalized phenomena. We shall now look more closely at the actual character of the connection between administrative departments and private groups. Contact is not random nor engaged in desultorily. It is well-structured and routinized. The creation of stable ties is aided by the formal pairing of public agency and interest group. Each private organization has its "sponsoring" department which serves as its link to government. Thus, the National Farmers Union has bonds with the Ministry of Agriculture, the Trades Union Congress with the Ministry of Labour, the now defunct Iron and Steel Federation was "sponsored" by the Ministry of Power, most industrial associations treat with the Board of Trade, while the commercial banks maintain ties directly with the Treasury (as well as acting in concert with the Bank of England). Because of its heterogeneous membership, the C.B.I. (formerly F.B.I.), Confederation of British Industries, has interchange with several ministries—the Board of Trade on general matters pertaining to some sector of industry, and with the Treasury on broad policy issues. (The C.B.I. is a sort of holding-company for industrial associations organized on a production basis. Its format is that of a loose coalition, and its vaguely worded public pronouncements are compromise resolutions that do not truly reflect the hard interests of its component groups. Its officials, who are chosen because of their tact and experience, in both government and business, serve as buffers between the state and the world of commerce.)

These departments are known as "vertical ministries" with special responsibilities for some productive sector of the economy except for the Treasury, which has more embracing responsibilities. They are charged with keeping their respective groups informed of government intentions in relevant areas of economic policy, with communicating the views of these groups to the Treasury or to the Cabinet, and with cooperating in the routine implementation of administrative programs. The notion of "sponsorship" is taken so seriously that, for example, even when the British Electronics Allied Manufacturers Association is engaged in consultations with the Treasury on some pressing matter, protocol demands that a representative from the appropriate department in the Board of Trade must be present and that duplicate memos must be sent to his ministry.

Interchange occurs at two levels, depending on the importance of the issue under discussion. Daily contacts on detailed regulatory matters are made between the private association's permanent staff and the middle-range administrators, who perform a largely service function. The great bulk of business is transacted here, and usually over the telephone. It is uncontroversial, well within the scope of established practice, and the decisions reached are little influenced by personalities.

On other occasions, when reform proposals come under consideration or discontents are brought to the fore, the pattern of contact changes. If the initiative is that of the private group, more prominent officials are brought into the picture by each side. The practice among business associations is for the director-general to make a more formal written approach to the undersecretary or assistant secretary. Individual points of contention are dealt with expeditiously on a personal basis. If the problem raised proves to be a thorny one, the two might well thrash it out over lunch at the United Universities or Reform Club. Needless to say, these consultations are conducted with the utmost discretion and the exchanges remain unpublicized. At other times talks are instigated by the ministry on its own volition or under prodding by its political head, to sound out the association as to its views on some aspect of economic policy. In this way reaction among economic groups is anticipated when the government is contemplating a policy departure. In either instance, the issue might be sufficiently broad in scope as eventually to require a series of meetings to examine jointly the problems at hand. They will usually be attended by civil servants up to the assistant secretary level (supervised by the permanent secretary) and their counterparts in the private organization.

Most discussions of this nature unfold in an atmosphere of cordial informality symptomatic of a very considerable mutual respect. The "old-boy net"—an idea now enshrined in the Valhalla of political clichés—is not in any literal sense the unifying force, however. The phrase only has significance if it is understood to refer to a certain community of values shared by men from similar social backgrounds who probably, although not always, are the product of an Oxbridge education. Contrary to the legend, they almost certainly do not preface their consultations with reminiscence about schoolboy pranks. Trust and understanding are more likely the products of longtime professional contacts, often as colleagues and collaborators in government service, especially during World War II when many executives from private industry took up public posts. Thus, the three top officials of the British Electrical and Allied Manufacturers Association held administrative posts in which they dispensed functions very similar to those now being undertaken by the men with whom they treat. Indeed, the vestiges of wartime experience can be seen in the fact that liaison offices within trade associations are still known by their wartime name of "production sections." Parenthetically, it can be noted that here is one of the sources of the uniformity of attitude on major issues that constitutes the famous "Establishment" opinion. It is in settings like this that the basis is laid for an informal, uncoordinated thrashing out of national problems—whether the individuals involved are formally responsible for the decision or not.

Despite the apparent informality of the relationship, the role separation between public officer and private official is maintained. Discretion dictates that the official representative never entirely reveal his intentions, just as the intentions of the minister are not made known to him in all their particulars. The civil servant is concerned, above all else, that in his efforts to improve liaison he should not suffer the embarrassment which would ensue from public, premature disclosure of information about "intention" that is communicated to the private official. In a sense, we can observe the principle of divided spheres of responsibility at work here. The existence of these proprieties should not detract from the intimacy of the relationship. The process of interchange is informal and conducted in confidence. Yet the public official is careful to keep in mind that his ultimate loyalty is to higher administrative authority and to his political superior. In this effort he is aided by the private official who accepts administrative independence as a *quid pro quo* acknowledgement of his own organizational rights and principles. British corporate politics is thus remarkably free of the type of conspiratorial cabal between interest and department whereby the two work hand in glove for advancement of the interests concerned and the expansion of bureaucratic empires. The "administrative class" civil servant's definition of his responsibilities in terms of national service minimizes this tendency commonly experienced elsewhere.

Parallel examples of cooperation can be seen between trade unions and the Ministry of Labour. The personal rapport to be found between many trade association officials and civil servants is usually lacking. Even there, however, the cumulative effect of years of regular contact and protracted dialogue on a range of common problems produces a similar capacity for free communication without fear of retribution. As for the N.F.U. and the Ministry of Agriculture, the very specialized character of the subject-matter and the technical decisions it demands assures the greatest degree of cooperation. The Agriculture Act of 1947 set up a complicated price review machinery that calls for an extensive series of meetings throughout the year. They proceed in two stages. Price Review Technical Meetings between economists on both sides undertake the laborious task of reaching agreement on the statistics that will serve as the basis for fixing price guarantees and deficiency payments. These are set by the main Review Committee that brings together officers of the N.F.U. and the leading administrators of the Ministry. The specificity of the Ministry's obligations and the resulting common perspective on national economic questions shared with the N.F.U. produce the closest thing to interest group-department collusion to be found in Britain.

Question III.   What resources are available to each party in its efforts to influence the other?

In speaking of resources we are asking two questions: what powers are held by interest groups to command the attention of policy-makers and influence a course of action?; and what powers do officials have to resist influences while promulgating programs of their own? The impact made by private associations can be estimated in the light of four factors: (a) the practical need of officials for their specialized knowledge; (b) the value of their cooperation in making a given economic policy successful; (c) the rights accorded them by the system; and (d) the political pressure they can bring to bear. Official resources can be judged by reference to: (e) the level of expertise and specialized information they possess; (f) the scope of their institutional authority to initiate and apply policies; and (g) their political backing.

Our foregoing discussion indirectly provided information on most of these points. Cooperation to the extent and in the detail that characterizes relations between the parties cannot but increase knowledge of each other (a, b, e). The staff of interest groups are thoroughly familiar with the workings of the relevant ministry; civil servants are knowledgeable about the operations and desires of the private association; statistical information is usually public knowledge. There is no doubt that the effectiveness of government could be markedly impaired if the interest group were prepared to deny the government the benefit of information as to its plans in such areas as investment and salary claims. Similarly, by refusing to cooperate on matters such as technological development it could undermine the government's most ingeniously conceived programs. To counteract these steps, economic departments could fall back on their own experience and practical understanding to gain their desired ends. The long tenure of many senior officials in their ministries would assist them in this undertaking. Moreover, the government can bypass interest groups, resort to legislation, and impose its will directly on corporations, workers, or agriculturalists.

But this entire hypothetical discussion assumes a state of open conflict between interest and government that would be a most extraordinary development in Britain. The flexible system of contacts we outlined has, as one of its purposes, the prevention of direct conflict. "Continuity" and "trust" are the two words most crucial to an understanding of these relations. Over the years a mutual confidence is built up as to the sincerity and responsibility of each party. It is not based merely on personalities. It is based on the belief that mutual benefit is to be derived ultimately from the connection, whatever the short-term disagreements. Nothing could be more detrimental to this quasi-diplomacy among friendly powers that is constantly going on in the interstices of government than a freezing of the channels of communication as the consequence of attempts on either side to undercut the position of the other. For his part, the head of an economic association recognizes the restrictions under which the administrator acts, and knows that, if he is to benefit from the connection, any rupture of this must be carefully avoided.

Two further considerations that reinforce pressures to reach consensus enter into the situation. The public values of contemporary Britain proscribe government attempts at destroying the effectiveness of private associations in the area of their primary concern (c). As discussed in our remarks on jurisdictional spheres, it would be deemed a radical departure from accepted practice if the government were to bypass groups completely in the formation of policy, or to pursue policies that severely harmed the interests concerned. This is a principle of administrative practice that has its counterpart in the realm of party politics. Neither major party can afford completely to alienate a major sector of society (d). Electoral necessity demands otherwise, and a perceived obligation to protect constituent elements of the national community emphasizes the desirability of reconciling interests and conciliating groups.

At the same time, those officials—permanent and political—responsible for national economic policy are charged with advancing the common good. In the Treasury, for example, top level officials are supposed to think in terms of the long-term health of the economy, and to deal with existing structural defects. At all times cognizant of the views expressed by particular interests, they are nevertheless given the authority to formulate policies that are something more than syntheses of the desires of private associations. There exists, then, the real possibility of a contradiction between the national "good" and the welfare of its individual components. To achieve this end might well require a concerted effort on the part of government to implement drastic measures without the full cooperation of all interests. The ultimate determination to proceed in this way will depend in large measure on the will and dedication of political leaders (f). In balancing the perceived need to move ahead with an innovative policy against the views of private groups or with their grudging approval only, the forcefulness of influential civil servants and the decisiveness of politicians will probably be the critical variables. (The Labour Government's austerity policy—its formulation and implementation—would make an excellent case study in this regard. Without detailing an analysis of a topic that is beyond the scope of this paper, we should note the very definite strain between an executive assessment of economic need and a deep-seated reluctance not only to restrict programs of benefit to party supporters but also for the state to impose measures in the form of a wage freeze on a major organized group that constrains severely their group activity.)

CONCLUSION

This outline of the ties between interest groups and administrative departments in Britain was meant to delineate the outstanding features of a relationship which, in its form and concept, expresses both the practical logic of public policy where government acts as manager of the national economy and the customary logic of long-established procedural norms and political values. To acquire an understanding of the phenomenon of functional representation as it appears in the British context required, therefore, that careful attention be paid to the distinctive manner in which the government exercises its powers of economic decision-making, the dominant concepts of what constitutes a proper level of activism, and the manner by which traditional beliefs nuance present institutional arrangements. In each national setting, it might be expected that the peculiar mix of political and economic elements in that system will produce its own form of interest-administrative department relations. One can imagine several alternative models, and national experience does offer a variety of patterns. In France, for example, one finds a more activist philosophy of administration, technocratically disposed civil servants, the use by government of coercive sanction, and greater disparity in the strength of the various interests.

The rather general propositions presented in this article represent an attempt at developing an approach to the study of interest groups in industrial democracies that emphasizes their logical place in societies where the calculus of economic productivity has been a major responsibility of government. In so doing, the article aimed at avoiding stylized methods of approach. There is no pretense to comprehensiveness. Qualifications likely would be made if its more general conclusions, even as regards British practice, are applied to specific instances in a case study. Just as this analysis sought to specify aspects of a political phenomenon often treated in isolation from the broad flow of national politics and public policy, so might it be expected that the richness of detail provided by an empirical study would suggest further refinements.

Neither the uniqueness of national circumstance nor the peculiar features of a given department-group linkage is an argument against the development of general theory. The unfortunate tendency for research to be narrowly focused on a discrete interest group or issue is both a cause and effect of the paucity of systematic theory, substantive hypotheses, or viable models. Where theory is employed in a group study, the theory is likely to be either (a) overdrawn in extending the group principle to political life in general (Truman); or (b) only tangentially concerned with the activities of economic associations (pluralist theory a la Dahl); or (c) so abstract as to lack structure and specificity (Almond). And, in almost all instances, the theory will offer little in the way of reference to the various policy areas on which group activity centers.

Although this essay offers no formal theory or model, it might be useful to suggest four guidelines (or, perhaps more accurately, four points of reference) for the study of interest politics at the administrative level.

1. Careful distinctions should be made between interest group behavior in the legislative sphere from group ties to administrative departments. Critical differences exist in the mode of exchange, the content of issues, and the level of partisan concern.

2. Functional representation can be most fruitfully studied when it is viewed as the interplay of institutional forces sharing a frame of action and performing interdependent functions. The action-reaction models that emphasize the structural independence of the actors distort the process of interest articulation by disregarding the community of purpose that is a major feature of the department-group relationship.

3. Integral to any theory of functional representation should be an acute awareness of the policy context. Without reference to the broad movement of government into new areas of economic management, the normal danger of creating stilted models, logically precise but of limited utility, is accentuated. For this reason, there would appear to be a sound basis for expanding analyses to include the political changes associated with the governance of an industrial economy.

4. The elements of political culture which in each national setting exercise a considerable influence on the manner of group-agency interchange should be

examined. It is clear that functional representation does not follow formal rules in a highly-structured context. Rather, both form and substance of the relationship are dependent in good part on unwritten norms and values that help determine powers and prerogatives.

These are but a few touchstones for analysis and theory-building. It is hoped that theory developed along these lines could further the analysis of national systems while also suggesting elements for a cross-national comparison of interest groups.

J. P. NETTL

Consensus or Elite Domination: The Case of Business

This article attempts to demonstrate a general thesis from a particular segment of society. The general thesis is that the famous British consensus is not a sort of social or political ectoplasm which emanates from, and hovers over, the consentient, but a social institution with its own structure, procedures, attitudes, beliefs. Nor is it equally shared. Instead, like a magnet, it sucks in members (or servants) from the periphery—away from their own self interested groupings. In doing so it emasculates these groups, while preserving their outward shell of autonomy and independence. Pressure group politics are therefore less 'real' than they seem—their very success in Britain, which has thrilled (American) political commentators searching for limited and orderly struggle as the highest form of organized democracy, may indeed depend on this element of shadow-boxing. It will be argued moreover that the consensus has its peculiar and particular exponent, both vehicle of consensus attitudes and ideal type—the higher civil service. It does

Reprinted from *Political Studies*, 13, No. 1 (February 1965), pp. 22-38, 41-42, by permission of the author and the Clarendon Press, Oxford. Footnotes omitted by the editors.

not create the consensus, nor is it created by it; nonetheless it is the centre of its magnetic field, its institutional expression.

This general thesis is examined in the particular context of the business community in its relations with Whitehall. The relationship is discussed in its various aspects—social, procedural, structural, legal, and from the point of view of policy, public and sectional. The usual practice in such cases is to use the tunnel method: broad general proposition—particular and 'narrow' application including 'proof'—restatement of broad general proposition with 'proof' of the validity of the connexion between the particular and the general. I shall be less orderly, shuttling back and forth from the general to the particular all the time. I believe the one makes no sense if divorced from the other, even for a short space of time.

It is a large subject and I can only sketch the problem in an article, ask more questions than I can answer and, even where an answer is attempted, indicate the manner of answering rather than provide the substantive answer itself. But perhaps this manner of approach will, if found valid, enable others to screw out answers from the intractable plethora of social relations in England.

Before we get down to any *relationship,* we must briefly examine the state of the related. I hope to show that as far as the business community is concerned, it is a state of remarkable weakness and diffuseness—compared, say, to organized labour or the professions. Lacking firm sense of their distinct identity, and belief in their distinct purpose, businessmen have been particularly vulnerable to the pressure of the consensus as emanating from Whitehall. (I have of course to show, and not merely to assume, the latter's strength and cohesiveness—indeed its very existence). The whole problem is largely virgin soil. There is a certain amount of factual material concerned with the structure and methods of government in order to be able to study its relations with the structure and methods of business. The new (in Britain) subject of pressure groups has again opened up certain aspects of business-government relations, but not in an exclusive sense; pressure groups are part of the political input process (in the broadest sense of 'political') in which business is an also-ran. Significantly the best detailed studies of pressure groups in Britain do not relate to business at all, but to professional organizations. Then there is the amorphous field known as 'economics', particularly policy and planning, in which government action on the economy has been discussed—the economy being a nameless, faceless, passive honeycomb of 'firms'. Finally business has been studied *per se*— with the government now in the role of faceless though active juggler of the parameters. Thus there is much incidental information on the relationship between government and business, but usually with the one serving as a vaguely limiting or activating factor of the other. No specific study of the dynamic, exclusive and precise relationship exists. Nor, of course, has this relationship been used as evidence of wider social problems.

THE IMAGE OF BUSINESS

Let us start with that mythical beast, the rugged entrepreneur: individualistic, non-conformist, aggressive, anti-social—the spider who sits at the centre of all the symmetrical webs of economists' models relating to perfect competition or the market economy. Historically, he is the product of ignorance and neglect; the government and the social forces behind it were hardly aware of his social or political existence until he had created his revolution—in the North, at the far end of the kingdom. For a long time, most of the legislation which took note of his existence was designed to inhibit him rather than positively to help those who worked for him, not to speak of helping him. The significant difference between the industrial revolution in England and elsewhere in Europe was the indifference of the central government, its failure for a long time to see any but undesirable consequences in what was happening—the ruin of agriculture. It seems to be a valid generalization in Europe that the later industrial takeoff and drive to maturity took place, the greater the extent to which governments got in on the act. And, just as many of our constitutional forms relate to the eighteenth century—a gap bridged by myth—so does the popular picture of the businessman still portray the rugged individual with the Yorkshire accent, with his aggressive contempt for the bewildering allurements of wicked London. We still find him occasionally in the fiction best-sellers of the less sophisticated kind ('Room at the Top'); monotonously he croaks and snaps at us from the television screen and out of the pages of serialized fiction—where, incidentally, we must look primarily for the personalization of our more massive myths, not in the sophisticated novels of Iris Murdoch or C. P. Snow. Curiously enough we also find him deeply embedded in the common-law view of business, which holds that the only possible function of businessmen is to make money—and be very frugal about spending it.

Such a man dislikes and fears government and has as little as possible to do with it. A few real specimens of the type still exist, on sociological parole from Manchester and Bradford. But nowadays the rugged entrepreneur hardly exists any longer, and certainly is typical of nothing but a sentimental attachment to eccentricity. Why then does fiction predominate so grossly over fact? The reason is that this hundred-plus-year-old figure is in fact the only example of a specific business identity that we have. Nothing equally specific or exclusive has ever taken his place. There has, in fact, been a vacuum and he has survived in it. Nor is it an entirely accidental vacuum. The sturdy British businessman to whom successive Presidents of the Board of Trade refer—this is he; Harold Macmillan's reminder that exporting is fun could only have been nostalgically addressed to such as him—he being a man uncouth enough to derive satisfaction out of 'doing' foreigners. As a type the rugged entrepreneur exists largely in the mind of the remoter members of both political parties—and in popular fiction.

This is not an image that businessmen like or even accept, but the point is that try as they might, they have never been able to find a better common image with which to displace it. Literature has not helped. In England, unlike America, business novels are not a recognized literary form; business *characters* in novels do not usually rise above the grotesque antics of John Braine's Brown. 'It is simply that here [in England] we know our audience. Any reading public is a tiny minority of the whole population; with us . . . the minority shares enough assumptions to be a good audience'. And one of the assumptions shared is expressed by one of C. P. Snow's own fictional characters in 'Strangers and Brothers': 'I'm still convinced that successful business is devastatingly uninteresting'. The pathetic best that advertising has tried to do for business is the figure of the benevolent public benefactor (the Bank Manager who really looks like a doctor and family solicitor rolled into one, and apparently working for no fee) or the anonymous corporation whose only concern is working for the benefit of the public—and occasionally its employees.

Business in England thus lacks a social identity of its own. The effects are far-reaching. I have, in a different context, previously dealt with the *economic* impact of this problem on profit maximization. In our society there is a general and a more particular reason for this lack. The general reason—extending beyond business—is that while we like to think of ourselves as essentially 'individuals', and both admire as well as sustain the articulation of eccentricity—laughing at regimented nations like the Germans—the real social situation is precisely the other way about. It is the Germans who are educated and trained to accept individuality and loneliness—hence the Hegelian State as substitute father—while our education is towards group activity, public virtues, team spirit, and the fancy that we are sufficiently cohesive not to need such a state. Having a notion of the public good instilled into us, we do not need to search for it—it emerges. Having group identities *ab ovo* we do not need to create them artificially. Thus there are existing social cohesions which surpass the strength of any specific group identity for businessmen—or teachers or farmers or politicians. One is *either* a rugged individual entrepreneur *or* a public figure, full of public spirit and consensus illumination, who happens to spend working hours in a business firm (but could just as well do so elsewhere).

The more specific reason lies in our attitude to ascription of merit. We do not recognize 'separate but equal' or parallel careers; like the American Supreme Court—though with more success—we enforce integration, at least at the top. Our honours list is a general one, barely divided into civil and military at odd points; businessmen get the same honours as scientists, footballers, professors, politicians—and, most important, civil servants. This applies to an O.B.E. as much as to a peerage. In France, and even more in Germany and Austria, the businessman has, or had, until recently, his own hierarchy of status and honour. The British businessman thus competes for honours designed for entirely different social groups. He is expected, in return, to adopt some of the attitudes that go with, say, membership of the House of Lords—to follow the example of the more regular and 'normal' recipients of honours. The granting of honours—at least higher ones—thus becomes a co-option more than a reward. A well known sub-category of the rugged entrepreneur in literature—charged with special functions of hilarity—is the rugged entrepreneur in ermine. I have always wondered whether the honours scandal under Lloyd George was not so much due to the manner of obtaining the peerages in question as the *continuing* 'rugged' and unreconstructed behaviour of the recipients. Once more we have the well known absorption effect of British society embracing the business world—but at a price of group self effacement.

It is an extraordinary and unique feature of British society that those considered worthy of higher bracket honours—a growing 'safety valve' category—should thereby be promoted to the legislature as well. A title can be a reward—and always was; appointment as royal counsellor was another reward for entirely different services, and one imposing obligations of service; only a special kind of philosophy assumes that both needs can be met with one and the same reward. A philosophy which assumes people—certain people—to be capable of playing a variety of quite different roles with equal distinction, and without conflict between one and the other. This notion necessarily reduces roles to the inferior status of a charade (a typically British game), limited and controlled by that obstinate, pervasive insistence of the common good ('general will' if you like) emerging through all institutional and role disguises by virtue of—what? The public virtues of education, of team spirit, of social cohesion, in short of consensus.

CONSENSUS

This I believe to be the central mechanism of British society and its sub-function, government. The notion of a division of powers originated in this island, from where it was transported into the practice of the American constitution and the theory of Montesquieu. Here in the last 150 years it has been neither applied nor specifically contradicted, it has simply been gobbled up by the assumption that its positive benefits can somehow always be retained by the unique British capacity for charades. A civil servant can be a judge, a minister of the crown can be a legislator, a businessman can be a civil servant or tax collector, an arts graduate can be a science boss—providing he declares his role and providing he adopts the relevant procedures. Institutional and personal separation, the classical division of powers applied in America and now revived by De Gaulle in France, became an unnecessary (and unspoken) nuisance in Britain and was quietly but effectively emasculated. Today only lawyers and very old fashioned professors of Government discuss it as a factor to be reckoned with. What counts are people—flexible, independent, selfless people able to fill any role with unblemished distinction. The only similar notion I have ever discovered elsewhere in the modern world is in the Soviet Union where party members are supposed to be equally able to tackle any assignment with the virtuosity of the allrounder (i.e. Communist).

In C. P. Snow's *The Masters* and again in *The Affair* there is a very pompous and irritating Master of a College, Crawford, who prefaces almost every one of his pontifical, uninteresting and usually obvious remarks with the phrase: 'Speaking now as a scientist' (or 'as a private individual' or 'as Master of the College' or 'as an impartial judge'). None of the characters in the book, or Snow himself, ever for one moment challenge his right to change hats in this fashion—for Crawford only says what others do without saying. A great critic has called *The Masters* 'a paradigm of political life',—and so it is, for the roles and functions of the college officers are—and are intended to be—perfectly capable of transplantation into Government, or for that matter into business. I make, incidentally, no apology for the frequent subpoena of C. P. Snow because he has lived in the stratosphere of the higher consensus and has tried to report it—in all its implications.

This then is the declaration of roles. In practice it operates very much as in literature. Only the English civil service and armed services have developed the special ghost category of 'acting' and 'temporary' positions, in which someone plays a superior role with all the attributes of the acquired rank save one—permanence (and partly pay). The impartial tribunal or commission, indiscriminately composed from among the higher consensus and confronted by the 'expert' (i.e. committed) witness, is another example of role-playing. Of course, experts sit on commissions or tribunals too, but those who become deeply committed (i.e. criticize the government too strongly) are often left to cool off in a commissionless tundra for a while. Unpaid magistrates, drawn from a very wide consensus list, are another example. And finally, as we shall see, most extraordinary and least known of all, businessmen 'regulating' their industry on a ministry's behalf.

The other necessary condition is the adoption of the relevant procedure that goes with the role. Examples of this, too, are legion, especially in the adoption of judicial procedures (including representation), by administrative tribunals or local housing inquiries. One of the most piquant examples was the procedure evolved in 1946-7 for assuring the continued internment of dangerous Germans not actually found guilty of specific crimes, a procedure in which amateur judges, prosecution and defence—temporary Control Commission officials and army officers—went through mock trials to deck up a political proceeding in luridly legal colour, to the utter bewilderment of participating German lawyers. And the procedure won; it proved very difficult to 'convict' anybody—

because the legal charade required a burden of proof that was simply (and by definition) not available.

In emphasizing role-playing as the structural myth of the British Constitution or polity, I believe that I am close to the central lubricant of British political and social life, for this seems to be the explanation of how the system works, why it works at all. The whole institutional paraphernalia of functional differentiation has been vitiated or scrapped, yet we speak of Executive, Legislature and Judiciary as though they were distinct entities; we speak of business, the professions, government as though these were wholly separate worlds. To see the real potential of our constitution we need only look at daughter versions operated without our myths—Ghana or South Africa. Yet the role playing capacity of the amateur is a myth—unless the British really are a kind of *Herrenvolk*. All roles cannot be equal, one must dominate, for procedural reasons if no other, but more probably because, as Khrushchev has stated, no men are neutral. Just as every conversation between two people is a mild form of tussle for control, so every role played conflicts somewhere with another, played already or yet to be played. As an adequate political system charades, however well acted, are not good enough.

Sociology, though much exercised by the concept and problem of roles, has surprisingly little to offer on this particular problem. The basic concept (an anthropologist's) is one person one role at one time; the problem is how to relate it to the social structure, and how to identify its specific attributes and consequences. In our more sophisticated societies, multiplicity and even conflict of roles has, of course, been recognized. But the accent is still mainly on the role itself (role consensus means agreement about a role, and not different roles within our present type of consensus); on the level of commitment to a single role or to one of several conflicting roles rather than on any multiplicity of sub-roles or, as I have dubbed it, charades. Neither conceptually nor terminologically does role theory cater for a consensus in role expectations that calls for the ability to tackle a host of sub-roles with no more commitment to each than a little stylized and temporary dressing up—adopting procedures and sitting in a chair labelled according to the role. Hence charades, once more.

The consensus I have in mind is not therefore simply an emanation of some unique British quality—though it has something of that too. Nor is it just the product of conscious compromise and group self-denial. I believe that to have a consensus *at all*, you need an ideal type, a model of attitudes, procedures, institutions—an elite. This must not be socially so remote as to make emulation and effective entry impossible. You also need a vehicle that will effectively carry the consensus into society. In Britain this is the higher Civil Service. It has the access. Its methods, social and functional attitudes, values are being ever more widely adopted. It allocates honour and rewards much in accordance with its internal scale. It has all the strength of adulation in popular as well as sophisticated literature.

Now from the general to the particular. As I have already stated, the relationship of government and business has not been examined in this context. On the input side (Business to Government) the student of politics has briefly identified pressure groups. On the output side (Government to Business) it has been the economists' pigeon. I believe, and will try to show, that in the social relationship between the institutions of government on the one hand and business on the other, the lack of social identity of the latter has been fostered, exploited and pre-empted by government (i.e. the Civil Service), and that this has led to something like schizophrenia in the world of business.

STRUCTURE

The first problem is a structural one. In a society which approves of growing economic regulation and on the whole sees its libertarian requirements fulfilled by checks on policy orientation through public discussion and a notion of popular representation or even mandate, the structure of administration will proliferate almost unseen. Contrary to the general belief implicit in an *ad hoc* philosophy of government, agencies are created not in the wake of urgent requirements but early on in the articulation of need; the *ad hoc* or higgledy-piggledy predilection is fulfilled by the informality, the untidy manner of their growth, and by the extraordinary unreason of their 'Subordination' (*podchinenie*; the Soviet Russian word for the place at which any institution is hooked on to the hierarchical chart). But the point is that the growth of administrative and governmental structure takes place from the centre outwards, not inwards from the periphery. The need is central and the structural remedy universal. With business particularly, the government's obligation (often statutory) to consult has led to the dilemma of having no one very obvious or representative to consult with. A planet cannot deal with satellites, it can only control them. Thus historically, we find ministries, especially the Board of Trade, encouraging the formation of representative industrial organizations and associations, especially during the time when government regulation of the economy was growing most rapidly. This was the period of the Second World War and the lean years immediately following, but it has continued ever since. As the need for contact between business and government grew, more industries organized for representational purposes; in many industries where representation was split or divided the relevant government department cajoled the industry into a representational structure which would make a suitably Procrustean bedfellow for itself. Representation was not of course the sole purpose of organization, nor its only historic cause, and very often (as in the motor industry as well as in Calico Printing) internal regulatory or oligopolistic functions provided a structure on which representation could readily be superimposed. But the whole point about representation is that it is so largely government-sponsored—

or at least government-encouraged; neither offensive nor defensive but essentially participatory.

Nothing shows this more clearly than the functional division of organizations; by industry, by product, by industrial process. It is a breakdown along technical lines. It is also a form of organization that unites what are essentially direct, complete, irreconcilable competitors at their most precise point of conflict. This aspect has almost entirely escaped attention. After all, industrial organization can be vertical as well as horizontal—above all it can be (and elsewhere often is) regional. And there are regional organizations in this country too, of very ancient vintage (Chambers of Commerce and Trade) but now with little power or representational influence. Industry has a respectable regional tradition in this country; the fact that industrial associations do not follow a basically regional pattern seems to indicate the connexion of associational purpose with government. Yet the form chosen (technical horizontal organization) happens also to be the most conducive to oligopoly and restraint of trade. This is part of the schizophrenia to which I shall return later. Meanwhile it is worth pointing out that this makes Britain uniquely comparable to countries with a false mythology of free trade covering what is in fact a highly organized market, like Switzerland or Austria—the most rigidly corporative economy of them all. The organizational emphasis is very similar; all that differs—a big difference though—is public policy.

That the flow of influence is greater from the government towards organized industry than from industry inwards can be seen from the position of the very big corporations. In industries organized for defence or attack these would be the natural 'leaders' of the organization. In fact, they are no more than participants, whose size is reflected by the provision of services and personnel to the association rather than by any shouldering of combat responsibility. Firms like I.C.I. and Lever Brothers in fact carry out a 'civil service' function for many of the associations to which they belong—with all the attributes of compromise and neutrality that this implies. I.C.I. belongs to 80 associations, Lever to between 40 and 50. 'They are at pains to avoid dominating associations . . . [and] for large firms the benefits of membership are often difficult to define.' PEP, the authors of these statements, recognize the predicament of such scattered membership for very large firms, and the difficulty of pinpointing the purpose of their membership. But they did not investigate the corollary: that none of these big firms use associations in order to talk to the government about their business concerns, nor does the government in order to talk to them. Membership of an association means participation in regulating the market (in the minority of cases where this is done); it always means a listening post with competitors; above all it is an additional means of government influence on industry as a whole—only the one big firm has then to be persuaded in its role as association 'uncle'.

The most flagrant example of colonization of 'big firms' by Whitehall—even without benefit of association—is the function of the joint stock banks as agents of the Bank of England. With little discretion or authority of their own, their job is to pass on applications, to sniff out transgressions—how right the French are to use the word *agent* for policemen—and to process inward demands for obvious irrelevance and unlikelihood of eventual acceptance. The result? Joint stock bank procedures mirror those of middle and lower-middle Whitehall. One wonders to what extent it is this that provides a rapidly growing market for Merchant Bankers.

Business divides into two; firms large enough to deal smoothly and regularly with government direct, and the atomized world which can only articulate or be addressed through an organization. Differences in size caked with an egalitarian philosophy unrealizable in practice (equality before the law etc.) are anyhow conducive to schizophrenia and this built-in class difference between a direct and an indirect-collective approach to government only enhances it. One has to have been in industry to appreciate the occasional humiliations involved for the medium-sized firm—for instance in being told by Whitehall with a slight (and falsely modest) frown: 'We seem to recollect dealing with this point in correspondence with your association's Mr. Snooks a little while ago . . . ' Not that access is denied to smaller firms; it is the gentle reminder that one has come and disturbed unnecessarily, and the difficulty of finding the right man in Whitehall in the first place. Dealing with Whitehall is a professional business, or rather an institutional one; odd occasional visitors have neither status nor privilege. Only associations and very large firms can institutionalize their Whitehall contacts.

The extent to which industrial associations take over governmental functions—and are universally understood to do so—becomes clear from this rather smug sentence: 'The (Government) department knows that a reputable association would not take up a case unless the *responsible officers* of the association believed that it should be pressed.' Responsible—to whom?

PROCEDURE

Procedures correspond to the charade rules. It is said that the difference between White and Indian in South America is not race, colour, religion, or even class; it is the manner of living, the role. One 'lives' white or Indian. Similarly in this country one 'acts' like a civil servant. No one will challenge the existence of informal but well-defined civil service procedures. There are no business procedures to compete with them.

Now it may be said that civil service procedures are optimal, the product of large size and great experience, and that to say there are no business procedures to compete with them is merely to admit the predominance of the best over the second best. There may indeed be such a thing as optimal procedure for large organizations and they may conceivably even apply equally to government and industry (but surely not necessarily)—in America, however, it is business that claims to originate and develop them, and is usually admitted to do so. We have, therefore, a double problem. Whether business calls for the same procedures as government (no one claims judicial and administrative procedures to be similar or substitutable; indeed it is mainly by procedure that Crawford the civil servant can be distinguished from Crawford the judge) I am not competent to answer. The other problem is the direction of procedural influence. In this country it is clearly outwards, government to business.

There seem to be at least two main factors. In explaining government policy to 'our people' association officials increasingly use government terminology and methods. They are, after all, temporary civil servants for much (an increasing part) of the time. They see and hear from their opposite numbers in Whitehall much more frequently than many of their own members. In many associations the proportion of the industry represented is small, the proportion who participate actively in the affairs of the association even smaller. The 'permanent' association officials (how they do get re-elected) are solicitors or accountants. The *Lorelei* appeal of the predictable and well-mannered Whitehall methods has a great and often natural appeal. They will bargain hard for the industry's obvious interests where these are clearly threatened—or can in some way be indentified (this question belongs to public policy) but it is through the small change of regular contact that Whitehall exercises its influence. And this small change is essentially procedural. Where civil servants with real if not official powers to negotiate 'cannot commit their ministers to more than this', businessmen with equally real powers 'cannot commit their boards to less than that'. The one is the consequence of the other. Thus the board of directors becomes the businessman's deterrent in response to the procedural strategy of Whitehall. The validity of the pre-war distinction between 'officials' and 'unofficials' has largely disappeared. The weapon of constitutional *non possumus*, with which American diplomats used to ward off dangerous foreign commitments by conjuring up an implacable Senate, has become an everyday fiction in the relationship between government and business.

The second factor arises from the situation that Whitehall has a distinct social identity and business has not. The value of official procedures is not only based on performance but on ascription—which, sociologists keep telling us, has an obstinate capacity for survival in an otherwise increasingly achievement-orientated society. I have attended at least half a dozen lectures by senior business negotiators on 'how to deal with government'—and while these lectures purported to be technical, they were in fact social: restraint, moderation, give-and-take, 'never overstate your case'. All the lecturers were phenomenally agreed (consensus). And the ideal type that emerged from their revealed wisdom was the precise opposite of the rugged entrepreneur. It is not merely that if you want things from government you have to follow its methods of going about its business, but the secondary spread of these habits into the internal conduct of business—especially in large firms. For instance, the rapid growth in the functions and status of secretaries, the impersonal award of status symbols and privileges to go with the job and not the individual, the vital destruction of the old business principle of dealing whenever possible with the boss—all are Whitehall habits.

Finally we must differentiate these contacts between government and business as regulator and regulated from those of government as purchaser or seller with industry as supplier or consumer. The charade will have it that here—and here only—commercial considerations must apply. Civil servants are under constant pressure to act as businessmen, as rugged entrepreneurs. In fact they are expected to outdo businessmen at their own profession. It is here that the latent role conflict inherent in charades—usually subsumed only by the admitted recognition of the postulated 'public interest'—comes out into the open. Businessmen in the role of civil servants must, to be successful, be wholly committed to their role—and even as businessmen they are often expected to behave à la façon de Whitehall—but civil servants in the role of businessmen must outdo businessmen and yet not cease to be civil servants. That surely is the essence of the implied philosophy behind the Nationalized Industries in Britain; the combination of business acumen and efficiency with public accountability and all the glare of publicity—a combination that is in fact a conflict. Especially in recent times the commercial rationality has been emphasized more strongly than ever, yet it has been matched by greater demands for parliamentary control (Committee on Nationalized Industries). Beeching has to make his profit—but at the same time follow the tortuous system of consultations and public appeals against his decisions.

Yet contacts between civil service and industry must not on the other hand become too loose and informal. Fourteen years ago a select committee examined the structure of commercial contact with government in detail, with special reference to the temporary problem of administering post-war scarcity. On the subject of our problem, the Committee had nothing but praise for the logic of industrial association. 'As the scope and extent of government activity . . . has increased, it has been only natural for the government to consult bodies which it *knew to be representative* of the interests which government activity increasingly affected.

THE SOCIAL ASPECT

Important as it is, the social aspects of any confrontation between structured groups are the most difficult to identify behind and around the more formal aspects of institutions and procedure. I can offer little evidence other than direct observation and—yet again—the informal illuminations of literature. But as this social aspect is central to my argument I am bound to try and deal with it.

The division between big business (plus business negotiators and administrators) and small business is most noticeable in social terms. Within firms like the I.C.I., Lever and the big oil companies, there is an immense hierarchical break between the centre and the periphery (Main Board and Divisions in I.C.I., Main Board and subsidiary boards in Lever, Main board and field units in the oil companies). I well remember an immensely successful I.C.I. Divisional Sales Director, enlivened by alcohol, explaining that he had everything—power, salary, perks—except the slightest chance of promotion to Main Board. 'As a successful Sales director I am not the type.' And he wasn't. *In whisky veritas* he saw his disability not in terms of capacity or technical education, but as a social bar. Yet it was not simply a matter of 'class' but a matter of his capacity for playing the essential charades. As Sales Director he was expected to play at (and with) rugged entrepreneurs; this was one role that could not be combined with the easy flexibility required at the centre. In his own words, he 'was not the sort ever to be *persona grata* in Whitehall'.

So he and many others are shunted off into the 'expense account' world. This is *not* the top of the business pyramid, as is often believed (largely by academics) but the resting place of those who will never get to the top. Insidiously the tax system and the philosophy behind it, which have created the expense account world, recognize the consolation aspect; they despise it and yet permit it, almost as necessary sop for social deprivation. Thus I think most senior civil servants would privately agree with Titmuss about the the inequitable distortion of our tax laws, but underlying this disapproval of the expense account mentality is a feeling of relief at the diversion of the wild beasts into hedonistic channels instead of those of social or (still worse) political ambition. The 'top' businessmen would never be seen dead at a typical expense account establishment—and those few who choose to be seen there alive often get their come-uppance with a savagery out of all proportion to any technical offence which they may have committed (Sir Bernard Docker). The rugged entrepreneur—the real one—would not go there either, and would not be expected to go. The ostentatious expense account businessman is really a social deviant, assisted by specially framed tax laws. It is curious how the real expense account industries (Films, Ladies' fashions) are still socially taboo.

Again I have found that members of (and aspiring candidates to) Main Boards move socially in Whitehall circles to a remarkable extent. The consensus operates even more strongly in silence (socially) than in speech (politically). Unlike America or Germany, where social entertainment is professionally enclosed all the way up the pyramid, it opens out in England to that platform where everyone can play charades—and where people are 'themselves' only in their own homes. It would be invidious to give names, but all the top business-men I know would never move in what they would describe as 'business' circles (except bankers who alone have a recognizable social identity of their own, and move in something called 'Bankers' circles', but which in turn are permeated by Whitehall mores). Perhaps the best way of obtaining a grip or focus on the imprecise is to study its negation; the sons of the rugged entrepreneurs (thrift) support and drive forward the teenage consumption boom (spendthrift); the offsprings of the higher consensus, including top businessmen (public spirit) wear jeans and help motivate the total negation of consensus (extreme egocentricity). There emerges an ideal type of personality representing this upper social platform of consensus—immaterial whether he be lawyer, civil servant, doctor, don, or businessman. One of the rare British novels interested in this problem of the indifference of profession compared to the importance of the role, a novel which emphasizes the ability of the ideal type to substitute one role for another with equal success, describes the type like this—through the eyes of a jeans-wearing detractor: 'London man, 1959, middle to upper class, brain worker . . . but functional, entirely functional . . . only this is what makes him interesting.' And from the inside, from the platform itself, comes this demand on the consensus member: the businessman who wants to be heard in Whitehall must 'moderate the direct selfish interests which it is his duty to promote by a decent sense of his obligations to the community at large'.

It is obvious that the consensus is not one of organic growth, of fusion; it is essentially the role of the public servant, of Upper Whitehall, that dominates it. 'Public interest', the sense of the community at large, is their peculiar property, goes naturally with the job, but it does not go naturally with business—indeed the rugged entrepreneur is almost by definition barred from suffusion by it. The extreme disparity of roles demanded here must produce either schizophrenia or the more common phenomenon of ceasing altogether to be a businessman and simply becoming a civil servant in business. It is this latter drift which has caused the frequent ministerial (mostly Tory) wails against a background of dollar crises and relatively declining exports; 'What has happened to the traditional (sturdy, aggressive, etc.) British businessman?'

As in the case of the nationalized industries, charades do not apparently trouble the consensus member called upon to play entrepreneur. The obvious example is the large number of senior civil servants who not only join industry (at Main Board level of course) but fit the role beautifully. The only recent case of incompatibility was that of Lord Mancroft (a former junior minister)—and it was his company that was incompatible (with their 'commercial' viewpoint and their rash statements in public) not Lord Mancroft (with his restraint, his anonymity, his conscience). In fact, stripping away all racial and religious overtones, we are left with widespread public assumptions about the compatibility or incompatibility of the roles of Lord Mancroft as director of a strongly Zionist group of firms, and Lord Mancroft as director of a neutral and hopefully ubiquitous international insurance company. More explicitly, the same problem was ventilated by the Bank Rate Tribunal examining the impartiality of Mr. Keswick's roles. But perhaps the most remarkable example of the expected capacity of consensus role-players is the case of Dr. Beeching, invited to leave the I.C.I. Main Board and outdo all rugged entrepreneurs at rugged entrepreneurship in publicly owned British Railways, and in the course of executing public policy to make the railways pay. For he is not a rugged entrepreneur at all, but a consensus figure acting like one—by order. We have already noted the curious lacuna in consensus attitudes where the government's commercial operations are concerned. . . .

CONCLUSION

Though specially strong in Great Britain, the notion of consensus is not uniquely British. It is a feature of all sophisticated societies. But the first problem is: whose consensus? For consensus is not so much the product of compromise as of elite ascendancy and its acceptance. In Britain it is, I maintain, presently a Whitehall consensus. It was not always so. But the political emasculation of the aristocracy as a condition of its survival, together with the remarkable decline of importance of formal politics (House of Commons, Party Conferences, grass roots) in favour of the executive and its chief, the Prime Minister, have led to the quiet emergence of the Snowmen, the upper civil servants and their mores. Their influence on the professions was socially logical and predestined, their influence over business a more drawn-out and difficult process. Efforts are being made to draw in the Trade Unions and the arts, though with only limited success as yet.

In America it is just the other way about. There is consensus too (though weaker) and it comes *from* the business community. Top businessmen join the administration—not to be businessmen (like Beeching) but to be administrators (Macnamara). When Americans think of 'organization' or 'administration', they visualize big business as often as government, at least they did until the end of the last war. Significantly the dichotomy individual/organization in American fiction is a business problem, from Theodore Dreiser to John P. Marquand; it was not until the McCarthy era that Merle Miller first used government as the personality-crushing octopus of fiction. Not that the theory of organization meets with universal approval in literature; the optimal view is size and growth *plus* a 'mood of nostalgic reverie for the company town, the home of paternalistic order, domestic virtue and productive work . . . assumptions—far from being 'capitalistic' or contemporary—are actually Populist and Veblenian'. There is here a view of business as a social philosophy, and both nostalgic 'good' and contemporary 'bad' are more sophisticated—and a much more popular subject for fiction—than the rugged North country millowner of Britain.

In American fiction and in European fact, the choice is between the individual and the corporation—with a happy ending ensuring the triumph of the former (integrity) over the latter (corruption)—or his utter degradation. Only in the English novels of C. P. Snow do the needs of individual and organization have to be reconciled; justice for the former, respectable self-preservation for the latter. The Continent has been fascinated by Snow's proposition, indeed by the whole 'typically English' problem. There the consensus (in so far as it exists) is not concerned either with business or with administration but with questions of political philosophy; business and government are—and are expected to be—in a state of permanent friction, fighting and subverting each other (influence is too polite a word).

I think only Sweden can fairly be compared with Britain. Those, like Gunnar Myrdal, who believe that consensus, self-regulation and widespread charades are the hope of civilized democracy (with perhaps more tolerant public policies in the international 'state of nature') put Sweden first as an example, then Britain. But it seems to me that this system is in many ways a self-denying ordinance, which Switzerland and Sweden have accepted (one might suggestively for once list the things these countries have to do *without*) but for which this country is not yet ready. For Britain, the austere consensus at home is not at all austere in the field of international relations, public policy still demands greatness (at least the equipment that goes with it). Hence the importance of the essentially British make-believe of charades, propagated and best played by Whitehall.

5 JOHN ARDAGH

Rural Change in France: The Young Farmers' Revolt

French agriculture today is an absorbing human drama, not merely a technical affair of subsidies and fertilisers. Nowhere else in the life of the nation are the human conflicts between change and tradition more acute, or more revealing of post-war France as a whole. An old peasant society is dying; and a new, surprisingly energetic one of modern-minded young farmers is painfully taking its place.

The delayed industrial revolution in France has provoked sudden transformations that in Britain or Germany were spread gently over several decades. The vast and static community of small farmers, once a source of stability to France, is suddenly an anachronism and a burden. Industrial wages and prices have risen far more sharply than food prices, so the farmers are more bitterly aware than before of their own poverty. Mechanisation of the farms has made economic nonsense of the huge agricultural population, and since the war about one-third of it (three million people) have moved to the towns where life is easier and labour short. Of those who remain

Reprinted from John Ardagh, *The New French Revolution* (Copyright © 1968, 1969 by John Ardagh), pp. 67-75, by permission of Harper and Row, Publishers, Inc.

on the small farms, many of the older ones are sunk as deep as ever in their seclusion and fear of progress; they are the pariahs of the nation, rather than the paragons of an idyllic and simple life. But a strange thing has happened: a new generation of young farmers, with a totally different outlook from their parents, has arisen, not from the rich estates of the northern plains but from the desolate smallholdings of the south and west. They have promoted a new creed of modernisation and technical progress, and are forming themselves into producer groups and co-operatives. They have seized from their elders most of the key posts in the farmers' unions and pressure groups; and they have even impressed some of their ideas on the Ministry of Agriculture. Whereas in industry this kind of impetus has come above all from official technocrats, on the land much of it has come from the farmers themselves. They have already done something to break down the old idea of les paysans[1] as an isolated social class, and to bring the small farmers closer into the community. Even cautious scholars have described their movement as a 'revolution'. This chapter is largely the story of their struggle: of how they are trying to pull peasant farming, in one generation, from the Middle Ages to the point where it can profit from the new competitive outlets of the Common Market and meet the consumer needs of a modern urban society.

THE JACISTS, PISANI, AND THE ARTICHOKE WARS

France is the richest agricultural nation in Western Europe, and also one of the poorest. Blessed by her climate, by a fertile soil and plenty of space, her output is far greater than any of her neighbours'; yet the standards of her subsistence farming would be unthinkable in Britain, Holland, or Denmark. For in France there are two agricultures, as it is often said. On the one hand, the big wheat and cattle farms of the Paris basin and the north-east plains, which for some decades have been as modern and rich as any in Europe; on the other, the small farms of much of the rest of the country, poorest of all in the Massif Central, the extreme south-west, and most of Brittany. The pattern is diverse, varying by region and produce, and this makes it hard to generalise even about the poorer areas. In Brittany and the Vendée, for instance, there are still far too many people on the land, and few local industries to draw them away; yet in parts of the Massif Central the rural exodus is nearing its safe limits, with barely enough young people left to replace the old when they retire. The small but flourishing fruit and vegetable plantations of north Finistère and the lower Rhône Valley contrast sharply with the larger but more barren farms of upland areas, often wasting their resources on uneconomic mixed farming.

The laws of equal inheritance, dating from Napoleon and earlier, have been one main cause of the small size of farms. Even until recent years, so great was the peasant's suspicion of town and factory that a son would stay tamely to receive his share of his father's land rather than seek his fortune elsewhere. Today, the laws are still valid, but the sons move away more readily. Farms have gradually been growing larger. The average size has almost doubled since 1882, while the total number has dropped in the same period from 3.5 to under two million, but most are still too small to make economic sense under modern conditions. Four-fifths of all farms have less than fifty acres, and of these the average is under twenty acres. Yet in the United States, anything less than 200 acres is often considered unprofitable.

Before the war, all but a small sector of agriculture lay sunk in a kind of lethargy and fatalism. The gulf between the peasant and the new industrial workers in the towns grew steadily wider; *paysantisme* was more than a profession, it was a way of life, a doctrine that nothing could or should disturb 'the eternal order of the fields'. The notorious 1892 reforms of Jules Méline, then Minister of Agriculture, had pushed up high tariff walls round France to protect the farmers from outside storms—but they simply caused stagnation. Later Governments then followed the Méline line. Agriculture was bolstered at the expense of industry, with tax relief and subsidies, so that the farmers could at least make a living. But it did not stop their discontent. In the 1930s the peasant world, hitherto dispersed and inarticulate, began for the first time to produce vocal leaders from its own ranks, mainly reactionary figures like the sinister Henri Dorgères and his 'greenshirts'. The Popular Front Government of 1936-8 realised that these were symptoms of a genuine *malaise* and helpless poverty, and so it drew up some imaginative reforms to encourage the farmers to modernise; but few were ever applied.

It was not until that weird interregnum, the Vichy period, that the stalemate really began to be broken. In agriculture, the influence of Vichy is a subject of some controversy. Led by Pétain himself, a man from a peasant family, Vichy promoted a massive 'back to the land' movement, and tried to set up a regionalised 'corporatist' structure, with the peasants forming a kind of state-within-the-State. This, by modern thinking, is pure fascism, and it had some parallels in Italy and Germany at that time; and yet in its French context it may have done some good. The system had not in practice got very far by the time Vichy ended, and the local farmers' syndicates it had set up to deal with local problems were quickly swept away by the Liberation. But even Vichy's harshest critics sometimes agree that these syndicates may have helped to sow the seeds of the practical peasant collaboration and local unity that was lacking in France hitherto and is developing, in a different way, today.

When peace came the immediate task, as in industry, was physical reconstruction. In 1945 food production was down to half its pre-war level, due to the fighting and especially to the mass deportations to Germany. The First Plan made farm machinery its top priority outside industry, and the results were striking. The number of tractors rose from 35,000 or so in 1938-45 to

230,000 by 1954, and farmers were encouraged by law to form State-aided groups for the joint buying and use of machinery. Productivity rose rapidly, and output was soon well above its pre-war level. At the same time, the much-needed rural exodus was gathering pace. It began to look as if French small farming might make some progress at last. But after about 1948 the real danger emerged: rapid industrial growth and its attendant inflation hit the farmer badly, for food prices did not keep pace. By 1950 industrial prices had risen 50 per cent higher than agricultural ones, compared with their pre-war level; by 1959, the disparity in growth was more than three to one. Yet for much of their spending, for fertilisers and machinery as well as clothes and household goods, farmers had to pay industrial prices out of a rural income. It is true that, thanks to much higher productivity, the farmers' overall standard of living did show a 25 per cent rise between 1938 and 1958. But this was most unevenly shared. In 1958, at least half the peasantry was still barely above the bread-line.

The 1950s were marked by continual rural protests and disturbances, with tractors barring the main roads. The leaders were Right-wing demagogues of the old school, men like Dorgères in Brittany and Paul Antier from the Massif Central. They demanded the remedy of higher price-supports and other forms of direct aid, but were utterly opposed to the real, more drastic solution of changing the structure of the small farms. Here the old peasant leaders found alliance with the rich farmers of the Paris basin who controlled the main union, the Fédération Nationale de Syndicats des Exploitants Agricoles (FNSEA). Together they formed a powerful lobby in Parliament: Antier was Minister of Agriculture himself in 1956. And so until its death in 1958 the Fourth Republic gave them what they asked for: price supports, based on a sliding scale that pegged food prices to rises in industrial ones. The farmers welcomed this system, but it helped the big well-organised farms more than the small ones, unable to compete with the chaotic system of marketing. Discontent went on, reaching a peak of violence in 1957. There were tractor blocks, the angry slogans, the mild stoppages, the burning of surplus crops, the wild-mouthed demagogues—inevitably these gave French townsfolk, as well as foreigners, a picture of the French farmer as a comic and ignorant anarchist, always complaining, his head firmly in the sand. Yet his plight was genuine, even if partly his own fault. It was time for a new outlook, and new leadership.

And it came. All this time the new young radicals were quietly marshalling their forces in the background. By about 1957, they began to make their presence felt. It was not a haphazard movement. Like so many of the progressive influences in post-war France, it was rooted in militant Leftish Catholicism: nearly all the young leaders came from the Jeunesse Agricole Chrétienne.

The JAC youth movement had been started by the priesthood in 1929. Its aim was to combat the spread of atheism, at an epoch when the conflict in rural France between clergy and Marxists was at its height. In the 1930s, village priests ran the local JAC branches and devoted them to prayer and Bible meetings, with a little social activity on the side. But during the war the JAC took on a different tone, more secular, but no less serious. Among the very young sons of small farmers, mostly still in their teens, there occurred one of those strange psychological changes that seem to have marked the destiny of France at that time. The danger and responsibility of their wartime activities, often in the Resistance, gave them an early maturity and seriousness. Many of them began to ponder deeply on how they could avoid a life of certain hardship and poverty, short of leaving the soil which they felt was their home. Some, deported to Germany, saw there the example of small farms that *could* be run on modern lines. But how could it be done in France?

From about 1942, little groups began to form to plan the future. The JAC's secretary-general, René Colson, an inspired young peasant from the Haute-Marne, toured the country organising meetings and firing other young peasants with his ideals. The initiative in the JAC was now out of the hands of the priests, and the accent was on learning economics, self-help, and sharing of labour. A liberal-minded priest from the Aveyron department, in the south of the Massif Central, has told me: 'Young boys who had left school at twelve or so were thinking and deciding for themselves—it was amazing, and quite new in France. The war had produced a surge of independence, both from family and from priests. The role of the priests in the JAC now changed—instead of a didactic leader, he became an equal. Most priests, of course, resented this. But for me, it was an eye-opener to meet these uneducated young Jacists who yet had far more calibre and more *sérieux* than my most gifted *lycée* pupils of the same age. They were determined to cure their sense of inferiority and make themselves articulate. One boy round here taught himself public speaking by treating his cows as an audience; another, a very rough type, kept his beret on at meetings so he could be forced to make a speech as a penalty. That was how he cured his shyness.'

One aim of the JAC in the early post-war years was to give its members something of the general culture they had missed through leaving school so young. A Breton farmer has described how the JAC 'changed his life' by introducing him to art and history, by widening his horizons outside the brutish world of the farm, and giving him some hope that the peasants *could* improve their lot. The JAC organised amateur theatricals, singing contests, and sports, for there were few cars and no television in those days, and young peasants had to find their own ways of fighting loneliness and boredom. The JAC's most important work, however, was professional. Local groups set about studying modern accountancy and the latest farming techniques—all much neglected by the older peasant generation. But the Jacists soon found that to apply these new ideas in practice was not so easy. On most farms the way was blocked by fathers who would have nothing of new methods and in many cases even tried to stop their sons leaving home in the evenings to study. In this patriarchal society the conflict of generations grew acute, and many Jacists saw little hope save to wait maybe ten or twenty years for father to retire. But the JAC was well organised nationally, with central committees and a newspaper; a rally in Paris in 1950 drew 70,000 members. The next step, so it seemed by the mid 'fifties, must be to carry their campaign into national farming politics and press for reforms of the whole structure of agriculture.

This was especially the view of Michel Debatisse, who took over the leadership of the JAC soon after Colson's early death in 1951. Debatisse, today one of the most influential farmers in all France, was typical of the JAC of those days. He was born in 1929 in the village of Palladuc, in Auvergne, near the cutlery town of Thiers. His parents had a thirty-five-acre farm on a hill, where the soil was almost as thin as the wooded landscape was lovely. The few dairy cows, poultry, and vegetables barely gave them a living; and in winter the family would sit round a stove in a little workshop behind the austere farmhouse, fitting handles on to knives for a firm in Thiers. Michel grew up without toys or much comfort, though he was lucky that this was one of the 25 per cent of French farms that had running water. He left school at thirteen and joined the JAC. Soon he was running a local drama group, touring the villages by bicycle on summer evenings. He was a squat, thin, badly dressed youth, but his ugly face had—and has—a fierce kind of strength, and he rapidly began to develop wider ambitions. There was little he could do, so he felt, in Palladuc, but he saw that in Paris no-one was really trying to help the small farmers constructively. He began to write articles for the JAC paper, and by 1950 was in Paris part of each week, editing it.

By about 1955 Debatisse and his friends were reaching the age when people generally leave the JAC and settle down to raising a family of their own and running a farm. Yet they felt that their campaign had hardly begun. Where could they carry it next? The main union, the FNSEA, was in the hands of much older and richer farmers from the north, and seemed hardly likely to welcome them. But the FNSEA had a moribund youth section, which the Jacists saw as a stepping-stone. When they made some innocent proposals for reviving it, the FNSEA leaders saw no objection, little suspecting what a Trojan horse they were letting in. So in 1957 the Debatisse faction took over the key posts of the Centre National des Jeunes Agriculteurs (CNJA) and began to use it as a militant and vocal pressure group. As a first step towards breaking down the isolation of the peasant, joint meetings were held with industrial workers' unions; a most unusual step in France. Debatisse toured the country, stirring up the support of young farmers, Marxist and Christian alike: though a practising Catholic, he was no sectarian when it came to farming. Other CNJA leaders were despatched to glean the latest ideas and techniques from Kansas, Denmark, or the Ukraine; today, it is rare to meet a member of that team who is not widely travelled.

The FNSEA leaders viewed all this activity with a cool suspicion, but made little move to expel the rebels. Meanwhile, and most significantly for the future, the CNJA began to form new links with the Plan and with the young technocrats who came to power with de Gaulle in 1958. Immediately they discovered a similarity of language and interest. Planners and civil servants began to consult the CNJA on what to do about farming; and Debatisse was elected one of the youngest-ever members of the Government's Economic and Social Council. The breakthrough was beginning.

Debatisse and his friends proposed that Government policy be switched from price supports to investment and structural reform. Above all, they questioned the hitherto sacred rights of property ownership, which they saw as a strait-jacket round French farming: they wanted drastic measures to persuade older farmers to retire, to take land away from unproductive hands and give it to new tenant farmers working in groups. They were still basically in favour of the family farm, as opposed to industrial-scale farming, but they saw that it must change its nature. And whereas many of the older FNSEA leaders still clung to the pre-war Mélinian doctrine that the rural exodus was a grave social danger, the CNJA saw it as necessary and good, but asked simply that it be 'humanised' to avoid distress.

The new Gaullist régime soon ran into trouble with the older and richer farmers. The Rueff financial reforms of December 1958 had stripped away many of the precious price supports, including the sliding scale. Rural discontent again grew, this time embracing even the rich farmers of the north, who were hit by the new measures: the Amiens riot of February 1960, where more than one hundred police and farmers were injured, was one of the worst since the war. But the Gaullists did not placate the old guard as the Fourth Republic had done. Michel Debré, the reform-minded Prime Minister, had an ear for the CNJA's ideas: he drew up a *loi d'orientation* partly inspired by them, and in the summer of 1960 narrowly succeeded in pushing it through Parliament, despite active opposition from the FNSEA and its allies. Above all, this law proposed a new Government agency to buy up and redistribute land; a modified form of what the CNJA wanted. For the first time, a French Government committed itself to tackling the question of farming structures, and turned its back on the heritage of Méline.

But the orientation law was no more than an outline of principle, and the Government proved very slow in applying the decrees that would put it into force. The CNJA began to suspect sabotage by Ministry officials in league with the FNSEA. The Young Farmers' rising irritation suddenly reached flashpoint at the end of May 1961, when a seasonal glut knocked the bottom out of the potato and vegetable markets in western Brittany. At Pont l'Abbé on 27 May farmers set fire to ballot-boxes in local elections and filled the streets with tons of potatoes sprayed with petrol. Then at Morlaix, a market town in north Finistère, 4,000 young farmers invaded the streets with their tractors at dawn on 8 June, seized the sub-prefecture in protest, and held it for several hours. This was the epoch of *putsches* in Algiers, and the newspapers delightedly drew the parallel. But these farmers were not terrorists: they were relatively prosperous growers of artichokes and other early vegetables, in the rich coastal plain between Morlaix and St.-Pol-de-Léon. When their two leaders, Alexis Gourvennec and Marcel Léon, were arrested by the police, sympathy riots spread throughout the west. Down as far as the Pyrenees and Languedoc, roadblocks and banners were out in force. It was the largest and most effective peasant manifestation in post-war France, and it marked a decisive turning-point.

For the first time, French farmers were demonstrating *for* progress, instead of against it. For the first time the riots were led and organised by the new leaders, not by the old demagogues. 'L'Agriculture de Papa est morte' read the triumphant banners in the streets of Morlaix. Gourvennec, an ex-Jacist, was only twenty-four; an arrogant, well-spoken young man with something of the looks of Gérard Philipe. He and his fellow-Bretons were protesting at the marketing system, and not for the first time: the previous year, in a rather less violent version of their famous 'artichoke wars', they had sent lorry-loads of artichokes straight to Paris to sell on the streets, after the Breton middlemen had refused them a fair price. The growers were furious because the Government had continually urged them to produce more, and yet had done nothing to reform the archaic marketing system, so that prices always collapsed in a good season. Gourvennec and the farmers of his region were highly organised and far from poor; their actual problems were rather different from those of a region like Debatisse's. But both types of young farmer shared the same dynamism and the same reforming zeal, whether the reforms they needed most were of markets or of land.

The Government responded quickly after the Morlaix affair. Gourvennec had friends in the Ministry, and it is often alleged that some of them had secretly advised him to stage the riot in order to get things moving! In August, de Gaulle dismissed the Minister of Agriculture, Henri Rochereau, a mild liberal-conservative of the old school, and replaced him with the most forceful and modern-minded figure to have filled that post in this century.

Edgard Pisani, tall, black-bearded, eloquent and flamboyant, looks something like a cross between Ustinov and Svengali. He is an ex-prefect, and very much in the new 'technocratic' mould. During his four-and-a-half years (1961-6) in the usually unwanted job of Minister of Agriculture he showed a greater understanding of the farmers' real needs than any of his predecessors. He is an ambitious man, too, and was determined to leave his mark on the scene. He at once drew up a *loi complémentaire* of decrees to activate the 1960 law, and got them approved. This Pisani Law, as it is called, established a new pension fund to encourage old farmers to retire; an agency for buying land (already outlined in the earlier law); stricter rules against absentee landlords; and measures to encourage farmers to form into groups both for marketing and for shared production. There have been a few other innovations since then (notably, in 1961, the wider extension of health insurance and social allowances to farmers), but in essence the Pisani Law is still the basis of Government policy for farming. It has often been described as the boldest and most realistic step yet taken to reform French agriculture. But in practice its application has been slow because of lack of funds and bureaucratic delays, some of them, possibly, deliberate.

The Pisani Law marked a victory for the Young Farmers, who rapidly began to infiltrate the FNSEA council itself through departmental elections. By 1961 they were so strong that one of their numbers, Marcel Bruel, a young cattle breeder from the Aveyron, was elected secretary-general of the FNSEA. Today the new leaders share the power evenly in the Federation with the big northern farmers, and the old-style peasant demagogues are everywhere falling away. But if Debatisse and his friends have won a political battle in Paris, they have not yet won the war in the fields. There is a new mood today in French farming; but, inevitably, the old structures are giving place more slowly.

FOOTNOTES

1.   The word *paysan* denotes the whole social class of poorer people who earn their living from the land, whether as farmers or labourers. It is a less archaic and pejorative term than 'peasant'. 'Countryman' might be a fairer translation.

6

JOSEPH LA PALOMBARA

In Defense of the Church: The Role of Catholic Action

PERCEPTIONS OF RELATIVE GROUP IMPACT

It is widely believed in Italy—and the belief is overwhelmingly confirmed by our interviews—that the single most powerful interest group operating in the political system is Catholic Action. Over half of the group leaders, four-fifths of the political leaders, and one-third of the bureaucrats interviewed identify Catholic Action as being in a class by itself in this regard. A national leader of Confindustria asserts that, from the vantage point of his Confederation, Catholic Action is more influential in public administrative circles than are even those trade unions supported by the Christian Democratic Party. One of C.G.I.L.'s [the major communist labor organization—eds.] officials tends to play down all groups except Catholic Action, arguing that because of the position it holds within the Christian Democratic Party, it is responsible for the increasing clericalization of Italian society and government. A director of the

Reprinted from Joseph LaPalombara, *Interest Groups in Italian Politics* (Copyright © 1964 by Princeton University Press), pp. 349-355, 404-407, 421-428, by permission of Princeton University Press. Footnotes omitted by the editors.

86

Christian Democratic C.I.S.L. [the Catholic counterpart to C.G.I.L.—eds.] who has himself been a Catholic Action leader generalizes that Catholic Action is immensely powerful in the bureaucracy because it is increasingly able to influence bureaucratic appointments, determine who will be awarded major academic chairs in the universities, place its own people on state-owned radio and television organizations, and receive its quota of appointments to the directive boards of the state-controlled industries of I.R.I. The editor of a political weekly, acknowledging that there has been great tension between Catholic Action and the Amintore Fanfani group, stresses that the tension grows out of the degree of control over the D.C. that Catholic Action managed to achieve between 1946 and 1958. A director of one of I.R.I.'s major divisions claims that it is not Catholic Action that is conditioned by the D.C. or other Catholic organizations but really Catholic Action that sets limits on the behavior of others. Many other statements that make similar points could be adduced. The general perception is aptly summarized by one group leader who remarks: "Catholic Action constitutes a fundamental problem for Italy. That organization is no longer merely spiritual or apostolic, but an enormous political and economic force in the country. It is an organization that succeeds in dominating important sectors of Italian society. It wants to control what is written in the newspapers, what kinds of books are published, what kinds of motion pictures are produced, what kinds of programs appear on television, what kinds of recreation we Italians engage in, what kinds of persons are elected to communal councils and the Parliament, what kinds of individuals will have the opportunity to make careers in the public administration—that is, it is interested in everything except spiritual things."

As far as the intentions of Catholic Action are concerned, the above observation is reasonably accurate. In their interview responses, national leaders of most branches of the mammoth organization are quick to articulate that creating the proper kind of citizen—the "civic man"—is a central purpose of Catholic Action activity. In the single-minded pursuit of this goal it is apparent that Catholic Action, in one way or another, will seek to intervene anywhere in the society or the polity. This orientation can best be illustrated by an examination of some data concerning the public licensing of motion picture theaters in Italy.

A national leader of A.G.I.S. (Italian General Association of Entertainment) points out that for several years the Catholic unit within the Association has tried to increase its relative power position. He indicates that the general strategy is based not merely on the force of numbers that the Catholics can muster within the organization but particularly on the use of political and bureaucratic influence to increase Catholic weight in the entertainment industries. The degree of influence exerted in the postwar years can be adduced from information concerning the disposition, by the Ministerial Committee that grants licenses to motion picture theatres, of requests to operate such new enterprises, or to enlarge those already in existence. During the period October 1, 1954, to January 31, 1955, the Committee handled and disposed of 1,817 such requests as shown by the table.

Disposition by Ministerial Committee of Requests to Open New Theaters or to Enlarge Existing Ones, October, 1945—January, 1955

Type of Organization	Requests	Granted		Rejected		New Theaters
		Number	Percent	Number	Percent	
Private enterprise	1,189	774	65.2	415	34.8	477
Parish churches	628	564	89.9	64	10.1	477

The most striking aspect of this table is not that the number of parish church requests rejected is less than one-third the rejection level for private entrepreneurs, it is that, during the period covered, as many parish as private theaters came into existence. According to our A.G.I.S. respondents, this trend has been true for some years, and by 1958 fully one-third of all the motion-picture houses in Italy were those owned and operated by the parish churches. He adds that there is more than a quantitative aspect to consider, in the sense that the newer parish churches are no longer tiny, dingy places but full-blown and often elegant theaters that seat large numbers of people. At the beginning of this evolution—say, in 1953—the private theaters outnumbered the parish enterprises seven to one; the fact that in just a few years the ratio has changed so dramatically is said to have certain ominous long-run implications for the Italian motion-picture industry.

It is apparent on close examination that the rules promulgated by the Presidency of the Council of Ministers and applied by the Ministerial Committee clearly favor the continued and disproportionate growth of parish theaters. For example, one general rule states that before a new theater can be authorized in a particular area, a five percent growth in motion-picture attendance must be demonstrated for the previous year. However, additional regulations stipulate that where there does not eixst any theater, or where the only theaters in existence are privately run, new parish theaters can be authorized. This regulation alone is sufficient to provide organized Catholicism with the opportunity to achieve a position of unchallenged dominance in this activity.

A.G.I.S. leaders assert, and officials of Catholic Action agree, that the strategy here is to make it difficult or impossible to produce in Italy motion pictures that are not acceptable to Catholicism. By exercising strong control over the places where motion pictures are shown, Catholic organizations can achieve a degree of direction of what motion pictures are produced that has thus far eluded them. If the balance is very heavily tipped in Catholicism's favor, it is unlikely that such motion pictures as *Don Camillo* or *La Dolce vita* would ever again materialize. On the other hand, as the Italian film output of recent years suggests, Italian affluence may now be such that most Italians can afford to attend commercial theaters, without having to be dependent on cheaper parish theaters.

Catholic Action's position is that, in addition to meeting strict standards of morality, motion pictures should not focus on man's baser instincts, his social degradation, his hopeless economic plight, or his struggles with religion, society, and government. Motion pictures should be happy, not sad; they should amuse and uplift the spectator and not cast him into a mood of defeat and depression. In short, motion pictures should not be too realistic and should not dwell on themes that increase a sense of discontent. The point here, however, is not whether the Catholic Action view is right or wrong but that as a result of the influence the view can exercise on the Christian Democratic Party and the upper bureaucracy, an important medium of communication has to some extent fallen under the control of one of Italy's ideologically isolative and sectarian interest groups. It is to developments such as this that Italians—and the respondents in this study—point when they underline the power of Catholic Action and the integralist intentions of organized Catholicism in general.

It is significant that the image of Catholic Action as the most powerful organized group in the Italian polity is held not only by Catholicism's major detractors but also by other Catholic group leaders, conservative members of the bureaucracy, and leaders of Confindustria. Several of the latter openly express their fear that Catholic Action will eclipse the industrial Confederation in the Ministry of Industry and Commerce, making of that key administrative sector "yet another vehicle at the service of Catholic interests." Within Catholic Action itself there is frank and self-confident appraisal of the vast influence exercised by the organization. As an example of this, a national leader of *Gioventù Femminile,* the young women's segment of Catholic Action, asserts that Catholic Action is far more important in the legislature and the bureaucracy than the Christian Democratic C.I.S.L., or for that matter any other Catholic group. She indicates that this is true not only because of Catholic Action's greater size but also because the organization carries on an important educational function in connection with several million persons in Italy. Contrasting Catholic Action and C.I.S.L., she says: "C.I.S.L. *organizes* its members; Catholic Action *forms* its own, shapes new attitudes in them, requires its membership to adopt new attitudes, requires its membership to dedicate themselves to the kind of work that demands sacrifice; and it works out this program of indoctrination and action not merely through occasional meetings but through frequent regular meetings, through personal and profound contacts. Catholic Action imbues its membership with principles."

This respondent adds that the best proof of the strength of the organization is that Communism considers it and not Christian Democracy or any other Catholic organization its greatest enemy. For this reason, she adds, it is probably Catholic Action and not the D.C. that, in a political emergency, would provide the greatest amount of cohesive opposition to a threat from the Communist Party. . . .

PERCEPTIONS OF REALITY: CATHOLIC ACTION

For several reasons, it is difficult to generalize about the content and meaning of the perceptions of reality manifested by the leaders of Catholic Action. In the first place, Catholic Action is officially described as the apostolic arm of the Catholic clergy and is by most measures completely subservient to the wishes of the Vatican. The top-level leaders of A.C.I. branches are never elected but chosen by the clergy; presumably, on all matters involving doctrine or policy—as opposed to action or methodology—it is the clergy, through the net-work of ecclesiastical assistants who oversee A.C.I. activities at all levels, that sets the direction of the organization. For this reason, it is necessary and logical to note reality perceptions as they are officially formulated and handed down by the Catholic hierarchy itself. Our interviews with both clerical and lay leaders of Catholic Action clearly indicate that the Catholic Church is anxious to assure that only limited freedom to interpret and evaluate reality is permitted. This simple and basic relationship of Catholic Action leaders and members to the clerical hierarchy is simply and pointedly stated by a leader of the *Movimento Laureati,* that branch of Catholic Action that recruits intellectuals and university graduates. "By taking out a membership card, one does not merely show one's interest in the Movement's activities. One also engages himself toward the Church hierarchy; he places himself at the disposition of the hierarchy in order to act according to the latter's direction."

Secondly, and despite what I have just said, it is clear that Catholic Action is an immense organization consisting of units that are ideologically and temperamentally somewhat dissimilar. For example, there is a significant gulf that separates the extremely conservative *Unione Donne* (Union of Women) or the *Gioventù Femminile* (Young Women) from the Movimento Laureati or the F.U.C.I. (Federation of Italian Catholic University Students). The former two units are less politically oriented than the latter, more exclusively tied to the apostolic rather than the secular dimension of Catholic Action. The latter organizations are self-consciously committed to the exploration of intellectual and political problems, much more determined to maximize the amount of freedom of philosophical as well as methodological initiative that can be expressed within the rather narrow confines of an admittedly authoritarian organization.

Thus the Movimento Laureati leader cited before is careful to distinguish his unit from others within Catholic Action. The Movement, he says, differs from other Catholic Action branches in the sense that it is willing openly to confront any problem, without the typical kind of Catholic Action prejudice that leads to choices on a completely a priori basis. Skirting very close to a basic criticism of the way in which Catholic Action is managed, he says: "The message of the gospel needs translation into a language that is differentiated according to the time and place in the total life of the Church in which an effort is made to communicate the message. It is the major responsibility of the priesthood, the ecclesiastical hierarchy, to guard the substantive integrity of the message. It is the duty of the lay members of the Catholic Church to elaborate that message so that it conforms to the exigencies of the time in which the elaboration takes place. It is specifically the task of the cultured or intelligent segment of the laity to conduct this elaboration."

This claim for relative freedom of action is echoed by a national leader of F.U.C.I., who claims that his organization is somewhat separated from the rest of Catholic Action and that, like the Movimento Laureati, it experiences less interference from the Catholic clergy. He says: "F.U.C.I. has a spirit of its own that the other branches of Catholic Action, with the important exception of the Movimento Laureati, do not share. For example, F.U.C.I. places great emphasis on the rule of free discussion as the most important internal educational device. Free discussion is simply not permitted in the four great branches of Catholic Action [i.e., U.D.A.C.I., Union of Women; U.U.A.C.I., Union of Men; G.I.A.C., Young Men; and G.F., Young Women]. The other branches of Catholic Action are highly articulated organizations where a rigidly hierarchical and authoritarian method of leadership and membership relationships is maintained."

He goes on to say that F.U.C.I. seeks an open dialogue with the laical forces of the country, that it seeks to liberalize the internal structure as well as the policy orientations of Catholic Action, and that it persists in these two orientations notwithstanding opposition from the rest of Catholic Action or the discouraging fact that little headway has been made.

I cite these respondents not to suggest that each branch of Catholic Action is free to perceive realities as it chooses but to caution against easy generalizations and to emphasize that organized Catholicism is not an absolute monolith even in that organizational sector over which the clergy can and does exercise the most assiduous and pervasive control.

Thirdly, it is necessary to understand that, for many practical and operational purposes, Catholic Action is essentially what each bishop, operating at the level of the diocese, decrees that it will be. One of the most significant internal struggles within Catholic Action (which we cannot examine in detail) is between those who would centralize authority in the General Presidency (i.e., Secretariat) at Rome and others who wish to maximize both functional divisional and geographic autonomy. For the latter, there always tends to be entirely too much ideological and tactical direction from the Center; for the former, the long tradition of autonomy under the direction of local bishops is felt to be dangerous and chaotic. The point to bear in mind is that, even under the highly centralizing designs of Pope Pius XII and Luigi Gedda, who ran Catholic Action as tightly as possible, many bishops could and did interpret for themselves the most efficacious way of implementing in the diocese the evangelical and (unofficially) political mission of Catholic Action. . . .

BEHAVIORAL RESPONSE: CATHOLIC ACTION

Given the perceptions, ideology, and organizational self-image of Catholic Action's leaders, it is not surprising that they should seek to develop a form of operational activity that will leave no sector of society untouched. If the society is shot through with evil, evil itself must be eradicated wherever it is found; if the Catholic Church is besieged by enemies, they must be sought out and combated wherever they may lurk; if the message of the Church is total, applying to every facet of human existence, there is no sector of social organization and behavior that should remain ignorant of it.

One obvious implication of this formulation is that Catholic Action must be a mass movement. What began in the mid-nineteenth century as a relative handful of ardent young Catholics is now one of Italy's vastest organizations. One national leader proudly asserts that A.C.I.'s three and one-half million members account for over six percent of the Italian population. In some of the regions of northern Italy, the proportion is much higher. Although membership falls off in the strongly left-wing central regions of Tuscany, Emila-Romagna, and Umbria, it is certain that Catholic Action is a factor to be reckoned with in all of the country's 311 dioceses and in most of the more than twenty thousand parishes they contain. Even after one discounts for natural membership figure exaggeration, it is certain that A.C.I. ranks as one of the top three interest groups in the country.

Moreover, as one of A.C.I.'s national leaders points out, those who are in the organization are *real* and dues-paying members. In addition, they understand that membership carries with it the responsibility to carry out assignments when they are given. The criteria of selection and retention to membership are such that those who remain or survive to join an adult unit are highly militant and devoted followers.

Catholic Action philosophy would also argue for organization by sector. The four great branches of the organization recruit young men, young women, older men, and older women. In addition, there are three major branches that involve university students, college graduates and intellectuals, and teachers.

There is considerable disagreement, however, as to whether there should be further functional divisions or subdivisions in the organization. For example, our interviews with leaders of the G.I.A.C. revealed considerable tension between those who manage the age-group divisions and others who are in charge of subunits dealing with industrial workers and rural inhabitants. At the time of this study at least, there existed the strong feeling that neither President Luigi Gedda nor the ecclesiastical hierarchy under Pius XII approved of functional divisions that were broken along social class lines. The line of "interclassism" is strong, and Gedda clearly did not want Italian Catholic Action to emulate class-conscious organizational patterns typical of French Catholic Action.

In a sense, this type of functional division is unnecessary. As we noted earlier, there now exist in Italy interest groups to cover every conceivable major social, professional, and economic category. Many of these groups maintain close liaison with Catholic Action branches and are to some extent influenced and guided by it. Nevertheless, there are Catholic Action leaders who feel that other Catholic groups lack the doctrinal purity and strong sense of devotion that marks A.C.I. For this reason, we can expect some pressure for greater functional articulation to continue.

Another possible implication of Catholic Action assumptions is that the work of the organization should be managed and integrated under a highly centralized national administration. Under the presidency of Luigi Gedda, a major effort was made to increase the powers of the General Presidency at Rome at the expense of territorial and functional units. One of Gedda's closest collaborators admits that the drive for centralization—the great emphasis on organizational structure—was a source of great internal tension and controversy. In support of the idea of greater centralization, this individual spoke of "compact unity" and "harmonious operations." In fact, he really meant that more critical policy and tactical decisions should be made at Rome and not left to the bishops in the dioceses or to the seven major divisions.

What this respondent describes as the atomistic tendencies in A.C.I. are said to be traceable to the Fascist period. Throughout that era, in order to be able to offer more effective resistance to attempts of the Fascist government to interfere with Catholic Action activities, the Vatican decreed a major decentralization of the organization. This tactic would presumably have made it more difficult for the Fascists to wreck A.C.I. than if it were a highly centralized unit. The decision to effect organizational atomization is not unlike that followed by Communist parties when they are under direct and immediate assault.

Following World War II, Luigi Gedda attempted to reverse this trend. He ran into opposition, not only from lay leaders of Catholic Action but also from many bishops who had become key figures in diocese-level A.C.I. activities during two decades of Fascism. In this latter sense, the organizational controversy was caught up in the even more fundamental Catholic question of how much autonomy in fact is to be permitted the powerful bishops, on which foundation the organizational apparatus of worldwide Catholicism really rests. As several A.C.I. leaders are quick to assert, the bishops of Italy retain great power and cannot easily be directed from the A.C.I. General Presidency at Rome. For this reason, as well as for reasons of strong internal opposition, the Gedda drive for centralization never reached the degree of implementation to which he and his devoted associates and collaborators aspired.

One might compare this situation to the controversy within Confindustria over the manner and form of political participation. Just as Confindustria's bureaucrats are subtly able to oppose open political participation, the unit leaders of Catholic Action are able to resist centralization; just as Fiat and Montecatini are able to intervene politically in their own right and outside the Confederation, the bishops are able to guide Catholic Action units in their dioceses pretty much as they wish and dictate. Perceptions of reality at the national level may call for a particular organizational and behavioral response. However, local perceptions—or, in any case, internal organizational maneuvering— may make such a response impossible. This is only one of the bitter dilemmas that confronted Luigi Gedda.

Another source of tension within Catholic Action is whether and to what extent there should be intervention in politics. Another way of putting this question is to ask whether A.C.I.'s mission is essentially apostolic or whether the organization is to be the major secular arm of the Catholic Church. Catholic Action leaders, who share perceptions of reality, are divided on this question. When I asked one of the national ecclesiastical assistants how he would define the A.C.I. mission, he quickly replied that "the ends of Catholic Action are equated with the ends of the organized Church. . . . There is some feeling in the hierarchy that it has failed to bring about a day-to-day relationship with its flock. Catholic Action is construed as one of the means of evolving modern Christianity in terms of adopting the ends of the Church to the real conditions in which the Catholics find themselves in Italian (as well as other) society." Many other lay leaders also emphasize the apostolic or evangelical purpose of A.C.I. They sharply shun the political or secular interpretation—namely, that A.C.I. is an important instrument for gaining and maintaining a certain amount of political power. While every unit of Catholic Action is conceded to be spending some time in the civic training of members (i.e., in their preparation for responsible participation in the country's political life), education is said to be as far as the organization goes in this direction.

Luigi Gedda responds in the same vein, holding that Catholic Action represents laical apostolic work adapted to modern conditions. He notes that it is the purpose of A.C.I. to learn to communicate the message and the teachings of the Church to the specialized categories of Italian society.

Gedda adds, as do other leaders, that Catholic Action does not directly engage in politics, that this is prohibited by the A.C.I. constitution, as well as by the 1929 Concordat that was incorporated into the Constitution of the Italian Republic. "This means," he says, "that Catholic Action's political activity is indirect. However, even if Catholic Action does not directly tell its members to vote for Christian Democracy, the members are conditioned to do so. This is a form of conditioned reflex—as in the case of Pavlov's dog."

The view that Catholic Action is not directly involved in the political process is shared by almost no one outside the organization. A former leader of Catholic Action asserts that A.C.I., like all Catholic groups, aims at "integralism," which implies a total—and totalitarian—control of society. Catholic Action represents a new form of the Church's intervention in the political life of the country, after the Church lost the temporal power it exercised prior to Italy's unification. Another ecclesiastical assistant points to the essentially political origins of Catholic Action when he remarks: "Catholic Action came into existence with the precise goal or purpose of defending the liberty and rights of the Church against the incursions of eighteenth-century liberalism. The Church increasingly felt the need of defending itself against the attacks of liberalism run rampant."

It is needless to pursue at any length the question whether Catholic Action is or is not directly in politics; it most obviously is. On the critical point of A.C.I.'s relationship to the directly political civic committees, it is widely understood that they were Luigi Gedda's creation. Moreover, a national leader of A.C.I. frankly admits the committees' origins in and ties to it, and adds that the National Civic Committee has no formal constitution, in order to avoid any difficulties concerning the Concordat's prohibition against Catholic Action's engaging in politics!

The more pertinent question, then, is *how* Catholic Action should engage in politics. Until now, the major patterns have been direct representation in Parliament and trading on *parentela* relationship to the D.C. However, as we have noted, *parentela* can be an ephemeral power base, not merely because the hegemonic Party may lose political control but also because an antagonistic faction may capture the Party. Fanfani represented the latter kind of threat for Catholic Action. Aldo Moro is less of a threat but still not completely reliable. Were one to go by the utterances of *Il Quotidiano,* A.C.I.'s semi-official and strident organ, Amintore Fanfani is no different from the Socialists and other forces of darkness loose in the society. Indeed, many Catholic Action leaders are frank to comment that, in their eyes, many of Christian Democracy's leaders are as morally reprehensible as the laical politicians of the country. The mission of integralism must be carried out within the D.C. as well.

Most of A.C.I.'s realists recognize that there is no complete alternative to continuing to capitalize on a *parentela* relationship with the D.C. No matter how strong men like Fanfani might be or remain, the Party apparatus cannot function under its own power and must continue to rely on the civic committees, Catholic Action militants in the parishes and dioceses, and the bishops. . . . As long as Christian Democracy remains the strange amalgamation of groups that it is, a group like A.C.I. that is based on outright and unequivocal confessionalism is certain to make its weight felt in a Catholic party.

However, there are now strong pressures aiming at *clientela*—at establishing the kinds of relationships to the bureaucracy that would transcend the term of office of a single party or, indeed, compel that party to come to terms with the bureaucracy. Catholic Action leaders frankly want "our people" on committees that award university professorships, on committees that advise ministries, on boards that govern publicly controlled enterprise, and spread about in the bureaucracy itself. As one A.C.I. representative who emphasizes *clientela* points out, "contacts with the ministries turn out to be particularly fruitful where the functionary involved comes from one of the Catholic Action branches." For men and women who share an image of themselves as involved in a noble mission with religious overtones, the argument is very persuasive that no avenue of possible effectiveness in the execution of that mission should be left unexplored.

It may well be, as one former A.C.I. leader claims, that the behavior of the organization brings about in its members and others a complete blocking of effective discourse and interaction (*blocco e chiusura reciproca*), and that this phenomenon has a nefarious influence on Italian society. It is also true that this type of *blocco* is one of the basic conditions of Italy, in which all the groups are compelled to operate. In these circumstances there is much to justify Catholic Action's implementation of the Church's unrelenting will to power. It is fair to say that because the secular State may permit the Church less control than previously, Catholicism's effort to maximize political power is undiminished. Catholic Action is clearly an important instrument for reaching this goal—not blindly, but on the basis of a fairly realistic appraisal of the limits on behavior, and on the attainment of power, imposed by any given situation. The Church can be and is often defeated, but it never relinquishes its claim to power. This is the *elan* that drives Catholic Action. It is also one of the critical reasons why the interest-group phenomenon in Italy does not yet contribute, as it might, to the maintenance of democratic stability.

7 VAL R. LORWIN

Working-Class Politics and Economic Development in Western Europe[1]

How far has economic development conditioned working-class politics in Western Europe in the last century and a half? Are there stages of economic development in which protest is always sharp and others in which it is dull? To what extent are the differences in protest among the nations due to differences in economic growth, to what extent to different patterns of general historical development caused by other factors? What types of studies may promote our understanding of these questions? These are questions I propose to raise or to discuss here.

The study of economic development has had a tremendous revival in the last decade. This revival springs largely from considerations of public policy, an honorable stimulus to scholars' quickened interest. One source is the pressure of the economically underdeveloped countries, those we used to call "backward" countries

Reprinted from *The American Historical Review*, LXIII No. 2 (January, 1958), pp. 338-351, by permission of the author and the publisher.

but which are often extremely "forward" these days. Another is the threat of economic stagnation in older industrial nations. A third is the concern of the democracies for their very survival in the face of the vast economic growth of the Soviet Union and, in the offing, of Communist China.

"Economic development," the economist James S. Duesenberry says, "seems to be one of those peculiar phrases whose meaning everyone knows without the aid of any formal definition. Onward and upward expresses the term's meaning as well as anything else."[2] Here I should like to consider the effects of long-range economic change, which includes some regression as well as the "onward and upward" which generally marks our period. Not only are changes in total national product and product per head important, but so are the types of industry, the size of enterprise, the structure of ownership and quality of management, the sources of the labor force, the patterns of occupations, the distribution of income, and the nature of the industrial and urban communities.[3]

The other side of the problem is the politics of labor, particularly the politics of protest. I shall include in political protest primarily fundamental protest against the social and political order (what Otto Kirchheimer has called "the opposition of principle"), but also the loyal opposition within the framework of the existing regime, and even some pressure group politics.[4] The distinctions have not always been clear to those who protest; often they have been even less clear to those to whom petition or clamor has been addressed— government, bourgeoisie, or fellow workers.

Working-class protest, like economic development, has been a matter of some agitated public concern since the Second World War. But people have been proclaiming it a chief problem of modern times since Carlyle wrote of the "bitter discontent gone fierce and mad, the wrong conditions therefore or the wrong disposition of the Working Classes of England"[5] and Harriet Martineau warned that "this great question of the rights of labor . . . cannot be neglected under a lighter penalty than ruin to all."[6]

A few hardy souls have sought to identify historical truth on these matters by quantitative methods, shrinking neither from the paucity of data nor the conceptual difficulties of the task. For all but very recent periods the data are sketchy, and "guesstimates" are difficult and shaky. Comparisons in time multiply the difficulties, as the composition of what is being compared changes—but the efforts are worth making. Economic growth may be measured in figures of national income or industrial production, in national totals and per head. We may try to measure not only the community's income but—still more difficult—the workers' shares of the community's income. People do not revolt against averages, however. We must try to separate groups of workers whose special grievances may set off widespread protest when the economy as a whole is moving forward. We must recognize the lags in political responses to objective conditions. Attitudes generated by economic regression may not manifest themselves in behavior until after economic recovery.

W. W. Rostow, in his valuable book on the nineteenth-century British economy, has a "social tension chart" for the years 1790-1850.[7] The chart records quantitatively factors that produce, or might produce, social tensions (wheat prices and the trade cycle, for unemployment), but not the tensions or manifestations of tension themselves. We are here, moreover, in the short-run ups and downs of business cycles, rather in stages of economic growth.

On the axis of protest, too, measurement is difficult. It is easy to over-estimate the evidence that is quantifiable. In recent decades many nations have recorded the man-days lost by strikes, but these numbers represent no uniform quantities; there are great differences in the intensity of protest, and political content, from one strike to another.

Political protest can be measured in some of its more orderly forms: party membership, election results, and—for the most recent years, in many nations—whatever it is people tell to those who take public opinion polls. For periods before the working class attained full suffrage, however, the test of votes is only partially applicable, and complete and equal manhood suffrage was not attained until the First World War in most of the advanced European nations. We do not know how workers voted, moreover, or who voted for the parties claiming to represent the working class, except in some one-industry areas like the miners' constituencies. Nor have all Socialist votes or all Communist votes been of equal intensity as protests. Some votes have implied rejection of the social order; others, merely hopes of immediate economic self-interest; still others, vague and diffuse frustrations.[8]

On the eve of the Industrial Revolution, Henry Fielding remarked: "The sufferings of the poor are less observed than their misdeeds. . . . They starve, and freeze, and rot among themselves, but they beg, and steal, and rob among their betters."[9] Soon the laboring poor were able to do more, when they were thrown out of work or their wages were cut, than "beg and steal and rob among their betters." Modern economic development created a new sort of political protest by generating the industrial, essentially urban, wage-earning groups in such numbers and force that they were, for all their medieval and early modern predecessors, in most ways a new class—as yet only "camped in society . . . not established there."[10] This was, said the ex-worker Denis Poulot, "the terrible sphinx which is called the people . . . this great mass of workers which does not know what it is, except that it suffers."[11] Huddled in the wretched new factory towns or in the slums of renowned old cities, oppressed by long hours of work, arbitrary shop rules, and monotony, sorely tried by recurrent unemployment, unlettered, this mass inspired more fear than solicitude. Lord Liverpool, congratulated by Chateaubriand on the solidity of British institutions, pointed to the capital outside his windows and replied: "What can be stable with these enormous cities? One insurrection in London and all is lost."[12]

Hunger will turn political. In the hard year of 1819 the banners of the crowd at Peterloo, before the Yeomen rode them down, typified the mixture of the economic and the political: "A Fair Day's Wage for a Fair Day's Work," "No Corn Laws," and "Equal Representation or Death."[13]

It was not hunger alone. "The poor have hearts as well as stomachs," said Cooke Taylor but deemed it a fact not known to many who passed for wise men.[14] Carlyle knew it: "It is not what a man outwardly has or wants that constitutes the happiness or misery of him. Nakedness, hunger, distress of all kinds, death itself have been cheerfully suffered, when the heart was right. It is the feeling of injustice that is insupportable to all men. . . . No man can bear it or ought to bear it."[15]

Michel Chevalier looked at manufacturing and said: "Fixed points are totally lacking. There is no bond between superior and inferior, no rapprochement between equals. . . . Nothing holds, nothing lasts."[16] Slowly, "fixed points" were established; the working classes gained in education, self-discipline, and political experience. In the course of industrialization in every Western country, despite crises and wars, workers' levels of living improved vastly. Did this resolve working-class protest?

Continuing economic development would resolve the very protest it brought into being, Marx argued, but only by the inevitable substitution of a new order for the capitalist society, which would prove incapable of continuing the triumphant progress of economic growth. Until the coming of the new order, declared the *Communist Manifesto*, "the development of class antagonism keeps even pace with the development of industry," and in *Capital* Marx affirmed that "there is a steady intensification of the wrath of the working class." (I use a few of Marx's significant statements as beginning points for discussion, not attempting an analysis of Marx or Marxism.)

These predictions have been contradicted by the experience (thus far) of all the Western nations except France and Italy—nor do France and Italy actually support the prophecy. Here is one of the ironies of the history of Marxist prediction.[17] Only in the two countries where, among all the great industrial nations of the free world, capitalism has shown the least sustained dynamism has the "wrath of the working class" permitted the Communist party to take and hold a preponderant position among workers.[18] These two countries require a closer look.

In France and Italy, economic growth alone could not resolve the noneconomic problems created by wars, religious tensions, social distance, and the relations between the individual and the state. We cannot go into the noneconomic factors here. But the sense of injustice in these countries also grew, in part, out of the qualities of economic growth: the character of entrepreneurship, the distribution of income, and—even more—the nature of employer authority. The bourgeoisie of France and of Italy were insistent in their demands for protection against labor as well as protection against competition. Niggardly and tardy in concessions to their workers, they flaunted inequalities by their style of living. Their class consciousness helped shape the class consciousness of workers.

Workers, moreover, doubted the ability of their superiors to fulfill their economic functions as an entrepreneurial class. The slowness of economic growth evoked protest, particularly in France. Before the First World War, labor leaders shared with many orthodox economists and publicists the impression that their country was stagnating,[19] although it was progressing in the two decades before the war. The gloomy view arose in part from comparisons with the industrial growth of the United States and with the industrial and military growth of Germany. That view also reflected the state of labor organization, greater in the stagnant old industries such as building and in the thousands of small workshops of Paris than in the newer industries such as the booming steel mills of Lorraine. Later, in the interwar period, the labor movement was strong in the civil administration and public service industries rather than in the new and technically progressive branches of private industry—chemicals, synthetic fibers, automobiles.

French employers groaned constantly about their high costs, especially of labor, and their inability to compete with foreign producers.[20] Labor leaders argued, however, that the employers' difficulties really came from their sterility; "their very slow progress, from their timidity; their uncertainty, from their lack of initiative. We ask the French employers to resemble the American employer class. . . . We want a busy, active, humming country, a veritable beehive always awake. In that way our own force will be increased."[21] But the unions' own force remained weak. Their weakness, along with pessimism about the country's economic growth, gave to French labor that curious combination of low immediate hopes and utopian dreams which has characterized it during most of this century.

Management's own leaders praised smallness of scale and slowness to mechanize. In 1930 the president of the General Confederation of French Manufacturers congratulated his members on "the spirit of prudence in the management of firms, which is the surest guarantee against the dangers of a fearful crisis," and on "the French mentality of counting on regular and steady dividends, rather than on the saw-toothed variation of dividends fashionable in some great industrial nations."[22] The year of this speech marked the beginning of fifteen years of economic decline and stagnation in France.

The dramatic inequalities between the poorer, agricultural areas and the industrialized regions of both Italy and France created further tensions in each nation. Finally, the bourgeoisie showed a fear of the people and a political bankruptcy at history's critical hours. Workers in Italy and France tended to merge judgments of the political and the economic performance of the powers that were. Their doubts as to the competence and courage of the bourgeoisie deepened their feelings of both the injustice and the fragility of the social and political order. Here let us leave France and Italy to return to the general question.

Some would turn the Marxian assertion upside down and argue that there is a "hump of radicalism" early in a nation's industrial development and that once the economy, by a big "initial push," surmounts its early difficulties, protest inevitably falls off. The history of a number of countries gives support to this analysis. But, despite Marx and many anti-Marxists, in the history of social relationships the several factors never long "keep even pace" with each other. In England the working class has not seriously threatened the political order since Chartist times, to be sure; but the syndicalists of the immediate pre-1914 period and the Socialists of the post-1918 period were far more critical of the social and economic order than the New Model unionists and the "Lib-Labs" of the 1850's, 1860's, and 1870's. France and Italy show a series of humps of radicalism.

Economic development has attenuated early protest by changes in the structure of the working classes. "Within the ranks of the proletariat," announced the *Communist Manifesto,* "the various interests and conditions of life are more and more equalized, in proportion as machinery obliterates all distinction of labor, and nearly everywhere reduces wages to the same low level. . . . The modern laborer, instead of rising with the progress of industry, sinks deeper and deeper below the conditions of existence of his own class."[23] Marx was observing a period of development in which the machine was breaking down old skills, especially in the textile trades. The historian was being unhistorical in assuming that the trend must continue.

By the turn of the century it was already clear to a good observer like Eduard Bernstein (who was aided by residence in England) that economic growth and social reforms were blurring the sharpness of class among wage and salaried workers.[24] This is the now familiar phenomenon of the rise of the "new middle class." (Let us accent the word "new," for we use the old, imprecise words "middle class" for lack of a more descriptive phrase.) George Orwell spoke of the "upward and downward extension of the middle class" and of the growing importance of the people of "indeterminate social class."[25] This is the result of the swelling of the so-called tertiary sector of the economy— of public administration, commerce, services, and, within the industrial sector itself, the expansion of professional, technical, and administrative jobs.[26] Even among those in traditional forms of wage employment, middle-class attitudes have flourished, made possible not only by higher real wages and greater leisure but also by enhanced security, housing in socially mixed communities, longer schooling, and an increasingly classless culture wafted on mass communications.

The people of the new middle class have most often sought individual rather than collective solutions. Their political preferences have been divided —although unevenly—among almost all the parties. On the Continent in crisis times, fearful of being dragged down to proletarian status, many have hearkened to authoritarian voices. The new middle class called into question many of the traditional appeals of working-class politics. The parties of labor were obliged to appeal to other classes and to more complex attitudes than, rightly or wrongly, they formerly took for granted among workers.

Another change which came with economic growth was the differentiation between the economic and the political organizations of the working classes. Early forms of action had confused the economic and political. Then there generally came a separation between unions and political parties and, allbeit with interlocking directorates and memberships, a cooperative division of function. France, Italy, and Spain, however, did not achieve this division of labor; while England was developing "Sidney Webbicalism,"[27] they developed syndicalism. This was the confounding of politics and economics in the name of "a-political" action. Anarcho-syndicalism, with its refusal to recognize the reality of politics and its disdain for parliamentary democracy, had fateful consequences. It prevented an effective working relationship of the unions with the socialist parties, to the great mischief of both, and helped leave workers poorly prepared later to distinguish between democratic political protest and communist politics.

Politics could not be denied, however much some workers' leaders might plead the sufficiency of economic action. No movement came to be more dependent on political action for economic gains than the "a-political" French unions. Even the robust British workers' consumer cooperatives, founded on the Rochdale principle of political neutrality, formed a Cooperative party (which became a small tail to the Labour party kite). When British labor attempted in the 1926 general strike to solve by industrial action a problem too big for industrial action alone, the result was catastrophe. Even there, moreover, the Trades Union Congress used its economic power in only a halfhearted way for fear of damaging the nation's political foundations.

The once lively anarchist and syndicalist movements practically disappeared under the hammer of economic development. The libertarian movements could not survive in the climate of assembly line production, modern industrial organization, or the modern welfare state. It was the communists, opposed though they were to the deepest libertarian impulses, who by their militant rejection of bourgeois society claimed most of the anarchists' and syndicalists' following. To the completely power-centered movement fell the heritage of those who had refused to come to any terms with political power.

Among the socialists, the bearded prophets gave way to the smooth-chinned organizers, parliamentarians, and planners. Socialist militancy was a victim of socialist success, itself made possible by economic growth. Economic growth produced a margin of well-being and facilitated the compromises and generosity which reconciled groups to each other in most of the liberal democracies.

Along with socialist militancy, socialist certitudes faded. The motto of "Socialism in our time" was amended, at least *sotto voce,* to "Socialism . . . but not in our time." Socialism became less than ever a doctrine and more a political temper. Despite an addiction to worn-out slogans, it was mellowed and strengthened, particularly after the First World War, by its identification with the noneconomic values of national life against threats from extreme left and extreme right.

Where it was most doctrinal, socialism was least effective—and often least true to its own doctrine. It proved most effective where it was most pragmatic, in the lands where the habits of civic responsibility and political compromise were strong; these were all (except Switzerland) constitutional monarchies. In France and in Italy, however, the Communist party rushed into the gap between socialist reasonableness and workers' old resentments, between socialist uncertainties and workers' pent-up hopes. Spain and Portugal were limiting cases; their hours of democracy were of the briefest, in part because of long economic stagnation.

"Modern industrial labor, modern subjugation to capital, the same in England as in France, in America as in Germany, has stripped [the proletarian] of every trace of national character. . . . National differences, and antagonisms between people, are daily more and more vanishing," said the *Communist Manifesto.* Instead, the working-class movements have all followed different national patterns. For many years it could be said that the only thing the socialists had nationalized was socialism.

Britain developed a labor movement of class solidarity and class organization without class hatred; France and Italy, class hatred but ineffectual class organization. Scandinavia developed on the British pattern, overcoming class conflict and moving on to an even higher degree of class restraint and responsibility than Britain's. The Belgian, Dutch, and Swiss working classes have shown a remarkable degree of responsibility, although their highly developed class organizations have followed the religious and political cleavages in each nation. The Communist Internationals have exercised central controls, but over parties which have differed not only from continent to continent but also from nation to contiguous Western European nation.

"A number of things govern men," said Montesquieu, "climate, religion, laws, maxims of government, the examples of things past, customs, manners; from all this there is formed a general spirit."[28] Economic development was only one of the factors that influenced social structures, cultural patterns, political habits and institutions, and what for short we call national character.

National character is often a bundle of contradictions, however, and it changes in time. The form and temper of working-class action also change. In Norway, for example, the tremendous onrush of industrialization early in this century evoked a radical protest which gave the union movement a syndicalist turn and took the Labor party into the Communist International.[29] But the party soon broke with the Comintern, and party and unions developed into one of the most solid—yet independent and imaginative—labor movements in the world.

In Belgium, about 1891, social conflict seemed so irreconcilable that Paul Vinogradoff thought revolution must break out in this "overcrowded country, where the extremes of socialist and Catholic opinion were at that time most in evidence,"[30] and that such a revolution would touch off a general European war. But before the First World War, Belgian workers had somehow assimilated their conflicts in a structure of compromise and appeared as among the most moderate in Europe.

The study of differences and similarities between the nations, as well as change within the nations, sheds light on our problems. One may, for example, compare France and Belgium, separated by a rather artificial frontier but by many historical differences. The reconciliation of the Belgian working class to the political and social order, divided though the workers are by language and religion and the Flemish-Walloon question, makes a vivid contrast with the experience of France. The differences did not arise from the material fruits of economic growth, for both long were rather low-wage countries, and Belgian wages were the lower. In some ways the two countries had similar economic development. But Belgium's industrialization began earlier; it was more dependent on international commerce, both for markets and for its transit trade; it had a faster growing population; and it became much more urbanized than France. The small new nation, "the cockpit of Europe," could not permit itself social and political conflict to the breaking point. Perhaps France could not either, but it was harder for the bigger nation to realize it.

Comparisons of different groups within nations and among nations are of the essence too. Some occupations seem prone to long phases of radicalism.[31] Dangerous trades, unsteady employment, and isolation from the larger community are some of the factors which make for radicalism among dockers, seamen, lumbermen, and miners in many—though not all—countries. Yet radicalism has had successes among the more stable occupations too.

It is not generally those who are in the greatest economic distress who are the leaders in protest. First, one may recognize the element of chance in the occupational selection of leaders of protest (as in all selections of leadership).

It is happenstance that the lifelong leader of the French unions, Léon Jouhaux, came out of a match factory and that the great leader of Danish Social Democracy, Thorvald Stauning, came out of the cigar maker's trade. Beyond the chance elements, however, there is a process of selection for leadership of protest from strength rather than misery, by the capacity of the group rather than its economic distress. First those in the skilled artisan trades (notably the printers and building craftsmen), then the metal workers, miners, and railroad men have been in the vanguard in many lands. In relation to economic development, some of the leaders have come from the groups of skilled operatives menaced by technological change, others from skilled or semi-skilled workers in positions of continuing opportunity or in stable, strategic locations in the industrial process.

Urban and regional social history and political history for the industrial age mostly remain to be written.[32] Description may be aided and informed by comparison. Birmingham may be compared with Manchester and Leeds, Birmingham with Lyons; Asa Briggs has done both for the early nineteenth century.[33] Comparisons within nations may point up the importance of factors quite different from those which emerge from comparisons between nations. In France and Italy, syndicalism seems related to comparative national economic retardation. In Spain, syndicalism was strong in the economically most advanced region of a country as a whole terribly retarded; the reasons were in the Catalans' political autonomism as well as in their economic advance.[34]

Apparently similar economic trends may give rise to, or at least be accompanied by, different consequences of protest. British miners' protest mounted bitterly as the coal industry sank into the doldrums of the 1920's. On the other hand, the porcelain workers of Limoges, vigorous socialists at the turn of the century, became torpid as their industry declined into torpor.

If only in passing and by inference, I hope to have recalled some examples of the particular subjects which invite the historian and some of the values of comparative studies.[35] We need to study many more individuals, in biographies, and many more occupations and industries, in their settings of period and place, as, with fond intensity and imaginative erudition, Georges Duveau has studied the workers of the Second Empire,[36] before we can safely generalize. But men will, as men should, generalize long before they can safely generalize.

Here I have thought that modest ground-clearing considerations would be most useful. To assume my share of responsibility, however, I offer a few working hypotheses. For some of them, the nature of the evidence has been hinted at in the preceding pages; for others, not even that. They are not meant to be "laws" or "universal" but merely to sum up a few aspects of the experience of the past 150 years in one area of the world, an area full of intriguing differences yet with enough homogeneity in culture and industrial development to make generalization valid and comparison significant.

Economic development is process, environment, and goal; it provides a framework, and sets problems, for man's capacities for political and social action.

Rapid growth in the early stages of industrialization generates protest by reason of the bewildering dislocations and (for many) the sacrifices out of current consumption which it imposes. Continued economic growth permits the satisfaction of much of this protest. But some attitudes of protest persist well beyond the economic conditions which aroused them.

Sluggish economic growth may generate the deepest and longest lasting protest by reason of the society's inability to provide well-being and social justice to match social aspirations and by reason of the economic elite's failure to inspire confidence. Slow growth of cities and slow recruitment of the industrial work force facilitate the carry-over of traditions of protest from generation to generation.

The gradual delineation of the separate (but overlapping) spheres and organizations of political and industrial protest makes for reconciliation and absorption of protest in each sphere.

The labor movements most dependent on the state may show the greatest hostility to the state. The working classes best integrated with their national communities are those which have built labor movements that are more or less autonomous centers of power.

The successive phases of a nation's economic development are not inevitably reflected in corresponding attitudes and behavior of labor protest. Moreover, different phases of development exist side by side in the same regions and industries. Different forms of working-class politics also exist side by side.

National differences shape the response of workers and labor movements to economic change. These differences are only in part due to the differences in patterns of economic development. In large part they are due to noneconomic factors—politics and religion, cultural patterns and class structure—and to historical accident and personalities. ("Everything is dependent on everything," however, and most of the noneconomic factors are themselves conditioned by economic change.)

These are a few of the problems on which we need further descriptive findings and further comparative analysis. Comparative studies may remind those of us who wear monographic spectacles to look up to the horizon from time to time and may remind those who strain at the horizon to put on the spectacles occasionally for closer observation.

It is to the more modest forms of comparative historical work that I refer, not to the abused "grand manner" of universal history. Yet even modest comparative studies will help put our problems in their broader settings of the history of man's relation to his work and his fellows, of the history of social organization and political striving, of the endless searches for justice, order, and freedom.

FOOTNOTES

1.   An earlier version of this paper was read at a session of the annual meeting of the American Historical Association, St. Louis, December 30, 1956. I thank the Inter-University Study of Labor Problems in Economic Development for making possible much of the research on which this paper is based.

2.   *Papers and Proceedings of the American Economic Association, 1951,* p. 558, a discussion of papers on economic growth in the United States. Economists, as M. M. Postan remarks, "have now moved into regions which historians have always regarded as their own. Yet, so far, the growing proximity has not done much to bring historical and theoretical study together." See his "Economic Growth" ("Essays in Bibliography and Criticism," XXIII), reviewing W. W. Rostow, *The Process of Economic Growth,* in *Economic History Review,* 2d ser., VI (1953), no. 1, 78-83.

3.   For recent discussion of some of the relevant considerations, chiefly by economists see Simon Kuznets, "Toward a Theory of Economic Growth," in Robert Lekachman, ed., *National Policy for Economic Welfare at Home and Abroad* (Garden City, 1955), pp. 12-103; Kuznets, Wilbert E. Moore, and Joseph J. Spengler, eds., *Economic Growth: Brazil, India, Japan* (Durham, N.C., 1955), which includes general essays; Universities-National Bureau Committee for Economic Research, *Capital Formation and Economic Growth* (Princeton, 1955); Norman S. Buchanan and Howard S. Ellis, *Approaches to Economic Development* (New York, 1955); S. Herbert Frankel, *The Economic Impact on Under-developed Societies* (Oxford, 1953); W. W. Rostow, *The Process of Economic Growth* (New York, 1952); Colin Clark, *The Conditions of Economic Progress* (2d ed., London, 1951); Bert F. Hoselitz, ed., *The Progress of Under-developed Areas* (Chicago, 1953); Léon H. Dupriez, ed., *Economic Progress,* Conference of International Economic Association (Louvain, 1955); and W. Arthur Lewis, *The Theory of Economic Growth* (London, 1955). Specifically discussing labor, see Wilbert E. Moore, *Industrialization and Labor* (Ithica, N.Y., 1951), with descriptive material from Mexico; Clark Kerr and Abraham Siegel, "The Structuring of the Labor Force in Industrial Society: New Dimensions and New Questions," *Industrial and Labor Relations Review,* VIII (Jan., 1955),

151-68; Clark Kerr, Frederick H. Harbison, John T. Dunlop, and Charles A. Myers, "The Labor Problem in Economic Development," *International Labour Review,* LXXI (March, 1955), 223-35; Reinhard Bendix, *Work and Authority in Industry, Ideologies of Management in the Course of Industrialization* (New York, 1956); and R. L. Aronson and J. P. Windmuller, eds., *Labor, Management and Economic Growth* (Ithica, N.Y., 1954).

4.   For a distinction between labor "pressure group" and "political" action, see Adolf Sturmthal, *The Tragedy of European Labor, 1918-1939* (New York, 1943).

5.   Thomas Carlyle, "Chartism," *Critical and Miscellaneous Essays,* in *Works* (30 vols., New York, 1900), XXIX, 119.

6.   *A History of the Peace: Being a History of England from 1816 to 1854* (4 vols., Boston, 1866), IV, 622.

7.   *British Economy of the Nineteenth Century* (Oxford, 1948), pp. 123-25. Cf. E. J. Hobsbawm, "Economic Fluctuations and Some Social Movements since 1800," *Economic History Review,* 2d ser., V, no. 1 (1952), 1-25.

8.   For criticism of an attempt at quantitative analysis of protest in earlier periods, see Crane Brinton, *The Anatomy of Revolution* (rev. ed., New York, 1952), p. 28.

9.   *A Proposal for Making an Effectual Provision for the Poor, 1753,* in *Works* (16 vols., New York, 1902), XIII, 141.

10.   Michel Chevalier, *De l'industrie manufacturière en France* (Paris, 1841), p. 37.

11.   *Le Sublime* (3d ed., Paris, 1887; first pub. in 1870), p. 27.

12.   Chateubriand, *Mémoires d'outre-tombe* (Brussels, 1849), IV, 210.

13.   F. A. Bruton, ed., *Three Accounts of Peterloo by Eyewitnesses* (Manchester, 1921); William Page, ed., *Commerce and Industry* (2 vols., London, 1919), II, 47.

14.   *Notes of a Tour in the Manufacturing Districts of Lancashire . . .* (London, 1842), p. 157.

15.   "Chartism," pp. 144-45.

16.   *Op cit.,* p. 38.

17.   Cf. D. W. Brogan (in a different connection): "It is one of history's favorite jokes to invert Marxian prophecy." Introduction to Alexander Werth, *The Twilight of France* (New York, 1942), p. vii.

18.   Nor, clearly, has the experience in the Soviet orbit borne out the Marxian prophecy any better, since revolution won in countries in early stages of industrial capitalism and had to be imposed from without on more advanced countries.

19.   For one excellent example of such writing, see Henri Truchy, "Essai sur le commerce extérieur de la France de 1881 à 1902," *Revue d'économie politique,* XVIII (1904), 543-87.

FOOTNOTES (continued)

20.   American protectionists groaned too, but they paid relatively high wages while groaning.

21.   Victor Griffuelhes, "L'Inferiorité des capitalistes français," Mouvement socialiste, no. 226, Dec., 1910, pp. 329-32.

22.   René-P. Duchemin, Organisation syndicale patronale en France (Paris, 1940), pp. 64, 68.

23.   Lack of space prevents discussion of the obviously related theme of the proletarianization of middle-class strata and the polarization of classes.

24.   Evolutionary Socialism: A Criticism and Affirmation, trans. by E. C. Harvey (London, 1909), esp. pp. 103-106, 206-207, 219. See also Peter Gay, The Dilemma of Democratic Socialism: Eduard Bernstein's Challenge to Marx (New York, 1952).

25.   The Lion and the Unicorn (London, 1941), pp. 53-54.

26.   Michel Collinet, Essai sur la condition ouvrière, 1900-1950 (Paris, 1951); Hans Speier, Social Order and the Risks of War (New York, 1952), a collection of earlier essays, esp. pp. 19-26, 53-67; Reinhard Bendix and S. M. Lipset, eds., Class, Status and Power: A Reader in Social Stratification (Glencoe, Ill., 1953); G. D. H. Cole, Studies in Class Structure (London, 1955); Raymond Aron, "Social Structure and the Ruling Class," British Journal of Sociology, I, nos. 1-2, 1-16, 126-43; Georges Friedmann, ed., Villes et Campagnes: Deuxième Semaine Sociologique . . . (Paris, 1953); Michel Crozier, "Les Tertiaires et le Socialisme," Esprit, XXIV, no. 238, 706-15; E. F. M. Durbin, The Politics of Democratic Socialism (London, 1940), Pt. II, sec. 4.

27.   The term is Punch's, quoted by G. D. H. Cole, The World of Labour (4th ed., London, 1920), p. 3. In Italy syndicalism was important but not the dominant current.

28.   The year 1956 reminded us again, in hope and tragedy, of the "general spirit" of peoples. Upsurge against Soviet rule came, where if anywhere among the satellites one might have expected it, from the "brave" and "romantic" Poles and Hungarians.

29.   Walter Galenson, Labor in Norway (Cambridge, Mass., 1949) and "Scandinavia," in Galenson, ed., Comparative Labor Movements (New York, 1952).

30.   H. A. L. Fisher, "Memoir," in The Collected Papers of Paul Vinogradoff (2 vols., Oxford, 1928), I, 19.

31.   See for example Clark Kerr and Abraham Siegel, "The Interindustry Propensity to Strike," in A. Kornhauser, et al., eds., Industrial Conflict (New York, 1954), pp. 189-212; K. G. J. C. Knowles, Strikes (Oxford, 1952).

32.   On the need for regional and local studies, see Carl E. Schorske, German Social Democracy, 1905-1917 (Cambridge, Mass., 1955), pp. 341-42; Georges

Duveau, "Comment étudier la vie ouvrière," in *Revue d'histoire économique et sociale,* XXVI, no. 1 (1940-1947), 11-21; J. -D. Réynaud and Alain Touraine, "Les ouvriers," in Maurice Duverger, ed., *Partis politiques et classes sociales en France* (Paris, 1955), pp. 34-35, 41-42; Gabriel Le Bras, *Études de Sociologie religieuse* (2 vols., Paris, 1956), esp. II, 546-57.

33.   "The Background of the Parliamentary Reform Movement in Three English Cities, 1830-2," *Cambridge Historical Journal,* X (1952), 293-317 and "Social Structure and Politics in Birmingham and Lyons (1825-1848)," *British Journal of Sociology,* I, no. 1 (1950), 67-80.

34.   Gerald Brenan, *The Spanish Labyrinth: An Account of the Social and Political Background of the Civil War* (Cambridge, Eng., 1944).

35.   Cf. the report of the Social Science Research Council Seminar on Research in Comparative Politics, *American Political Science Review,* XLVII (Sept., 1953), 641-75; Roy Macridis, *The Study of Comparative Government* (Garden City, 1955). On comparative labor history, see Selig Perlman, *A Theory of the Labor Movement* (New York, 1928); Adolf Sturmthal, *Unity and Diversity in European Labor* (Glencoe, Ill., 1953); Walter Galenson, ed., *Comparative Labor Movements* (New York, 1952), pp. ix-xiv; Lewis L. Lorwin, *Labor and Internationalism* (New York, 1929), esp. chap. XXIV. In "Recent Research on Western European Labor Movements," *Proceedings of the Seventh Annual Meeting of the Industrial Relations Research Association* (Madison, 1955), pp. 69-80, I have summarized a few of the main lines of labor history in publications since 1946.

36.   *La Vie ouvrière en France sous le Second Empire* (Paris, 1946) and *La Pensée ouvrière sur l'éducation pendant la Seconde République et le Second Empire* (Paris, 1948).

JOHN H. GOLDTHORPE
DAVID LOCKWOOD
FRANK BECHHOFER
JENNIFER PLATT

The Politics of Affluence: A Study of British Workers

In this chapter our main concern will be with the thesis that working-class affluence leads, via a process of *embourgoisement,* to an erosion of Labour political loyalties. The circumstances which first lent force to this thesis are part of the familiar history of the 1950s and we need to refer to them here only briefly. Economically, these years were characterised by a relatively rapid rise in living standards and, most significantly perhaps, by a marked increase in the number of families achieving 'middle range' incomes.[1] This resulted in a considerable overlap, in terms of income, between those in manual and nonmanual occupations. Furthermore, important changes also occurred in the pattern of working-class consumption. Manual workers considerably increased their ownership of most kinds of durable consumer goods and for many items—such as TV sets, record players, washing machines and refrigerators—wide differences in the spread of ownership ceased to exist between the more prosperous manual and the lower white-collar strata. A sharp

Reprinted from John H. Goldthorpe, et al., *The Affluent Worker: Political Attitudes and Behavior* (Copyright © 1968 by the Cambridge University Press), pp. 33-35, 38-48, by permission of Cambridge University Press.

increase also occurred in the number of manual workers owning, or buying, their own homes and in the number possessing motor vehicles.

Politically, these years of growing prosperity were, of course, ones of undisputed Conservative dominance. In 1951 the Conservatives were returned to power with a majority of 26 over Labour; in 1955 they increased this figure to 67, and in 1959 raised it still higher to 107. These three successive victories, with rising majorities, were unparalleled in British electoral history. At the same time, the Labour vote showed signs of secular decline, falling from 49% of the total poll in 1951 to 46% in 1955 and to 44% in 1959. Moreover, there were indications that in those areas of the country which were economically the most progressive, this fall in the Labour vote was due to some significant extent to loss of support from among the industrial working class, either through defections or through new voters failing to follow in the traditional pattern.

In these circumstances, then, it can scarcely be regarded as surprising that the thesis of the progressive *embourgeoisement* of the British working class should have proved an attractive one. The argument that British society was becoming increasingly middle class provided a convenient means of linking together the outstanding economic and political developments of the period. It was, in fact, an argument accepted by spokesmen of both the right and left, by numerous journalists and social commentators, and by not a few political scientists and sociologists.[2] However, the existence of this general consensus of opinion did not alter the fact—though it may have served to obscure it—that the thesis of 'the worker turning middle class' lacked any satisfactory validation. It remained merely an assumption, or at best an inference, which it seemed reasonable to make in interpreting the socio-political situation in Britain at the end of the 1950s. Although the circumstantial evidence might be persuasive, very little direct evidence—and that of a relatively unsophisticated kind—could be presented to support the specific proposition that it was affluence *per se* that was chiefly responsible for the decline in the working-class Labour vote.

Perhaps the clearest statement of the 'affluence thesis' that has been made was that put forward by Butler and Rose in their study of the General Election of 1959. They begin with the observation that 'a significant number of skilled workers may be called class hybrids—working class in terms of occupation, education, speech and cultural norms, while being middle class in terms of income and material comforts'. They then go on to claim that those who are in this way 'on the threshold of the middle class are in some ways divided by conflict between their past and present, between their family and occupational traditions and their aspirations. They are thus exposed to conflicting political pressures. Voters subjected to such cross-pressures are particularly likely to abstain or to switch their voting allegiances.' According to this argument, then, a 'middle-class' standard of living produces a sense of social marginality; and this social marginality in turn leads to a lower Labour vote, either by way of abstention, or by way of a higher Conservative or Liberal vote. It is only fair to add that while Butler and Rose lay greatest stress on the workers' acquisition of a 'middle-class' standard of living, they also suggest that the effect of affluence will be more pronounced among those workers who have moved outside the sphere of influence of traditional working-class communities into new neighbourhoods, and who have developed new styles of consumption associated with a 'home-centred' existence.

It may be noted that this account of the political consequences of *embourgeoisement* is rather more advanced than that which is involved in the familiar idea of the working-class 'prosperity voter'. The latter concept implies that erstwhile Labour supporters among the affluent working class are likely to become Conservative voters or to abstain from voting Labour as a direct result of their experience of rising standards of living under a Conservative Government. Thus the intermediate stage of social marginality that is postulated by Butler and Rose does not enter into this particular version of the affluence thesis. From the point of view of our study, however, the difference between the 'prosperity' and the 'social marginality' arguments is not especially significant. For the workers we studied were not only affluent but they tended to lead the relatively 'home-centred' lives that Butler and Rose regard as being conducive to a sense of social marginality. . . .

If the affluence thesis is correct, then it ought to follow that these manual workers should be clearly less left-wing in their political sympathies than are manual workers in the country at large. However, as we have already seen [in an earlier chapter—eds.], this conclusion is not supported by our data. Despite the fact that the men in our sample undoubtedly earn higher wages, are more often house-owners, and have more durable consumer goods than the majority of manual workers, they also register a notably high and solid Labour vote.

This general conclusion is, of course, open to the possible objection that the sample of manual workers we chose was not 'sufficiently affluent' to test the affluence thesis properly. To this, we would reply, first, that in terms of the thesis itself our workers should clearly qualify as a critical sample since they can be shown to be enjoying at least a 'lower middle-class standard of living'; and secondly, that, if by this measure their standard of living is not regarded as 'middle class' enough, the burden of proof lies with the affluence theorists, who must specify the exact level of affluence that is needed to produce the results that they postulate. It is also worth making the obvious point that the difference in support for Labour between our manual and white-collar samples cannot be readily interpreted in terms of their relative economic conditions. It might conceivably be argued, of course, that the role of affluence is not something that operates 'across the board' but is only important among manual workers. However, here again, it could be said that the exponents of the affluence thesis have never in fact specified this limitation; and in terms of the underlying logic of the thesis it is not clear why it should exist.

The fact that the workers in our sample exhibit overall a relatively high Labour vote may, then, be regarded as at all events highly inconsistent with any unqualified affluence thesis. However, within the sample it is of course possible to distinguish between men who are, so to speak, more or less affluent than others. By dividing up our sample in terms of such factors as income and house-ownership we can therefore test the affluence thesis further; and we can in this way partly take into account the possible objection that the men who fell into our sample were 'not affluent enough' to constitute a proper test of this thesis.

As can be seen from Table 1, differences in family income have almost no effect on Labour voting, but differences in husband's earnings produce a slightly lower intended Labour vote among the higher income group.[3] While the latter

Table 1

Voting intention by income

	Voting intention						
	Lab.	Cons.	Lib.	Uncertain (incline to Lib. or abstain)	Abstain	Total	N[a]
	Percentage						
Husband's earnings							
Less than £18	79	12	5	0	3	99	96
£18 or more	74	14	8	2	3	101	110
Family income							
Less than £21	77	10	6	2	5	100	103
£21 or more	75	16	8	0	1	100	103

[a]N = 206.

finding could be constructed as evidence in favour of the affluence thesis, the effect is not very marked; and from the point of view of this thesis it is in any case not entirely obvious why it should be the husband's rather than the family income which affects Labour voting. And, even if we isolate a particularly affluent group—men earning more than £21 a week—Table 2 shows that still no very marked decrease in Labour voting is produced.

Table 2

Voting intention by husband's earnings

	Voting intention						
	Lab.	Cons.	Lib.	Uncertain (incline to Lib. or abstain)	Abstain	Total	N^a
	Percentage						
Husband's earnings							
Less than £18	79	12	5	0	3	99	96
£18 or more but less than £21	74	11	7	3	4	99	70
£21 or more	73	17	10	0	0	100	40

[a]N = 206. See note [a], Table 1.

The association between house-ownership and vote is presented in Table 3. Here it is at once apparent that the affluence thesis is supported by the fact that house-owners are less prone to vote Labour than are men living in council houses and other rented accommodation. Nevertheless, the differences in intended Labour voting are again not great, being in fact of much the same order as those associated with differences in husband's earnings.

However, if we combine income and house-ownership as in Table 4 it can be seen that the differences in voting intention between the most and least 'affluent' of our workers becomes rather more pronounced. The house-owners earning more than £18 a week have an intended Labour vote of

Table 3

Voting intention by house-ownership

	Voting intention						
	Lab.	Cons.	Lib.	Uncertain (incline to Lib. or abstain)	Abstain	Total	N^a
	Percentage						
House-owner	74	13	9	1	3	100	119
Other	80	13	3	1	3	100	88

[a]N = 207.

Table 4

Voting intention by husband's earnings and by house-ownership

	Lab.	Cons.	Lib.	Uncertain (incline to Lib. or abstain)	Abstain	Total	N[a]
	Voting intention						
	Percentage						
Husband's earnings:							
£18 or more							
House-owner	73	14	9	1	3	100	74
Other	75	14	6	3	3	101	36
Less than £18							
House-owner	76	13	9	0	2	100	45
Other	82	12	2	0	4	100	51

[a]N = 206. See note [a], Table 1.

73%, while for men earning less than this amount, and not owning their own houses, the figure rises to 82%.

These findings are certainly consistent with the affluence thesis. However, it is the specific claim of this thesis that it is the loyalty of the Labour supporter that is strained by the fact of his prosperity. Therefore, it is of some interest to see whether the relationship between affluence and intended voting just noted also holds among those men in our sample who voted for Labour in the election of 1959. In Table 5 we make this comparison between the voting intentions of 1959 Labour voters of greater and lesser affluence, as measured by husband's earnings and house-ownership. From this table, it is clear that there is no systematic relationship between level of affluence and stability of Labour voting. Thus, the most affluent group propose to give 93% of their votes to the Labour Party, while for the least affluent group the figure is 95%. Since there can be no question that the former group of workers have attained, if not surpassed, the level of income and material comfort enjoyed by a great many employees in the white-collar middle class, the fact that these affluent workers show no particular tendency to abandon their support of Labour is inconsistent with what the affluence thesis would predict.[4]

Yet another possible way of testing the argument that prosperity is a force weakening working-class support for Labour is to compare the voting behaviour of men who have always lived in Luton with that of men who have been attracted to Luton from other parts of the country. We have good reason to

Table 5

Voting intentions of Labour voters of 1959 by husband's earnings and by house-ownership

Labour voters of 1959	Lab.	Cons.	Lib.	Uncertain (incline to Lib. or abstain)	Abstain	Total	N[a]
			Percentage				
Husband's earnings:							
Less than £18							
House-owner	88	3	6	0	3	100	33
Other	95	2	2	0	0	99	40
£18 or more							
House-owner	93	2	4	0	0	99	45
Other	100	0	0	0	0	100	24

[a]N = 142. There were five respondents who were unsure about their voting intention.

believe that those men in our sample who migrated to Luton did so in the majority of cases because of the lure of higher wages and better housing. Therefore, if the migrants have comparable incomes and possessions to the 'native' Lutonians, the former group might be expected in the main to have experienced a greater relative improvement in their standard of living than the latter group. And since in the last resort the undermining of Labour loyalties that is postulated by the affluence thesis must result from the worker's own perception of his improved standard of living, the migrants should have a lower propensity to vote Labour than the 'native' Lutonians.

In Table 6 we compare the voting intentions of these two groups, holding constant level of affluence as measured by husband's earnings and house-ownership. We see that in every case except that of the least affluent workers the migrants intended to give a higher proportion of their votes to the Labour Party than did the men who had always lived in Luton. Thus, for example, 75% of the most affluent migrants intended to vote for the Labour Party as opposed to 68% of the comparable group of native Lutonians. Moreover, differences in level of affluence would appear to have less effect upon voting among the migrant workers, even though from the point of view of the argument under consideration one might expect just the opposite. Yet while there is a difference of only five percentage points between the proportions voting Labour in the most and the least affluent groups of migrants the corresponding figure for the comparable Lutonian groups is fourteen percentage points.

Table 6

Voting intention by husband's area of upbringing, by husband's earnings and by house-ownership

Husband's area of upbringing	Husband's earnings	House-owner	Lab.	Cons.	Lib.	Uncertain (incline to Lib. or abstain)	Abstain	Total	N[a]
					Percentage				
Lutonians	£18 or more	Yes	68	16	10	0	5	99	19
		No	67	33	0	0	0	100	9
	Less than £18	Yes	68	16	10	0	5	99	19
		No	82	12	6	0	0	100	17
Migrants	£18 or more	Yes	75	13	9	2	2	101	55
		No	78	7	7	4	4	100	27
	Less than £18	Yes	80	12	8	0	0	100	25
		No	81	12	0	0	6	99	32

[a]N = 203. See note [a], Table 1. No information on area of upbringing was available for four respondents; and one of these respondents was also still ineligible to vote.

Any conclusion that we may draw from these data is bound to be highly tentative. But we can at least say that those workers in our sample who have been attracted to Luton by the prospect of a higher standard of living, and who have actually succeeded in finding it, are not less likely to support the Labour Party than the workers who have not had to move house and home in search of prosperity. The fact that a higher proportion of migrants than Lutonians intended to vote for the Labour Party does not, of course, demonstrate that the proportion of Labour supporters among the migrant group—and especially among the most affluent migrants—has not declined by comparison with what it was before they moved to Luton. On this point, our data can provide no conclusive answer. But in the voting histories of the most affluent migrant workers there is no indication of any marked swing away from voting Labour to voting Conservative, Liberal or abstaining. On the contrary, the proportion voting for the Labour Party seems to have been remarkably stable.[5] Migration, whatever its effects on other aspects of our workers' lives, does not seem to have had any noticeable consequences for their political allegiances; even among the men who have crossed the threshold of a 'lower middle-class' standard of living.

A final test of the affluence thesis can be attempted by examining the relationship between voting and our workers' own estimates of the changes in their living standards. We asked our respondents: 'Would you say that over the past ten years your standard of living has gone up, or down, or stayed about the same?' This question was followed by another which asked: 'Well, comparing yourself with other people, would you say that you have done better than they have, worse, or about the same?' In this way, we obtained measures of our workers' perceptions of their 'prosperity' relative to both their own previous positions and those of others.[6] The response to these questions provides us with data that are highly relevant to the argument being considered because, unless the worker feels that he is affluent, especially by comparison with other manual workers, he is unlikely to start thinking of himself as potentially 'middle class' in the way that is assumed by the affluence thesis.

In answer to the first question 78% of the sample thought that their standard of living had gone up; 19% thought that it was more or less the same; and 3% believed that they were now worse off than they had been ten years ago. On the whole, then, our workers' subjective estimates of changes in their standards of living are in line with what on the basis of their objective position as earners and consumers we should expect them to be.

When comparing their own living standards with those of 'other people' they were, however, less optimistic: 35% thought that they had done better than others as against 61% who judged that they had done equally well. On the other hand, though, only 2% considered that they had done worse, while a further 2% were unable to make the comparison.

As a result of correlating our respondents' replies to these two questions we find that the large majority of the sample (87%) fall into three main groups: (i) those who thought that their standard of living had risen and who also thought that they had done better than others; (ii) those who thought that their standard of living had risen but not appreciably more than that of other people; and (iii) those who thought that they were more or less in the same position as before and had done neither better nor worse than other people. The first group—the self-rated 'achievers'—were a sizable minority, and indeed by objective measures of house-ownership and husband's earnings they were in fact relatively more affluent than the other two groups. If the affluence thesis is correct, it is this particular group of workers in our sample that should be least committed to the Labour Party. As may be seen from Table 7, they do actually have the lowest intended Labour vote. But it should be noted that this is only fractionally less than the proportion of votes intended for the Labour Party in the second group, and not very much lower than the Labour vote of the third group, that is, of the men who were not very impressed by what they had gained as consumers. Although these findings are in line with the affluence thesis, they can hardly be regarded as constituting a very powerful confirmation of it. Moreover, when we take into account *both* objective measures and subjective estimates of standard of living a very different result

Table 7

Voting intention by evaluation of change in standard of living

Standard of living		Voting intention						
Change over last ten years	Compared with 'other' people	Lab.	Cons.	Lib.	Uncertain (incline to Lib. or abstain)	Abstain	Total	N
		Percentage						
Up	Better	74	11	7	2	7	101	61
Up	Same	76	14	8	1	1	100	93
Same	Same	80	12	8	0	0	100	25

is obtained. If we single out those of our respondents who not only felt themselves to be comparatively well off but who were also among the most affluent in that they owned their own houses and earned £18 or more a week, we then find that 81% of this group intended to vote for the Labour Party at the next General Election.[7] This particular piece of evidence cannot of course be regarded as a conclusive refutation of the affluence thesis, but it is nevertheless a striking fact that the workers who were most affluent *and* relatively most satisfied with the improvement in their standard of living over the last ten years were also considerably more pro-Labour than the sample as a whole.

As we have said at the beginning of this chapter, our study does not allow us to make as thorough an investigation of the effects of affluence on voting as would be desirable to test the affluence thesis decisively. We have noted that this thesis itself is in some respects imprecise, and would need clarification and refinement in order to be tested in any definitive way. However, since we ourselves do not embrace it, we shall leave this task to those who do. We have seen that, as a result of the various analyses we have made, some—albeit slight—evidence can be produced that is consistent with the thesis as we have interpreted it. In the case of the workers we studied, there is some relationship between particularly high earnings and house-ownership, on the one hand, and the likelihood of not voting Labour on the other. By far the strongest differentiation in Labour voting was produced by a measure of affluence that combined husband's earnings and house-ownership. At the same time, though, differences in family income, geographical mobility, and subjective estimates of changes in standard of living appear to have no very great effect so far as party allegiance is concerned.

Moreover, in this respect we must not lose sight of the basic fact that even the most affluent group within our sample—men earning £18 or more a week take-home pay and owning their own houses—still registers a high Labour vote relative to manual workers in the country at large. If we consider the votes which this most affluent group had prospectively committed to the three main parties in 1963-4, we find that no fewer than 75% were intending to support the Labour Party. This then brings us back to the main finding with which we started: namely that our sample as a whole, while clearly affluent by comparison with lower white-collar and other manual workers, is strong and stable in its allegiance to Labour, as indicated both by voting history and by voting intention at the time of our interviews. So far as politics is concerned, this is the most important conclusion of our study and it provides no backing at all for those who claim that affluence is incompatible with a continuing high level of support for Labour among the industrial labour force.

Finally, before leaving our discussion of the affluence thesis, we would like to draw attention to what we believe to be its shortcomings from a theoretical point of view. The major flaw in the thesis, in our view, lies in the assumption that a certain level of income and possessions (itself never clearly specified) leads to a feeling of social marginality among manual workers. But why, one may ask, should this be so? Neither actual membership nor an aspiration to membership in social, as opposed to statistical, groups is an automatic consequence of having a certain level of income and possessions. Therefore, since individuals do not develop orientations or attachments to abstract statistical collectivities, such as the 'middle income bracket', it is difficult to see in what sense an affluent worker is cross-pressured between his 'middle-class standard of living' and his role as a manual wage-earner. To be sure, the latter role does involve him in social relationships which lead to characteristic experiences and attitudes which differ from those, say, of men who are salaried nonmanual employees. In this sense, being a manual worker does orient the individual towards actual collectivities which from his point of view may be either 'membership' groups or 'reference' groups or both. But a certain standard of living, measured simply by income and possessions, does not likewise result in any direct way either in participation in different membership groups or in the adoption of reference groups other than those which derive from his role as a manual wage-earner. Being affluent does not mean that the worker becomes a member of middle-class society or even aspires to such membership. To take one obvious example: no amount of relative affluence in the past appears to have led to any diminution of class solidarity in communities of mine-workers, even though class feeling may have become weaker in these communities of late as a result of changes which are the concomitants of growing prosperity. In brief, then, the confusion in the affluence thesis stems basically from the ambiguous phrase 'middle-class standard of living', which merely begs the question of whether such a standard of living makes a family middle class in any social, as opposed to a statistical, sense. The auxiliary hypothesis that affluence is only a necessary, but not a sufficient, condition for the development of middle-class aspirations and the worker's assimilation into middle-class society, is, of course, more plausible. But this qualified affluence thesis is even more vague than the original one because it lacks specification of the other factors involved in such a process of *embourgeoisement,* and it still makes the questionable assumption that, given these other factors, affluence remains a highly relevant consideration.

Our own view is that the role of affluence in working-class politics, even as a necessary condition of non-Labour voting, has still to be proven. A worker's prosperity, or lack of it, is only one element entering into the formation of his class and political awareness; and, when compared with the experiences and influences to which he is daily exposed at his place of work, in his local community, and within his own family circle, the effect of such purely material factors as level of income and possessions may well be a relatively minor one. The weakness of the affluence thesis is that it fails to take account of the worker's social relationships, and particularly of the way in which they affect the *meaning* which the individual worker places on the fact of his prosperity or privation. Indeed, the role of these social factors may be so strong as to override considerations of affluence altogether. For, even though it may be possible to find some degree of association between affluence and voting, it may still be the case that, if one controls for other, more theoretically relevant factors, this association no longer exists.

FOOTNOTES

1.   See John H. Goldthorpe and David Lockwood, 'Not So Bourgeois After All', *New Society,* vol. 1, no. 3 (1962).
2.   See the references given in Goldthorpe and Lockwood, 'Affluence and the British Class Structure' and in W. G. Runciman '*Embourgeoisement,* Self-rated Class and Party Preference,' *Sociological Review,* vol. 12, no. 2 (July 1964), p. 158 n. 8.
3.   Since our data on income and house-ownership refer to our respondents' economic situation at the time of the study, the following tables relate differences in level of affluence to our respondents' voting intentions. However, it may be said that cross-tabulations substituting voting in the General Election of 1959 for voting intention produced very similar results. This reflects the fact of the high degree of stability in the voting behaviour of our sample. It should also be noted that in all subsequent tables relating to voting intention, the 16 men in the sample whose voting intention was 'don't know' have been excluded, so that unless otherwise indicated the total size of the sample is reduced from 223 to 207. In fact, the inclusion or the exclusion of the 'don't knows' does not materially affect any of the conclusions that are

reached. Following the argument of Butler and Rose, however, we have included abstaining as a possible form of 'non-Labour voting'.

4.   It appears also inconsistent with the finding of table 4 that a relationship is to be found between level of affluence and level of Labour voting. But as we shall see in the following chapter, this relationship is in fact largely capable of being 'explained away' by the introduction of a third variable: namely, the extensiveness of a worker's 'white-collar affiliations'. When the latter is controlled for, the relationship between level of affluence and level of Labour voting almost disappears.

5.   We recorded all changes in voting, including changes from voting for a particular party to abstaining and *vice versa,* for all our respondents from the General Election of 1945 to the election of 1959 inclusive. Among the most affluent migrant workers there were 16 such changes in voting: two of these involved a change from voting Labour to voting Conservative (1) or Liberal (1); and three involved a change from voting Conservative to voting Labour (2) or abstaining (1). It may also be noted that at the General Election of 1955—some eight years prior to the time of our research—71% of those eligible to vote among the most affluent immigrants gave their vote to Labour as opposed to voting Conservative, Liberal or abstaining. From table 6 above it will be seen that the corresponding figure for voting intention is 75%.

6.   These two questions were designed to lead on to a third: 'Who is it that you're thinking of when you say that you've done (better) (worse) (the same)?' This last question was aimed at discovering the actual reference groups of our respondents in their role as consumers. The results of this analysis will be reported elsewhere. Here it may simply be noted that their reference groups were overwhelmingly people in the same class as themselves—neighbours, workmates, friends, and relatives.

7.   The number of respondents falling into this category was twenty-six; the rest of their intended votes were distributed as follows: Conservative Party, 8%; Liberal Party, 8%; abstain, 4%.

9 RENATE MAYNTZ

Germany: Radicals and Reformers

W est Germany seems an unlikely place for the growth of a protest movement. There is no notably oppressive political regime; there is nothing like a Vietnam War; and there are no major socio-economic problems such as large-scale poverty, disadvantaged racial or ethnic minorities, etc. If, therefore, the protesting students define Germany as ripe for a revolution, they can only point to less tangible issues. There is, for example, the "immobilism" of the Bonn Government, especially in matters of foreign policy. Anticommunism has lost its appeal, the failure to recognize the East German regime has been judged to be unrealistic, and the continuing dependence on the United States, a power which has lost its moral claim to leadership through the war in Vietnam, has been increasingly resented. The exceedingly slow progress of certain reforms—such as the revision of the penal code or educational reforms—has added to the feeling that inertia is the dominant force. When the CDU [Christian Democratic Union] and SPD [Social Democratic Party] joined in the Great Coalition, the possibility of successful opposition within the existing parliamentary system seemed to be further reduced. The dice appeared to be loaded and the rules of the game favored the established authorities. From this a minority

Reprinted from *The Public Interest*, No. 13 (Fall, 1968), pp. 160-168, 170-172, by permission of the author and National Affairs, Inc., © 1968.

drew the radical conclusion that the whole system had to be overthrown. Among the advocates of what has come to be called the "extra-parliamentary opposition," students are numerically the strongest.

The extra-parliamentary opposition's main problem is that what *they* perceive as an unbearable situation seems sufficiently satisfying to the large majority of the population. Hence one of their main tasks is seen to be the "enlightening" of the masses and changing their "false consciousness." Some of the protest actions are deliberately intended to serve this purpose. If the police, for instance, are provoked to use their power brutally, their popular image will change; if authority can be made to act repressively or to look ridiculous, respect for it will wane. With *such* an end in view, many of the protest actions are indeed shrewdly chosen and are not the infantile expressions of self-indulgent activism which some critics have judged them to be. They are efforts at establishing a self-confirming hypothesis.

The protest actions have had some positive effect. The established authorities have reacted—after the first shock of challenge wore off—with a greater sensitivity to the need for legitimation. Shortcomings and the necessity of reforms are more readily admitted today. There are changes in the style of public speech: fewer empty phrases are uttered, or are uttered with less unthinking assurance. Some of the ceremonious pomposity has disappeared from public life. The mass media take the young and their claims more seriously than before. This is not much, perhaps; still, there is the feeling of a small, fresh breeze.

But if so, it is too small to satisfy the impatient, and it has been dearly bought. The protest actions have provoked a considerable amount of public resentment against the radical students. The unsympathetic reporting by some newspapers helped foster such hostility, but it would be a gross exaggeration to say they produced it. The plain fact is that the working class, for example, was all along quite hostile to the students. With the exception of some small groups of young laborers, the workers and the unions utterly failed to respond to the students' battle cries. The events in France, early this summer, raised new hopes among the students that solidarity with the working class might yet be achieved, and the imminent passing of the Emergency Laws (since enacted), which some union leaders continued to oppose vociferously, seemed to provide a favorable opportunity. It is estimated that the "extra-parliamentary opposition" was able to mobilize about 150,000 demonstrators in the course of their protest against the new legislation, but no public uprising took place, and the controversial laws were passed. When the striking workers in France settled for mere "material advantages," and de Gaulle returned to power with a large majority, the young German rebels saw their hopes of fomenting a revolution dashed. For the time being, they are redirecting their efforts to university reform, where they are likely to meet with at least partial success.

PROBLEMS IN THE UNIVERSITIES

The situation in the universities is thought by many to have produced the present movement. The problems are indeed real, but I would suggest that they only created a readiness, and provided a first target, for the protest.

Compared to some other highly industrialized nations, the German Federal Republic has been relatively late in making concerted efforts to adapt its educational system to the requirements of a scientific civilization and to modern democracy. The universities fall short of efficiently fulfilling their training and innovative functions; their traditional structure prevents more widespread participation in academic affairs, even where this would be pragmatically justified; and they fail to play a focal democratic role in educating for responsible political participation, providing equal opportunities to the capable irrespective of their social origin, and serving a political control function by offering independent guidance and criticism.

These different needs were recognized by those who, early in the history of the Federal Republic, tried to make reform proposals. They held it necessary to redefine the relationship between the university and the state, and in particular to strengthen academic autonomy in order to make the universities politically less dependent and subservient than they had proved to be during the Nazi regime. The right of the universities to self-government, and the academic freedom of teaching and research, were reaffirmed and secured by law; but the early efforts at internal structural reforms remained largely ineffective. The professorial "chair" still is at the pinnacle of university organization, and administration is highly centralized.

Externally, the federal government had left control in the field of education to the *Länder* or state governments, which—acting singly or through the joint Conference of the Ministers of Culture—felt it impossible to impose reforms upon the universities after having just affirmed their autonomy. Within the universities, on the other hand, no spontaneous reform movement developed. The Conference of University Rectors was institutionally ill-adapted to the task of planning comprehensive reforms. The professional association of university teachers functions mainly to defend the privileges of its members. The student organization VDS (*Ferein Deutscher Studentenschaften*) did develop some reform plans, but at that time its voice carried little weight.

This left the field of planning university reforms open to the initiative of the *Wissenschaftsrat*, a council founded in 1957 by the federal government together with the *Länder*, for this purpose. Though only an advisory body its recommendations have been largely followed as if they were binding law. The first recommendations, published in 1960, were designed to expand facilities for teaching and research. The *Wissenschaftsrat* aimed to provide teaching facilities for 200,000 university students, to increase the number of full professors by one-third, to triple the numbers of positions intermediate between professors and assistants, and to double the number of assistants. These goals were realized within three years, but it soon became obvious that they had not been ambitious enough.

For one thing, the number of students increased much faster than expected. The target figure of 200,000 was surpassed several years ago; a projection by the Conference of the Ministers of Culture concludes that by 1980 there may well be 500,000 university students in the Federal Republic and West Berlin.

The second shortcoming of the *Wissenschaftsrat's* recommendations was its concentration on quantitative matters. The *Wissenschaftsrat* was well aware of the structural weaknesses of the established universities. In 1962, for instance, it criticized in no uncertain terms the inadequacy of the traditional forms of university administration, the parochialism of the faculties, the oligarchy of the full professors, and the autocracy of the directors of institutes. But the *Wissenschaftsrat* was also conscious of the resistance it would meet if its first recommendations aimed to upset the traditional structure. Ironically, the quantitative expansion sharpened the structural problems and increased the potential for conflict. The power of the full professors, for instance, was significantly enhanced as they received more assistants and more research funds under their control; and consequently they became an even more visible target for student protests. Similarly, the numerical expansion of the ranks below the full professor has created a strong "third party" who, feeling themselves relatively deprived, have sided with the students in their claims for radical reforms.

In 1966, the *Wissenschaftsrat* published some new recommendations but sidestepped plans for a comprehensive structural reform. Though these recommendations for student participation were similar to plans previously advocated by the student organization, they were now met with harsh criticism, especially where the mobilization of student unrest had started to develop into a sustained protest movement. None of the recommended measures would provide the students with more influence in determining course content, curriculum, personnel policy, or give them a greater chance to participate in and co-determine current research. These are some of the criticisms which had been made, but clearly the student protest movement is no longer interested simply in a better education. More now is at stake.

THE POST-WAR GENERATION

Since the situation at the universities did not suddenly deteriorate in the middle of the 1960's there must be other reasons that account for the sudden mobilization of dissatisfaction. The motivational structure of the radical students seems characterized by a curious lack of realizable, concrete, and self-oriented life goals, combined with a pronounced need for engagement and activity in favor of a cause. At the root of it all seems to be a generational factor. The radical students of today belong to the generation born after the war. Raised predominantly in middle and upper-middle class homes by parents who were more permissive than previous generations of Germans, growing up in a peaceful and relatively affluent society, nothing in their early experience taught them to appreciate or comprehend the skepticism which characterized the first generation—born, say, in 1935—of post-war youth in Germany. They did not experience in their childhood the presence of misery, fear, brute power, and violence, nor the fierceness of the struggle for survival under such conditions. They take the satisfaction of their basic needs so much for granted that they can show disdain for their parents' avid striving for economic security and material well-being. Nor do they regard the present condition of order, legality, and more personal freedom than their parents ever experienced anything to be particularly grateful about. They are optimists and idealists, and lack any sense of the precariousness of social order and the vulnerability of social institutions; they are, on the contrary, impressed with their seemingly unshakeable solidity. This may account for their belief that nothing short of a revolution can move the established institutions, while their elders fear that only a small push can bring them toppling down—a feeling which motivated their hysterical reactions to the threat posed by a few thousand demonstrating youths.

The first, true post-war generation was willing to be mobilized, but it still needed something to spark the movement, and it needed additional sustaining forces to keep it going. But before coming to this, it ought to be recalled that only part of the present student generation has in fact become actively engaged in the movement. A larger group participates only occasionally, and there are also those who remain passive and are even hostile to their radical classmates, even if their opposition is neither organized nor vocal. Those for whom going to the university is a means for upward social mobility, especially the small percentage of workers' children, are less inclined to engage in the radical movement. Of equal importance is the differentiation in field of study. The unrest is most pronounced among students of the social sciences and at the faculties of philosophy (which also include languages and history), while by and large the natural sciences, engineering, and faculties of law and medicine have remained relatively quiet. More or less the same differentiating factors appear to be at work in the student movements of other countries, too.

THE "CRITICAL THEORY"

To come back to the question of what may have provided the spark, it is very likely that the example of the Berkeley rebellion, of the developing student movement in the United States, and possibly also the Dutch "provos" have all been important stimuli. The mass media provide for an instant contagion, bringing together in one "global village" Le Bon's "crowd." To this day, the German students use such American terms as "sit-in," "teach-in," etc. It may also be revealing that the first occupations of university offices at the Free University happened after this had occurred on a large scale at Columbia.

The sustaining factors, on the other hand, those which made the spark catch on, are more or less peculiar to the German situation. For one thing, there was a theory ready to be used by the students to articulate their criticism—the "critical theory" taught by the so-called "Frankfurt school of sociology"—and there was a hard organizational core around which the movement could crystallize: the socialist students' federation, SDS. The SDS, expelled in 1961 from the Social Democratic Party because of its opposition to moderate reformism, had been a small and marginal group among the student organizations, a circle of convinced neo-Marxists, adherents of the "critical theory" of T. W. Adorno, Max Horkheimer, and Jürgen Habermas. These students could be identified by the special terminology they used and appeared rather esoteric to most outsiders. For many years, only a few would listen to them, but this changed with the restlessness among the students, during the Vietnam War, and with the growing sense of political stagnation in Germany. Thus the SDS became the theoretical leader of the movement, and often the main organizer of demonstrations and other protest actions. The SDS leaders have become public figures, written about in the papers and discussed on TV, and a disproportionately large number of SDS members are found among the elected student representatives in many universities.

The "critical theory" is itself a serious intellectual doctrine but it does fulfill the functions of an ideology rather than a philosophy for many of its student adherents. As developed by Adorno and Habermas, this theory opposes a "value-free" social science in the name of a "committed" rationality whose ultimate justification lies in the unfolding of history. To appreciate fully this rather opaque theory requires a good deal of philosophical training. This, as well as the style in which it is written, makes it difficult reading. Many of the newer converts have in fact turned to Marcuse, whose popularity is partly due to the fact that he has supplied such catchwords as "repressive tolerance" and "one-dimensionality." In the end, however, Marcuse too has disappointed those students with an activist temper, for like Adorno, he has been unable to give new, concrete and positive goals and tell the students exactly what to do. The activist element of the student movement is better served by such models as Mao and Ché Guevara.

THE SEQUENCE OF EVENTS

A general readiness to protest, an issue, a theory, and an organizational core— these are important conditions, but they do not fully explain the growth of the movement. One must turn therefore to history, to the sequence of actions and reactions which feed the movement. The first large-scale student protests took place in West Berlin in 1965. The students insisted on the right of their elected representatives to conduct an extra-curricular program of "political education" (which, by that time, had become predominantly and rather one-sidedly "critical") and on the right of the student council to take an official stand on general political questions. To underline what they called their "political man-date," the students took to the streets. In 1964, they had already demonstrated against Tshombe when he visited the city. Now, in early 1966, the first large anti-Vietnam demonstration took place. Clashes with the police, the hostile attitude of the public and of the press, the criticisms voiced and sanctions imposed, only strengthened the opposition by convincing a growing number of students of the authoritarianism of the established powers.

But the students not only sought a free hand in their political activities. They also demanded improvements in their conditions as students and the initiation of reforms within the university. At first, their demands were modest; but they became increasingly radical through the peculiar mixture of failure and success with which they were met. Reforms, even of the most pragmatic and necessary kind (e.g., certain curriculum changes, the publication of course descriptions, changes in teaching methods, etc.), were extremely slow to start. This impressed students with the futility of rational argument and made them feel that nothing much would be gained until they themselves had won a voice in the decision-making bodies of the university. Thus they started to ask for more participation, and to resort to pressure tactics to give emphasis to their claims. The pressure tactics proved successful, and this prompted their increasing use, to the point where students now present their far-reaching demands together with an announcement of the measures they will take—sit-ins, boycotts, occupation—if they are not immediately met.

Berlin had remained the center of student unrest until 1967, when a student, Benno Ohnesorg, was killed during clashes with the police on the occasion of a demonstration against the visiting Shah of Persia. This death—and the sharply repressive reaction of the public authorities to the demonstration—precipitated the eventual downfall of the Berlin mayor and produced a wave of student solidarity in the major West German universities. The students could not fail to notice the extent of the fears they were able to produce. Together with the repeated successes of their actions, if not on a national scale then at least on the local and university level, this produced a sense of power among them which occasionally assumed the proportions of a delusion.

An important process of learning and unlearning is involved in this whole development. The students have learned that the social institutions are not so stable and impervious to attack after all. They have learned how simple it is to paralyze the complicated mechanisms on which their functioning depends—how easy to break up an academic ceremony or meeting of the faculty committee, to disrupt a lecture, a public concert, or theater performance, to bring city traffic to a stand-still. They have learned that they can bring down a mayor or cause a rector to resign, that authority can be successfully challenged and concessions be achieved through threat.

To learn that all this is possible implies also the unlearning of attitudes and behavior patterns acquired in earlier life. It is not only that students now know from experience that authority is vulnerable—they have also lost any ingrained respect for it. This can be seen in many small ways, such as the disappearance of the accustomed forms of deference shown to professors. Students in Berlin, for instance, have started spontaneously to address their professors as "Mr." X instead of "Herr Professor," and they will criticize him to his face, apparently without having to overcome strong inhibitions. Similarly, the technique of violating rules, frequently employed for the purpose of provocation, has the effect of making the respect for, and unthinking compliance with, all kinds of rules disappear. Rules suddenly appear as arbitrary creations which can be broken and dispensed with if they seem no longer justified. This is perhaps salutary up to a certain point, and positive effects can be seen in the informality and self-assured spontaneity which has come to characterize the behavior of many students. But carried to an extreme, the growing disrespect for rules also has dangerous implications. Already it happens quite often that an argument against a given action on the grounds that it would be illegal only provokes ironical laughter. It is not only traditional authority, but also rational-legal authority (speaking in Weberian terms) which is entering a crisis of legitimation. . . .

POLITICAL GOALS

If the students have a difficult time identifying their true enemy, they do have a conception of the "good society" they wish to realize. This would be a non-bureaucratic, radical democracy, based on a socialist economy. The West German student radicals reject the model of the USSR and look with contempt on such "socialist" countries as Eastern Germany. But they feel that, while socialism alone is not enough, it is a better starting point than capitalism for the development of their ideal society. Thus many followed with hope and intense interest the events in Czechoslovakia which they had believed might lead to a true socialist democracy.

The real issue behind this image of the good society is less a protest against capitalism in its late phase than a crisis of democracy in highly advanced industrial nations. In East and West, the tendencies in a technocratic direction make democratic participation increasingly difficult to maintain. The student movement is thus somewhat like a fundamentalist's protest against a church that still professes, but does not any longer follow, the commandments of the Holy Scripture. The principle of direct and full participation—a rally slogan also in France this summer—is the negation of the bureaucratic principle.

It is hardly surprising that, in view of the functional prerequisites of a technologically advanced society, this image of a radical democracy with its implications appears utopian. The sociologist Erwin K. Scheuch has gone so far as to call it a social theology, and to suggest that it is particularly attractive to students with histories of disturbed personalities. Other critics point out quite correctly that it is typically the sons of a satiated bourgeoisie to whom such an ideology, with its impressive lack of production-orientation, appeals. The charges of romanticism, often connected with that of utopianism, is, on the other hand, only superficially correct. The analogy with the romantic German youth movement of the early nineteenth century, which was characterized by the withdrawal from the claims of adult society into a communal sub-culture of youth and a cult of emotionality and self-expression, might in fact fit certain elements in the American student movement better than the German. The latter are political activists and do not wish to withdraw. Nor have I yet heard a German student rave about the glorious experience of community, as some of the Columbia University occupants did this past spring. The much publicized "communes" of German students are marginal phenomena, smiled at and even rejected by the more serious radicals.

UNIVERSITY GOALS

The goals of the students in the German university are less utopian and much more precise than their aims for a social revolution. For a short while it seemed that the movement's major point of attack had shifted away from the university, whose structure after all only reflects the condition of the whole society. But university reform has recently often become the focus of attention—a development which, in particular, the city government of West Berlin seems to welcome heartily. As one harassed professor put it privately in a burst of exasperation: "They let us happily run into the open knives of the SDS as long as the students only stay away from the Kurfürstendamm."

What the students want is, for one thing, the abolition of the *Ordinarienprinzip,* i.e., the institution of "the chair" whose incumbent, the full professor, has complete control of the financial means of administration; of buying books, of research, and full control over the assistants belonging to his chair. It is clear that this privileged position, which constitutes for many the attractiveness of a full professorship, will not be relinquished voluntarily. Though myself an "Ordinarius," I cannot find much by way of rational arguments in its defense. The abolition of the exclusive rights of the full professor needs to be combined with a redistribution of teaching, examination, and administration duties among all ranks of the full-time staff. The students, however, would not be satisfied with a change which would give independence to the lower ranks of the full-time staff but would not increase their own influence. Their idea, therefore, is to form departments, or institutes, which are governed by a board on which the students are represented and which would decide about the distribution of funds, selection of personnel (including the nomination of candidates for a full professorship), course offerings, and research to be undertaken. An "adequate" representation of students means at least one-third (though 50 per cent is occasionally being asked), the other third going to the full professors and to the lower ranks of full-time staff, including assistants. At the Free University, a model for such an order has recently been worked out for the institute of political science and voted for by the majority of the students, assistants, and professors concerned. It was rejected by the Academic Senate which must approve it; but similar reform plans are already being discussed in other departments. The most radical students want to give to the board, the *Institutsrat,* mainly executive functions, reserving the right of decision-making in all major questions for the plenary meeting (*Vollversammlung*) of all students and staff members of the department or institute. This would give the students the overwhelming majority and make the staff virtually dependent on them. The ultimate utopian goal of such demands is the "free university," where students elect their professors and tell them what to teach, how to conduct examinations, and what research to do. It is the model of "radical democracy" applied to the university.

In view of their practical and legal implications, such demands for radical structural change are often simply rejected as utterly utopian. But quite aside from this, it is felt that such changes would inevitably result in a loss of efficiency, a decline in the quality of training and research. Such fears are also expressed in the "Marburg Manifesto." The students either do not realize these dangers or they do not greatly care, since efficiency in performing these services to the society is for them no guiding value. In fact, they have a very different notion of the university's relation to society. The university is to be a center of social change, a "critical" rather than an affirmative institution. They do not wish to influence what is being taught and what kind of research is being done for the sake of participation per se, but to use this influence to sponsor a "politically engaged" curriculum. This movement against "value-free" science started in the social sciences, where it has been a hotly debated issue between neo-positivists and adherents of the dialectical approach of "critical theory," but it is now also being applied to other fields, even though the notion of "politically engaged" archeology, art, history, or biology seems absurd to many.

The connection between structural reform and demands for a partisan orientation to knowledge has stimulated the most severe criticism. The reforms, it is felt, would amount to a restriction in the constitutionally guaranteed freedom of teaching and learning. Parallels to the Nazi regime or to one of the totalitarian Communist regimes are being drawn, and even quite a few students feel uneasy about it. The radicals deny that they want to restrict this freedom, arguing that they only want it extended to the students instead of reserving it for the professors; but this is not convincing. And yet, in spite of the obviously dangerous implications of a demand for a politically engaged knowledge, it is incontestable that in a society where knowledge is increasingly and ever more directly involved in political decision-making, the abstinence from making rationally argued normative judgments, practiced by many social scientists, will simply no longer do.

10 MICHEL CROZIER

French Students: A Letter from Nanterre-La Folie[1]

This is a hard time to be a sociologist, especially a French one. Sociologists have been forced out of their traditional *voyeurist* position and made part of the sad game of survival politics, and they don't know yet how to behave.

This should be, of course, the time of sobering up and facing bravely the real meaning of one's own analyses. But sociology meanwhile has become fashionable. Abstract jargon at last is *in*. The most naïve girl of Passy, after a couple of years at Nanterre, can terrorize a general assembly of engineers from the Polytechnique with a few cliches about "alienation." Who can resist such evidence of the success of one's own trade? Sociologists are men, after all, and there's a time and place for everything including sociology.

Strange times: responsible people day-dreaming in the streets; swarms of people talking, talking, talking; and nobody ever listening. Several times I made the experiment of contesting the confrontation. I had to repeat myself again and again, until my audience barely understood that I did not agree with them. Since I was a

Reprinted from *The Public Interest,* No. 13 (Fall, 1968), pp. 151-159, by permission of the author and National Affairs Inc., © 1968.

sociologist, and presumably therefore part of "the movement," it was regarded as just a temporary misunderstanding.

My comments on the French scene will be biased, as should be obvious by now. Whatever my desire for change, my hatred for the old system, and my sympathy for the students, I simply couldn't help resisting the fashionable trend; maybe I was just cold-headed, or too damn conservative. In any case, mine is a minority opinion, in my profession and in my intellectual milieu. Remember, therefore: I am not representative.

As I write, only a month has passed, and the first question that comes to my mind whenever I look back at "the events"—*les évènements*[2]—is always: Did it really happen? One is very hard put to find proof. Of course people don't stop talking about it. Some are still obsessed. But it seems as if it were a theoretical revolution they are commenting upon, not a real one. Professors say: *La rentrée* will be impossible, what are *they* going to do; Students say: We can't accept that *they* should impose something on us; what are *their* intentions? Corporation executives say: *They* are as crazy as usual, but business after all may finally pick up, we have to wait. Intellectuals say: Something *irréversible* has come; the world will never be the same again. But everybody has already gone back to his own professional, organizational, political, and cultural family life; and they act just the same as before.

Of course there are still some elements of uncertainty. The General may have gone really crazy with his "participation" schemes. Or the students' anger will be enough to make life miserable for everybody. But, at the moment, it is as if some members of the family had had a terrible, hysterical, but passing fit. They will be awkward with each other for a while; but whatever they say outside, they have to behave at home as if nothing had happened.

This surface of things, however revealing it may be, of course is only the surface. We know: something has really happened, and it is serious. Every Western country has had student troubles—enough to mobilize the police, moral leaders, public consciousness. But these were limited turbulences. "Culture" and "civilization" were in trouble; but culture and civilization are not part of daily life, and one can live a long time while they rot. With Cartesian logic, however, French students have put first things first. If culture is corrupt, society is sick, and only prompt, total revolution will bring purification.

And, in a way, they have demonstrated the possibility of building a real link between intellectuals and the proletarian revolution. For a little while it really worked. In the temporary void of authority, the magic Leninist formula: *students, workers,* and *poor peasants*—it seemed at last real. For the French intellectuals—Catholic, Marxist, and skeptic alike—this was enough; students were viewed as the new Christians bringing to a tired and *blasé* world the flame of a living faith. A new era had begun, the era when man will finally meet man and recognize his brother. Maybe it is not for tomorrow; maybe we are only in 1905 Russia or in 1919 China; but the long march has begun.

You may smile; but if one does not take this pathos seriously, what kind of meaning is one to ascribe to such an incredible thunderstorm in the blue sky of a prosperous, developed-developing nation?

A REBELLION WITH CAUSES

Western civilization was "confronted," but Western civilization as such is just a figure of speech. French students were not at first rebels without cause. They were lonely, bewildered youngsters entering, without preparation and possibility of understanding, a world of higher learning that had become a caricature—a world consisting of gigantic teaching factories pretending to be loyal to the ideal of a great humanist culture that they negated in every aspect of their behavior, a world of solemn stupidity.

The Nanterre explosion was not accidental; it had to happen there. Suppose you take the children of the best neighborhoods of Paris and oblige them to go to a college in a suburban slum area where you have built, especially for them, the barest and ugliest functional concrete structure.[3] Suppose you have chosen for a landscape, low-cost housing projects, railroad tracks, gas-tanks and construction sites; and you locate, only half a mile away, the worst shanty town in the whole Paris region, if not Western Europe, where thousands of North African and Portuguese migrant workers live in the mud. Who would not suspect that you intend to create, among the students, both personal resentment and enormous guilt?

This took place, furthermore, in a social context that has always been characterized by student apathy and isolation. French students are traditionally docile and passive. They barely know one another and have meaningful human relationships only outside the university building. With the new buildings at Nanterre, the "outside" was just suppressed, and with it the compensating folklore of turbulent cafes, narrow streets, and gay boulevards. If you then further tip the scale with a rigid bureaucratic reform of the curriculum, imposed from above without consultation, that deprived the students of their traditional freedom of choice as regards courses and exams, the amount of disgust and frustration built up is such that you may well wonder why it took them so long to start the explosion.

Something fundamental was wrong, and no serious-minded student could accept the situation as the natural order of things. French students had been too naïve and too docile for a long time; when they woke up, the shock was bound to be terrible.

A SOCIETY PARALYZED BY BUREAUCRACY

But why should an understandable and, in a way, legitimate student rebellion bring about such an explosion—one that threatened the very foundations, not of the Gaullist regime, but of modern capitalist society?

In order to understand this, one should look at the internal functioning of the French university system. There are no French autonomous universities, only one huge state system that is organized according to the basic principles of a monopoly. Only one school in each geographical area, and only one full professor for each discipline in any given year. Competition between universities, between departments, and between professors cannot be suppressed but is barely tolerated. The students are a captive audience. The system is perfectly self-contained, with no possibility for outsiders to interfere.

Such a system, of course, tends to be the corporative preserve of the different vested interests, especially the professors. Since these interests are extremely conservative—monopoly is the only game they know—whatever innovative force there is tends to come from the national ministry in Paris. This means that all the forces of progress and change will generally work in favor of centralization.

The upshot is a system that is an uneasy compromise between feudal corporative privileges and bureaucratic centralization. Its power of resistance is tremendoux; its only motor of action—the ministry—is blind and erratic.

This could work well enough for a stable and hierarchical society, where the main function of higher education was to select people for higher-status positions, while providing a real freedom to think for small groups of learned men. Other European, old-fashioned systems, such as the German, have at least been able to prevent the entry of the "barbarian" mass, thus preserving some kind of aristocratic symbiosis between research and teaching. But the French system had been built upon the equalitarian principle of free tuition and free entry, with the examination as the only barrier. So, gradually, a triple-standard system has developed. Research is being carried on outside the university in separate "institutes" whose members don't have any students to be bothered with. The best students will spend their time in the great professional schools, whose selective examinations are appallingly severe, even worse than the Japanese. Only the run-of-the-mill students will then go to the conventional *Facultés,* whose diplomas do not carry much prestige compared to the privilege of being an alumnus of such professional schools as the *Polytechnique* or *Normale supérieure.* As a result, conventional university education could all the more easily be sacrificed to demagogic pressures. Selection was too hot an issue to be debated: but expenditures to match the tremendous increase in numbers was not economically feasible. As a result, the number of university students increased almost three times in ten years, whereas the amount of money spent per student is now but a small percentage of the amount spent for secondary school children! At the same time, no meaningful reform was ever attempted in order to adapt universities to the task of mass education and to counter the estrangement from active research that has demoralized the professorial corps.

Only a major crisis could stop the continuous degradation of the system. But the French bureaucratic state itself was unable to provoke and handle such a crisis. Although of course much more efficient, it also is over-centralized and rigid. This rigid—apparently modern but in reality conservative—Gaullist bureaucratic state had suppressed all these indirect channels for settling grievances and introducing innovations. It boasted of courage and clarity, but could ignore and neglect problems that would have brought down any government of the Fourth Republic. Which means that it was to be completely helpless when, finally, a major crisis became the only solution to those problems.

Its basic weakness was then revealed. An over-centralized bureaucracy, with no safety valves, will always be the victim of a sort of "multiplier" effect that develops whenever a crisis disturbs it. Every group will rush in to have its grievances discussed at the bargaining table. Since this may be the only chance to change the basic equilibrium during the next few years, one has to be part of the final settlement at any cost.

THE TWO CULTURES

The institutional setup and the patterns of decision-making I have described are certainly basic for French society. A clearer understanding of them might have enabled one to predict the coming crisis. But to what kinds of problems was the crisis responding to, and what kind of changes was the revolution longing for? To give a tentative answer, I would like to speculate for a moment on the meaning of culture in a post-industrial society and on the conditions of its development.

"Culture" is no longer a luxury for the privileged or gifted few. It is the basic instrumentality of action in a world increasingly rationalized. But not every type of culture can be used in such a way. France has had for a long time a great tradition of *culture classique,* rationalist and humanist at the same time. But this *culture classique* has become inadequate; it is gradually being eroded by specialization while it retreats more and more into formalism.

Modernist reformers in France have been attacking classicism vigorously, but with some uneasiness and without proposing anything to replace it. They completely overlook the need for a new "general" culture that could make it possible for people to understand their world, to use this understanding in an active and experimental way as citizens in order to adjust to change and to innovate rationally and meaningfully. Paradoxically enough, there is now much more of such "general" culture in good American universities than at such temples of classicism as *La Sorbonne*. Recent attempts at "modernization," as in the Plan *Fouchèt,* only succeeded in accelerating the trend toward narrow specialization.[4] These basically retrograde decisions were pushed by reformers simply because they permitted an increase in the so-called modern fields, without attacking directly that classical training which remains the only common cultural basis for the French elite, i.e., the literary-mathematical and philosophical curriculum of the secondary school that is the preserve of the most powerful university group, the *agrégés.*[5]

The May revolution expressed to a great extent the revolt of students against the dilemma they were trapped in: formalistic-classical culture or narrow specialization. Incoherent grievances were presented on this score, all of them with great violence and sincerity. Half the revolutionists complained that their training was too abstract and remote from worldly problems; the other half, that it was too narrowly professional.

But the longing for a general culture that could be useful for our post-industrial society does not concern only the content of a curriculum. It is also, and perhaps especially, a question of social and human relations; methods of teaching, types of relations between students and teachers, the students' status and their capacity for initiative.

The French university is a caste-ridden system governed by social distance and impersonal, functional relationships. This is deeply linked with the abstract-formalistic content of the curriculum and the way that curriculum is inevitably taught. Formal lectures cannot be very effective in training students to understand new modes of reasoning. If they are addressed to large captive audiences, they are even a hindrance to real communication. The same is true of rhetorical examinations that will test memorized knowledge at the expense of creativity. French students traditionally protect themselves by passive docility in their official role and by rebellion outside it. Professors withdraw into formalism.

The whole process is completely inadequate for adapting creatively to the second half of the twentieth century. The inefficiency of French public administration, and of most French business, is deeply rooted in this inadequacy. Thus, the French elite is still a kind of caste, much less based on class origin than the English one, but more rigidly based on professional training. And this elite is completely segregated from the rungs immediately below it. We have the most brilliant generals, who impress all our foreign allies; but behind them there are deserts of mediocrity.

It is around this problem that, I feel, the student rebellion was really contributing something to French society. This rebellion has been the triumph of spontaneous, easy-going, comrade-like relationships. It has opposed in its own very existence the stuffy, outmoded, ridiculous, formal relationships that still prevailed in the university hierarchy (and even in the various left-wing elites).

REVOLT OF THE MIDDLEBROWS

It has also been a revolt of the middlebrows, of the masses of people who were supposed to benefit from the vastly increasing supply of higher education, but who felt cheated of this reward just when they got it—the multitude of white-collar and lower middle-class job holders whom Frenchmen call *cadres* (lower executives, supervisors, technicians) and who are taught in the university not to accept traditional bourgeois relations anymore, but who could not define a meaningful role for themselves in the building of the new society. One did not pay enough attention to this sudden influx of thousands of young people to the universities. They came, not from the working-class, but from the lower middle classes, from the old French *petit bourgeoise* that has lost its feeling of inferiority and now feels it can compete on equal terms with the real *bourgeoise.* But at the same time, these *petits bourgeois* enter the temples of culture to discover bureaucratic factories and to encounter the tremendous aggressiveness of the *bourgeois* children, who have not made it in the *grandes écoles* and thus have no place in the meritocracy.

All Western countries have these problems. But none of them has organized its recruitment of university students in such a humiliating way. None has disregarded with such equanimity its human responsibilities. None has covered up for its deficiencies with such a blatant equalitarian demagogy. This is why I think the students' explosion has struck so deep in the French consciousness and why so many people have followed its lead in very different sectors. For what has not been so well publicized, even in France, is the extraordinary turmoil that inflamed hundreds of intellectual institutions; research and study groups, consulting firms, economists' bureaus, planning agencies, urban development bureaus, marketing agencies, cultural institutions. These people are part of the great masses that have always been, and probably will be, the stalwarts of *bourgeois* order. But they express at this time their fears and anxieties, their dreams and their frustrations.[6]

SHALL WE OVERCOME?

French society had been much too tightly run, and it is not surprising that it lost its nerve when it encountered its first great difficulty. But once the crisis has developed, what can be its outcome? Will it have brought enough change to permit a gradual shift to a new and stronger equilibrium that could ensure more flexibility and innovative capacity to the social system; or will it just lead to a general regression to earlier and "safer," i.e., more authoritarian patterns of government; or will it be only the first move in a new cycle of violent crises?

Surprisingly enough, there are many more people who have reacted in a positive way than could have been predicted. Leading corporation executives now ask for more experiments in participative structures. Civil servants are questioning the nature of their own organizations. Even finance ministry officials wonder about the cost of their traditional imperative constraints. And university innovators are being listened to.

But will it be enough? Are the conditions favorable for a successful new deal? Or can we wait long enough before they are favorable? The real tragedy of the recent crisis seems to me this: while the whole society has been deeply disturbed, the only voices that have expressed the desire to change are so violent, naïve, and unpredictable that they could strike but very few responsible echoes.

In circumstances such as these, two dangerous trends are going to develop:

1. The obsessive regression of most forces of renewal among the young, and especially in the intellectual world, toward the impossible dream of total change. The French intellectual world is much more important strategically than people may think, inasmuch as the basic crisis *is* a cultural one.

2. The temptation for the government and for the elites to buy social equilibrium—and to isolate the extremists—at the expense of a real renewal. There is an easy way to placate the resentment of the middlebrows: by imposing on the whole society the bureaucratic rules that already protects them from competition in public administration. This is already a strong tendency among Gaullists and traditional bureaucrats: it meets socialist dreams and middlebrow anxieties. And already revolutionary student leaders are campaigning *against* the introduction of competition between and within the universities, while professors will be all too happy to accept just anything to keep their sacrosanct rights of corporative cooptation.

The real risk in post-crisis in France is that of declining into a closed society, with its traditional double standards of irresponsible radicalism and corporative complacency.

The French elites of today are going to bear a terrible responsibility during the next few years. On their conscious choices, as well as from their instinctive behavior, will depend whether the crisis will have been the last great melodramatic gesture of a romantic nation before entering the world of rationality, or whether France will have lost for a long time to come her chance to remain creative in the world of the future.

FOOTNOTES

1.   The Faculte des Lettres of Nanterre, where the student revolution first broke out, was built four years ago in the section of Nanterre called "La Folie," which means in modern French: "madness."

2.   Notice the vocabulary. Books advertise *la révolution* but people talk about *les évènements.*

3.   In an effort to "deconcentrate" student populations, the French authorities promulgated a rule whereby students of parents living in the sixteenth-century *arrondisement*—the fashionable districts of Passy and Auteuil—had to go to the new University of Nanterre, rather than to the Sorbonne.

4.   Specialization during the last two years of high school now seals off students completely at the first year of university.

5.   The *agrégation* is still theoretically the basic competitive examination for recruiting secondary school teachers. The very high standards of this classical examination give *agrégés* a great deal of prestige. Half of them at least have left the *lycées* for university professorships or for more glorious fields. Many politicians (for example, Pompidou) are *agrégés.*

6.   Readers may be puzzled to see me emphasize the middlebrows' revolt while it was the working class that went on strike. But I am ready to argue that the puzzled and covertly hostile behavior of the Communist party expressed the attitudes of the working class much better than the enthusiasm of the Catholic trade union leaders who are typical examples of the left middlebrows.

Political Parties in
the New Europe:
Adaptation and
Resistance

Political parties are an inherent feature of democratic political systems. They are institutions through which competition and choice—the touchstones of democracy—are operationalized and structured. They are also the vital representational bodies linking the various constituencies of society with the decision-making institutions of the political system. As such, political parties are particularly useful indicators of change occurring both within society and the processes of government.

The historical image of European party systems has been one of marked fragmentation. The familiar spectre of multipartyism was a witness to the many cleavages with which the continental nations found it necessary to contend. In contrast to the American example, in which the various sectional, religious, ethnic, and economic divisions were subsumed within a two-party framework, the same rifts in the European social fabric tended to become politicized.

The result of this politicization was a collection of ideological party organizations, many of which claimed to serve as public spokesmen for clearly delineated segments of society. Not infrequently the goals championed by one or more parties were held to be irreconcilable with the aims of other parties. The confrontation between parties with Marxist orientations and those representing the urban and rural middle classes is a familiar example of this situation. Even where visions of fundamental socio-political conflict were not central to a party's ideology its objectives were commonly infused with doctrinaire qualities which produced expectations of unswerving partisan loyalty. This was true, for example, for many of the religious parties in Western Europe.

The multitude of political parties with their insulated clienteles frequently acted to debilitate the effectiveness of political regimes. Great amounts of energy were consumed by efforts at coalition building and shoring up shaky governmental executives, leaving little time or room for responsive policy-making endeavors. Certainly, there was no absence of criticism directed at this condition. Yet, so long as a relative stability prevailed in the socioeconomic patterns which had initially given rise to and sustained Western European party systems, the prospect for transformations in character remained limited.

In his seminal article, Otto Kirchheimer argues that a number of contemporary Western European political parties are in fact undergoing noticeable and significant changes. It is Kirchheimer's thesis that parties from diverse philo-sophical and historical backgrounds are increasingly exhibiting common charac-teristics and becoming what he labels "catch-all parties."

The impetus for this transition is found in the changing nature of European societies. For one thing, the various divisions upon which the parties of integration fed are to Kirchheimer's way of thinking losing much of their political force. Class differences, which perhaps more than any other single factor divided Europeans into highly structured and often antagonistic partisan groupings, have been reduced by the general wave of economic prosperity in which virtually all the democratic nations of Western Europe have shared. Of particular importance is the fact that the traditional triumvirate of class politics—that is to say, the proletariat, the independent farmers, and the urban self-employed—are widely in relative decline. It is the so-called "new middle class," a term encompassing the armies of white-collar employees in both private and government service, which is enjoying increasing numerical as-cendency.

While the non-manual character of their occupational roles leaves the white-collar workers removed from the proletarian ranks, their status as employees rather than owners sets them apart from the traditional bourgeoisie. For many of these citizens identification with a particular class has become obscured. The objective and subjective ambiguity of their status and the growing weight of their numbers have made the members of the new middle class attractive targets for the mobilization efforts of all major parties. The result has been two-fold: 1) A convergence in the content of the programmatic appeals of parties as they enter into competition for elusive white-collar votes, and 2) a conscious effort on the part of these parties to divest themselves of their traditional class trappings in favor of emphasizing their broad representational basis. It is this last development which stands at the core of Kirchheimer's "catch-all" formulation.

The transformation discussed by Dr. Kirchheimer is not equally evident in all of the Western European political systems. West Germany is a country in which the process of party convergence appears to have reached an advanced stage. As Peter Merkl points out, Germany has experienced a history of multi-party politics rooted in traditions of social and economic dissension. Yet, in contrast to its Weimar predecessor, the Federal Republic of West Germany has experienced few ideological confrontations. Much of the credit for this can be traced to the atmosphere of mutual respect established between the two dominant parties, the Christian Democratic Union and the Social Democratic Party, and the growing similarity of their strategies and aims.

Care should be taken, however, that the arguments concerning the trends toward party convergence and moderation not be exaggerated or overextended. That is to say, there is no reason to. believe that the logical outcome in any context need be political parties stripped of differences in clientele orientations and philosophical perspectives.

In comparison with the nations of the continental core area, Great Britain has experienced a lengthy period of basic two party domination. Perhaps the principal ingredient allowing for this partisan duality has been the broad consensus among most Englishmen regarding fundamental political procedures and values. While this general agreement has restricted the successful development of highly ideological parties of the type familiar to the French and Italians, it has not left the Labor and Conservative Parties without enduring points of philosophical difference.

According to James B. Christoph, the consensus which forms such a vital part of British political culture is counterbalanced by sets of attitudinal cleavages which, while not constituting generalized *Weltanschaungen*, provide cohesive alternatives for political action. In large measure, these points of contention receive institutional form in the two British parties which continue to display a distinctiveness of clientele and program.

Unlike West Germany and Great Britain, Italy and France remain beset by extreme partisan fragmentation and ideological contention. The Italian party system, for example, extends across a broad spectrum that stretches from the party remnants of Italy's monarchist and fascist past on the right to the Communist Party on the left. The latter, the Partito Comunista Italiano (PCI), is the largest communist party in Western Europe and probably the largest outside the communist world.

According to many political observers, the communist parties of Europe stand as prototypes of unrelenting and uncompromising organizations of particularistic and highly ideological appeal. Yet the article authored by Sidney G. Tarrow brings into question whether the revolutionary, conspiratorial characteristics assigned to communist parties in general and the anti-system orientation attributed to the PCI in particular remain valid contemporary interpretations. Most notable, perhaps, is the reformist, practical approach which the PCI has adopted toward the accumulation and exercise of political power. The immediate goal of the Italian Communists appears to be to demonstrate their responsibility and their capacity to govern in a democratic context. Among other things, this has produced overtures to the ruling Christian Democratic Party which, while not always reciprocated, are indicators of the degree to which the ideological gulf separating the two has narrowed. Whatever the outcome of this dialogue, Tarrow's article demonstrates in a clear fashion that the contemporary Italian Communist Party understands the importance of adapting itself to the requirements of its immediate milieu and has in practice done so.

A somewhat contrary picture is painted by Frank L. Wilson in his study of the parties of the French democratic left. Historically at odds, the members of the non-communist left in France have experienced recurring failures in their efforts to create a broader, and hence more formidable, political front. The most recent and ambitious attempt to rally these parties, the erection of the Federation of the Left in the middle 1960's, appears to be in near total disarray in the face of the Gaullists' overwhelming electoral victory in 1968 and Pompidou's presidential triumph in the following year.

Wilson's piece succinctly traces the pattern of forces which have kept the French parties of the left locked into their separate ideological grooves. By clinging to traditional ideological formulations, these parties have placed themselves out of step with the processes of socioeconomic change in France which have turned the attention of the general electorate away from fighting the old class battles and toward the attainment of more limited personal ends. Yet, despite declining electoral fortunes, the parties of the French left have proven reluctant to cast off their narrow political perspectives and adopt postures more in keeping with the "catch-all" model.

Like the class parties of Western Europe, postwar religious parties have also encountered environments which have tested their capabilities for philosophical and organizational adaptation. As Margot Lyon points out, these challenges have been met with varying degrees of success. In Germany, for example, the CDU has been able to broaden its basic Catholic underpinnings to encompass Protestant values. By means of a highly pragmatic approach to most economic and social questions, the CDU has built up a mass following drawn from all sectors of West German society. The result has been a record of electoral prosperity.

The prospects appear less optimistic for those Christian parties which have been unable or reluctant to relax their ties to the Catholic Church or modify their religious images and adopt more "catch-all" configurations. The Italian Christian Democrats, while still in power, have suffered a gradual erosion of support in recent years. And the French MRP is for all intents and purposes dead as a viable political force. Throughout Western Europe the forces of secularization which accompany economic modernization are striking at the historical bases of legitimacy and influence upon which religious parties were erected. In the end, the political future of these parties, as with so many institutions in Western Europe, is likely to depend upon their ability to reconcile long-established traditions with the innovative spirit which transitional times demand.

11 OTTO KIRCHHEIMER

The Transformation of the Western European Party Systems

THE ANTEBELLUM MASS INTEGRATION PARTY

Socialist parties around the turn of the century exercised an important socializing function in regard to their members. They facilitated the transition from agrarian to industrial society in many ways. They subjected a considerable number of people hitherto living only as isolated individuals to voluntarily accepted discipline operating in close connection with expectations of a future total transformation of society. But this discipline had its roots in the alienation of these parties from the pre-World War I political system whose demise they wanted to guarantee and speed up by impressing the population as a whole with their exemplary attitudes.

Reprinted by permission from Otto Kirchheimer, "The Transformation of the Western European Party Systems," in *Political Parties and Political Development,* eds. Joseph LaPalombara and Myron Weiner, Social Science Research Council (Copyright © 1966 by Princeton University Press; Princeton Paperback, 1968), pp. 182-200. Some footnotes omitted by the editors.

During and soon after the First World War the other participants in the political game showed that they were not yet willing to honor the claims of the working-class mass parties—claims based on the formal rules of democracy. This discovery was one of the primary reasons why the social integration into the industrial system through the working-class organizations did not advance to the state of a comparable political integration. Participation in the war, the long quarrels over the financial incidence of war burdens, the ravages of inflation, the rise of Bolshevist parties and a Soviet system actively competing for mass loyalty with the existing political mass organizations in most European countries, and finally the effect of the depression setting in at the end of the decade—all these were much more effective agents in the politicization of the masses than their participation in occasional elections, their fight for the extension of suffrage (Belgium, Britain, Germany), or even their *encadrement* in political parties and trade union organizations. But politicization is not tantamount to political integration; integration presupposes a general willingness by a society to offer and accept full-fledged political partnership of all citizens without reservations. The consequences of integration into the class-mass party depended on the responses of other forces in the existing political system; in some cases those responses were so negative as to lead to delayed integration into the political system or to make for its disintegration.

Now we come to the other side of this failure to progress from integration into the proletarian mass party and industrial society at large[1] to integration into the political system proper. This is the failure of bourgeois parties to advance from parties of individual representation to parties of integration, a failure already noted in France. The two tendencies, the failure of the integration of proletarian mass parties into the official political system and the failure of the bourgeois parties to advance to the stage of integration parties, condition each other. An exception, if only a partial one, is that of denominational parties such as the German Center or Don Sturzo's *Partito Popolare*. These parties to a certain extent fulfilled both functions: social integration into industrial society and political integration within the existing political system. Yet their denominational nature gave such parties a fortress-type character seriously restricting their growth potential.

With these partial exceptions, bourgeois parties showed no capacity to change from clubs for parliamentary representation into agencies for mass politics able to bargain with the integration-type mass parties according to the laws of the political market. There was only a limited incentive for intensive bourgeois party organization. Access to the favors of the state, even after formal democratization, remained reserved via educational and other class privileges. What the bourgeoisie lacked in numbers it could make good by strategic relations with the army and the bureaucracy.

Gustav Stresemann is the politician who stood at the crossroads of this era, operating with a threefold and incompatible set of parties: the class and the denominational democratic mass integration parties; the opposition-of-principle parties integrating masses into their own fold against the existing order; and the older parties of individual representation. Forever on the lookout for viable compromises among democratic mass parties, old-style bourgeois parties of individual representation, and the powerholders outside the formal political party structure, Stresemann failed. For the party of individual representation from which he came could not give him a broad enough basis for his policies.

Not all bourgeois groups accepted the need for transformation to integration parties. As long as such groups had other means of access to the state apparatus they might find it convenient to delay setting up counterparts to existing mass parties while still using the state apparatus for keeping mass integration parties from becoming fully effective in the political market. Yet after the second World War the acceptance of the law of the political market became inevitable in the major Western European countries. This change in turn found its echo in the changing structure of political parties.

THE POSTWAR CATCH-ALL PARTY

Following the Second World War, the old-style bourgeois party of individual representation became the exception. While some of the species continue to survive, they do not determine the nature of the party system any longer. By the same token, the mass integration party, product of an age with harder class lines and more sharply protruding denominational structures, is transforming itself into a catch-all "people's" party. Abandoning attempts at the intellectual and moral *encadrement* of the masses, it is turning more fully to the electoral scene, trying to exchange effectiveness in depth for a wider audience and more immediate electoral success. The narrower political task and the immediate electoral goal differ sharply from the former all-embracing concerns; today the latter are seen as counterproductive since they deter segments of a potential nationwide clientele.

For the class-mass parties we may roughly distinguish three stages in this process of transformation. There is first the period of gathering strength lasting to the beginning of the First World War; then comes their first governmental experience in the 1920's and 1930's (MacDonald, Weimar Republic, *Front Populaire*), unsatisfactory if measured both against the expectations of the class-mass party followers or leaders and suggesting the need for a broader basis of consensus in the political system. This period is followed by the present more or less advanced stages in the catch-all grouping, with some of the parties still trying to hold their special working-class clientele and at the same time embracing a variety of other clienteles.

Can we find some rules according to which this transformation is taking place, singling out factors which advance or delay or arrest it? We might think of the current rate of economic development as the most important determinant; but if it were so important, France would certainly be ahead of Great Britain and, for that matter, also of the United States, still the classical example of an all-pervasive catch-all party system. What about the impact of the continuity or discontinuity of the political system? If this were so important, Germany and Great Britain would appear at opposite ends of the spectrum rather than showing a similar speed of transformation. We must then be satisfied to make some comments on the general trend and to note special limiting factors.

In some instances the catch-all performance meets definite limits in the traditional framework of society. The all-pervasive denominational background of the Italian *Democrazia Cristiana* means from the outset that the party cannot successfully appeal to the anticlerical elements of the population. Otherwise nothing prevents the party from phrasing its appeals so as to maximize its chances of catching more of those numerous elements which are not disturbed by the party's clerical ties. The solidary element of its doctrinal core has long been successfully employed to attract a socially diversified clientele.

Or take the case of two other major European parties, the German SPD (Social Democratic party) and the British Labour party. It is unlikely that either of them is able to make any concession to the specific desires of real estate interests or independent operators of agricultural properties while at the same time maintaining credibility with the masses of the urban population. Fortunately, however, there is enough community of interest between wage-and-salary earning urban or suburban white- and blue-collar workers and civil servants to designate them all as strategic objects of simultaneous appeals. Thus tradition and the pattern of social and professional stratification may set limits and offer potential audiences to the party's appeal.

If the party cannot hope to catch all categories of voters, it may have a reasonable expectation of catching more voters in all those categories whose interests do not adamantly conflict. Minor differences between group claims, such as between white-collar and manual labor groups, might be smoothed over by vigorous emphasis on programs which benefit both sections alike, for example, some cushioning against the shocks of automation.

Even more important is the heavy concentration on issues which are scarcely liable to meet resistance in the community. National societal goals transcending group interests offer the best sales prospect for a party intent on establishing or enlarging an appeal previously limited to specific sections of the population. The party which propagates most aggressively, for example, enlarged educational facilities may hear faint rumblings over the excessive cost or the danger to the quality of education from elites previously enjoying educational privileges. Yet the party's stock with any other family may be influenced only by how much more quickly and aggressively it took up the new national priority than its major competitor and how well its propaganda linked the individual family's future with the enlarged educational structures. To that extent its potential clientele is almost limitless. The catch-all of a given category performance turns virtually into an unlimited catch-all performance.

The last remark already transcends the group-interest confines. On the one hand, in such developed societies as I am dealing with, thanks to general levels of economic well-being and security and to existing welfare schemes universalized by the state or enshrined in collective bargaining, many individuals no longer need such protection as they once sought from the state. On the other hand, many have become aware of the number and complexity of the general factors on which their future well-being depends. This change of priorities and preoccupation may lead them to examine political offerings less under the aspect of their own particular claims than under that of the political leader's ability to meet general future contingencies. Among the major present-day parties, it is the French UNR (National Republican Union) a latecomer, that speculates most clearly on the possibility of its channeling such less specialized needs to which its patron saint De Gaulle constantly appeals into its own version of the catch-all party. Its assumed asset would rest in a doctrine of national purpose and unity vague and flexible enough to allow the most variegated interpretation and yet—at least as long as the General continues to function—attractive enough to serve as a convenient rallying point for many groups and isolated individuals.

While the UNR thus manipulates ideology for maximum general appeal, we have noted that ideology in the case of the *Democrazia Cristiana* is a slightly limiting factor. The UNR ideology in principle excludes no one. The Christian Democratic ideology by definition excludes the non-believer, or at least the seriously non-believing voter. It pays for the ties of religious solidarity and the advantages of supporting organizations by repelling some millions of voters. The catch-all parties in Europe appear at a time of de-ideologization which has substantially contributed to their rise and spread. De-ideologization in the political field involves the transfer of ideology from partnership in a clearly visible political goal structure into one of many sufficient but by no means necessary motivational forces operative in the voters' choice. The German and Austrian Social Democratic parties in the last two decades most clearly exhibit the politics of de-ideologization. The example of the German Christian Democratic Union (CDU) is less clear only because there was less to de-ideologize. In the CDU, ideology was from the outset only a general background atmosphere, both all-embracing and conveniently vague enough to allow recruiting among Catholic and Protestant denominations.

As a rule, only major parties can become successful catch-all parties. Neither a small, strictly regional party such as the South Tyrolian Peoples' party nor a party built around the espousal of harsh and limited ideological claims, like the Dutch Calvinists; or transitory group claims, such as the German Refugees; or a specific professional category's claims, such as the Swedish Agrarians; or a limited-action program, such as the Danish single-tax Justice party can aspire to a catch-all performance. Its *raison d'etre* is the defense of a specific clientele or the lobbying for a limited reform clearly delineated to allow for a restricted appeal, perhaps intense, but excluding a wider impact or—once the original job is terminated—excluding a life-saving transformation.

Nor is the catch-all performance in vogue or even sought among the majority of the larger parties in small democracies. Securely entrenched, often enjoying majority status for decades—as the Norwegian and Swedish Social Democratic parties—and accustomed to a large amount of interparty cooperation, such parties have no incentive to change their form of recruitment or their appeal to well-defined social groups. With fewer factors intervening and therefore more clearly foreseeable results of political actions and decisions, it seems easier to stabilize political relations on the basis of strictly circumscribed competition (Switzerland, for instance) than to change over to the more aleatory form of catch-all competition.

Conversion to catch-all parties constitutes a competitive phenomenon. A party is apt to accommodate to its competitor's successful style because of hope of benefits or fear of losses on election day. Conversely, the more a party convinces itself that a competitor's favorable results were due only to some non-repetitive circumstances, and that the competitor's capacity of overcoming internal dissension is a temporary phenomenon, the smaller the over-all conversion chance and the greater the inclination to hold fast to a loyal—though limited—clientele.

To evaluate the impact of these changes I have found it useful to list the functions which European parties exercised during earlier decades (late in the nineteenth and early in the twentieth centuries) and to compare them with the present situation. Parties have functioned as channels for integrating individuals and groups into the existing political order, or as instruments for modifying or altogether replacing that order (integration-disintegration). Parties have attempted to determine political-action preferences and influence other participants in the political process into accepting them. Parties have nominated public officeholders and presented them to the public at large for confirmation.

The so-called "expressive function" of the party, if not belonging to a category by itself, nevertheless warrants a special word. Its high tide belongs to the era of the nineteenth-century constitutionalism when a more clear-cut separation existed between opinion formation-and-expression and the business of government. At that time the internally created parliamentary parties expressed opinions and criticism widely shared among the educated minority of the population. They pressed these opinions on their governments. But as the governments largely rested on an independent social and constitutional basis, they could if necessary hold out against the promptings of parliamentary factions and clubs. Full democratization merged the opinion-expressing and the governmental business in the same political parties and put them in the seat either of government or an alternative government. But it has left the expressive function of the party in a more ambiguous state. For electoral reasons, the democratic catch-all party, intent on spreading as wide as possible a net over a potential clientele, must continue to express widely felt popular concerns. Yet, bent on continuing in power or moving into governmental power, it performs this expressive function subject to manifold restrictions and changing tactical considerations. The party would atrophy if it were no longer able to function as a relay between the population and governmental structure, taking up grievances, ideas, and problems developed in a more searching and systematic fashion elsewhere in the body politic. Yet the caution it must give its present or prospective governmental role requires modulation and restraint. The very nature of today's catch-all party forbids an option between these two performances. It requires a constant shift between the party's critical role and its role as establishment support, a shift hard to perform but still harder to avoid.

In order to leave a maximum imprint on the polity a party has to exercise all of the first three functions. Without the ability to integrate people into the community the party could not compel other powerholders to listen to its clarions. The party influences other power centers to the extent that people are willing to follow its leadership. Conversely, people are willing to listen to the party because the party is the carrier of messages—here called action preferences—that are at least partially in accord with the images, desires, hopes, and fears of the electorate. Nominations for public office serve to tie together all these purposes; they may further the realization of action preferences if they elicit positive response from voters or from other powerholders. The nominations concretize the party's image with the public at large, on whose confidence the party's effective functioning depends.

Now we can discuss the presence or absence of these three functions in Western society today. Under present conditions of spreading secular and mass consumer-goods orientation, with shifting and less obtrusive class lines, the former class-mass parties and denominational mass parties are both under pressure to become catch-all peoples' parties. The same applies to those few remnants of former bourgeois parties of individual representation which aspire to a secure future as political organizations independent of the vagaries of electoral laws and the tactical moves of their mass-party competitors.[2] This change involves: a) Drastic reduction of the party's ideological baggage. In

France's SFIO, for example, ideological remnants serve at best as scant cover for what has become known as *"Molletisme,"* the absolute reign of short-term tactical considerations. b) Further strengthening of top leadership groups, whose actions and omissions are now judged from the viewpoint of their contribution to the efficiency of the entire social system rather than identification with the goals of their particular organization. c) Downgrading of the role of the individual party member, a role considered a historical relic which may obscure the newly built-up catch-all party image. d) De-emphasis of the *classe gardée,* specific social-class or denominational clientele, in favor of recruiting voters among the population at large. e) Securing access to a variety of interest groups. The financial reasons are obvious, but they are not the most important where official financing is available, as in Germany, or where access to the most important media of communication is fairly open, as in England and Germany. The chief reason is to secure electoral support via interest-group intercession.

From this fairly universal development the sometimes considerable remnants of two old class-mass parties, the French and the Italian Communist parties, are excluding themselves. These parties are in part ossified, in part solidified by a combination of official rejection and legitimate sectional grievances. In this situation the ceremonial invocation of the rapidly fading background of a remote and inapplicable revolutionary experience has not yet been completely abandoned as a part of political strategy. What is the position of such opposition parties of the older class-mass type, which still jealously try to hold an exclusive loyalty of their members, while not admitted nor fully ready to share in the hostile state power? Such parties face the same difficulties in recruiting and holding intensity of membership interest as other political organizations. Yet, in contrast to their competitors working within the confines of the existing political order, they cannot make a virtue out of necessity and adapt themselves fully to the new style of catch-all peoples' party. This conservatism does not cost them the confidence of their regular corps of voters. On the other hand, the continued renewal of confidence on election day does not involve an intimate enough bond to utilize as a basis for major political operations.

The attitudes of regular voters—in contrast to those of members and activists—attest to the extent of incongruency between full-fledged participation in the social processes of a consumer-goods oriented society and the old political style which rested on the primordial need for sweeping political change. The latter option has gone out of fashion in Western countries and has been carefully eliminated from the expectations, calculations, and symbols of the catch-all mass party. The incongruency may rest on the total absence of any connection between general social-cultural behavior and political style. In this sense electoral choice may rest on family tradition or empathy with the political underdog without thereby becoming part of a coherent personality structure. Or the choice may be made in the expectation that it will have no influence on the course of political development; it is then an act of either adjusting to or, as the case may be, signing out of the existing political system rather than a manifestation of signing up somewhere else.

THE CATCH-ALL PARTY, THE INTEREST GROUP, AND THE VOTER: LIMITED INTEGRATION

The integration potential of the catch-all mass party rests on a combination of factors whose visible end result is attraction of the maximum number of voters on election day. For that result the catch-all party must have entered into millions of minds as a familiar object fulfilling in politics a role analogous to that of a major brand in the marketing of a universally needed and highly standardized article of mass consumption. Whatever the particularities of the line to which a party leader owes his intraparty success, he must, once he is selected for leadership, rapidly suit his behavior to standard requirements. There is need for enough brand differentiation to make the article plainly recognizable, but the degree of differentiation must never be so great as to make the potential customer fear he will be out on a limb.

Like the brand whose name has become a household word, the catch-all mass party that has presided over the fortunes of a country for some time, and whose leaders the voter has therefore come to know on his television set and in his newspaper columns, enjoys a great advantage. But only up to a certain point. Through circumstances possibly outside the control of the party or even of the opposition—a scandal in the ranks of government, an economic slump—officeholding may suddenly turn into a negative symbol encouraging the voter to switch to another party as a consumer switches to a competitive brand.

The rules deciding the outcome of catch-all mass party competition are extremely complex and extremely aleatory. When a party has or seeks an almost nationwide potential constituency, its majority composed of individuals whose relation to politics is both tangential and discontinuous, the factors which may decide the eventual electoral outcome are almost infinite in number and often quite unrelated to the party's performance. The style and looks of the leader, the impact of a recent event entirely dictated from without, vacation schedules, the weather as it affects crops—factors such as these all enter into the results.

The very catch-all character of the party makes membership loyalty far more difficult to expect and at best never sufficient to swing results. The outcome of a television contest is dubious, or the contest itself may constitute too fleeting an exposure to make an impression that will last into the election. Thus the catch-all mass party too is driven back to look out for a more permanent clientele. Only the interest group, whether ideological or economic in nature or a combination of the two, can provide mass reservoirs of readily accessible voters. It has a more constant line of communication and higher acceptance for its messages than the catch-all party, which is removed from direct contact with the public except for the comparatively small number intensively concerned about the brand of politics a party has to offer these days—or about their own careers in or through the party.

All the same, the climate of relations between catch-all party and interest groups has definitely changed since the heyday of the class-mass or denominational integration party. Both party and interest group have gained a greater independence from each other. Whether they are still joined in the same organization (like British Labour and the TUC [Trades Union Congress]) or formally enjoy complete independence from each other (like the German SPD and the DGB [Workers' Federation]), what matters most is the change of roles. Instead of a joint strategy toward a common goal there appears an appreciation of limited if still mutually helpful services to be rendered.

The party bent on attracting a maximum of voters must modulate its interest-group relations in such a way so as not to discourage potential voters who identify themselves with other interests. The interest group, in its turn, must never put all its eggs in one basket. That might offend the sensibilities of some members with different political connections. More important, the interest group would not want to stifle feelings of hope in another catch-all party that some moves in its direction might bring electoral rewards. Both party and interest group modulate their behavior, acting as if the possible contingency has already arrived, namely that the party has captured the government—or an important share in it—and has moved from the position of friend or counsellor to that of umpire or arbitrator. Suddenly entrusted with the confidence of the community as a whole, the government-party arbitrator does best when able to redefine the whole problem and discover solutions which would work, at least in the long run, in the favor of all interest claimants concerned.

Here there emerges a crucial question: What then is the proper role of the catch-all party in the arbitration of interest conflicts? Does not every government try to achieve best tactical position for exercising an effective arbitration between contending group claims? Is the catch-all party even needed in this connection? Or—from the interest viewpoint—can a society dispense with parties' services, as France now does?

A party is more than a collector of interest-group claims. It functions at the same time as advocate, protector, or at least as addressee of the demands of all those who are not able to make their voices felt as effectively as those represented by well organized interest groups: those who do not yet have positions in the process of production or those who no longer hold such positions, the too young and the too old, and those whose family status aligns them with consumer rather than producer interests.

Can we explain this phenomenon simply as another facet of the party's aggregative function? But functionalist phraseology restates rather than explains. The unorganized and often unorganizable make their appearance only on election day or in suddenly sprouting pre-election committees and party activities arranged for their beneift. Will the party be able and willing to take their interests into its own hands? Will it be able, playing on their availability in electoral terms, not only to check the more extreme demands of organized groups but also to transcend the present level of intergroup relations and by political reforms redefining the whole political situation? No easy formula will tell us what leader's skill, what amount of pressure from objective situations has to intervene to produce such a change in the political configuration.

In this job of transcending group interests and creating general confidence the catch-all party enjoys advantages, but by the same token it suffers from an infirmity. Steering clear of sectarianism enhances its recruiting chances in electoral terms but inevitably limits the intensity of commitment it may expect. The party's transformation from an organization combining the defense of social position, the quality of spiritual shelter, and the vision of things to come into that of a vehicle for short-range and interstitial political choice exposes the party to the hazards of all purveyors of nondurable consumer goods: competition with a more attractively packaged brand of a nearly identical merchandise.

LIMITED PARTICIPATION IN ACTION PREFERENCE

This brings us to the determination of action preferences and their chances of realization. In Anthony Downs's well-known model action preference simply results from the party's interest in the proximate goal, the winning of the next election. In consequence the party will arrange its policies in such a way that the benefits accruing to the individual members of the community are greater than the losses resulting from its policy. Downs's illustrations are frequently, though not exclusively, taken from fields such as taxation where the cash equation of political action is feasible. Yet Downs himself has occasionally noted that psychological satisfactions or dissatisfactions, fears or hopes, are elements in voters' decisions as frequently as calculations of immediate short-term benefits or deprivations. Were it different, the long-lasting loyalty of huge blocks of voters to class-mass integration parties in the absence of any immediate benefits from such affiliation could scarcely be explained. But can it be said that such short-term calculations correspond much more closely to the attitudes connected with the present-day catch-all mass party with its widely ranging clientele? Can the short-term benefit approach, for example, be utilized in military or foreign-policy issues?

In some countries in the last decade it has become the rule for catch-all parties out of office simply to lay the most recent shortcomings or apparent deterioration of the country's military or international position at the doorstep of the incumbent government, especially during election campaigns: thus in the United States the Republican party in 1952 with regard to the long-lasting indecisive Korean War, or in Germany more recently the Social Democrats with regard to Adenauer's apparent passivity in the face of the Berlin Wall. In other instances, however, the opposition plays down foreign or military issues or treats them in generalities vague enough to evoke the image of itself as a competitor who will be able to handle them as well as the incumbent government.

To the extent that the party system still includes "unreformed" or—as in the case of the Italian Socialist party—only "half-reformed" class-mass type integration parties, foreign or military issues enter election campaigns as policy differences. Yet even here the major interest has shifted away from areas where the electorate could exercise only an illusory choice. The electorate senses that in the concrete situation, based in considerable part on geography and history, the international bloc affiliation of the country rather than any policy preference will form the basis of decision. It senses too that such decisions rest only partially, or at times nominally, with the political leadership. Even if the impact of the political leader on the decision may have been decisive, more often than not election timetables in democracies are such that the decision, once carried out, is no longer contested or even relevant to voter choices. As likely as not, new events crowd it out of the focus of voters' attention. Few voters still thought of Mendès-France's 1954 "abandonment" of Indo-China when Edgar Faure suddenly dissolved the Assembly in December 1955. While a party may benefit from its adversary's unpopular decisions, such benefits are more often an accidental by-product than the outcome of a government-opposition duel with clearly distributed roles and decisions.

A party may put up reasonably coherent, even if vague, foreign or military policies for election purposes. It may criticize the inept handling of such problems by the government of the day, and more and more intensively as it gets closer to election day. But in neither case is there a guarantee of the party's ability to act as a coherent body in parliament when specific action preferences are to be determined. Illustrative of this dilemma are the history of EDC in the French Parliament and the more recent battles within the British parties in regard to entrance into the Common Market (although the latter case remains inconclusive because of De Gaulle's settling the issue in his own way, for the time being). Fortuitous election timetables and the hopes, fears, and expectations of the public do not intermesh sufficiently with the parliamentary representatives' disjointed action on concrete issues before them to add up to the elaboration of clear-cut party action preference.

The catch-all party contributes general programs in the elaboration of domestic action preferences. These programs may be of a prognostic variety, informing the public about likely specific developments and general trends. Yet prognostics and desirability blur into each other in this type of futurology, in which rosy glasses offer previews of happy days for all and sundry among the party's prospective customers. These programs may lead to or be joined with action proposals in various stages of concretization. Concrete proposals, however, always risk implying promises which may be too specific. Concretizations must remain general enough so that they cannot be turned from electoral weapons to engines of assault against the party which first mounted them.

This indeterminacy allows the catch-all party to function as a meeting ground for the elaboration of concrete action for a multiplicity of interest groups. All the party may require from those who obtain its services is that they make a maximal attempt to arrive at compromises within the framework of the party and that they avoid coalescing with forces hostile to the party. The compromises thus elaborated must be acceptable to major interest groups even if these groups, for historical or traditional reasons, happen not to be represented in the governing party. Marginal differences may be submitted to the voter at elections or, as older class-mass parties do on occasion, via referenda (Switzerland and Sweden). But expected policy mutations are in the nature of increments rather than major changes in intergroup relations.

It is here that the difference between the catch-all and the older form of integration party becomes most clearly visible. The catch-all party will do its utmost to establish consensus to avoid party realignment. The integration party may count on majority political mechanisms to implement its programs only to find that hostile interests frustrate the majority decision by the economic and social mechanisms at their disposal. They may call strikes (by labor or farmers or storekeepers or investors), they may withdraw capital to safe haven outside the country, they may undermine that often hypocritically invoked but real factor known as the "confidence of the business community."

INTEGRATION THROUGH PARTICIPATION IN LEADERSHIP SELECTION—THE FUTURE OF THE POLITICAL PARTY

What then remains the real share of the catch-all party in the elaboration of action preferences? Its foremost contribution lies in the mobilization of the voters for whatever concrete action preferences leaders are able to establish rather than a priori selections of their own. It is for this reason that the catch-all party prefers to visualize action in the light of the contingencies, threats, and promises of concrete historical situations rather than of general social goals. It is the hoped-for or already established role in the dynamics of action, in which the voters' vicarious participation is invited, that is most in evidence. Therefore the attention of both party and public at large focuses most clearly on problems of leadership selection.

Nomination means the prospect of political office. Political office involves a chance to make an impact via official action. The competition between those striving to influence official action puts into evidence the political advantage of those in a position to act before their political adversaries can do so. The privilege of first action is all the more precious in a new and non-repetitive situation where the political actor can avoid getting enmeshed in directives deriving from party action preferences. Much as the actor welcomes party support on the basis of revered (but elastic) principles, he shuns specific direction and supervision. In this respect the catch-all party furnishes an ideal background for political action. Where obtaining office becomes an almost exclusive preoccupation of a party, issues of personnel are reduced to search for the simplest effective means to put up winning combinations. The search is especially effective wherever the party becomes a channel by which representatives of hitherto excluded or neglected minorities may join the existing political elite.

The nomination of candidates for popular legitimation as officeholders thus emerges as the most important function of the present-day catch-all party. Concentration on the selection of candidates for office is in line with an increasing role differentiation in industrial society. Once certain levels of education and material welfare are reached, both intellectual and material needs are taken care of by specialized purveyors of communications and economic products. Likewise the party, which in less advanced societies or in those intent on rapid change directly interferes with the performance of societal jobs, remains in Western industrial society twice removed—through government and bureaucracy—from the field of direct action. To this state of affairs correspond now prevailing popular images and expectations in regard to the reduced role of the party. Expectations previously set on the performance of a political organization are now flowing into different channels.

At the same time, the role of the political party as a factor in the continued integration of the individual into the national life now has to be visualized in a different light. Compared to his connection with interest organizations and voluntary associations of a non-political nature and to his frequent encounters with the state bureaucracy, the citizen's relations with the political party are becoming more intermittent and of more limited scope.

To the older party of integration the citizen, if he so desired, could be closer. Then it was a less differentiated organization, part channel of protest, part source of protection, part purveyor of visions of the future. Now, in its linear descendant in a transfigured world, the catch-all party, the citizen finds a relatively remote, at times quasi-official and alien structure. Democratic society assumes that the citizen is finally an integral and conscious participant in the affairs of both the polity and the economy; it further assumes that as such he will work through the party as one of the many interrelated structures by which he achieves a rational participation in his surrounding world.

Should he ever live up to these assumptions, the individual and society may indeed find the catch-all party—non-utopian, non-oppressive, and ever so flexible—an ingenious and useful political instrument.

What about the attitude toward the modern catch-all party of functional powerholders in army, bureaucracy, industry, and labor? Released from their previous unnecessary fears as to the ideological propensities and future intentions of the class-mass party, functional powerholders have come to recognize the catch-all party's role as consensus purveyor. In exchange for its ability to provide a clear-cut basis of legitimacy, functional powerholders are, up to a point, willing to recognize the political leadership claims of the party. They expect it to exercise certain arbitration functions in intergroup relations and to initiate limited political innovations. The less clear-cut electoral basis of the party's leadership claim and the closer the next election date, the smaller the credit which functional powerholders will extend to unsolicited and non-routine activities of the political powerholders impinging on their own positions. This lack of credit then sets the stage for conflicts between functional and political leadership groups. How does the catch-all party in governmental positions treat such conflicts? Will it be satisfied to exercise pressure via the mass media, or will it try to re-create a militant mass basis beyond the evanescent electoral and publicity levels? But the very structure of the catch-all party, the looseness of its clientele, may from the outset exclude such more far-reaching action. To that extent the political party's role in Western industrial society today is more limited than would appear from its position of formal preeminence. Via its governmental role it functions as coordinator of and arbitrator between functional power groups. Via its electoral role it produces that limited amount of popular participation and integration required from the popular masses for the functioning of official political institutions.

Will this limited participation which the catch-all party offers the population at large, this call to rational and dispassionate participation in the political process via officially sanctioned channels, work?

The instrument, the catch-all party, cannot be much more rational than its nominal master, the individual voter. No longer subject to the discipline of the party of integration—or, as in the United States, never subject to this discipline—the voters may, by their shifting moods and their apathy, transform the sensitive instrument of the catch-all party into something too blunt to serve as a link with the functional powerholders of society. Then we may yet come to regret the passing—even if it was inevitable—of the class-mass party and the denominational party, as we already regret the passing of other features in yesterday's stage of Western civilization.

FOOTNOTES

1.   Integration into industrial society: while the worker has accepted some aspects, such as urbanization and the need for regularity and the corresponding advantages of a mass consumer society, powerlessness as an individual and the eternal dependence on directives by superiors make for strong escapist attitudes. The problems are discussed in detail in André Andrieux and Jean Lignon, *L'Ouvrier d'aujourd'hui*, Paris, 1960. The ambiguous consequences to be drawn from these facts and their largely negative impact on the political image of the workers are studied in detail in H. Popitz, *et al.*, *Das Gesellschaftsbild des Arbeiters*, Tuebingen, 1957.

2.   Liberal parties without sharply profiled program or clientele may, however, make such conversion attempts. Val Lorwin draws my attention to the excellent example of a former bourgeois party, the Belgian Liberal party, which became in 1961 the "Party of Liberty and Progress," deemphasizing anticlericalism and appealing to the right wing of the Social Christian party, worried about this party's governmental alliance with the Socialists.

12

PETER H. MERKL

Party Government
in the Bonn Republic

A comparison of parliamentary government in Great Britain and
France directs attention to the pivotal role of political parties
and of the party system in the various types of executive-legislative
relations. German parliamentary government is no exception to
this rule. No other verbal formula, perhaps, can express the different
attitudes toward the penetration of representative institutions by
political parties as succinctly as the contrast between the English
term "party government" and the German "party state" (*Parteienstaat*).
Both concepts denote a modern democratic state with political
parties in the Government and the Opposition. To English and
American ears, "party government" is an ideal political system in
which parliamentary government merges with a system of stable,
moderate parties which take turns at governing and criticizing
governmental policies so that the voter can make an effective
choice between alternative sets of leaders and policies. Responsible
party government has been the model for most of the older nations
of the British Commonwealth and has preoccupied American political
scientists since the days of Woodrow Wilson.

Reprinted from Peter H. Merkl, "Party Government in the Bonn
Republic," in *Lawmakers in a Changing World*, Elke Frank, ed.,
© 1966, by permission of Prentice-Hall, Inc., Englewood Cliffs,
New Jersey. Some footnotes omitted by the editors.

On the other hand, the term "party state" of German constitutional jurisprudence, from its earliest use in the days of the Weimar Republic, mirrored the misgivings of many Germans about the unfamiliar ways of parliamentary democracy. To begin with, the term lacked the well defined character of the English "party government." It set no limits to the number or character of the parties included. Parties hostile to democracy and to the parliamentary system were just as much considered a part of the "party state" as the parties loyal to the system. Neither did it set forth any rules of the political game or establish such roles as Government and Opposition with any precision. But there was no mistaking the note of suspicion in the term "party state"—the distrust in the parliamentary figures and party politicians who were inheriting power from the *Kaiser,* the aristocrats, and the trusted bureaucracy of the old regime. In the phrase "party state" one can also discern the distaste of many Weimar Germans for the bargaining and what they considered the disorderly haggling among the parties. Even the terms party or partisan interest were contrasted unfavorably with the public interest or the common good by most of the literature of that period. Being partisan meant being selfish, or placing the interest of a partial group above those of the whole community.

The party state of Weimar parliamentary democracy finally succumbed to the impact of the Great Depression and to the rising Hitler movement. Today, more than forty years after the birth of the Weimar Republic, Western Germany in many ways approaches British style "party government." Looking back at the decades of crisis and transition, it may be well to reflect on the difference between executive-legislative relations in the "party state" and in "responsible party government." Why was it so difficult for the Weimar Republic to achieve this latter system? Just what makes the Bonn system a closer approximation of party government than the Weimar Republic could ever have hoped to have been?

THE FAILURE OF THE WEIMAR PARTY STATE

Regarding the setting for British-style party government in the Weimar Republic of Germany, there are many unfavorable circumstances to account for. First of all, there had not even been a national German parliament until 1871. By the end of World War I, this Parliament, the *Reichstag,* had as yet acquired very little control of the executive branch. In particular, the *Reich* chancellor and his cabinet were not responsible to the *Reichstag* but only to the monarch until a few weeks before military defeat and the revolution pulled down the whole monarchic edifice of Imperial Germany. The political parties of the Imperial *Reichstag,* consequently, viewed themselves primarily as instruments of the representation of the people against a government they could not control.

Each *Reichstag* party and every deputy considered himself the spokesman of a particular electoral district or a clearly defined group of German society. It was his function to stand up for the interests of those he represented: to protest, to oppose, even to propose, but not to govern. This notion was not at variance with nineteenth-century liberal views of representation, or of state and society. Governmental responsibility was thus left to the *Kaiser* and his chancellors and ministers, who were generally men without a parliamentary or partisan profile of their own.

With the downfall of autocracy and the advent of the Weimar Republic, the political leaders were well aware of the fact that under the new parliamentary constitution they were supposed to take on governmental responsibility. Yet old habits die a slow death, and there were many circumstances that conspired to perpetuate the oppositional attitudes of the past.

The framers of the Weimar Constitution were evidently plagued by considerable doubts about the wisdom of turning over a monopoly of decision-making power to the parliamentary executive, chancellor and cabinet, and by implication to the parties supporting them in the *Reichstag*. Instead of centering the chief policy-making power in a British-style cabinet, therefore, they divided it between the parliamentary executive and a strong *Reich* president. Popularly elected to a term of seven years, the *Reich* president represented the new sovereign—the people—as the *Kaiser* had represented the old sovereign—the monarchy. The *Reich* president thus could actually point to a more popular mandate than the *Reich* chancellor and his cabinet. The framers of the Constitution naïvely assumed that the identity of the electorate of both *Reichstag* and president would make dualism or conflict between the two executives unlikely. They also expected the spheres of executive power to remain separated neatly, since the *Reich* president was to appoint chancellor and cabinet for the making of governmental policy, and then to keep in the background until a state of emergency would require his intervention. Little did the framers of the Constitution expect that the use of the ill-defined presidential emergency powers would be so frequent and indiscriminate as to determine the character and fate of the Republic. What had been designed as an executive "emergency brake" on the wagon of the party state turned out to be more important than the steering wheel.

The lesson of distrust in the ability of the *Reichstag* parties to exercise governmental responsibility was not lost on the party leaders who frequently preferred to remain outside the Government, even though their parties might support it. Their own diffidence often manifested itself also in selecting nonpartisan experts for ministerial posts. The Weimar Constitution showed its suspicion of parties also with its recurring use of the popular referendum and the initiative which enable the voter to take direct action over the heads of their elected *Reichstag* deputies. Thus, the temptation was great for the parties to leave weighty and unpopular decisions to the *Reich* president or to the electorate itself.

A Fragmented Party System

If, on the one hand, the executive-legislative relations evolved by the Weimar Republic discouraged the parties from taking on governmental responsibility, on the other hand, they spared no effort to facilitate the task of opposition and obstruction from many sides. By questions and interpellations which called cabinet ministers on the carpet, and by unprecedented parliamentary investigations of the once sacrosanct executive branch, the *Reichstag* could make the most of its power to harass the Government. Several significant groups in the *Reichstag* used all means to oppose and obstruct not only the Government of the day, but parliamentary democracy itself. The economic and political crises of the Weimar Republic likewise made it far more attractive for a party to remain in opposition, or at least to avoid being blamed for circumstances beyond its political control, by avoiding governmental responsibility.

The rampant proliferation and particularistic character of German parties comprised another major factor in propagating older attitudes. Right at the end of the war, to be sure, many party leaders thought of merging several smaller parties into one in an effort to build a broader political base. A number of traditional party names were changed so as to end with "people's party" (*Volkspartei*) to denote the quest for a mass following from many layers of society. Throughout the Weimar years, the different parties in the *Reichstag* strove to develop their own trade unions, farm organizations, and veterans' organizations in order to strike broader roots in many parts of German society.

Despite these efforts, the number of parties condemned each one to a permanent minority status. Too many parties were competing with each other, as the following brief glance at the political spectrum will illustrate. Starting from the left wing, there were the Communists (KPD), the Social Democrats (SPD), and, for a while, two further Socialist groups. Next came the Catholic Center Party (Z) whose Bavarian branch (BVP) insisted on maintaining a separate party. The two Liberal parties (DDP and DVP), and at times several smaller middle-class groups, represented a variety of economic interests. Finally, the German Nationalists (DNVP) and smaller conservative groups shared the spotlight on the right with numerous tiny right-wing extremist parties from among whom the National Socialist Movement (NSDAP) of Hitler rose in a great landslide in the last years of the Weimar Republic.

At one time, close to forty distinct parties competed in the national elections. Even the largest of them generally received no more than 15 to 20 per cent of the popular vote, and only on rare occasions as much as 30 per cent. Such a permanent minority status at times of crisis, when successive governing coalitions invariably got blamed for economic breakdowns and political emergencies beyond their control, was very unlikely to encourage the taking on of a stance of governmental responsibility. Only a party with a popular majority or within reach of winning a majority can fully know what governmental responsibility means, through years of crisis or of triumph, for better or for worse. A permanent minority is naturally inclined to regard the larger questions of statesmanship with the myopic eyes of particularistic selfishness. Even for stalwart friends of the embattled Republic it seemed much safer to ride out the years of crisis in the opposition, or by merely tolerating rather than participating in the Government in office.

The Problem of Missing Consensus

Responsible party government was frustrated also by the obvious lack of consensus on the fundamentals and procedures of government. The Communists on the extreme left and the so-called "folkish" groups on the extreme right were plotting for the violent overthrow of the Republic. At times, the sizable groups of the Independent Socialists on the left and the conservative German Nationalists on the right definitely favored forms of government other than the parliamentary democracy of Weimar. The original three-party coalition of Weimar—the Social Democrats, the Center Party, and the Democrats—which wrote the Weimar Constitution and constituted the first provisional government after the war, lost their popularity in the first *Reichstag* elections, and regained it only sporadically.

In the declining years of Weimar, a new tide of popular disaffection with parliamentary democracy rose at the same time that emergency decrees and cabinets without parliamentary support signified the abandonment of the basic executive-legislative ground rules of the political system. The assertion of presidential emergency powers was taken even by the moderate parties of the Republic as a sign that they did not really have to take on governmental responsibility while the *Reich* president was taking charge. In 1932 a clear majority of German voters actually turned out to vote for the totalitarian parties of Communism and National Socialism in a pointed protest against the failure of the "party state" to steer the country through the mounting economic crisis of the Great Depression.

While the masses thus cried out for an authoritarian replacement of the bankrupt "party state," ironically enough, Weimar constitutional lawyers were still debating whether parties really fitted into a system of true representative government. They seriously discussed the relative merits of such alternatives to party government as corporatism, or the authoritarian, or administrative state. The parliamentary parties indeed had never quite become the depositories of governmental responsibility in the First German Republic. The Constitution attempted to deny them the right to impose party discipline on the individual deputy. The extraparliamentary parties and even the organized interests constantly interfered with the parties' autonomy. Even in such fields as labor legislation or foreign policy, where notable decisions and legislative enactments were made in the 1920s, it was generally not a particular party or coalition of parties that was responsible for the achievements, but more often *ad hoc* blocs made up of interested segments of several major parties. Considering the fact that well organized interests and lobbies had frequently broken up the existing major parties along functional lines behind the scenes, toying with schemes of corporate representation as an alternative to the party state was not as absurd as it may seem today.

All of these facts and considerations played a significant role in the thinking of party leaders after 1945, and especially in the deliberations of the framers of the Bonn Constitution. There was a widespread conviction that the system of executive-legislative relations under the Weimar Republic had been a failure, although it was not entirely clear what particular aspect of it had been at fault. Of the seventeen coalition governments with legislative majority support or its equivalent in the years from 1919 to 1932, three had fallen on a question of confidence, one upon the dissolution of the *Reichstag,* three after an election, another four because of foreign policy crises or internal revolt, and no less than six cabinets fell because of internal convulsions or instability in one of their coalition parties. Were the parties to blame or was it the institutional design? To supply a background for an understanding of the present development, the dilemmas raised by the crises of the Weimar Republic have to be compared with the details of the design decided upon at Bonn. By the same token, only a thorough analysis of what caused the "party state" of Weimar to fail can open up insights into what is stable and enduring about party government in the Bonn Republic.

THE WEST GERMAN PARTY SYSTEM

Following World War II, no other factor was as important to the eventual development in the direction of responsible party government in the Bonn Republic as the actual changes in the party system. The difference is particularly obvious in the number, the size, and the character of the parties represented in the West German *Bundestag,* the Parliament of the Federal Republic of Germany. In fact, the entire system of social, cultural, and economic cleavages that used to supply the particularistic divisions among the Weimar parties has undergone extensive changes.

From Multiparty System to Two-Party Government

The returns of the state and local elections of the early postwar period gave every indication that the Weimar multiparty system would be revived.

The first *Bundestag* of 1949-53 still consisted of representatives of nine parties, including the Communists (KPD), the regional Bavaria Party (BP), the conservative German Party (BP), the Economic Reconstruction Party (WAV), the revived Center Party (Z), and refugee representatives who later joined the Refugee Bloc (BHE), as well as the three largest parties, the Christian Democrats (CDU/CSU), the Social Democrats (SPD) and the Free Democrats (FDP). Decimated from election to election by restrictive electoral laws and by the successful drive of Adenauer's Christian Democrats for an electoral majority, the number of parties shrank to the last named three by 1961.

Of these three parties, the Christian Democrats (CDU/CSU), Social Democrats (SPD) and Free Democrats (FDP), the first two have each demonstrated a definite capacity to win a majority of the popular vote. Their combined total of the vote has grown from about 60 per cent to over 90 per cent. It therefore seems appropriate to speak of a two-party system in West Germany at the present time, even though there is still a third party, the FDP. Not unlike the British Liberal Party, which has survived in spite of the two-party system, the German FDP is clearly a minor party with little growth potential. In fact, it may well fall victim someday to the clause in the West German electoral law which denies representation to parties polling less than 5 per cent of the vote. It is also conceivable that the two major parties may change the prevailing electoral law in order to deprive the FDP of what they consider its undeserved key position.

Contemporary Party Orientation

The West German parties of today also differ from their Weimar predecessors in their basic character. The futile attempts of 1919 to transform many of the particularistic, hidebound parties of old into broadly based "people's parties" have wrought fundamental changes in the two major parties after 1945.

The CDU/CSU was built on the basis of the old Weimar and pre-Weimar Center Party which already had succeeded in recruiting its members and voters from all different social classes in the midst of the prevailing system of class parties. There had been one severe limitation, however, which had kept the Center Party imprisoned in a tower of exclusiveness in spite of all its efforts at becoming a Christian People's Party in 1919: the Party was limited to the Catholic minority, for one of the chief reasons for its rise had been the discrimination against Catholics under Bismarck. This limitation kept the Party from ever polling more than about 20 per cent of the nationwide popular vote throughout the Weimar Republic. The Christian Democrats of 1945, on the other hand, made a determined and by and large successful effort to attract Protestants as well as Catholics which soon resulted in a share of the popular vote of 30 per cent and more.

When Adenauer's determined drive for a majority of *Bundestag* seats was successful in 1953 and 1957, it not only made the CDU/CSU the first German party to get a majority of the popular vote, but also rallied a body of voters so evenly distributed over the main social groupings of German society, including the blue-collar workers, as to approximate a cross section of the electorate.[1] Only a few groups, such as farmers, women, and Catholics, are still rather disproportionately represented among the CDU/CSU voters.

The Social Democrats took longer to shake off the rigidity of their old Marxist orientation and restriction to labor votes. But in recent years they also have come around to a determined attack on their sources of electoral weakness. Their Bad Godesberg Program of 1959, in particular, was a landmark in the effort to change the public image of the party to that of a broad "people's party." Since 1959 the new emphasis on selecting attractive candidates and on wooing rural voters and even members of the Catholic church have confirmed the significance of the Bad Godesberg Program as a reformation. The electoral success of the party, long confined within the "magical 30 per cent barrier," has demonstrated with nearly 40 per cent in the 1965 elections that this second major party of the Bonn Republic is well on its way to contesting the headstart of the CDU/CSU.

The third party, the FDP, is the only one that has not followed the trend toward becoming a broadly based "people's party." It is still in many respects a liberal "party of representation" of the old style, a party made up of individual-istic notables who are as reluctant to become involved in matters of party bureaucracy and organization as they are to accept party discipline in the *Bundestag* or the state diets. The FDP was in virtual eclipse during the years 1953-1961 when the governing CDU/CSU majority made the cooperation of the FDP superfluous. Since 1961, however, the party has enjoyed the accidental advantage of being the balance between the two almost evenly matched major parties. In the government coalition since 1961, the FDP was repeatedly able to get its way on various issues in spite of the embittered resistance of its coalition partner, the CDU/CSU, which has four times as many deputies in the *Bundestag*.

Along with the number and character of the more important parties, it should be emphasized that the basic nature of the social and political cleavages typical of the Imperial and Weimar years has changed. The most important cleavage before the rise of Hitler was the class antagonism between bourgeoisie and proletariat. This cleavage defined the confrontation of labor and manage-ment. It also defined the embattled position of bourgeois parliamentary democracy, bourgeois civilization, bourgeois morality, and bourgeois family life. There were legions of militants who regarded themselves proudly as the "vanguard of the proletariat" and further millions of veterans, including the extreme right wing, who were clamoring for the day when the bourgeois civilization would disappear along with white shirt collars, neckties, and the institution of bourgeois marriage. Today even the symbols of this belligerent confrontation of three decades ago seem to have lost their significance in the public mind. In public opinion polls, it has turned out, nobody wants to call himself a "proletarian" any more. The word that once defined class antagonism is now considered quite negatively, or as a synonym of vulgarity. Its opposite term of reference, "bourgeois," is similarly hazy, though vaguely positive, in meaning. A majority of respondents in public polls who identified themselves as regular SPD voters, for example, call their party bourgeois.

The voting habits of the different socio-economic groups today show the extent to which the old lines of social cleavage have been obliterated. German blue-collar workers turn out to vote for the CDU almost as heavily as for the SPD. White-collar voters and public employees also split their allegiance between the two major parties. If it were not for the needs of a part of the remaining fraction of the German electorate, one might say that a two-party system would be quite sufficient for West German society. The remaining part of society—farmers, businessmen, and professional people—divide their votes between the CDU/CSU, the FDP, and a number of small, regional, and generally right-wing groups which are no longer represented in the *Bundestag.*

As German sociologists have pointed out, the new basic political alignment in West German society owes much to fundamental structural changes that have occurred since the 1920s. The destruction of the landed nobility east of the Elbe River and the old aristocratic ruling class in general has left ample room for the rise of new elites, a motley group of business tycoons, politicians, movie stars, professors, judges, and so forth. The new social elites are not very conscious of their status, but firmly committed to parliamentary democracy. The arrival of mass consumption has also dissolved some of the older patterns of group collectivism and made the average German rather individualistic, intent upon personal success and material possessions, and pragmatic rather than idealistic—or ideological. It is small wonder, then, that the age of ideological commitment and fanaticism in Western Germany has given way to a more distant, general identification with a particular party because of its candidates, its general image, or specific bread-and-butter issues.

The programmatic differences between the major parties also bear out this thesis. In subjects as loaded with heated controversy as foreign policy and defense, the two major parties today are substantially in agreement. What little dissension is left, such as between the "Gaullists" and "Atlanticists," or on relations with Eastern Europe, generally does not separate the major parties, but may create opposing factions within each of them. The economic and social policies of CDU/CSU and SPD, while differing somewhat in matters of emphasis and degree, are also so close as to be in substantial agreement. The Socialist plans for the nationalization of basic industries, for example, were abandoned as early as 1952, and their commitment to free enterprise and competition has never been in doubt since then. There is very little apprehension among German businessmen today about the consequences of a possible Social Democratic election victory.

What the SPD seems to be saying in effect with every election is that it can do anything and will do anything the voters have found attractive about the CDU/CSU; and, in fact, the SPD will do it better. Real dissension between the parties seems to have been transferred to program details and peripheral issues.

FOOTNOTES

1.   In the 1961 elections, for example, approximately 20 per cent of the CDU/CSU voters were drawn from unskilled labor, about 33 per cent from skilled labor and lower white-collar groups, about 33 per cent from the middle layer, and another 14 per cent from upper-middle and upper classes of West German society. SPD voters were composed of 20 per cent unskilled workingmen, 55 per cent skilled and white-collar workers, 22 per cent middle layer and 3 per cent upper-middle and upper class.

voluntary association into disciplined and deployable political agents," and its "adoption of subversion" and "penetration and manipulation of institutional targets." While the model is most relevant in societies in which Communist doctrine is remote and unappealing to the population, Selznick, like Duverger, holds that it "provides a fair interpretation of the Communist vanguard or combat party, wherever it is found."

Each of these approaches extrapolates a marxist party model out of a single political setting—the West before 1950—and a single party strategy—the Leninist strategy of *What is to be Done?* Neither writer considers the elementary marxian proposition that both party strategy and political setting can vary greatly, and that a model of a marxist party can emerge only from the interaction of the two. This article is an attempt to elaborate this proposition in one rich empirical setting: Italy, and particularly southern Italy, where the Italian Communist Party (PCI) is very different from the party of devotion and combat envisaged by Duverger and Selznick. I hope to show (1) that the party's role differs sharply between advanced, industrial North and backward, traditional South; (2) that these variations can be ascribed both to Italy's dualistic political setting and to party strategy; and (3) that these two variables—political setting and party strategy—are the key to understanding marxist parties wherever they are found.

THE ITALIAN COMMUNIST PARTY

When we turn to the Italian Communist Party, we find most students close to the Selznick-Duverger view. For example, in his paper "European Political Parties: The Case of Polarized Pluralism," Giovanni Sartori shares Selznick's emphasis on the party's capacity to withdraw members from other group loyalties ("the ability of the party's organizational network to produce a culturally manipulated isolation of given social groups in given areas") and his concern with the dual nature of Communist organization—a party of elite with mass following. He also shares Duverger's emphasis upon organization but implicitly recognizes the weakness of the cells ("the organizational incapsulation and cultural saturation that a Communist *network* is capable of producing"). And while both Selznick and Duverger concentrate upon the subversive aspects of Communist activity, Sartori concludes that the PCI is outside the system altogether. He writes, "We thus come to the uncomfortable paradox that the Communist party would make for an excellent opposition if it were an opposition, i.e., a possible alternative government. But since it would replace the *system* as well as the people, the net result is that the country is deprived of its best potential elites. . . . "

While no one would deny the Italian Communist Party's opposition to the present Italian regime, we gain nothing by substituting the scientific word "system" for the less inclusive term "regime." Secondly, Sartori overstresses the disruptive effect of the PCI. In a series of manipulative hypotheses, he maintains that "an extreme centrifugal development is very likely wherever the political system accepts not only as legal but also as a legitimate and somewhat equal and normal competitor a party . . . which opposes the very system, such as a Communist Party." He adds that "Such a centrifugal development will not necessarily follow . . . if the existence of anti-system parties is legally prohibited."

Apart from the fact that these "hypotheses," if realized, would not make for a very democratic theory, are we justified in concluding that the PCI is a devotee party and an anti-system party simply because it is the PCI? I would argue that, so contrary is the evidence and so rare the historical examples of flourishing parties of the type Duverger and Selznick describe, the burden of proof is on the other side.

What is the PCI like in very general terms? Under the guidance of Togliatti and Longo its strategy since 1944 has been a broad national one, rather than the strategy of proletarian revolution and hegemony developed by Togliatti's predecessor, Antonio Gramsci. Returning from Moscow in 1944, Togliatti said "We are the party of the working class; but the working class has never been foreign to the nation," thereby launching what has come to be called the *Via Italiana al Socialismo*. Its general characteristics are: (1) constructive participation in parliament and in elections and local government; (2) a strategy of alliances which has at the same time emphasized the party's proximity to the Socialists, "sincere democrats" and the progressive wing of the Christian Democratic Party; (3) an ideology of "reform of structure" as the preferred means of constructing socialism in Italy; and (4) activity in local government, cooperative associations and stores, which both develops an efficient class of PCI administrators and ties the economic interests of large numbers of people to the party.

Three general points should be made about the *Via Italiana al Socialismo*. First, it was developed by Togliatti as a strategic response to a particular political setting: a modern, industrial society which had been torn by twenty-two years of reactionary extremism. It was possible to interpret the party line in merely tactical terms in 1944 when the presence of Allied troops made revolution impossible, but the party's revisionism has, if anything, increased between that time and the present.

Second, it is not clear that there is anything about the PCI which would justify its classification as an anti-system party or a centrifugal force. I would argue that the symbiotic stability of the Italian political system (which is often confused with the instability of the French Fourth Republic) depends precisely upon the existence of a Communist Party like the PCI. Its broad, popular strategy and stress upon reform have both prevented the formation of radical leftist groups and forced a conservative government upon a path of reform that it would have avoided if left to its own devices.

Third, and most important, it is impossible to talk reformism for twenty years and then carry off a revolution. What we see in the PCI is something we may tentatively call the institutionalization of strategy. The communication of its militants, its image among the population and the structure of loyalties at the local level have been conditioned by the party's strategy over the last two decades. Once a commitment to vote-getting is made, a political party, marxist or otherwise, routinizes certain roles and behaviors and endows them with legitimacy. Were these roles and behaviors to suddenly shift, a complicated structure of loyalties based upon personal and group interest, and not upon the devotion of militants, would come tumbling down.

The party's strategy has had an impact upon its membership, its organization, its behavior and its internal unity. First of all, the typical party member is not a dedicated militant whose entire life is devoted to party work. Interviews and questionnaires carried out with PCI federal secretaries in 1964 showed that only 10 to 15 per cent of party members are full-time activists. Moreover, the number of party members has decreased sharply since 1956 and the ratio of members to voters has changed from one member for every three voters in 1956 to one member for every 4.8 voters in 1963. Finally, the ideological preparedness of even the most militant party cadres is very weak. In 1962, a party report concluded that "the problem of launching an elementary activity of ideological education in the party on a wide scale remains an urgent one."

Second, the classical unit of disciplined party activity—the cell—has been progressively weakened in the post-war years, while the party section has become more prominent. The shift is not coincidental; the *Via Italiana* is geared more closely to the loose, horizontally-linked party sections than to the narrow, vertically-linked cells. Between 1950 and 1963, the number of PCI cells decreased from 54,000 to 33,000 while party sections increased from 10,200 in 1951 to 11,000 in 1961. Factory cells have become less important in contrast to the more heterogeneous neighborhood cells and sections.

Third, the PCI pays *primary* attention to parliamentary and electoral activity and has not been observed to dedicate itself to conspiratorial activities more than any other Italian party in the rather Byzantine Italian Party system. The increased importance of the party section is related to this emphasis, for the traditional cell structure is useless in winning elections, while the section functions as a typical party club. In the trade-union field, the party-dominated Confederazione Generale Italiano del Lavoro (CGIL) now shuns the political strike weapon and concentrates upon bread-and-butter union issues. The infiltration of non-Communist organizations, which Selznick postulates as an essential element of combat party strategy, is nowhere evident in Italy, despite the party's substantial popularity.

While the PCI is by far the most disciplined party group in Parliament, its voting patterns in secret parliamentary committees are far less rigid. A research group at Bologna recently estimated that PCI parliamentary committee members vote with the government on a large majority of committee votes. This high level of compromise voting was maintained even during periods of maximum intransigence in the Chamber.

The party administers over eighty communes in the central provinces of the country—the so-called "Red Belt." These local units perform all the typical functions of local government and maintain majorities which depend upon the satisfaction of concrete personal and group interests. The party administers a whole range of profit-making cooperatives which are essential to relations with workers and peasants. Major dislocations would occur in the economic life of thousands should the PCI suddenly turn to revolutionary strategy. Despite the possible tactical origin of its pattern of participation in Italian politics, the institutionalization of these tactics transforms them into commitments.

Several attitude studies have suggested that Communist leaders and followers have developed political attitudes which correspond to the party's broad strategy. A study of Italian parliamentarians carried out in 1963 revealed that Communist deputies scored lower on the Rokeach dogmatism scale than Christian Democrats. Further evidence was provided by a CISER public opinion survey in the same year which demonstrated, first, that PCI supporters reflect the reformist doctrinal line of the party and, second, that certain key divergencies may be seen within the sample with regard to their presumed support for the PCI in a hypothetical two-party system; for example, only 60 per cent of the sample would choose the PCI in a bipolar choice between their own party and the Socialists! Third, Almond and Verba have pointed out that supporters of the left are more likely to be "open partisans" than supporters of the right. They write, "Opposed to the Constitution is a left wing which, at least in part and at the rank-and-file voter level rather than among the party elite, manifests a form of open partisanship that is consistent with a democratic system."

In other words, the following of the PCI is far more pluralistic than has been generally acknowledged. The same appears to be true of the leaders, if the factional strife currently raging in the party is any indication. The right, led by Giorgio Amendola, would go further than Togliatti in examining the crimes of Stalin, in condemning the Chinese and in adapting the PCI to a reformist strategy. The left, on the other hand, returns ideologically to Gramsei's emphasis upon the factory and the trade unions, but seeks more internal democracy in the party and wants to empower the party Congress to make theoretical decisions in place of the bureaucratic Central Committee.

Two facts are indicative of the relationship of the two factions to the PCI's *Via Italiana al Socialismo*. First, the left is neither the old sectarian Stalinist left, nor, as is sometimes imagined, a pro-Chinese group. It arose out of the crisis generated by the anti-Stalin campaign and the Hungarian Revolution and does not criticize the fundamentals of the *Via Italiana*. Second, the new left arose in part with a basis of support in the Communist Youth Movement (FGCI), in whose publication, *Nuova Generazione*, they found an excellent forum, and in the trade unions, whose late leader, Giuseppe de Vittorio, was fond of telling Togliatti that the labor movement is *not* the transmission belt of the party. In other words, the internal diversification of a party which takes up the tasks of day-to-day operation in a parliamentary system encourages the development of internal differences which, if not themselves democratic, are at least competitive.

But the internal differentiation of the PCI is not merely ideological; it is structural and behavioral as well. The *Via Italiana* strategy opens the way to a variety of influences from the political setting. The most important such influence is the dualistic nature of the Italian political system itself. If the analysis up to this point has indicated that the PCI is not a devotee or combat party, it is only an analysis of what happens to the *Via Italiana* strategy in its two political settings which can suggest what the party *is*.

THE CONTEXT: THE TWO ITALIES

"Italy," Joseph LaPalombara writes, "represents two distinct cultures, the relatively dynamic and industrial North and the relatively stagnant South." The disparity between the regions is not merely one of degree; it is a structural cleavage, observed by generations of statesmen and intellectuals, extending into the economic, social and political systems and presenting concrete obstacles to political integration. While exhaustive analysis of Italian dualism is impossible in this context, several basic indicators may suggest the breadth of the economic, social and political gap between North and South.

Economically, Italy has long been a "dual economy," with a dual labor market and a dual structure of industry. The North is industrial, the South agricultural: out of fifty-eight northern provinces, thirty-five have more than half of the working population in non-agricultural activities, while in the South only four provinces out of thirty-two have more than 50 per cent of the active population outside agriculture. In the industrial sector, most southern workers (500,000 in 1951) work in the small-scale traditional sector, while only 200,000 are employed in the large-scale modern sector. In agriculture, the stable and productive commercial and family farms of the North contrast sharply with the unstable tenancies and *latifundia* of the South.

Socially, we find a rather mobile highly organized society in the North and a fragmented developing society in the South. Briefly, what the latter term designates is a social structure which has lost the functional coherence of tradition and has not yet achieved a modern organization of social roles. Historically, we can trace the emergence of modern social organization in the North to the typical western processes of commercialization and industrialization; commercialization set up a marketing and credit network while industrialization re-shaped social stratification through the discipline of the factory process.[1]

The South, in contrast, remains a fragmented developing society because commercialization, caused by the influx of northern goods after national unification in 1861, was not accompanied by industrialization; traditional social roles were undermined by commercialization, but in the absence of industrialization, they remained transitional and disorganized. Without industry, the attention of all major social groups focused upon the land, with results that soon became pathological. The middle class, urban, aggressive and entrepreneurial in the North, was unproductive, provincial and land-oriented in the South. The family retains an importance in socialization and economic allocation in the South far greater than its equivalent in the North; in a society in which modern forms of social organization have failed to crystallize, the family is a solidarity unit of almost pathological consistency.

If we search for indicators of the South as a fragmented developing society, we can find them in the atomization of business enterprise and in the network of unstable and transitional roles in agriculture. The average industrial firm in the South employs 2.4 workers, as opposed to 7.5 workers in the North; only 13 per cent of southern firms have joint-stock ownership, as compared to 46 per cent in the North; and twice as many southerners (27.3 per cent) working in industry are owners and directors than in the North (12.8 per cent), suggesting the dominance of the family enterprise over modern forms of business.

In agriculture, the situation is still more symptomatic. Until the agrarian reform of 1951, much of the land was operated by small renters, share tenants and day laborers on plots with no farmhouse or equipment. These marginal operating units are not "farms" in any significant sense of the word, nor are they commercial operations. Many peasants shift from one occupational role to another, while others (figure miste) hold several occupational roles at once.[2] The fragmentation of contractual ties between owners and peasants prevents the formation of horizontal secondary organization, inhibiting both economic development and political aggregation.

In the political system, the fragmented nature of southern Italian society has critical effects. Politics in the North have long been organized according to typical western patterns, with groups and parties growing out of the broad functional and class groupings of an industrial society. In the South, in contrast, a formal representative system disguised what amounted to a massive system of clienteles. Clientelismo grew out of the narrow vertical ties of a fragmented agricultural system. Organized by the liberal middle class of the provinces, which held a strategic role in landholding, it used the fulcrum of local government for patronage, and sent local notables to parliament to make up willing majorities for regional politicians. The ties between leader and follower are highly personal; an American research group found that in seventy-six towns of the South where the vote had shifted greatly,

. . . the voters were motivated by strictly local and personal issues, that ideology and national issues played little part in determining their voting behavior, and that many shifts were simply the result of *clientelismo*, voters following a personal leader from one party to another.

Structurally, the clientele pattern means that broad functional interests are not readily represented in politics, where personal favors and patronage are dominant. The failures of the system are patent; one reaches the apex of authority not by merging one's demands in a horizontal membership group, but by linking up to a hierarchical chain of personal acquaintance which may begin in the network of neighborly relations and reaches up to the state bureaucracy with little adjustment in structure. The clientele chain soon grows too long for effective political allocation. It is this, and not a conspiracy by the industrialists of the North, which has made the South ineffective in the national political arena; faced by the well-organized interest groups of Milan, Turin and Genoa, southern clienteles are unable to bargain effectively since they can trade only in personal favors. The lack of political integration between the regions is not simply a matter of political culture, but is a *structural* factor; the clientele system is actually congruent with the South's fragmented social structure and resists or modifies the forms and techniques of a modern party system. Even a "monolithic" party like the PCI is profoundly affected by the dualism of the political system in Italy.

DUAL POLITY AND DUAL PARTY

Four dimensions are particularly interesting in comparing the PCI in northern and southern Italy: (a) the composition of the membership; (b) the party organization; (c) the leadership; and (d) its ideology.

(a) *Membership.* The membership of the PCI in northern Italy is concentrated in the medium and large-sized cities, while party membership in the South is dispersed in the countryside. Northern membership is consistent as well as concentrated: new members in the North composed less than six per cent of regional membership in 1961. In the South, in contrast, the party suffers from rapid turnover, with new members amounting to 13.9 per cent in 1961, during a period in which it was losing an average of 45,000 members a year.

The sharpest difference in the membership of the PCI in North and South stems directly from the different social composition of the two regions: a working class cadre is strong in the North and weak in the South, while the peasantry is the bulwark of the party in the South (with 42 per cent of the members) and much weaker in the North (30 per cent). A historical factor colors the composition of the PCI membership in the South: the absence of an important labor movement to provide the experience and the cadres for political activity today. In this reversal of historical roles, the Communist Party in southern Italy resembles many marxist parties in non-western nations. In northern Italy, the PCI profits from the long experience of labor organization in the region.[3]

Secondly, Communist Party membership in southern Italy differs radically in its composition from the northern wing of the party in the relative importance of intellectuals and students in its membership. While 25.8 per cent of the PCI's members live in the South, 40 per cent of the intellectuals registered in the party and 60 per cent of its student members are southerners. The importance of intellectuals in the South increases as we move up the hierarchy from ordinary members to active cadres. Figures released in 1954 indicate that over 30 per cent of the members of the party's federal committees in the South were students, technicians, intellectuals or other professionals, as compared to less than 18 per cent in the North.

Turning to youth in general, we find that 34 per cent of the members of the party's Federations of Young Communists of Italy (FGCI) are found in the South, 10 per cent higher than the region's share of total party membership. This factor perhaps reflects the deep frustration of youth in a developing society, where the symbols of affluence have recently become visible but the means of achieving them are not available. Women members of the party, in contrast, are concentrated in the North. Eighteen per cent of the party's female members live in the South as opposed to 82 per cent who live in the North. These figures reflect the traditional role of women in the South and their relative emancipation in the North.

Perhaps because of its largely peasant composition, PCI membership in the South is less closely related to electoral success than in the North. Relating the percentage of the population registered in the PCI to the party's share of the provincial vote, we find that membership rises rapidly with electoral success in the North, while it is almost unresponsive to the polls in the South. Party membership ranges from 0.3 per cent of the provincial population in the lowest voting province to 17.4 per cent in the highest province in the North, but from 1.7 per cent in the lowest province to 3.5 per cent in the highest voting province in the South. Moreover, the rise in party members bears an almost geometric relation to the vote in the North when the vote is above 30 per cent, suggesting that the Via Italiana in that setting is a successful organizational and electoral strategy. In the South, in contrast, at no point in the electoral curve does membership rise above 4 per cent of the population, even when the vote is as high as 37 per cent.

The paradox of the Via Italiana in southern Italy is that the PCI has as its largest membership bloc a group with the poorest organizational potential.

Table 1

PCI Federal Committees Professional Distribution by Regions, 1954*

		North	South	Italy
Workers	(N)	1323	402	1725
	(%)	44.9	30.8	40.6
Agricultural workers	(N)	120	92	211
	(%)	4.1	7.1	5.0
Peasants	(N)	245	114	359
	(%)	8.3	8.7	8.5
Artisans	(N)	134	78	212
	(%)	4.5	6.0	5.0
White Collar	(N)	452	143	595
	(%)	15.4	11.0	14.0
Professionals, students	(N)	506	392	898
and technicians	(%)	17.2	30.1	21.1
Housewives	(N)	60	52	112
	(%)	2.1	4.0	2.6
Others	(N)	104	30	134
	(%)	3.5	2.3	3.2
Total	(N)	2943	1303	4264
	(%)	100.0	100.0	100.0

Source: PCI, *Forza del Attivita del Partito* (Rome, 1954), p. 67.
*More recent figures on the professional composition of federal committees are not available.

Rather than a popular mass party based upon the organized support of the urban proletariat, the PCI has the membership outline of a poor peasant's party in a fragmented developing society, with an intellectual leadership group and a scattering of worker and middle class groups on either side. Not only is its major membership group dispersed and poorly organized; unlike the urban and rural proletariat of the North, it is a group whose social aspirations belong to a rearguard and not a vanguard. The effects of this conservative center of gravity in the PCI membership group in the South can be noted in the inertia of its programs, which still insist upon the need for an agrarian reform at a time when thousands of peasants want only to escape from the land to the cities.

(b) *The Party Structure.* In its network of party sections, cells and factory cells, clear differences within the PCI between North and South are directly linked to the socio-political structure of each region. Seventy per cent of its party sections, 68 per cent of its cells and 92 per cent of its factory cells are found in the North. In the large-scale industries of the major cities and the commercialized agriculture of the central provinces, these units operate with relative regularity and precision. Moreover, a panoply of secondary units—recreational groups, adult classes, and economic organizations—are articulated around the nucleus of the party cell and section. The relevance of these secondary organizations to the economic life of the worker creates the natural basis for the differentiation of program between party and mass organization—one of the bases of the Leninist party.

In the South, party organizations are less numerous and less articulated than in the North, and the differentiation of program between party and mass organization is far less clear. While 30 per cent of the party sections are in the South, only 11.4 per cent of its cells, and less than 8 per cent of its factory cells are found there. The decrease in articulation from level to level means that the PCI organizational pyramid is virtually inverted with respect to that of the North. In many places, there are more sections than cells, and the cells are far too large to permit their political use.

Secondly, the number of secondary and mass organizations surrounding the party cells and sections is far smaller than in the North. In the absence of these groups, the section is often the single manifestation of the party in the southern village. The party member goes there to meet his friends and gossip, to play cards and watch television. Surprisingly, 42 per cent of the PCI sections in this impoverished region have television sets, as opposed to only 16 per cent in the North. It is significant that the only PCI units in which the southern portion of the party carries its organizational weight are the *Circoli* of the Communist Youth Federation: 22.1 per cent of the national total are found in the region. Women's cells, on the other hand, are extremely underrepresented in the South, with 7.1 per cent of the national total. To one party leader, this results not only from the modesty of women in the region, but from resistance from PCI leaders. He writes, "Conceptions which assign to women a subaltern and a marginal role in society are not yet overcome by the PCI."

A third organizational characteristic of the PCI in southern Italy which contrasts sharply with the North is the lack of the strategic differentiation between the programs of the party and the policies of the mass organizations. Launched in the region in an organizational vacuum, the party was compelled to recruit many members spontaneously and to fulfill many of the functions which normally fall to labor and other mass secondary groups. A number of party front groups were formed, but these inevitably drew upon the same cadres, and "very often the Communist Party, the Socialist Party, the Chambers of Labor and the Cooperatives were nothing but different faces of a single popular movement." In some provinces, the membership of the party exceeds that of the unions and in others the reverse is true. The division seems to depend upon which group arrived first after Fascism. "One of the defects in our organization is that the party today pursues directly many of the activities which should be fulfilled by the secondary mass organizations."

Organizational difficulties are encountered by all militant political parties in their early phases, but the PCI in southern Italy appears to have been permanently affected by these problems. Why this should be so relates to the socio-political milieu of southern Italy. As a party document states: "Experience has shown the great difficulty in organizing the masses of the southern peasants and, above all, of grouping them in organizations by category, because of their indeterminate social character." This is particularly true in the backward areas of the region. As a Sardinian leader writes, "Every social category is fragmented in a guise which is difficult to locate. . . . More than twenty or thirty people in a village who are tied to a clear identity of interests cannot be found."

The Communist Party in southern Italy has developed a style of organization distinctly different from its style in northern Italy. A resolution of the Central Committee defines it: "A multiplicity of popular assemblies, of committees for the land and other democratic organizations of an elementary type are necessary to give a primary and simple form of organization to masses of the people who are not socially concentrated and homogeneous." This pattern of organization reached its apogee in the PCI-led movement for the occupation of the *latifundia* in 1950. Yet twenty years after the party began its activity in the South, its organizations still have an amorphous and fluctuating character.

(c) *Leaders and Leadership Roles.* As might be expected when dealing with political leadership in dualistic political settings, the backgrounds and career patterns of Communist leaders in northern and southern Italy differ sharply. Southern Italian Communist leaders are mainly middle- or upper-middle-class individuals with urban backgrounds. In the North, 48 per cent of the party's national level leadership are of lower- or lower-middle-class origin, while only 34 per cent of the southern leaders come from these groups. Eighteen per cent of the northern leaders are of middle-class status, compared to 28 per cent in the South; and 19 per cent of the northern leaders are of upper-middle or upper-class origin, compared to 32 per cent in the South.

Northern and southern leaders differ in the size of the city of their origin, too. Northern leaders parallel the distribution of the population of the North in the cities of their birth; 15 per cent come from villages up to 5,000 in population, 26 per cent are from towns of 5,000-20,000, 12 per cent are from cities from 20,000-100,000 and 36 per cent are from large cities of more than 100,000 population. Most southern national leaders were born in the large towns and the cities from 20,000-100,000 population (31 per cent in the former

Table 2

PCI National Leadership Social Status of Family, by Region

		Lower	Lower Middle	Middle & Upper Middle	Upper Class	Total
North	(203)	18.2%	41.4	26.1	10.8	100.0%
Center	(134)	16.8%	37.9	28.5	10.2	100.0%
South	(107)	13.1%	25.2	35.5	23.4	100.0%
Islands	(66)	7.6%	22.7	42.4	19.7	100.0%

Source: Istituto Carlo Cattaneo, unpublished data collected from PCI parliamentarians and national officers, 1964.

and 36 per cent in the latter) with only 11 per cent from the small villages and only 20 per cent from cities over 100,000 in population. This distribution of southern leaders is hardly in keeping with the preponderantly rural membership of the party in the region.

Additional data on the leadership were collected by the author in a series of questionnaires and interviews with party secretaries on the provincial level. Social origins on this level do not differ significantly between leaders in North and South, with lower-middle-class backgrounds predominant in each group. Educationally, however, marked contrasts are apparent; while provincial secretaries in the North are evenly divided between elementary or medium level education and secondary or college backgrounds, almost two-thirds of the southern leaders have graduated from high school or college, and little more than a third ended their education in elementary or high school; indeed, there is a chronic overabundance of intellectuals in the PCI in this backward region.

The geographic (and presumably social) mobility of the leaders differs between North and South, too. Forty-three per cent of the southern provincial leaders grew up in cities other than those of their birth, while 25 per cent of the northern leaders changed residence during the formative period of their youth. The northern leaders are characterized by greater career localism; 38 per cent hold positions in the cities and provinces of their childhood, 47 per cent work in a different city but in the same province, and 15 per cent hold a post outside the province of their childhood. In the South, half as many (19 per cent) work in the city and province of their childhood, 52 per cent hold posts in the same province but in different cities, and twice as many (29 per cent) have positions in entirely different provinces. Related to this factor is the greater breadth of experience of the southern leaders; 40 per cent have held positions in two or more provinces, while only 28 per cent of the northerners have worked in several provinces.

The southerner is a relative newcomer to politics. Turning again to the national leadership, we find that 58 per cent from the South are full-time professional politicians, as opposed to 67 per cent from the North. Half as many southern national leaders are the sons of Communist Party members, and very few have siblings, wives and children who are members of the party. On the provincial level once again we find that 53 per cent of the northern leaders entered the party from the Resistance movement, compared to 24 per cent in the South. The largest group of southern provincial leaders were recruited into politics while in college or during professional careers (28 per cent), or from the peasant or labor movement (36 per cent). In the North, in contrast, 11 per cent came from intellectual pursuits and 19 per cent joined the party from the labor movement.

The roles assumed by the leadership differ between North and South. Since fewer paid officials are available in the South, the provincial leaders in that region function more as generalists than in the highly-articulated federations of the North. Interview and questionnaire responses indicate that 45 per cent of the southern federations employ only one to five persons, 40 per cent employ six to ten persons and only 15 per cent employ over ten. In the North, in contrast, only 13 per cent of the federations employ less than five full-time officials, 45 per cent employ six to ten, and 42 per cent employ over ten.

While the southern membership of the party is spread out in the countryside, the leadership tends to cluster in the cities. The most dynamic party workers gravitate to the federations, where they can find greater social prestige and better positions. In fact, party leaders have often noted that the dispersion of party cadres in the villages has slowed up the process of formation of a leadership group, since organizers forced to live in the villages become demoralized and isolated, frequently becoming involved in "clientelistic relationships with local figures." A disproportionate number of the full-time leaders of the PCI in the South are now stationed in the provincial capitals. Party sections in the villages often have a merely formal existence; they form and dissolve according to the issues of the moment and the season of the year—the peasant organizations are only truly militant in seasons when the planting and harvesting have been completed.

The disjunction between city and countryside, between middle class intellectual leaders and peasant members, is attitudinal as well as organizational. Southern leaders tend to view the peasants paternalistically. The failure of a substantial peasant cadre to develop in the party may be linked to such attitudes. As national leaders critical of the southern leadership maintain, "The party must advance further to liberate itself courageously from any elements of clientelism and paternalism which still exist here and there." As one leader complained, "The formation of a new type of cadre of popular extraction is bound to meet or even instigate a certain resistance and danger of distortion from the residues of clientelism in the bosom of the popular movement."

Southern provincial leaders are far more "political"—understanding "political" as public activity-orientation—and less "organizational" than their northern colleagues. There appears to be considerably more flexibility, less ideological closure and more discussion than in the northern federations. Southern leaders, one informant suggested, "have more political sensitivity than leaders in the North." Another informant, a member of the party secretariat said,

> The cadres in the South are more politically sensitive, more flexible, more sensitive to the political nature of their problems. In the South, traditionally, everything is decided politically, for in a disorganized society, it is the relations between individuals which solve problems. In the North, in contrast, we deal more with concrete classes and opposing groups, and less with contacts on a personal level. In the leaders of the South, therefore, political sensitivity and ideological subtleties are more important.

Yet the greater political capacity of the southern leaders, according to these informants, is damaged by their organizational incapacity. As another informant in the national party organization said,

> The differences between northern and southern leaders are the differences in the characteristics of the regions. The northerner is more of a formalist; the southerner is more versatile but he is less organizationally oriented.

The characteristic described as "political sensitivity" by party informants shades into personalism in relationships with followers and with the opposition. In interviews, provincial leaders in the South stressed such qualities as "prestige," "honesty," and "seriousness" as the factors which recommend them to the admiration of their fellow citizens. In the North, party leaders are more concerned with presenting a united face to the opposition. Southern leaders were far more conscious of the need to establish a network of ties with local elites than northerners, who interpret the Leninist policy of alliances as the affair of the party organizations themselves, pointing to relations with the Vatican rather than interaction with village priests.

In their relations with the rank and file, the southern leaders are personally oriented too. They spend much of their time helping job seekers, writing letters of recommendation for students and trying to resolve the legal disputes of the peasants. A leader writes, "There is a need to overcome the personalism, the tendency to divide into groups around one or another personality. This derives from the type of social organization of the South, and is a reflection of its social dis-aggregation in the files of our party."

Table 3

PCI Federal Secretaries Individual Role Perceptions (N = 80)

		Political	Labor Oriented	Organiza-tional	DK NA	Total
North	(N)	8	4	31	4	47
	(%)	16%	9%	66%	9%	100%
South	(N)	20	3	5	5	33
	(%)	61%	9%	15%	15%	100%
Italy	(N)	28	7	36	9	80
	(%)	35%	9%	45%	11%	100%

Southern leaders perceive their federations as more autonomous with relation to the party national office than do their northern colleagues. Each secretary was asked his opinion on the role a party secretary should play in relation to the national party organization. There were five alternatives presented, representing different degrees of autonomy or central direction. Northern leaders were ranged heavily on the side of central direction (66 per cent), with 17 per cent perceiving their role autonomously and another 17 per cent expressing moderate positions. In the South, in contrast, only 42 per cent were centralists, as many as 42 per cent were autonomists and 16 per cent were moderates.

In order to further explore the perceptions of their roles held by northern and southern leaders, provincial secretaries were asked in questionnaires and personal interviews: "In your work as party secretary, what are the most important things you do, in the order of their importance?" Responses were not contextually coded because of the small number of respondents, but were classified according to their political orientation, their labor orientation and their organizational content. The results are recorded in Table 3.

Naturally, all the responses contained a strong political element, but many incorporated elements which were specifically labor oriented, while many others were organizationally oriented. As the Table shows, two-thirds of the northern respondents perceive their roles predominantly in organizational terms, while almost two-thirds of the southerners include mainly political factors in their role perceptions.

(d) *Ideology.* Unlike French communism, which has been wholly dependent upon imported theory, the PCI was fortunate to possess its own theorist in Antonio Gramsci, whose writings in prison under the Fascists later became an important source for today's leaders. What is most interesting, however, is the extent to which the *Via Italiana al Socialismo* in both North and South was formulated *without* Gramsci's aid, for he died in prison and his writings were not publicly disinterred until 1948.

Gramsci contributed two important ideas to his party's future ideology: the idea of the party as the modern Prince, and the concept of the alliance of northern workers and southern peasants. Both were Leninist in inspiration if not in tone.

Gramsci saw in *The Prince* "a creation of concrete imagination which could work upon a dispersed and disintegrated society to stimulate and organize its general will." The modern equivalent of Machiavelli's Prince is the political party and its sublime role is organizing a new collectivity.

> The modern Prince, the myth-prince, cannot be a real person, a concrete individual; it can only be an organism . . . the political party, which, time and again . . . knows how to form a new type of state.

The party is a creative agent of education and revolution, "a collective intellectual," developing a new class of leaders out of an old and divided society.

A second aspect of Gramsci's thought regarded the backward and "disaggregated" nature of southern Italian society and its role in the future revolution. To Gramsci, North and South were not united nationally, but colonially; "The bourgeoisie of the North," he wrote, "has subjected the South of Italy and the Islands to the status of colonies for exploitation." The South is ruled by an agrarian bloc of landed proprietors and intellectuals who are paid off by their northern bosses through parliamentary deals. The peasant is helplessly tied to the agrarian bloc through clientele relations with the landholders. Semi-feudal contractual relations dominate economic life, preventing the peasantry's emergence as a modern social force.

Left to themselves, the peasants of the South will dissolve into a "disorganized mass, a chaotic disorder of exasperated passions." Organized by the proletariat of the North, they are the motor force of the revolution. "The proletariat," Gramsci wrote, "will destroy the southern agrarian bloc in the degree that it succeeds, through its party, in organizing ever larger masses of poor peasants in autonomous and independent organizations."

Several points are significant about this formulation of Gramsci. First, it separates North and South theoretically and admits that special factors condition the organization of the southern peasant. Second, the relationship is bilateral. "The workers of the factory and the poor peasants," he writes, "are the *two energies* of the proletarian revolution." Third, the alliance is revolutionary and socialist, rather than tactical and democratic and there is no doubt about proletarian hegemony. Instead of what he calls the "magic formula" of the division of the *latifundia,* Gramsci proposes a "political alliance between workers of the North and peasants of the South to overthrow the bourgeoisie from the power of the state."

The "organizational weapon" which emerged from these two central ideas—the party as the modern Prince and the alliance of northern workers and southern peasants—would have had a strong potential for revolution in an underdeveloped area like the South. Gramsci wanted the peasants to start an insurrection in the countryside to occupy the army, thereby leaving a clear field for a proletarian revolution in the cities. With allowance made for his unique style and sensitivity to Italian conditions, he is quite close to Lenin's model for a revolutionary party in a backward society. "Spontaneity" is rampant in the "dis-aggregated" southern peasantry, while the party as modern Prince is the embodiment of "consciousness." The parallel to Lenin's model, we may assume, was not lost on Gramsci.

In the North, Gramsci concentrated upon the factory. He wanted to transform society *from within,* as a preparation for the revolution. Gramsci's group in Turin wanted to establish the *Consigli di Fabbrica,* workers' councils which aimed at eventual assumption of the control of production. In 1919, he wrote:

> The socialist state already exists potentially in the institutions of the social life of the exploited working class. To tie these institutions together . . . means creating from then on a true and real workers' democracy.

These ideas, actually of anarcho-syndicalist derivation, were denounced as "reformist experiments" by Gramsci's extremist opposition in the party.

The essence of PCI ideology since 1945 is the cross-fertilization of Gramsci's ideas with Togliatti's *Via Italiana al Socialismo.* And since the latter is essentially reformist in nature—calling for action within the constitutional system through structural reform—the combination ranges from the comic to the bizarre, with a good deal of practical common sense in between.

Gramsci's idea of the party as the modern Prince has, in North and South, lost its Leninist components and is now interpreted almost entirely in terms of Togliatti's emphasis upon national solidarity. Togliatti wrote in 1944:

> The central idea of the political action of Gramsci was the idea of unity: unity of the working class parties in the defense of democratic institutions and the destruction of Fascism; . . . unity of the socialist working masses with the Catholic working masses of the city and countryside; unity of the workers; unity of workers and peasants; unity of workers of the arm with those of the mind. . . .

In the North we find the PCI operating with an increasingly reformist political ideology, with excellent results. For the *Via Italiana* is a strategy for industrialized societies. Emphasis is increasingly placed upon trade union action and structural reform within the capitalist system. Theoreticians have virtually adopted revised views on the evolution of capitalism, and party leaders talk of "insertion" in the processes of neo-capitalism to influence its direction. As a leading labor intellectual writes:

> The CGIL does not try to prevent the modernization of Italian capitalism. Instead of opposing neo-capitalist solutions *a priori*, we each time oppose more advanced and equally realistic and concrete solutions.

In the South, the synthesis of the *Via Italiana* with Gramsci's formulations has been less happy. The party has obliterated his concept of a creative working class impelling a peasant motor force to revolutionary action in a bilateral relationship directed by the party as a modern Prince. Instead, it calls for a pluralistic *system* of alliances between many social groups which *suppresses* the insurrectionary force of the peasants. A partnership-turned-coalition is expanded into "a system with the working class at its head . . . and an alliance with the southern peasants, first, with the petit bourgeoisie, the intellectuals and the progressive medium bourgeoisie, isolating the conservative and the large bourgeoisie."

The alliance also loses its revolutionary character. We learn retrospectively that "Gramsci reaffirmed the real unity between workers and peasants in the common battle for the *structural renewal* of the Italian state." There is a theoretical problem in the admixture of Gramsci and Togliatti: the first is revolutionary, the second reformist; taken together they are contradictory.

For example, the party inevitably impels the peasant "motor force" to action which is not revolutionary, for it simultaneously seeks the support of social groups whose interests would be threatened by a peasant insurrection. Moreover, lacking the "organizational weapon" of the Leninist party, PCI initiatives for the peasants do not enlist them in the battle for socialism, but support the peasants' own struggle to become petit bourgeois landowners. Hence, the limited agrarian reform which the party demanded in 1950 has aided the peasants of the South immeasurably, but not the party.

With neither a Leninist organizational weapon nor its revolutionary goals, the PCI in the South falls prey to the "objective conditions" of its political setting in a backward and fragmented society. The whole concept of the party changes from the creative catalytic agent envisaged by Gramsci into an amorphous movement which casts its net through diverse social strata, seeking issues which can unite them. As Togliatti wrote in a key theoretical article:

> Because of the social disorganization of the South, we need an organization of a conspicuously broad, popular nature, more than is necessary in the large industrial centres.

As a result, the PCI in southern Italy shares the personalism, disorganization and ideological weakness of other political parties in that setting. Having applied a strategy well-designed for the industrial North to the backward South, *where the same conditions do not obtain*, the PCI in the South is *neither* an effective Leninist party *nor* a well-organized mass party, but something very different again.

AN INTERPRETATION

Neither in North nor South does the Italian Communist Party have the attributes of the devotee-combat party described by Duverger and Selznick. This illustrates two things, one that we should have known all along and another that requires a great deal more thought and elaboration. First, the role and structure of marxist parties cannot be derived abstractly as Duverger and Selznick attempt to do. Second, a theory of Marxist parties will only result, in true dialectical fashion, from analysis of the interaction of party strategy and political setting under many different conditions. Turning to this second consideration, we may well ask, "What then are the 'models' with which we may understand the Italian Communist Party in North and South?" In the North, Duverger provides us with an answer: the mass party. In the South, we must turn to the experience of marxist parties in the underdeveloped world.

It is ironic that Communism in northern Italy at mid-twentieth century should vindicate the nineteenth century Western European Social-Democratic tradition. By 1900, the advances made in western society had negated many of the assumptions of Marx in the *Communist Manifesto*. These assumptions had "presupposed a pattern of events which experience had shown to be no longer possible in Europe—*or indeed in any advanced country*." The chauvinistic behavior of the Social-Democratic parties in 1914 and the failure of the revolution to spread to Western Europe in 1917 gave the finishing touch to Western European revolutionary socialism. Since then, every flourishing western socialist party has been a constitutional mass party, recruiting broadly and emphasizing parliamentary and electoral activity instead of the barricades and the *putsch*. The idea of the vanguard party, with which Marx had toyed in 1850 and Blanqui developed more fully, did not appear again until 1905 in Russia.

For just as advancing conditions in Western Europe caused the transformation of European Socialism, "the obverse also applied: where the pre-1848 situation still existed, the fire that had gone out in the West might still burst into flames." Lenin's double-edged contribution was to recognize the connection between political backwardness and revolution, and to develop an organizational weapon and a strategy tailored to these conditions. The Leninist party was the ideal weapon for making the revolution in a backward country, for it by-passed the weak and "spontaneous" proletariat and seduced the disorganized but potentially revolutionary poor peasantry. This is essentially the strategy Gramsci wanted to develop for southern Italy.

Lenin was convinced that the conditions of all backward societies demanded the strategy he had utilized in Russia. He told a group of Asian Communists:

It is imperative for you to make a success of applying Communist theory and practice under conditions where the peasant is the primary class of the masses, where the task of struggle pending solution lies in the fight against the remnants of mediaevalism, but not in the fight against capitalism. . . .

The solution to the above tasks . . . can . . . be seen in the over-all struggle already started in Russia.

Yet he failed to conclude the obvious corollary: that the strategy used in Russia *would no longer do* in the advanced nations of the West, where capitalism and liberal democracy had already proceeded too far in satisfying the masses.

It is Togliatti's great contribution to have recognized this "bright side" of Leninism and to have responded with the idea of the *Via Italiana al Socialismo*. His statement that "It is impossible to conceive realistically of the advance towards socialism outside the fabric of Italian democratic life, outside of the struggle for the objectives that interest the whole society," is typical of this attitude.

When we examine the membership, the organization, the leadership and the ideology of the Communist Party in northern Italy, we can only be impressed by its successful adaptation and struck by its essential similarity to the "sociological type" of the mass party presented by Duverger: membership is broad and relatively unselective; loyalty is class-based and weak as compared to the religious loyalty of the devotee party; the cell is replaced in importance by the section, and formal centralization disguises factionalism and ideological rivalry; and party strategy focuses upon parliament, the trade unions and the mass media, in contrast to conspiracy and infiltration.

The proof of the essential compatability of the PCI's *Via Italiana* with the conditions of an advanced industrial setting is found in its incompatability with the conditions of the backward agricultural South. Here membership is inconsistent and weak; commitment is personal and interest-oriented; neither the cells nor the sections are well articulated; leadership reflects the clientelistic nature of southern politics; and party ideology is dispersive and "catch-all" in nature.

If the PCI in the South cannot be described as either a Leninist party or a mass labor party, what then is its nature? Here we must turn to the experiences of marxist parties in today's developing areas; in the combination of an under-developed setting and a non-Leninist strategy, the PCI in southern Italy has emerged as a type very similar to political movements in the new nations. David Apter writes:

The central characteristics of the movements, whatever their forms, are their spontaneous and populist qualities, the direct relationship between the leadership and the people, the high degree of emotional appeal of their programs, and the simplicity of their aims.

Not only does the PCI in southern Italy reflect many of these characteristics, it also reflects the failure of this type of movement to grapple successfully with many of the needs of the underdeveloped areas. The problem is one which a careful reading of Lenin could have predicted to party leaders: a marxist party in a backward country which lacks a Leninist organization will advance the (not necessarily progressive) goals of the peasant population without advancing the goals of the party. It thus appears as a sophisticated structure of patron-client relations fortified by an ideology that is more populist than marxist and led by intellectuals who are more bourgeois than proletarian.

All this leads us back to the question of the relevance of Duverger and Selznick and other western theorists to the study of marxist movements. The foregoing analysis shows that *neither* in northern nor southern Italy do we find the devotee or combat party. In the first, the combination of a highly developed setting and an open strategy have led to the emergence of the PCI as a mass party. In the second, the same open strategy in a fragmented developing society leads to another sociological type—one closely related to the political movements we now see in the new nations. Had the party in southern Italy been more rigorously Leninist in its strategy, as Gramsci was, we would have seen a third sociological type: the vanguard party, which can overcome the "spontaneity" of a backward society with the "consciousness" of a revolutionary leadership.

Where does this leave the devotee or combat model developed by Duverger and Selznick? It leaves it a poor fourth, a historical mutant in which a strategy designed for underdeveloped societies was mistakenly applied to the West in its high stage of industrialization. That this combination was an unhappy one may be seen in the sorry history of the Communist Party in both Germany and the United States, where an elite of revolutionaries became a sect of devotees persecuted for their beliefs and "outside the system" in a scientific, as well as in a political way. Such a pattern is not inevitable however, as is evident upon examination of marxist parties in places like Italy.

FOOTNOTES

1.   David Apter writes, "Industrialization is that aspect of modernization so powerful in its consequences that it alters dysfunctional social institutions and customs by creating new roles and social instruments, based on the use of the machine": *The Politics of Modernization* (Chicago: Chicago University Press, 1965), p. 68.

2.   Vera Lutz writes: "The peasant is almost always what is called a mixed figure—small proprietor, tenant, share-cropper, wage earner. In the past, at least, the link between him and that part of the land which he farmed but did not own was in many cases a precarious one".

3.   While 42 per cent of the membership in the North are members of the working class, 32 per cent of the southern PCI members are workers. In the North, even in the agricultural regions, Emilia, Tuscany and the Marches, 36 per cent of the members are workers, more than the working class portion of the party in any southern region. See PCI, *Dati Sull' Organizzazione del PCI* (Rome: PCI, 1964).

15

FRANK L. WILSON

The Persistence
of Ideology
on the French
Democratic Left[1]

Much has been written about the decline of ideology in Western
democratic nations. While these discussions about the end of
ideology have sometimes been complicated by uncertainties about
the meaning of the term, the general argument has been that the
left-wing political parties in Western Europe have abandoned their
former Marxist and socialist ideologies in favor of more pragmatic
and less doctrinaire or programmatic approaches to politics. There
is strong evidence to support this thesis in the case of several West
European nations: Britain, West Germany, Austria, and the Scan-
dinavian nations. In France, however, the situation is somewhat
different. Despite some premature pronouncements of the death of

Reprinted from Frank L. Wilson, "The Persistence of Ideology on
the French Democratic Left," a paper presented at the sixty-sixth
annual meeting of the American Political Science Association, Los
Angeles, September, 1970, by permission of the author and the
American Political Science Association. (Copyright © 1970). Some
footnotes omitted by the editors.

ideologies in France, the ideological commitments remain firm in the parties of the democratic Left as well as in the Communist Party. It is not unusual to find a Communist party that is faithful to its ideology; it is somewhat unusual to find socialist parties that remain as rigorous in their commitments to Marxism as do the Socialists in France.[2] French socialists have refused to follow their socialist brothers elsewhere in Europe in moderating or abandoning their ideologies. Even though the ideologies of the parties of the democratic Left no longer arouse the masses in France, the leaders and rank-and-file members of these parties still have an emotional as well as a verbal attachment to their ideologies. This paper will indicate the nature of the ideological commitments of the democratic Left, the reasons for the continuation of ideologies, and the effects of this commitment.[3] The purpose is not necessarily to challenge the thesis of the end of ideology, but rather to explore the reasons for an exception to this thesis.

The democratic Left in France is divided into several parties, a number of political clubs and groups, and individuals who refuse to adhere to any of the formal organizations of the democratic Left. The major component of the democratic Left is the French Socialist Party (Section Française de l'Internationale Ouvriere—SFIO) which has the largest number of card-carrying members and receives the majority of the votes of the democratic Left. The Socialist Party remains firmly committed to its Socialist ideology. As the party reorganized itself after the Second World War, the Socialists explicitly rejected proposals by Leon Blum and others that would have given the party a less doctrinaire character. Instead, the Socialists chose to reiterate their acceptance of doctrinaire Marxism and elected as party secretary general the chief advocate of this left-wing position, Guy Mollet. In the course of his twenty-two years reign as head of the Socialist Party, Mollet wandered from one end of the political spectrum to the other in his political behavior, but never deviated from a verbal and emotional commitment to a fundamentalist view of socialism. While he spoke of class war, of nationalizations, and of the oppressions of capitalism, when he was premier in 1956 (heading the cabinet with the longest life in the Fourth Republic, seventeen months), Mollet's chief mark on history was the Anglo-French-Israeli invasion of Suez in October-November, 1956. One critic compared Mollet to de Gaulle and wrote of his attachment to doctrinaire socialism:

> He believes that he is the incarnation of socialism just as de Gaulle believes he is the incarnation of France. Both in fact are no more than opportunists. In the name of this socialism that must be carried through history from one end of the planet to the other like the Olympic torch, Guy Mollet climbs mountains, crosses oceans, defies storms and continues to smoke cigarette after cigarette in his little office near Place Pigalle.

It is often argued that the French Socialists maintained only a verbal commitment to socialism and practiced a pragmatic type of politics. If there can be no doubt that the Socialists' use of the term "revolution" was rhetorical and not a real aspiration, it nevertheless remains true that the French Socialists maintain a deep emotional commitment to the basic tenets of Marxism. If in the past they had compromised and allied with centrist or so-called reactionary parties, the Socialists did so *a contre coeur* [against their hearts] and were relieved to return to their ideological positions. During the Fourth Republic the ideological differences between Socialists and other democratic parties were the major source of the divisions among the *ministrables* that produced cabinet instability. The emotional attachment to their ideology can also be seen in the enthusiasm with which SFIO leaders and militants responded to the retreat into opposition in 1951 and again in 1959. By severing their governmental ties with the parties of the Center and Right, the Socialists could retreat into the defense of pure socialist goals.

It has also been suggested that the ideological commitment was stronger among active party members and militants at the base than among party leaders and elected representatives who were supposedly more responsive to the less ideologically oriented electorate. However, no evidence was found to support this argument in interviews conducted with a number of Socialist Party leaders at both national and local levels, the majority of whom were elected officials serving in the National Assembly, the Senate, and/or local government.

With only one or two exceptions, all of those interviewed expressed a deep, often emotional attachment to a fundamentalist view of socialism. Furthermore, it is unlikely that there was any great disparity between the ordinary party militant and the SFIO's elected representatives since in the 1965 municipal elections over forty thousand SFIO members were elected to local offices. That figure represents more than half the number of members claimed by the SFIO. The majority of the active SFIO militants were thus also elected officials.

The commitment of Socialists to their ideology is both verbal and emotional but it is not a practical commitment. Socialists serving in public office at both the national and local levels have not been constrained in their actions by their ideology. When serving in governing positions both at the local level and at the national level, Socialists have performed their tasks unhindered by ideological concerns. They have justified such activities as necessary because of coalition pressures or because general social conditions were not yet ready for a true socialist policy. This willingness to ignore socialism in the face of the demands of practical politics in no way detracts from the sincerity of their attachment to their ideology. Indeed, the compromises that are required for practical day-to-day politics are atoned for by intensified emotional attachments to socialism and by proclamations of this fidelity.

Since 1946, the Socialist Party has avoided internal debate on its ideology; there has been no serious attempt to revise the party's doctrines. Although many degrees of socialism are espoused by its members, the party is not divided on the basis of doctrinal differences over the content of socialism. Debate and division within the party have centered on questions of party policy on current issues rather than on doctrine. There were important internal party debates over issues such as the degree and wisdom of participation in cabinets at several points during the Fourth Republic, the policy toward Algeria, the party's attitude toward de Gaulle's return to power in 1958, the party's position on the institutions of the Fifth Republic, and the question of party reform from 1964 to 1969. While these debates had some ideological content, the divisions were not along a doctrinaire/revisionist line. Instead, advocates of doctrinal orthodoxy and revision were found on both sides. For example, Gaston Defferre, a leading advocate of revising the party's ideology, joined the most orthodox left-wing Socialists in opposing the Algerian policy followed by Mollet in 1956; Mollet in turn found support among both doctrinaire and revisionist Socialists. Perhaps the closest the Socialist Party has come to true ideological debate was the attempt by Defferre to reform the party during his abortive presidential campaign of 1964-1965. Here again, the division in the party was not along ideological lines, as Defferre's closest supporters included several party leaders whose sincere devotion to orthodox Marxism could not be questioned.

In sum, the French Socialist Party has not experienced a reexamination of its fundamental doctrines and Marxist commitment such as those endured by Britain's Labour Party, the German Social Democratic Party, and other socialist parties of Western Europe. It has avoided the internal divisions which accompanied such doctrinal revision elsewhere by maintaining its verbal commitment to the pure Marxist theory, while permitting its members and public office-holders to act without reference to party doctrine in practical politics. As one deputy expressed it: "The party doctrine has become like the Bible. There is the same refusal to change it and to believe in it." Thus, the Socialist parliamentary group could repeat in a statement of its goals that it was "essentially a revolutionary party, . . . a party of the class struggle," in terms not much different from similar statements of purpose made in 1905.

Among other political groups of the democratic Left, the dedication to doctrinaire socialism was at least as strong and usually stronger than that of the SFIO. The *Parti Socialiste Unifie* (PSU) is a highly ideological party composed of a variety of elements of the far Left including dissidents who had left the Socialist Party as a result of Mollet's policy in Algeria, former Communists, Trotskyites, followers of Pierre Mendes-France (who was himself a member of the PSU until 1968), and some Catholics of the far Left. The PSU places emphasis on the need to develop a modern socialism without abandoning the basic principles of Marx. However, the divisions within the party and the refusal to reexamine the validity of the basic assumptions of socialism prevent the PSU from revising its ideological commitments. The priority that is placed on doctrinal purity characteristic of the members of the PSU thus precludes success in modernizing socialism.

In its quest for ideological purity, the PSU has criticized both the Socialist Party and the Communist Party for their tolerance of pragmatism in political action. The PSU denounces such pragmatism by Socialist and Communist officeholders as compromise with the bourgeoisie and as acts of treason in the class war. It insists upon a dogmatic and ideological approach to politics. With its distinct intellectual flavor and its ideological bent, the PSU is accurately described by Stanley Hoffmann as: "a typically intellectual protest movement, marked by swift evolution toward an ideological and intransigent indictment of the regime and of society altogether: Here Marxist phraseology becomes, once more, a substitute for realistic analysis."

What is more surprising is to find this same ideological fundamentalism among the clubmen. Allegedly the new element in French politics, the men of the clubs demonstrate the same commitment to a traditional view of socialism. The clubmen call for a new presentation of socialism, but when they speak about doctrine, they do so in essentially the same terms used by the Socialist Party. They call for the modernization of the doctrine but are every bit as dogmatic as the SFIO in their opposition to "revisionism." This attachment to a rigid socialist ideology is characteristic not only of the more politicized "club" of Francois Mitterrand, the CIR, but also of most of those clubs which have remained faithful to their original goals of the study and discussion of political issues.

In its early years, especially between 1963 and 1965, the political club movement seemed to promise a wholesale revision of the time-worn ideologies of the French Left. The clubs seemed ready to forget the old terminologies, slogans, and shibboleths in a search for new approaches to the problems of the present, approaches which would be more readily accepted by people from a broad section of society and not simply by a single social class. To this end the early publications and statements of the clubs avoided the use of terms such as socialism, class conflict, expropriations, nationalization, etc. By 1968 this aspect of political innovation had virtually disappeared from the club movement with the possible exception of the small but prestigious Club Jean Moulin. Thus, at the October 1968 session of the CIR the most applauded speech was that of Marc Paillet on ideology, a speech that might well have come from the lips of the most doctrinaire old guard socialist, and Francois Mitterand's article in the first issue of the Convention's journal of political thought was a full-scale assault on the twin dangers of "the Left that calls itself modern" and "the Left that calls itself new." In part the reversion to doctrinaire socialism by the clubmen is typical of the French Left's tendency to fall back upon its ideologies at times of defeat. In part it is due to the clubmen's attempts to prove to the rest of the Left that they are truly men of the Left. Many Socialists are skeptical of the clubs' commitment to socialism particularly as a result of the large number of Catholics in the clubs. In response, many clubmen have become more rigid in their ideological commitments than even doctrinaire Socialists. Finally, the clubmen's reversion to ideology is partly explained by the fact that they have come to think of themselves as the chief line of defense in the democratic Left against the pragmatism and revisionism of certain Socialists and against the conservatism of the Radicals. This self-conceived doctrinal purity leads them to accept and indeed demand that the democratic Left remain faithful to the ideologies that prevented its adaptation to the modern world.

The Radical Party is the only part of the French Left that avoids a doctrinaire commitment to socialism or to any other ideology. For the Radical Party, anticlericalism came closest in the past to being the party's doctrine, and by the 1960s even this was no longer characteristic of much of the party. Indeed, the president of the party from 1965 to 1969, Rene Billeres, was a practicing Catholic. Composed essentially of local politicians who find the Radical label a convenient one in their quest for local elective offices, the Radical Party has been chary of adopting any ideology or even a well-defined program. In February 1970, the Radical Party adopted a new manifesto. While the manifesto proposed far-reaching changes (including the abolition of inherited wealth, which is a radical proposal for a party composed mainly of elderly middle class men), it is clearly a program and not an ideology. In addition, the document appears to be more a political statement designed to further the political ambitions of Jean-Jacques Servan-Schreiber, currently secretary general of the Radical Party, than a firm commitment by the party as a whole.

In summary, with the exception of the Radicals, the democratic Left in France remains faithful to its ideologies. This ideological attachment does not always make itself apparent in the activities of the moderate leftists, but it is far more than simply a verbal affirmation. There are strong emotional and psychological aspects of this ideological fidelity.

In seeking an explanation for the persistence of ideology on the French democratic Left, the answer is *not* to be found in a continuation of the social and economic conditions which originally fostered the growth and popularity of ideologies all over Europe. It might be expected that ideologies based on class conflicts, on comparatively deep social cleavages, and on the disadvantaged condition of the working class would lose their vigor and even disappear as socio-economic change removed the causes for the ideologies. This has not been the case in France. The political forces of the democratic Left retain their ideological convictions even though socio-economic change has removed most of the earlier bases for the ideologies. While class consciousness still is common, the most visible signs of class differences are disappearing. Higher salaries for workers have improved their standard of living and permitted them to enjoy what once were luxury items: cars, television, refrigerators, and vacations.[4] Issues which once were the objects of intense political conflict no longer are the causes of deep divisions among Frenchmen: laicite, nationalizations, the role of the state in the economy, etc. Public opinion studies indicate that while differences remain between the left and Right on these traditional issues, the cleavages are far less than might be expected. These studies also indicate that new issues such as aid to underdeveloped nations, support of the Common Market, and attitudes toward the United States are not producing new cleavages. There are differences among the political families on these new problems but new cleavages similar to those which in the past divided France are not emerging. Indeed, one of the features of the changing French society has been the gradual emergence at the level of the general public of a consensus on political issues including those issues that provided the fuel for ideological conflicts in the past. Yet, the appearance of this political consensus among Frenchmen in general has not produced the abandonment of their ideologies by the active political leaders and parties of the democratic Left.

Evidence of the voters' disinterest in party programs, doctrines, and ideologies can be seen in polls probing voters' motivations. In a poll taken in November, 1944, 72 percent of those questioned preferred to vote for a program rather than a man; only 16 percent preferred to vote for the man. By the end of the Fourth Republic the voters had abandoned this preference for party and program. Polls in January, 1958 showed that 52 percent would rather vote for a man and only 27 percent wanted to vote for a party. Before the 1967 and 1968 elections, polls sought the voters' primary objective in choosing a candidate. Only 28 percent in 1967 and 23 percent in 1968 wanted to choose the political family that most closely corresponded with the respondents political ideas. The majority indicated that their objective was either to vote for a deputy whom they trusted, or to vote for or against de Gaulle. One more poll can be cited to show the public's disinterest in ideologies. The poll taken in 1967, asked which of two statements best described the respondent's attitude: "In politics it is of no value to have grand theories; it is enough to have good sense and realism." Or, "Politics is not worthwhile if it is not in the service of an ideal and of a general philosophy of society." Fully sixty percent favored pragmatism over idealism. This percentage remained constant for all parts of the political spectrum from the far Right to the far Left.

The democratic Left is aware of the general public's disregard for ideology. It regards this as part of the process of depoliticization that has accompanied technocracy, the consumer society, television, vacations, and the Gaullist regime. Some socialists believe this is a temporary phenomenon that will eventually be followed by a return to ideological concerns; most despair of any such ideological revival. Whatever their evaluation of the permanence of this de-ideologization, few socialists regard the public's disinterest as a reason to modify or abandon their ideologies. The fact that there are still some Frenchmen who are ideologically oriented encourages the parties of the democratic Left to maintain their ideological flavor. It is this ideologically oriented section of the population which, although small in absolute number, makes up a large part of those who belong to these parties, who attend their public meetings, and who provide the core of their supporters. Since this is part of the general public that the leadership of the democratic Left is more likely to meet, the trend away from ideologies of the majority of the public is obscured from the vision of the leadership.

Since the explanation of the persistence of ideologies is to be found neither in the continued importance of sharp political or social cleavages nor in the general public's preference for ideology over pragmatism, the sources of the democratic Left's attachment to its ideologies must be sought within the parties of the democratic Left. There the explanation can be found in the nature of the appeal of ideology, the nature of inter-party competition on the French Left, and the practical uses of ideology in maintaining party unity.

The appeal of ideology to men of the Left is in part the product of the widespread French conviction that "there are general laws of principles which govern human affairs whose discovery would make the difference between chaos and order." This search for universal laws has increased the attractiveness of ideologies such as Marxism which claim to provide these universal laws. As de Tocqueville noted over a century ago, the Frenchman is "more inclined to think up grandiose schemes than to carry through great enterprises." This is certainly true of the democratic Left. As an example, the Federation of the Left spent the major part of its three year existence wrangling over one doctrinal statement after another.[5] First, the parties in the FGDS prepared a doctrinal charter for the new organization; then they elaborated a detailed program based on this charter, the Program of July 14, 1966. A year later, discussions on doctrine and ideology were undertaken in order to write a charter to serve as the basis for the fusion of the FGDS families into a single unitary party. These negotiations continued through the rest of 1967 and produced the "Charter of Bondy" (named after the city where it was signed). After the electoral losses in June, 1968 and the resulting problems for the Federation, new doctrinal negotiations began again. In short, the attempt to create a new and dynamic force of the democratic Left quickly became mired in the traditional pre-occupation with ideology and doctrine.

There is a practical side-effect of this doctrinal preoccupation that permits the democratic Left to accept its defeats. Socialism is a messianic ideology that gives its adherents idealistic goals which are recognized to be far in the future

and not immediately attainable. Such an ideology makes the absence of immediate results or achievements understandable and acceptable. For the socialist
militant, this ideology provides an explanation of the lack of success of the
party's efforts and assures final victory in the end. For parties in decline, as is
the case with the democratic Left, the ideology is very valuable in maintaining
the faith and diligence of its members.

The continued appeal of rigid socialist ideology is also attributable to the
place of Marxism in the French intellectual tradition. Marxism is not only
accepted in French intellectual circles, it is often a prerequisite for admission
into many of these circles. French intellectuals, including those actually engaged
in politics, are not noted for their ability to perceive the demands of practical
politics. Instead they prefer the abstract but perfect world of their ideological
preferences. The fact that pure socialism is still acceptable on an intellectual
level inhibits its revision in the light of practical politics.

The French socialists consider themselves the heirs of the French Revolution.
While they no longer seek to carry out a revolution, they deem it their duty to
defend past revolutions. One clubman expressed well the attitude of the French
democratic Left: "We always live by the spirit of the Revolution." In most
cases, fidelity to the revolutionary tradition becomes translated into defense of
the ideology. Marxism is viewed as the latest manifestation of the liberation of
mankind from its oppressions that started in 1789. To dilute socialism would be
tantamount to deserting the humanitarian and libertarian traditions of the
Revolution.

What makes this more important is the fact that there are at least four different parties or groups in France (the Socialist Party, the PSU, other socialist
groups and individuals, and the Communist Party) all claiming to be the one
true heir of the revolutionary tradition and the defender of pure socialism. The
competition among these rival claimants of socialism prevents any modernization of doctrine. Any revision of its doctrine by the SFIO (or any other party
of the democratic Left) would provide evidence of its abandonment of the
pure Marxist doctrine. Such evidence would be seized by its rivals to press
their claims to being the true and only repository of the Revolution and of
socialism.

The presence of a powerful Communist party is particularly important in
explaining the continued fidelity to a relatively pure socialism. Elsewhere in
Western Europe, the decline of political extremism has made possible the
abandonment of rigid ideologies. In France, the extreme Right has disappeared
but the extreme Left remains unabsorbed. It is institutionalized in the Communist Party which steadfastly resists any effort to modify its ideology and
which stands ready to capitalize on any relaxation in the ideological commitment
of the democratic Left. Confronted with a powerful Communist opponent
which claims to be the true defender of pure Marxism, the socialists are loathe

to change the slightest portion of their doctrine for fear of being denounced as revisionists. Unlike socialist parties in other countries which lack strong Communist parties, the French socialists fear the defection of their left wing to the Communists should they change their doctrine.

The democratic Left sees itself as the defender of the Revolution and of pure socialism not only for France but for all of Europe. With historical roots in the Jacobin traditions, this self-vision of being the European advocate of pure socialism encourages the French socialists to hold tenaciously to their ideology. They speak disparagingly of the welfare statism accomplished by the rule of social democrats in Britain and in Scandinavia; they are contemptuous of doctrinal revision and compromises that other social democratic parties have accepted. They reject social democracy as a compromise with the bourgeoisie and insist that their own goal is a pure socialist society. It is likely that by clinging to a pure socialism French socialists hope to maintain their claim to being the European advocate of the Revolution and also to explain their own lack of success compared to other European socialists whom they see as having succeeded only by compromising the principles that the French Socialists regard as sacred. Thus, in order to maintain the illusion of world leadership in the socialist movement the democratic Left retains its ideological purity.

For members of the Socialist Party, the ideological bond has deep emotional roots in the party's long history of struggling for socialism. French Socialists have an emotional tie to their ideology stemming from their heroes in the past who sacrificed, sometimes at the cost of their lives, to defend the doctrine. The Socialist Party regards its heroes of the past with a deep respect that demands fidelity to their principles. The memories of these heroes and their battles are often invoked in party congresses and debates to urge faithfulness to the pure ideology that they had defended. The valiant warriors of socialism must not be betrayed by changing the party's doctrine. Furthermore, the activities of its present militants in spreading socialism cannot be neglected. The Socialists regard the faithful old militants as the "consciences of the party." One venerable Socialist has even earned the title "pope of the party." The Socialists take pride in belonging to a "very sentimental party" which honors the memory and principles of their predecessors. Their respect for these heroes of the past and for the faithful activities of today's militants dictates a vigilant defense of the ideological convictions for which the heroes and militants have fought.

There are also certain practical reasons of party unity for maintaining the inherited doctrine. The Socialist Party is not as homogeneous a party as one might expect. Instead, it is a coalition of fragments from a variety of classes and socio-occupational groups. In the industrial departments of the north it is a worker's party; in the south and southwest it is the small farmers' anti-Communist force; in areas of high religious practice it is anti-clerical; in the southwest it is anti-Radical; in the cities it is the party of the postmen and the lower civil servants. For this coalition of varied interest, the major point of accord is on the continued advocacy of a pure socialist doctrine. Ideology serves to cement the groups together into a single party. Revision of the ideology might threaten the cohesion of the party and is therefore to be avoided.

The socialist ideology also serves as a defensive reflex. When confronted with electoral defeat, with disillusionment as a result of experiences in government, or with failure to expand the party's following, the Socialists can fall back upon their ideology. If they fail to achieve their goals in the outside world, they can assure the party's survival by emphasizing the ideal of the *dur et pur* party of old. This does not improve the party's chance to recoup its electoral losses or to regain its lost members. It is essentially a holding action against further decline. Although written about certain segments of the British Labour Party, the following accurately describes the French socialists' response to defeat: "Without the prospect of victory, nobility of cause and purity of doctrine become the means by which followers are gained and kept steadfast."

The result of the democratic Left's continued ideological fidelity has been to contribute to three adverse developments: its declining appeal at the polls; its inability to reform or unite itself; and its growing conservative nature. While the blame for none of these consequences can be placed entirely on the persistence of ideology, the refusal of the parties of the democratic Left to abandon their rigid ideologies has been a major contribution to the development of these problems and has prevented the checking of these adverse eventualities.

For the modern political party the most important objective is the winning of elections. Party leaders and outside observers judge the health of a party by its success at the polls. Electoral results are a good indicator of a party's adaptation to the political and socio-economic environment in which it performs. For the French democratic Left, the message from the polls is one of disease and maladaptation. Since World War II, the share of the vote obtained by the democratic Left in national elections has declined steadily in every election except one.[6] The percentage of votes received by the democratic Left has fallen from 33.9 percent in the first postwar election to 20.4 percent in 1968. While the electorate increased in size by three and a half million voters, the democratic Left received two million fewer votes in 1968 than it did in 1945.

There are undoubtedly several factors which must be considered in explaining the failing electoral fortunes: the appeal of de Gaulle, the decline of the immediate postwar revolutionary spirit, the lack of appealing candidates, etc. But the persistence of dated ideologies has also played its part. The postwar tendency toward pragmatic and technocratic solutions of economic problems has had influence on the political sphere also. De Gaulle's claim that ideologies are no longer valid and no longer needed finds responsive ears in all parts of the political spectrum as noted above. The continued attachment to these ideologies by the democratic Left and its refusal to modify them in any meaningful way in spite of public disinterest contribute to the inability of the democratic Left to expand or even maintain its electoral support.

The continued importance of ideology hinders party reform in two ways. First, it tends to blot out or distort the demands for party change in response to an altered socio-economic and political environment. Those who recognize the need to reform the style and structures of the democratic Left are viewed as revisionists who have been deceived by the bourgeoisie into accepting its corrupt practices and philosophies. Second, ideological considerations foreclose the possibility of making certain kinds of changes that might make the democratic Left more appealing to the general voting public. Indeed, the very persistence of ideology makes impossible the development of the catch-all type of party that has emerged on the Right in France and on the Left elsewhere in Europe since one of the requisites of this new type of party is minimal commitment to a formal ideology and maximum flexibility of doctrine. Ideology has thus first prevented the democratic Left from seeing the need to change, and then prevented the adoption of any kind of change that might compromise its purity.

Furthermore, ideology has impeded efforts to unite the Left. It is an obvious obstacle to any attempt to unite the democratic and Communist Lefts. It also hinders efforts to bring the democratic Left together as all do not share the socialist ideology and even those who do share it disagree on its content and on how to interpret it. Ideological differences ended the 1965 attempt of Gaston Defferre to create a grand federation extending from the Christian Democrats to the Socialists. They were also evident in the withdrawal of the Radicals from talks leading to a transformation of the FGDS into a new socialist party in the fall of 1968 and in the eventual collapse of these talks in 1969.

Finally, lingering ideology had the effect of increasing the conservative nature of the democratic Left. Under the Third Republic it was accurate to speak of the Left, as François Goguel did, as being the "party of movement" in contrast to the Right which was the "party of the established order." Since 1958 it appears that the Left has become the "party of the established order" and the Gaullists have become the "party of movement." The continued acceptance of ideologies which appear out of the past and irrelevant to modern concerns has played a part in making the democratic Left less dynamic and more traditional than the Gaullists. The leaders of the Left look back with fondness on the good old days of party militancy. They place the blame for the public's lack of interest in ideology and party activities on modern developments such as television, automobiles, and week-end vacations which take the militant away from his party duty and lull the public into complacency. At times the democratic Left gives the appearance of regretting these features of modern life because of their unfavorable effects on the public's interest in ideology. The Left's attempt to perpetuate or recreate the old role of the active party militant and of a tightly organized instrument of social combat rather than to modify its ideology leads the public to believe that the Left is fighting a rear guard action to preserve the old style politics of a discredited and unwanted political past.

The democratic Left therefore appears out of tune with the nation and tied to the past. The public's interest in old ideological battles is minimal; the symbols of these battles are still featured in the appeals of the parties of the democratic Left. The French reject revolutionary change; the parties of the Left still call for revolution if only on the verbal plane. While the public seems ready to accept new political forms, the Left is still wedded to the terminology, battles and ideologies of the past.

Another important effect of the refusal or inability of the democratic Left to review its ideological commitments is its lack of success in channeling the energy and dynamism of the young radicals into its movements and activities. The same inertia which prevents the moderation of ideological commitments also blocks revisions which would make the ideologies relevant to the sources of discontent and the goals of the new radicals of the 1970s. The result is that those who demand revolutionary change are not attracted to the democratic Left.

In spite of the persistence of ideologies which remain radical and revolutionary at least on the verbal and emotional levels, the democratic Left has failed to remain the leader of the forces of revolution and radical change. It lost its position as leader of French radicalism to the Communists in the 1920s. The Communists in turn have lost the leadership of revolutionary forces in the past few years as a "new Left" has emerged. Attempts by parts of the democratic Left (especially by the PSU and by some political clubs) to recapture the leadership of the revolutionary movements have been unsuccessful; attempts by the Communists to control the new Left have not been attractive to the new and youthful advocates of revolutionary and radical change. The new Left has rejected the Marxism taught and practiced by the democratic Left and by the Communists, yet it has not produced distinctive ideologies of its own. While it expresses a variety of ideological persuasions ranging from Maoism to anarchism, the new Left prefers the acts rather than the philosophies of revolution. Some Marxist thought and terminology are used by the new Left, but this is at least part the result of the conviction that a Marxist credo is the *sine qua non* of a leftist and revolutionary movement. The new extreme Left is openly contemptuous of the democratic and Communist Lefts' ideological discussions and prefers to be actively engaged in the revolution rather than to theorize about it.

To summarize, the continued fidelity to its ideologies poses two problems for the French democratic Left. On the one hand, the persistence of ideologies prevents the democratic Left from becoming a pragmatic political force capable of generating mass public support. On the other hand, the retention of ideologies which are radical and revolutionary has not permitted the democratic Left to retain leadership of those who advocate radical change and revolution.[7] The attachment to pure ideologies that appear more relevant to the Nineteenth Century than to the second half of the Twentieth Century makes it impossible for the democratic Left to appeal successfully to either the pragmatic voter or the revolutionary militant.

In the last analysis, the refusal of the democratic Left to abandon or revise its ideologies is indicative of the profound traditionalism and conservativism of the French Left. Leon Blum noted the conservative nature of the socialist insistence on a pure doctrine. After the 1946 AFIO congress had passed a resolution stating ". . . that all attempts at revisionism must be condemned, particularly those inspired by a false humanism whose real purpose is to mask that fundamental reality, the class struggle . . ." and had replaced Blum's protege, Daniel Mayer, with Guy Mollet, Blum told the congress:

> You are afraid of the voters, afraid of the men you will or will not designate as candidates, afraid of public opinion, afraid of failure. But more than anything else you are afraid of what is new. You are nostalgic for everything that might recall this party as you knew it in other days. . . . And the nostalgia takes you back to this past even though it no longer is relevant and even though everything around you has been renewed. . . . The vote for the motion of Guy Mollet [condemning revisionism], do you know what it is? It is the moral alibi by which you have sought to delude your bad conscience.

Twenty-four years later, this same harsh judgment could still be directed at the socialists of the French democratic Left, and not simply at the more traditional socialists in the Socialist Party but also at the supposedly new and modern elements of the democratic Left in the clubs and the PSU. The overall effect of the retention of its old ideologies is to prevent the democratic Left from responding to the recent socio-economic changes in France. It has been unable to create a political force that is capable of attracting broader electoral support and of serving as a viable alternative to Gaullism. It has also been unable to serve as a means of political expression and action for the new Left. As a consequence, not only does the democratic Left attachment to out-dated and unpopular ideologies.

Some political scientists, including both those who see a decline in ideology and those who reject that thesis, have raised doubts about the supposed beneficial effects of de-ideologization on the political system. It is suggested that the decline in ideological fervor will adversely affect the public's participation in politics. Without the firm convictions and passions of ideologies, motivation for political involvement may also decline. In addition, the lack of clear-cut distinctions between parties may result in lower voter turn-out and a reduction in the voters' sense of efficacy. It is feared that the disappearance of real choice and the decline in involvement will contribute to voter apathy and alienation. This may very well be the case. But the ideologies that persist on the Left in France do not appear to be effective in stimulating public participation or in providing real choice. All parties of the Left including the Communist Party, are suffering from declining memberships[8]—and they have never had large memberships. Those members that remain are not as actively engaged in party functions as in the past. The continued decline of the parties of the Left at the polls suggest that if their ideological positions do offer a choice to the voter, it is not a choice that the voter is ready to accept. It may be claimed that the reason that the ideologies of the French Left do not fulfill the hoped for tasks is that they are too often ignored, and the good effects are negated by the rigid party bureaucracies. This may be true of the SFIO and even of the Communist Party, but it is not so easily maintained in the case of those elements of the Left that insist on purity, such as the PSU and the CIR. They too have been unsuccessful in stimulating new participation, or in offering an acceptable choice to the voter. The conclusion appears to be that whatever the desirable effects that ideology might offer, the present ideologies of the French Left do not provide them. To increase public involvement and to offer a real choice, the democratic Left will have to either revise substantially their ideologies or find an entirely new set of principles.

FOOTNOTES

1.   This paper is based on parts of a forthcoming study of the French democratic Left tentatively titled: *The Attempted Unification of the French Democratic Left*, 1963-1969 (Stanford: Stanford University Press, 1971).
2.   Since not all those in France who claim to accept the doctrines of socialism are members of the French Socialist Party (SFIO), I will capitalize "Socialist" only when I refer explicitly to the SFIO, its policies and practices, and its members. When referring to those outside the SFIO who accept socialism and to socialists in general I will use the word "socialist" without capitalization.
3.   The term ideology is used here in its narrower sense as a particular type of belief system—one having a broad explanatory scope, requiring the total or near-total dedication of its advocates, and having a rational rather than an empirical basis.
4.   The following table indicates the workers' possession of important consumer goods with relation to the population as a whole in 1966. Source: Institut National de la Statistique et des Etudes Economiques, *Annuaire*

Statistique de la France 1967 (Paris: Ministère de l'Economie et des Finances, 1967).

	all	workers
car	48.5%	48.8%
television	47.3%	52.5%
refrigerator	60.6%	64.2%
washing machine	42.3%	48.3%
record player	31.5%	31.8%

5.   The *Fédération de la Gauche Démocrate et Socialiste* (FGDS) was composed of three "families": the Radical Party, the Socialist Party, and the political clubs of which the *Convention des Institutions Républicaines* (CIR) was the largest and most important. Presided over by François Mitterrand, the FGDS coordinated the national politics of the democratic Left from its creation in September, 1965 until its disintegration after the electoral defeat in the elections of June, 1968.

6.   The exception was in 1956 when the campaign of Pierre Mendès-France and a general desire to defeat the incumbents pushed the democratic Left's share of the vote up by almost six percentage points compared to 1951.

7.   While the question is beyond the scope of this study, it seems likely that these same problems afflict the French Communist Party.

8.   The PSU *may* be an exception to this decline in membership. The party claims modest increases in the number of members since 1965. See Michel Rocard, *Le PSU et l'avenir socialiste de la France*, (Paris: Editions du Seuil, 1969).

16 MARGOT LYON

Christian-Democratic Parties and Politics

Christian-democratic parties sprang to prominence only after the second world war, but their ancestry goes back to the Catholic movements of the nineteenth century, when industrialization and constitutional government were becoming the characteristic features of modern Europe. Against this background, new forces began to emerge, partly as champions of the new labouring masses; and Christianity was obliged to adapt itself to a new social and political situation.

The adaptation began in the social field. Christian social reform movements, particularly successful in rural areas, were slow to develop parallel political action. In general, the church hierarchy was wary of political participation in governments that had some of their roots in anti-clerical liberalism—although the church's attitude varied with the history of each government's relations with the Vatican. Once a working relationship had been established with Rome, the church came to tolerate, if not to encourage, the rise of Catholic parties. Throughout the nineteenth century, however, when the Vatican was fighting its long rearguard action to retain diplomatic influence in international affairs, Catholic parties were suspected of being pawns in the power game or even

Reprinted from *Journal of Contemporary History* (Winter, 1967), pp. 69-87, by permission of Harper and Row, Publishers, Inc.

agents of foreign interests: they lost popularity at home as nationalism gained ground. Only gradually did the church manage to establish a new relationship with the nation-states that was no longer dependent on support from political parties.

Paradoxically, however, the conflict between church and state was one factor in the rise of Christian-democracy. The phrase itself has meant different things since it was first used over a century ago; but it is not found in either Great Britain or the United States—precisely those countries where, in contrast to continental Europe, no long-standing church-state conflict now exists. Elsewhere, after the clash between the claims of the temporal and the spiritual world that marked the eighteenth-century Enlightenment and was heightened by nineteenth-century rationalism and individualism, it was largely atheistic liberals who seized political power. The fact that the church survived not only as a religious organization but also as a political force inevitably led the state to concern itself with the church and the church with the state. The determined assertion by governments of the lay spirit was in most cases matched by the church's hostility to constitutional government. This mutual enmity led to a serious moral dilemma for conscientious Catholics, torn between the claims of the church and their natural wish as lay citizens to share in political life. For whom were they to vote? When both left and right professed doctrines that offended the Catholic conscience, a political vacuum was created which many wished to fill with what was acceptable from both.

One of the charges, indeed, that is frequently made against Christian-democracy is that its doctrines are very much vaguer, in particular, than socialist or communist ideology. Catholic social doctrines are set forth in broad general categories based on the principles of 'natural law': they seldom have specific reference to concrete situations. Since they are imprecise guides for practical action, their adherents have developed extremely elastic and eclectic policies, borrowing from other parties and inevitably attracting the accusation that they are turncoats or trimmers. In some situations, moreover, the Catholic parties embrace social and political interests that have little in common on any but confessional subjects: if they are parties of the centre, their left and right wings are subject to sometimes victorious centrifugal pressures. Such constants as there are in the non-confessional aspects of Christian-democratic doctrine include on the one side a concept of authority that derives naturally from the inheritance of the Catholic church, and on the other a concern for the social conditions of workpeople that partly reflects the movement's powerful rival, socialism. At the same time, Christian-democracy's traditional ultramontanism and concern for Catholic universality has encouraged it to pioneer some of Europe's most enterprising postwar attempts to set up supranational institutions, for which it alone had both the concept and the contacts.

The constitutions of 1848 and the publication of the Communist Manifesto in the same year mark respectively the political revolution of the bourgeoisie and the first stirrings of the socio-economic revolt of the masses. Much less renowned, but cherished by modern Christian-democrats as an equal landmark, were the writings of Frederick Ozanam, a professor of commercial law at Lyon university and a disciple of Lamennais and Lacordaire. It was Ozanam who first used the expression 'Christian democracy' in the same year, 1848. 'I believe in the possibility of Christian democracy,' he wrote in *L'Ere Nouvelle*; 'let us give up our repugnances and resentments and turn towards that democracy, that people that does not know us; let us help them, not only with those alms that make men obliged to many, but with our efforts to obtain for them institutions that will set them free and improve them.'

The paternalism of this outlook is evident. It was to remain characteristic of Catholic action in the socio-economic field beyond the end of the century. In contrast to the socialists, who worked for both political democracy and social progress simultaneously, the first sponsors of the Catholic movements were alienated almost as much by the egalitarian aspects of democracy as by the atheism of continental socialism. Although the church admitted men's spiritual equality, traditional beliefs about the natural hierarchy of society were an accepted part of the Catholic outlook: socialist and communist advocacy of class war was anathema. So also was the attack on private property, which in Catholic eyes was one of the safeguards of individual and family rights.

But who was to guarantee such rights? In general the church was wary of the nineteenth century's constitutional governments, which for the most part were founded on anti-clerical liberalism and the beliefs condemned by Piux IX's 1864 Syllabus. So Catholic parties were slow to emerge in France and Italy, where there was open hostility between church and state; they developed faster in countries such as Germany, where Catholics were a minority seeking to protect their rights. Germany, paradoxically, became a model for state intervention in social matters. After Bismarck's unsuccessful attacks on the Catholic church, he pioneered state intervention in limiting working hours, enforcing Sunday rest, and introducing insurance against accidents and old age—thus outdoing the efforts of the Catholic Centre party, as of the socialists, to secure the welfare of the masses.

For many years his initiative found no followers. In the eyes of Catholics, the next important landmark in the social field was the issue in 1891 of Leo XIII's encyclical *Rerum Novarum*, the so-called 'workingmen's charter'. In it, Leo stressed the gravity of the modern social crisis in which two classes of men faced each other, one of them reduced to conditions little different from slavery. The state had the right and duty to intervene in order to ensure that the worker was paid a wage sufficient for him and his family to live decently. The encyclical also acknowledged the workers' right to organize themselves either in mixed guilds with employers, or in workers' trade unions.

Rerum Novarum gave a great fillip to the Catholic movements. Their social programmes increased greatly in scope and number: they now included minimum wages, factory regulations, factory hygiene, health protection for women and children and the limitation of their labour, the development of workers' and consumers' co-operatives, and the fostering of benefit societies. In all these activities, Catholics followed in the wake of socialist pioneering—except in the rural areas, where they took the lead, especially in developing credit banks and other aids for peasant agriculture.

By the turn of the century, the term 'Christian democracy' was widely used in Europe. It had been further popularized by an Italian professor from Pisa university, Giuseppe Toniolo, whose two-volume *Christian Democracy*, published in 1894, became something of a Catholic classic. Toniolo's conception of democracy, however, was both vague and social rather than political, unsuited to a rapidly changing era of industrialization. Essentially, it was based on the notion of reviving the communal and corporative democracy of the Middle Ages, and attempting to show the workers that they ought not 'to support the illusory, wicked, and impossible social-democracy in order to achieve their legitimate aims'.

Christian-democracy's rival bid for working-class allegiance was naturally enough condemned by socialists in the name of working-class solidarity. Conservative liberals, on the other hand, saw the more left-wing Catholics as dangerous allies of the socialists in their efforts to wring concessions through state intervention. It seemed as if the conservative wing had won when in *Graves de communi*, a new encyclical issued in 1901, Leo XIII restricted use of the name 'Christian democracy' to non-political organizations only, and decreed that all such organizations be placed under direct control by the bishops.

The Pope's exhortation was only partly heeded. With or without the name of 'Christian democrats', left-wing Catholics continued to develop political parties as well as social organizations, usually supported by workers' elites and a small number of the lower clergy. France, where Christian trade unions had been slow to appear, was the exception; there, left-wing Catholic movements had slowed down by the outbreak of war in 1914, not only because of the ferocious opposition of Catholic conservatives, but also because of the anti-clericalism unleashed by the Dreyfus case, which made Catholics close ranks. Most Christian-democratic leaders, moreover, shared the conservatives' anti-semitism and militarism; those more markedly left-wing, such as Marc Sangnier, were condemned for extremism by the church authorities, and made submissive.

During the first world war, Christian-democrats throughout Europe, like the socialists, fully shared in their countries' war efforts. After the war, women in Germany and Austria—as in Great Britain, the Commonwealth, and the United States—won the right to vote. The new constitutions of postwar Europe were broadly democratic, often with proportional representation; and those already in existence were also affected by a general move leftwards. All this stimulated the re-emergence of political Catholicism, and gave it a temporary leftist tinge. In Italy, in particular, the Vatican now dropped its ban on Catholic participation in government, and a new party, the *Partito Popolare Italiano*, rapidly rose to prominence, avoiding the name of 'Christian democrat' but seeking under the leadership of a Sicilian priest, don Luigi Sturzo, to make a more modern approach to Italy's political, economic, and social needs.

In Germany, the re-formed Centre became one of the leading components in the Weimar republican government, although its own right wing included some who did not fully accept either the republic or its democratic ideals. In Austria, the Christian-Social party allied with the socialists in the first coalition of the new Austrian republic. Czechoslovakia, Poland, Lithuania, and Hungary all had Christian-democratic parties, as did Switzerland and Spain. France's Popular-Democrat party, revealingly nicknamed 'the party of Catholic youth and the parish clergy', was founded in 1924 in alliance with the Social-Christian group in Alsace, whose main aim was autonomy vis-à-vis the centralized French administration. An important non-parliamentary group, more to the left and very internationalist, was the Young Republic led by Marc Sangnier. The majority of Catholics, however, continued to support right-wing parliamentary parties, while the clergy in general favoured the non-parliamentary Action Française. Consequently, Catholics offered little political cohesive force to the troubled French Third Republic.

Belgium had been one of the pioneers of Catholic political action, with a Catholic party that had played a leading role in Belgian parliamentary life ever since the country's independence in 1831. Towards the end of the century a left-wing movement had grown within the party; it came to prominence after the occupation years, and lived in uneasy alliance with the Catholic conservatives throughout the period between the two world wars. In Holland, the Catholic party was also divided between its conservative and its Christian-democratic wing—the latter closely linked, as in Belgium, with the trade union and co-operative movements.

In all these countries the Christian-democratic parties evolved in relative isolation from each other. It was not until 1925, with the coming of fascism, that Italians led by don Sturzo set up in Paris the International Secretariat of the Democratic Parties of Christian Inspiration, with the task, according to Sturzo, not only of coordinating activities but of warning the world against the dangers threatening freedom and democracy. Italy was represented on the Secretariat throughout the fascist era, but when the German Centre party dissolved itself at the onset of nazi rule, Hitler forbade Germans to take part. Austrians, Czechs and Yugoslavs similarly lost their freedom to attend; there were few Poles or Lithuanians; and it was the French, the Belgians, and the

Dutch who were the most constant in carrying the almost extinguished torch of Christian-democracy until the outbreak of war in 1939. Then, the International Democrat Union was founded in London, where it continued throughout the war years, with the support of exiles from the Christian-democratic parties of France, Italy, Poland, Czechoslovakia, Holland, Belgium, Catalonia, and the Basque provinces.

The greatest change, however, during the century of Christian-democracy's existence until the second world war was its gradual democratization. At the outset clerical and bourgeois, by 1939 the movement had become political and drawn closer to the working class. Authoritarianism and paternalism remained; the movement was indeed the main political haven for conscientious Catholic aristocrats, but by the time that war once more threw European politics into the turmoil of Occupation, Resistance, and Liberation, Christian-democracy was beginning to justify the use of the word 'democracy' in its name.

FRANCE

When the *Mouvement Républicain Populaire* was founded at Lyon, a Catholic Resistance centre, in 1944, it drew on the progressive Catholic groups that had flourished in the interwar years. Foremost among them was *Jeune République* of Marc Sangnier—which had supported the Popular Front in 1936—together with the Catholic trade union movement, the *Confédération Française des Travailleurs Chrétiens*, and such youth movements as the *Jeunesse Ouvrière Chrétienne* and the *Jeunesse Agricole Chrétienne*. In the urgent and dynamic postwar atmosphere the MRP set out not only to reconcile traditional Catholicism with the alienated workers, but also to create a new political climate within France, a bold attempt to regenerate political and social life after the demoralization of the Occupation years.

The party appealed to a larger cross-section of the French population than any other political force: its voters included businessmen, workers, white-collar employees, many farmers, and a high proportion of women voters (although women were not favoured for party offices). It also contained a sprinkling of French Protestants and Jews, many of whom were put in prominent positions in order to emphasize the non-confessional nature of the party. The country in general, however, continued to regard it as primarily Catholic. This was inevitable in view of the backing it received from the Catholic regions of France and from the organizations mentioned above, and because it took a traditionally Catholic stand on such questions as divorce, birth control, and above all the perpetually sore subject of the church schools.

At the outset, nevertheless, like the Christian-democratic parties of Italy and Germany, the MRP sought to offer something new in the political spectrum—a political movement with its own philosophy, equally opposed to Marxist collectivism and to right-wing conservative individualism. It aimed at ending the long hostility between church and state in France, and at purifying French public life by restoring confidence between the state and the citizen. But despite this sense of mission, the MRP found like other Christian-democratic parties that it was difficult to reconcile its aim of introducing high moral standards into public life with its need to achieve electoral success.

The MRP suffered, moreover, from the relative vagueness of the Catholic political doctrines on which all the Christian-democratic parties were based. 'Our political activity,' wrote Etienne Gilson in 1948, 'presupposes certain fundamental convictions that we implicitly admit without always being able to explain them . . . Being incapable of doing this is a weakness.' Basically, however, the party set its face equally against individualist liberalism and collectivism, 'the two facets of a single error'. It respected the individual, but 'each man is not only an individual but a person . . . that is, an individual endowed with reason . . . who can assume responsibility for his acts'. 'There is in the word *mass*,' continued Gilson, 'when it is applied to men, something insulting and repugnant . . . It is not the number of heads that counts but what there is in them . . . From this springs the precise meaning of the word *people*: a group of persons united for the conquest of the common good, which they pursue in the light of reason.'

The person, in this view, is linked with the wider community by a natural but complex and hierarchical social structure, within which the family is paramount. The role of the state is to be the protector and regulator of these natural groupings, without seeking to replace them. Such is MRP political theory. But when the party sought to define its policy on more concrete matters, including questions of economics, its main concerns remained social and psychological, and its policies unspecific. 'Economic democracy,' said the MRP's national council in 1945, 'is characterized by effective participation by everyone in the management of economic affairs, by a more equal distribution of income, and by respect for the rights of everyone . . . It is opposed to capitalism . . . and it is equally opposed to a totalitarian statism.'

Doctrine notwithstanding, in October 1945 the MRP itself was surprised by its overwhelming success at the polls: with over 4¾ million votes, it came second to the communists and a little ahead of the socialists. Much of its support, undoubtedly, came from voters who found nowhere else to register an anti-socialist or anti-communist vote, the parties of the right being temporarily discredited; others no doubt sought their own rehabilitation after a somewhat equivocal wartime past.

Influenced by the postwar political climate, the MRP voted with the other members of the coalition government for state control of the Bank of France and the bigger private banks, of insurance, gas, electricity, and the coal mines, as well as of Air France and the Renault car plants—although it believed that nationalization was justified only in the case of such key industries. It soon became evident, however, that the majority of the party's supporters were far less progressive than the MRP militants, and that many Catholics had been frightened into voting for it by their fear of communism. Early in its career, therefore, the MRP faced the problem of moving to the right in order to keep votes while trying not to betray its own reforming aims. These, according to the earliest party programme, included state planning, the nationalization of key industries, a great extension of the state's social role, and greater influence for trade unions, together with economic modernization and European co-operation.

After General de Gaulle's abrupt departure in January 1946, the MRP was temporarily France's largest party, although it lost its most conservative voters very soon after the General's *Rassemblement du Peuple Français* was launched in April 1947. The MRP quickly got onto bad terms with the RPF, whose outlook it opposed on most questions except that of state aid for church schools. On this, its uneasy alliance with the socialists was broken in 1951, when Gaullist pressure forced through the Barange bill for state aid—a project which it was impossible for the MRP not to support, although it cost the departure of the socialists from the coalition, and the consequent inability of the MRP to push through much of its social programme.

On other occasions, too, the characteristic difficulties of all multi-party systems checked the MRP's early hopes of setting a new style in French political life by following a clear-cut and coherent political line. By the very nature of coalition government, the party was forced to seek different allies for different aims, and only with difficulty did it insert itself into the political spectrum, against the will of the traditional parties, which all despised the MRP as a trimmer. After some years of life and a good deal of disillusion, the reforming fervour of the party's leaders seemed to become channelled exclusively towards European issues. Robert Schuman, MRP Foreign Minister, helped to launch the European Coal and Steel Community, with strong MRP backing, in 1950. The party also supported the proposal for a European Defence Community as a second step towards a federal Europe; but although the project was backed by the German, Italian, and Benelux Christian-democrat parties among others, it was defeated four years later in the French chamber in 1954. When the integration of Europe was re-launched from 1955 onwards, the MRP again took the lead in supporting and promoting a European Common Market as well as the six-nation nuclear energy authority, Euratom.

On colonial questions the MRP's policy was much less progressive: it opposed the independence movements in the Far East and in North Africa, and favoured the maintenance of French rule and influence. Georges Bidault and other MRP ministers bore much of the responsibility for repressive French policies in Tunisia and Morocco; they also opposed Pierre Mendès-France's termination of the Indo-Chinese war, and a few months later helped to bring down his government over the question of Tunisia. By this time, in the mid-1950s, the party was largely shorn of its extreme left wing. In number, its adherents had settled down to a faithful 2½ million. But this figure was to be shaken again as the Algerian war continued, when differences of opinion within the Catholic church had repercussions on the local electoral fortunes of the MRP. Gradually Bidault became isolated, branded rightly or wrongly as an extreme colonialist; and the party drew even further away from his views when the Algiers rebellion and mutiny plunged the Fourth Republic into its final crisis. Sternly condemning the rebels, the MRP approved Premier Pierre Pflimlin's resignation in May 1958 in favour of General de Gaulle, seeing it as the only alternative to civil war.

MRP ministers took part in the Gaullist governments of the Fifth Republic until May 1962, and the party recommended its electors to vote in favour of the General's referenda during this period. But its support was never unconditional: it sought to steer a middle course between systematic endorsement and systematic opposition. This grew more and more difficult as the nature of the General's regime and policies became clearer; and the General's press conference of May 1962, in which he poured scorn on European integration, touched off the resignation of Pierre Pflimlin and other MRP members of Georges Pompidou's government. The party was by this time in a state of disarray. Its electoral support was dropping, and new men—some of them with a trade union background—were advancing in its ranks. At its twentieth congress at La Baule it elected as its President the youngish Senator Jean Lecanuet, and unanimously voted in favour of a motion proposing that it be ready to dissolve itself into a broader 'democratic union'. This was proposed with one eye on the 1965 presidential elections; but the tempting potential prize of the floating voters of the centre was eyed by others besides the MRP. In the event, the attempt to create a centre federation was initiated by Gaston Defferre, socialist Mayor of Marseille; but his attempt to create a broad-based grouping with socialists, radicals, and MRP came to grief on 18 June 1965, when the participants failed to agree on relations with the Communist party, church schools, the timing of the operation, and even its name. MRP leaders rightly felt that their electorate would hesitate to follow them too far to the left. When in December 1965 Jean Lecanuet stood in the presidential election, it was as a centre candidate, but without the support of the socialists, which went to Francois Mitterrand. Lecanuet polled 3.7 million votes in the first round, and helped to force General de Gaulle into his victorious run-off against Mitterrand; but when the 'democratic centre' fought the legislative elections of 1967, it did only moderately well, and the future of the movement seemed both fluid and speculative.

GERMANY

'From the chaos of guilt and shame into which the idolization of a criminal adventurer threw us, an order of democratic freedom can grow only if we return to the cultural, moral, and intellectual forces of Christianity.' Thus the manifesto of the newly-formed Christian-Democratic Union, issued in Berlin in 1945 in a conquered Germany dominated by hunger, despair, and misery greater than any its people had experienced since the Thirty Years' War.

Fostered by the moves towards democratic reconstruction developed by the Occupation authorities from grass roots level to the boundaries of the *Länder* of the three western zones, the party's rise was spurred by the psychological effects of Germany's prostration. While the mass of the people were still preoccupied by the struggle for food and shelter, an active political minority aspired to found a new society based on human dignity, the sanctity of the individual person, Christian charity, the rights of man, and democracy. Democratic ideals were preached from church pulpits and academic chairs by men who felt themselves to blame for having looked on ineffectually at the rise of nazism. Parish clergy enthusiastically backed the CDU, despite the reluctance of some of the hierarchy to give its blessing to a party that included Protestants. The Protestant churches also hesitated, partly because they knew that the Catholics were now in a majority—the Eastern provinces being traditionally the home of Protestantism—and partly because the Protestant vote was habitually dispersed. Their eventual determination to work together was certainly inspired by fear of communism; but it was also the expression of a genuine religious revival and a wish for social regeneration which affected socialists and liberals also, lessening the traditional anti-clericalism of these two parties.

The CDU and later the Federal Republic itself recognized the validity of the 1933 Concordat between the Vatican and Hitler's Reich, although it was left to the various *Länder* to interpret for themselves such questions as schools legislation. Under the Concordat, denominational schools were to be set up where reasonable demand existed; furthermore, in agreement with the Protestants, the clergy were to take no direct part in political life. This latter stipulation was ill observed: some 11 million Catholics attended Mass every Sunday, and the clergy have never been silent on the need to support the CDU. The Protestant clergy have been more divided. Although not entirely happy in the CDU—which has always been considered by many something of a Catholic brainchild with Protestant window-dressing—Protestants were proud of the important part their leading co-religionists played in it from its earliest days.

At the grass-roots level, both Catholics and Protestant party groups wrote their own political programmes. All, however, asserted their basic belief in democracy and expressed their willingness to share in the difficult task of political reconstruction. They stressed their desire for a new social order based

on respect for individual rights; they called for the recognition of the family
as the vital social unit, for the protection of women and children, and for the
right of parents to decide on their children's education. On the subject of
economic reconstruction, some wanted nationalization, at least for certain
basic industries, while all saw the need for some degree of indicative planning,
decartelization, and effective government supervision of the economy. In general,
the party groups supported small-scale private property and aid for farmers,
artisans, and small businessmen; they also asked for relief for war victims, a
decentralized administration, and federalism. At national level, all this became
official CDU policy.

The recruits to the new CDU party and to its Bavarian counterpart, the
Christian-Social Union, were partly drawn from the older generation which had
been active in the democratic parties of the Weimar republic; they were joined
by Protestant conservatives from the northern *Länder*, particularly Lower
Saxony and Schleswig-Holstein, and from Protestant areas of the south-west
such as Württemberg. From its earliest days, the CDU/CSU attracted a large
cross-section of German society—from industry, the professions, and the
administration; from town-dwellers and farmers; from refugees from the East
as well as from native West Germans. It has always enjoyed a high proportion of
farmers' and of women's votes, the latter particularly important in view of the
preponderance of women in the postwar German population. The party also
made deliberate efforts to break down class antagonisms, helped by the rapidity
of social change as well as by the rival efforts of the socialists. Certainly, the
reconciliation and recruitment of contrasting social groups made good political
sense; but the attempt at co-operation was genuine. Its most notable achievement, in fact, was the political *modus vivendi* between the two Christian
churches; but it has been the proud boast of the CDU/CSU to this day that it
represents a cross-section of the whole German people.

For this reason, the party took pains to recruit into its structure numerous
Catholic and Protestant lay organizations, as well as the trade unions, which
wield a considerable degree of influence. The belief that the state should not
usurp functions that smaller social groups can fulfill is a basic part of Catholic
and Christian-democratic doctrine. By following this principle, the party hoped
to avoid classical liberalism's extreme emphasis on individualism and Marxism's
exclusive concern for the good of the collectivity.

The economic programme of the CDU/CSU aimed at a free enterprise
system preserving personal initiative, together with respect for the welfare of
the masses. It also included some degree of state socialism, although practical
policy turned out to be a very long way from the party's 1945 Bad Godesberg
programme, which had urged that 'the country's natural resources should be
given over to public ownership'. This was already modified by the Ahlen
programme of February 1947, which called among other things for decartelization

and the widespread participation of workers in the control of industry, as well as government control in the interests of public welfare; and the 1949 'social market' system adopted by Chancellor and CDU president Konrad Adenauer firmly set capitalist orthodoxy and free competition as the party's main economic aim. Workers' rights to joint control of enterprises were admitted with the proviso that this should not destroy managerial responsibility; social benefits were generous, but did not include family allowances until the mid-1950s. In the 1957 election campaign, Eugen Gerstenmaier declared that the limits of social legislation had been reached if Germany were not to become 'a charity state of the super-socialist type'. At the same time, the CDU admitted that it had abandoned its earlier aim of nationalizing at least the basic industries of coal, steel, and chemicals.

Partly responsible for the CDU's abandonment of its early socialistic thinking was the overwhelming influence of Adenauer, who was horrified by the state capitalism of the Eastern zone, and regarded socialism as a halfway house to atheistic communism. For more than ten years it was he who dominated the political life of Germany as its chancellor and of the CDU as its president. His authoritarian style, coupled with the weakness of Germany's parliamentary and democratic traditions and the CDU's lack of a clear-cut programme, made it difficult for the party to assert itself against his strong-willed leadership. But the CDU rank and file grew more and more restive, and after the succession crisis of 1959, when Adenauer announced his intention to resign as chancellor, then changed his mind on discovering that he could not hand-pick his successor, the tensions within the party became increasingly evident and severe. It already had little cohesion precisely because it was an amalgam of conflicting elements— although its power to sustain itself at the local level made some degree of confusion bearable at the top. And if the CDU/CSU became steadily more anti-socialist during this period, this was only partly due to Adenauer's imposition of his will. Growing affluence in Germany would in any event have moderated the party's early left-wing leanings, which were never strong, in particular among the majority of women voters. Today, there is a tendency to look back with a certain cynicism on these radical beginnings.

ITALY

When the long fascist interlude ended in 1943, the old Partito Popolare (PPI) was revived as the *Partito della Democrazia Cristiana*, and quickly rivalled socialism or communism in its popularity with the masses; it was the only major party that did not demand the immediate revolutionary transformation of Italy. Its policies were based on the aims of the old PPI: it favoured liberty and democratic principles, local and regional autonomy, the rights of the family, and advocated ambitious social reforms. Though in the abstract the DC acknowledged the right of workers to share in business management, little progress was made on this front; DC leaders justified their caution on the ground that in a country like Italy, where one-third of the votes go to communists or communist sympathisers, joint control by workers could be used to obstruct and undermine industry and even the democratic state itself. The rights of private property were to be guaranteed, though the DC in power retained several powerful nationalized and semi-nationalized enterprises inherited from fascism.

Relations with the Catholic church were closer than don Sturzo had ever advocated for the PPI, partly because in the postwar chaos the church and Catholic Action (the powerful organization of laymen, directly controlled by the hierarchy) had been the natural vehicles for rebuilding the party structure. The 'civic committees' of Catholic Action were set up to bring out voters at election time in favour of the DC—with the inevitable corollary that Catholic Action has sought to influence the formulation of party policies, always with emphasis on avoidance of any link with atheistic communism or socialism.

Other elements within the DC, however, had strong left-wing sympathies. Men like Giovanni Gronchi (an ex-trade unionist who later became President of the Italian republic) and Giorgio La Pira had a sincere and burning concern for Italy's underprivileged, and it was owing to pressures such as theirs that DC premier Alcide De Gasperi described his party as 'of the centre moving towards the left'. Before his death in 1954 the party had indeed undertaken bold land reform and regional development schemes, but in other fields was justly accused of immobilism. This was partly owing to the influence of the DC's own right wing, which included conservative landowners and big business-men, who had supported fascism and the monarchy. Between them, in the centre, were large masses of industrial workers, artisans, and peasant farmers, most of them very Catholic and not very reformist-minded. Within these three broad categories of left, right, and centre, the party in turn was splintered between innumerable pressure groups consisting of trade unionists, women, youth; industrial, rural, and urban lobbyists, and local factions of every kind with varying views on politics, economics, and social affairs. Indeed the party was virtually a microcosm of the entire Italian political scene—including elements suspicious of the West and anxious for better relations with the communist world. The only cement that held it together was a common respect for Catholicism.

Although the DC had won an absolute majority in the first free parliamentary elections, held in 1948, Premier De Gasperi chose to rule by coalition, so as to strengthen the solidarity of those political parties that explicitly championed the democratic republic. He formed a centre coalition which was to serve as the basis of most governments for fourteen years. As time went on, however, and especially after De Gasperi's death in 1954, the right wing of the DC party

246 Politics in Western European Democracies: Patterns and Problems

grew more restive and active, at a time when a shift to the left was taking place in popular feeling despite, or even because of, the gradual alleviation of massive unemployment and inflation. This move leftwards was stimulated by the schism between the *Partito Socialista Italiano* (PSI) of Pietro Nenni and the communists after the events of 1956 in the Soviet Union, Poland, and Hungary, and also by the accession to the papacy of John XXIII. All this gave a new respectability to the moderate left, and a new plausibility to calls for a Catholic-Socialist coalition as a way of breaking out of government immobilism. But the 'historical inevitability' of the DC's leftward evolution, forecast by the secretary-general of the party, Aldo Moro, at the national congress of 1959, was bitterly contested.

One of Italy's severest post-war crises was touched off in 1960 when DC premier Antonio Segni resigned after the Liberals had left the coalition. Typically, Segni withdrew because of a decision taken in the inner caucuses of the DC party, without a public vote of no confidence, or even a parliamentary debate. This, according to a Christian-democrat critic, Cesare Merzagora, reduced parliament 'to an organ without a voice at the crucial moments of Italian life'. Several cardinals intervened openly to prevent any collaboration between the DC and the socialists, while socialists and communists began a series of strikes in protest against neo-fascist participation in the government coalition.

After public order had been restored, a centre-left experiment based on Christian-democrat and socialist collaboration at the municipal level was carried out, beginning with the administration of the city of Milan; Catholic Action fought this developing trend bitterly, but without success. In 1962 the first government with a centre-left programme was formed with the 'benevolent abstention' of the socialists; it aroused the intense opposition of business circles and provoked a sharp decline on the stock market. At the next general elections in April 1963, the DC party was accused of betraying religion, morality, and western civilization. Despite this, coalition governments between the PSI and the DC have continued, uneasily, until the present time. However, there have been few striking moves to iron out the inequities and instabilities within Italian society; factional disputes have condemned Italian governments to relative immobility, in which neither parliament nor the parties enjoy great prestige. Much the same criticisms are made of all the parties. As for the DC, in an atmosphere of increasing public cynicism it is held together mainly by two factors: the external discipline imposed by the church, and the realization that an open split would mean the loss of power and all the perquisites of power. None the less, it is possible that the right and left wings of the DC may split apart before the general elections due in the spring of 1968. Socialists and communists have an evident interest in weakening the party by encouraging the present signs of impending schism.

The fortunes of the smaller European Christian-democratic parties largely followed, within their different national boundaries, the same evolution as their larger counterparts in France, Germany, and Italy, and faced the same problems of adaptation to post-war democratic life. These have rather strikingly illustrated the characteristic perplexities that beset any Christian-democratic party: in France the MRP found its influence whittled away by the increasing polarization of political life and the inherent difficulty of maintaining a moderate, or central, position; in Germany the party lost its regenerative force in a rising tide of affluence; Italy's great problem, still unresolved, was to free itself from the too-close embrace of the Catholic church. Italy, it is true, is in an exceptional situation as the home of the Papacy and also of western Europe's largest avowedly atheist political party. Other Christian-democratic parties, physically more distant and less closely involved in Vatican politics, have freed themselves fairly successfully from the control of the church hierarchy—to the point where they claim that the church is merely one of the interest groups that make demands on them. Yet it is in the conservative nature of the church to modify rather than to relinquish any authority that it enjoys; this poses a problem for all parties, and especially for the relatively young Christian-democratic movements of countries such as Spain and the nations of Latin America. It is a problem that is likely to become more pressing everywhere with the growth of a larger educated Catholic middle class that is increasingly restive under church authority.

The cases of France, West Germany, and Italy illustrate another characteristic difficulty: all of them tend in a greater or less degree to include men of different political sympathies, ranging from extreme conservative to radical, together with a host of pressure groups which may conflict with each other on any issue except loyalty to Catholicism. The difficulty of establishing internal cohesion in these circumstances is very great, especially as Catholic doctrine has no fixed economic or political ideology to compare, for instance, with that of communism. As a rule the Christian-democratic parties seek a position in the centre of the parliamentary spectrum; usually, moreover, they exist in countries which, unlike Great Britain or the United States, have no clear in-out parliamentary system. It is impossible to seesaw on a three-legged stool; the centre therefore is obliged either to seek a permanent majority for itself alone, or more frequently to find allies on either right or left. In either case a vote cast for the centre is one which delegates to the party machine the choice between political options that in other countries is made by the voter himself. This withdrawal of open democracy in favour of decisions made behind the scenes in party caucuses is one of the most serious charges levelled against Christian-democratic parties. It also tends to obscure the aims these parties genuinely stand for. Only on certain issues is the party line likely to be clear— notably on support for the family and on the right of parents to decide the type of education for their children. On divorce and birth control it appears likely that Christian-democratic attitudes will become more flexible. Like other democratic parties, they now accept the welfare state, economic planning, and a degree of government ownership. Very often their trade unions cooperate readily with those of socialists and communists.

One line of policy followed by the Christian-democratic parties of all countries is support for European integration. It is significant that three of the main architects of European union were all Christian-democrats and all men from frontier areas: Robert Schuman of Alsace, Alcide De Gasperi of the South Tirol, and Konrad Adenauer the Rhinelander. Their efforts expressed the widespread desire shared by others as well as Christian-democrats to make European boundaries into bridges between the nations instead of trenches. Together in 1950 they helped to launch the European Coal and Steel Community, pilot scheme for the common market organization that was to follow in 1958. The latter in turn was to be the foundation of a more ambitious political union, with Franco-German reconciliation as its cornerstone.

How much right have Christian-democratic parties shown themselves to have to call themselves by their chosen name? Insofar as Christianity means the precepts of the Sermon on the Mount, and insofar as democracy means the public choice of alternative policies by the electorate as a whole, it may be questioned whether these parties have the full right to either of the adjectives in their title. Nevertheless, if the Christian-democrats are neither fully Christian nor entirely democratic, of what other party can these words be used? At its best, Christian-democracy represents a real attempt to apply to political thinking something finer and more organic than the slogans of the class war. Its greatest tragedy has been that too often in its early days it was prone to foster another kind of social war; its greatest service could be to develop truly harmonious relations between church and state.

IV

The Governmental Response

An historical political problem encountered by many of the nations of Western Europe has been to strike a balance between the democratic ideal of representation and the need for a certain unity of authority. On one hand, a strong liberal tradition argued for a limited protectionist form of government with a legislative rather than executive orientation. Basically, the role of the political system was to provide a forum within which various interests could air their problems and attempt to resolve their differences. Parliamentarians were frequently local political luminaries whose legislative behavior was directed toward utilizing the machinery of national government to defend their constituencies against threatening forces—both domestic and foreign. The specter of an activist government involved in regulating the relationships between social groups and managing key socioeconomic processes was viewed with suspicion.

The image of government as limited in scope and primarily protectionist in nature was attractive and feasible for largely rural and agrarian societies. It became increasingly difficult to sustain, however, as the spreading impact of industrialization produced a growing number of diversified interests that were concentrated in urban settings and were at once highly contentious and highly interdependent. Legislative-dominated systems tended to lack leadership capacity and were, as a result, vulnerable to stalemates arising from confrontations between these interest sectors, some of whom came to the struggle with deep ideological commitments.

In response to the need for direction, pressures built up to assign greater interventionist powers to governmental executives and to confer on them the chief responsibility for reconciling the particularistic demands of the various socioeconomic constituencies with the preservation of national prosperity and progress. In some instances, where governmental immobility was chronic, widespread feelings of frustration triggered longings for imposed solutions. Only governments with a concentration of authority and a unity of will appeared to have the capabilities to break the obstructive deadlocks and minimize social disruption.

A familiar and classic example of this is the German case. The successful usurpation of power by Adolf Hitler and his followers was greatly facilitated by the failures of the highly splintered, legislative-centered politics of the Weimar Republic. A similar pattern is readily discernible in the political life of France. In that country a succession of what Professor Stanley Hoffman terms "heroic leaders" have alternated with periods characterized by weak and unstable executive authority.

The swings to concentrated, personalized power in France have traditionally proven to be stop-gap resorts. As political logjams are cleared away, Frenchmen have shown a tendency to lose their affinity for a strong executive, thus depriving the office of institutionalized legitimacy. The final judgment as to whether the de Gaulle years were only another "heroic" interlude in French political history or the forerunner of a lasting, if less grand, executive-centered formulation must await viewing from a more lengthy time perspective.

The British political system presents an interesting contrast to France's executive dilemma. Rather than a pendulum-like alternation between executive and legislative superiority, the English pattern over the last century has for the most part been one of steadily emerging prime ministerial influence. This has led several British political analysts to argue that there has now occurred an overconcentration of power in the hands of the prime minister.

In his article George W. Jones offers a useful review of the evidence put forward by those who claim that the prime minister has become too powerful. While Jones does not dispute the pre-eminence of the prime minister, he does contend that the picture can be overdrawn. In an effort to counterbalance the more extreme allegations of prime ministerial domination Jones endeavors to identify a variety of formal and informal constraints on the autonomy of the Queen's first minister.

The growing influence of executives in many Western European democracies has been augmented by a decline in the policy-making power of parliamentary assemblies. It is with some sense of alarm that Alfred Grosser concludes that Western European legislatures "are definitely in a state of crisis." Having lost the policy-making initiative to the executive branch, continental legislatures are, in the spirit of the times, faced with an identity problem.

In an accompanying piece Professor Samuel H. Beer suggests that the decline of the legislatures' law-making function need not drain these bodies of all political significance. On the contrary, Beer holds that legislatures can provide a valuable stabilizing service by mobilizing popular consent for governmental policies. In this sense, the redistribution of decision-making power between the executive and legislative branches may not so much signify the latter's obsolescence as call attention to the need for a re-evaluation of the legislature's functional contributions.

Just as there has been a reordering of power relationships between the executive and legislative arms of government, there has also been a noticeable shift in the relative importance of elected and non-elected officials within the executive realm. A dominant theme in the politics of Western European democracies has been the growing reliance of public office holders on bureaucrats possessing highly specialized technical and planning skills. This development appears to be a logical consequence of the push into the postindustrial age. As governments take on increasing responsibilities as guarantors and guardians of their citizens' well-being, a plethora of complex problems are created with which elected officials, both for reasons of time and expertise, are frequently ill-prepared to deal.

The growing bureaucratization of political life has not occurred without misgivings. It is sometimes argued, for example, that the nature of bureaucratic life, with its emphasis on formalized rules and regulations, leads to a concentration on the administration of existing policies. Thus it is a common contention that bureaucracies are limited in their abilities to innovate.

Using the French civil service as his subject, Alfred Diamant offers an interesting reappraisal of the bureaucratic capacity for creative planning. On one hand, Diamant demonstrates that the bureaucracy can serve as an innovative body. On the other, he cautions that its ability to do so is highly dependent on the nature of the issue and the existence of a supportive political environment.

Despite the visibility of the technocrat, the institutional response of Western European democracies to the challenges of the postwar decades has not been to convert themselves into wholly "administrative states." The traditions of economic and political liberalism have not been so easily supplanted. Still, the tasks confronting these nations have made it obvious that social harmony and sustained economic growth require a capability on government's part to exert a high level of control over the allocation of scarce resources. Consequently, most are demonstrating a serious interest in planned development.

The piece by A. H. Hanson, which concludes the readings in this section, serves as an introduction to the various patterns of governmental planning adopted by the major nations of Europe. Of particular value are the author's attempts to identify both the conditions conducive to and limitations on successful socioeconomic planning. One impression left by Hanson's survey article is that in attempting to foresee and shape their future images the countries of Western Europe cannot easily ignore or escape the characteristics left to them by their pasts.

17 STANLEY HOFFMANN

Heroic Leadership: The Case of Modern France

The heroic leader is, with reference to "routine authority," the outsider in two significant ways. He tends to be a man who has not played the game, either because he has had little contact with the political arena (an indispensable quality when the crisis that brings him to power amounts to the collapse, and not merely the stalemate of the regular regime) or, if he has been in it, because he has shown impatience with the rituals and the rules. He thus stands in contrast to a Franklin D. Roosevelt or even a Churchill. Pétain and de Gaulle fit, of course, the first category: although both had had governmental experience before June 1940, this experience merely heightened their sense of power and their distaste for the crippling conditions imposed by the Republic on the exercise of power. The second category includes Clemenceau, who was called to head the war government of 1917 precisely because he had the qualities that had made him obnoxious to his colleagues in peacetime,

Reprinted from Lewis J. Edinger (ed.), *Political Leadership in Industrialized Societies*, published by John Wiley and Sons, 1967: pp. 127-139, 143-154, by permission of the author and the American Political Science Association. (Copyright © 1966, The American Political Science Association.) Footnotes omitted by the editors.

253

and Mendès-France, who had been a sharp and intransigent, if loyal, censor of the Fourth Republic until the Dien-Bien-Phu emergency brought him to power.

Moreover, the heroic leader is a man who has been a rebel against the prevalent order of things or the prevalent ideas. In other words, when those ideas are found or proven bankrupt and that order breaks down, he has the kind of prestige that fits best with French notions of authority, the prestige that comes from defiance, from nonconformity, from not having participated (in the errors of the evil way). The heroic leader is a man whose personality and behavior have shown that he has in him the necessary ingredients of such leadership: he has maintained his independence from superior authority, he has said no, he has been right when such authority was wrong, and he usually suffered for it, either through setbacks to his career or through temporary withdrawals from the public scene.

And yet (here we find again the other side of occasional French willingness to lift customary restraints on leadership) there is a difference between "outness" and adventure, defiance and nihilism, being outside routine authority and being outside the over-all pattern of French authority. One turns to heroic leadership when there is no "normal" alternative; but the selection of the hero is not haphazard. Clemenceau had been in the wilderness through much of his career, yet he was a former Prime Minister and tested leader. Mendès-France had resigned with *éclat* from de Gaulle's cabinet in 1945 and mercilessly denounced the colonial and economic policies of de Gaulle's successors, yet he was in many ways a devoted servant of the parliamentary republic and of the Radical party. Pétain's military career before 1914 had suffered from his advocacy of a defensive strategy at a time when the high command was wedded to the offensive, but he had become one of the military glories, a minister and ambassador of the Republic. De Gaulle's career had known rough days for reasons inversely symmetrical to Pétain's, yet he too had tried to gain influence through the ordinary channels, not in plots against them. True, the temporary two-star general of 1940 literally stepped out of France's institutions and exerted a brand of heroic leadership pure, unbound, and self-made that is almost unique in French history; but his success in rallying the Free French and the Resistance around himself was due not just to his character and his statecraft: the rebel hero was not *n'importe qui*, he had served (however briefly) in the cabinet and had had a distinguished (if difficult) career. He was admirable, but he was also respectable. May one suggest a rapprochement between the willingness to endorse and applaud rebellion when the rebel appears not only vindicated but in other ways "notable," and the tolerance of adolescent rebellion because one knows it to be a prelude to conformity?

BELIEFS

With respect to the heroic leaders' beliefs, we find some interesting common features which contrast with those of the "routine leaders" mentioned before. First, we find areas of unshakable dogmatism: a conviction of possessing a certain number of truths whose prevalence is the condition of France's salvation and the purpose of heroic leadership. Indeed, it would be worth scrutinizing the words of the three leaders for references to perdition and salvation and for expressions of a therapeutic approach to leadership, France being the beloved patient badly treated by puny leaders but at last to be cured by a doctor who knows exactly what is wrong with the patient and what is to be done. To be sure, each leader had his own dogmas, and each one proved capable (or had to show himself capable) of flexibility in action. Yet Pétain's austere doctrine of authoritarian regeneration through suffering and the restoration of rural values, de Gaulle's doctrine of the strong state, above factions, engaged in a permanent struggle for greatness on the world scene, Mendès-France's dogma of the primacy of economics, all contrast with the skepticism of many parliamentary Premiers as well as with the willingness of many who held principles and ideals to set them aside when in power (often with a heavy rationalization of why they had to do so).

Second, in part because of their previous experience of having been right and unrecognized, the heroic leaders' self-perception is a peculiar blend of self-orientation and identification with a cause. Self-orientation is not exactly limited to the heroic leaders—French politicians' capacity to project their personality onto the center of the stage and to discuss issues in terms of the issues' impact on their psyches is remarkable. But there is a difference between the narcissism of a Herriot or Blum and the kind of vanity displayed by the three heroic leaders. Theirs was not narcissistic but active and self-transcending, for each one saw himself as the carrier of a message greater than himself. Mendès-France, the least vain of the three, had a serene confidence in his ability; Pétain "gave his person to France in order to alleviate her misery"; de Gaulle has turned himself into a "somewhat fabulous character" whom he discusses in the third person, who is clearly the agent of destiny, and whose moves must always be carefully thought through precisely because they shape France's fate.

Third, this self-perception goes with a coldly or caustically harsh perception of the nonheroes: there is, in all three cases, an undeniable sense of superiority (expressed differently in each case). Mendès-France once confided to the deputies that France had been unlucky in some of her leaders before him. Pétain's treatment of his foes, his indifference to the personal fate of his followers, his obvious lack of sympathy for the individual members of the very elites he was trying to shore up collectively were not just symptoms of that "shipwreck," old age. De Gaulle's way of handling his own followers as instruments or part of the "heavy dough" he has to knead, that attitude of "king in exile" detected by one of his superiors at an early age, the haughtiness which threw ice on the ardor of so many *Résistants* when they met him for the first time needs no elaboration. We have here a clue to their personalities: they are nongregarious men who exhibit in different degrees that melancholy quality so well described by the most self-analytic and gifted of them, de Gaulle: a propensity to solitude in the midst of action as well as in proud and bitter solace once duty has been performed. After all, is it not fitting that heroic leadership, because it is a reassertion of leadership, should be exercised by men who are by personality as well as origin distant from the pack?

BEHAVIOR

The following references to the leaders' behavior apply primarily to Pétain and de Gaulle. They are less true, or more unevenly true of Mendès-France, largely because he was operating within the constraints of the Fourth Republic; but to the extent to which they apply to him too, they show how far he had gone in trying to distinguish himself from the pattern of routine authority.

The political behavior of the heroic leaders seems, first to display a permanent contradiction. There is, on the one hand, the aspect of revenge often mentioned—the repudiation of and reprisals for the routine pattern and its servants. There is, on the other hand, the nostalgia for unanimity and reconciliation, partly tied to the revenge (since the routine pattern is blamed as divisive and denounced for having left unrepresented the "latent" general will of the French), but partly contradicted by the exclusion of the "old regime" from unanimity. The drive for consensus, however vague, mystical, or personal, is indispensable for the marshalling of support, for, as previously shown, the heroic leaders, who shun the kind of structured support that is provided by the ordinary channels (parties and established interest groups), would be at sea if faced merely with the sullen hostility of the discarded channels. The drive for punishment is, however, also necessary; it gives to the most enthusiastic supporters of the heroic leader a sense of accomplishment (as well as jobs), and it provides the new authority with an argument whenever support flags: "do you want a return to the old mess?" Hence heroic leadership always seems to have two faces: a sectarian one, which reenforces that vicious circle already described, and a Rousseauan one, both elusive and delusive, with the leader in a position comparable to Rousseau's legislator. In Vichy the sectarian face was particularly evident, yet there was a myth of latent unanimity or rather of self-evident reassertion of "natural" community structures hidden but never erased by the now defunct Republican superstructures. De Gaulle's rule offers the most clear-cut case of coexistence of the two faces—the constant flaying of the "parties of the past," and the celebration of the "will of the nation," which they do not represent. It is as if the heroic leader could establish his legitimacy only by getting the consent of the "routine authority," and by convincing himself thereafter that such authority is the abnormal, and he is the norm. Mendès-France could hardly "punish" the political forces that had fought him, yet there was an element of vindictiveness in his relations with the MRP and with right-wing Radicals, and in order to get the indispensable support of the organized channels he too resorted to the myth of unanimity, thus putting popular pressure on a restive assembly.

Second, the heroic leaders tend to behave in a way that constitutes a pointed reversal of routine authority. Even when punishment or revenge is ruled out, the heroic leader acts as the opposite of his ordinary "counterplayer." Thus, whereas the life of the ordinary Premier is absorbed by a kind of pure game of politics—defined almost entirely as a perpetual process populated by professional players—the heroic leader tries to make the public (presumably fed up with such politics) believe that he is not playing politics: they are politicians, he is a statesman (cf. Vichy's official designation as "l'Etat français" or de Gaulle's decision upon his arrival in liberated Paris first to "put the State back in its center, which was of course the Ministry of War" before meeting the leaders of the Resistance in the Hotel-de-Ville). Ordinary politics means a method rather than a set of goals, a procedure for making (or avoiding) decisions rather than a net of decisions; therefore the leader who aims at goals and lives for decisions denies that his policies are politics. To a social scientist, politics means difficult choices among values and confrontations of ideas; the heroic leader, even when he proclaims that to govern is to choose, tends to propose to the public *his* choice as a suprapolitical course of action dictated not by necessity, as in the parliamentary style, but by the higher good of the country. De Gaulle's "interest of France," Vichy's "eternal truths," even Mendès-France's technique of *le dossier*—of facts and statistics leading to necessary conclusions by the interplay of evidence and economic science—constitute three very different approaches to "depolitization": in reverse order, an economist's version, a mystical (yet basically right-wing) one, and an astutely political one. Politics also means bargaining and the public banter of horsedeals and barter. The heroic leader tries to maintain a façade of rigorous hostility to such debasing procedures, although a great deal of private trading goes on behind the scenes. Pétain, when the incessant clashes of personal cliques and clans had reached a temporary halt, liked to announce "his" decision in trenchant terms and terse decrees. De Gaulle's disdain for negotiation, his preference for unilateral offers (and vetoes) to which others must adjust and which preserve the appearance of his sovereignty, mark his handling of the Algerian war and of foreign affairs, his transfiguration of bargaining into "arbitration" marks his handling of domestic ones. Mendes-France, true enough, had to bargain far more than he originally wanted to, and to an increasing extent as his time in office ran out; but it cramped his style and proved the incompatibility between the "system" and heroic leadership.

As one punster has put it, the style of such leadership (often far more than its actual substance) is caesarian—and thus totally opposed to the gentle and often unnoticeable massage administered by ordinary Premiers. Politics, for them, is a French garden of rules and regulations within which they move with caution; the heroic leader, even when he observes the unwritten rules of French authority, refuses to be bound by the "ordinary" rules of the political system. Even Mendès-France, a normal Prime Minister, tried to tell the Assembly that he had his own conception of the Executive, one quite incompatible with the rules of a game that made Premiers the mice of the parliamentary cats. Pétain, to show his dislike of the "old regime," violated outrageously the terms of the delegation he had received from Parliament. De Gaulle, in a way, went even farther, since he has proceeded to a constant reinterpretation of his own Constitution—always in the same direction—reenforcing the President's position, and often in contradiction to the letter and procedures of the text.

Ordinary politics all too often means the demise of responsibility: dismembered and buried by the too numerous occupants of power, repudiated by a temporary leader who had a variety of good reasons for wanting to appear as merely the executor of collective compromises or as the foster parent of "other people's children." The heroic leader seizes responsibility as a sword instead of hiding behind the shield of committee procedures; he deliberately puts the spotlight on his acts and claims personal authorship even for measures actually instituted below him. Sometimes such claims are pathetic as well as a bit repulsive, as with many of Pétain's punitive "decisions," actually initiated by his entourage or forced upon him by German pressures. Sometimes there is an aspect of deliberate and (again) spectacular provocation, as when de Gaulle personally took the responsibility of vetoing Britain's entry into EEC instead of letting Mr. Macmillan's application get lost in the procedural sidestreets at Brussels. The heroic leader tends to thirst for responsibility, just as the routine leader longs for absolution: Pétain's proud statement to his judges and de Gaulle's claim to all the social and economic reforms of the Liberation are cases in point.

Ordinary politics, although confined to the "house without windows," really takes place in a fishbowl, and the ratio of words to deeds is extraordinarily high. Heroic leadership certainly does not shun words, but the flow of explanations and justifications is thinner, and above all such leadership depends to an extraordinary degree on secrecy and surprise. Secrecy and surprise are necessary ingredients of the spectacle, components of prowess, ways of renewing the alertness and applause of a people whose support is needed but whose participation is unwelcome. Moreover, the very obstacles found *below* the political surface, in the resistance of the relevant "strata" to change, oblige the heroic leader to concealment and cunning, for he has to preserve the myth according to which past inefficiency came only from the paralyzing rules of the political game—the myth of heroic omnipotence—and he must be able behind the scenes to conclude the deals and wage the retreats that, if public, would make the Emperor look naked, that is, he must disguise the reality of heroic limitations. Mendès-France's "style" of steeplechase suspense in dealing with Indochina, Tunisia and E.D.C. was both "functional" in the short run and dysfunctional à la (rather early) *longue*, in that it infuriated the parliamentarians, who were made to look silly. Because they had to fight heavy odds in extremely constraining situations where candor could have been fatal, both Pétain and de Gaulle have resorted to ambiguity, cunning, and deviousness, often making heroic leadership into the dubious art of deceiving all groups in turn. But when similar constraints confronted "routine" leaders, they could usually not even resort to that black magic: for cunning may well be a resource of the weak, but the parliamentary premiers were too weak even to use this resource; or when they tried it, they were often not able to keep control of events. "Routine authority" can best be characterized either by blustering statements in sad contrast with outcomes ("no German guns pointed at Strasbourg," "Algeria French forever," etc. . . . .) or by plaintive confessions of impotence ("we are condemned to live together," "my subordinates did not obey my orders"). Heroic leadership—and this speaks volumes both about the tragic circumstances in which the French turn to it and about the limits within which the hero must operate—can best be characterized either by Mendès-France's month-long self-ultimatum for a Geneva settlement, or by de Gaulle's dazzling first words to the Algerian crowd: *je vous ai compris.*

All these deliberate contrasts, by which heroic leaders seek to differentiate themselves from routine leaders, are part of what I call the vicious circle of heroic leadership. The style of these practices is of the essence of the French style of authority. The heroic leader is the man who decides, above the hagglers, in the general interest. And by such practices, the leader tries to ground his legitimacy in deeds: routine authority was legitimate because of what it *was*; he will be legitimate because of what he *does*.

The third aspect of the heroic leader's conduct refers to his behavior toward the citizenry as a whole, to the quest for effusive unanimity, not revenge. Here we find one feature, but one only, common to the three statesmen. It is what might be called the constant call to collective prowess. Heroic leadership is both the spectacle of the hero defying the Gods and the mobilization of the spectators' enthusiasm by presenting the hero's performance as a national undertaking. There is, for the rallying of support, a conscious attempt at promoting the identification of the audience with the character on the stage, thus wrapping his legitimacy in their complicity; yet such identification *ipso facto* evades the problem of organizing and channeling support: simply, each citizen is asked to feel like a hero. In Mendès-France's case, the quip reported by Alexander Werth is eloquent enough: that heroic rush after deadlines, those swift successive confrontations with France's enemies and allies, those slayings of the domestic dragons of alcohol and "Malthusianism," *c'était du cinéma*; although it would perhaps be more accurate to switch metaphors: it was like an Olympic race, for there was in the leader's own attitude and in the behavior of his supporters something of the ardor, good humor, and grim earnestness of competitive sports (alas, it turned out to be a 500 yard race, instead of a marathon). In Pétain's antiquarians' dreamhouse, based on the Maurrassian notion that the people had had altogether too much to say in recent French history, there was nevertheless a vigilant effort at rallying enthusiasm both by the tear-jerking display of the old man's self-sacrificing stigmata, and by the beating of drums for the National Revolution, key to France's regeneration: here, the appropriate metaphor (derived from an oddly cheerful song of Maurice Chevalier) is that of the workers who rebuild the fallen house under the guidance of the wise, stern old masterbuilder. In de Gaulle's Republic, although the population is kept in a state of mental and emotional alert by the leader's incomparable sense of personal drama—the well-spaced and well-prepared public announcements, the trips, sublime or familiar, the recurrent crises—there is always an effort to present his acts as the reaching toward and the unfolding of a "great undertaking," a *grande affaire*, a "national ambition," condition of France's role in the world and of France's cure from the national itch of petty in-fighting. Here, the simile most congruent with the General's own self-image (or at least—given the man's complexity—his public version of his self-image) would be that of a modern Moses guiding his flock toward a (very misty) Promised Land.

However, the public conduct of the three men was quite different in various other respects. Mendès-France's style was fascinating because it was a heterogeneous mix between the seemingly inescapable style of French authority reflected in his perception of self and others, and his personal ideal, which is much closer to the model of democratic face-to-face discussions in a "participant political culture." There was a tension between character and convictions: on the one hand, the man himself observed, between him and his aides in particular, the kind of distance that enhances the mystery and sense of fruitful solitude around the dominant personality; his rigor and uncomprising austerity in matters of basic importance to him (such as the fight against the alcohol lobby) projected the image of a confident loner unburdened by friendships and foibles. Yet his very emphasis on *le dossier*, the simplicity of his fireside chats, his plain and flat way of stating the unadorned truth as he saw it, his preference for clear contractual relations between Parliament and Premier—as if the Fourth Republic could be turned into the British political system—

pointed toward a very different political style, which his intelligence and democratic convictions admired even as his temper and training were rather unfit
for it. The qualities of his temper and training contributed to his popular
appeal; but those qualities and the direction of his beliefs contributed to his
parliamentary downfall. Whether the citizenry was more moved by his attempt
to treat them as rational human beings entitled to a faithful accounting of
public affairs by their trustee than by his personality and prowess—and whether
the citizenry was at all aware of a tension between the heroic activism of the
harried leader and his aspirations to merely effective leadership—is impossible
to know.

In the cases of Pétain and de Gaulle, however, no such tension exists. What
is remarkable about their style—above and beyond Himalayan differences—is
the scope and historical significance of common elements. Mendès-France,
whose problem of legitimacy was simplified by the very fact that he was a
regular Premier, could be satisfied with (and indeed democratically believed in)
the self-evident eloquence of deeds. But Pétain and de Gaulle needed and
wanted more. Conditional legitimacy based on achievements past and present
is fragile. Hence the attempt at giving it deeper roots by digging, so to speak,
into the archetype of the national psyche. Their style of heroic leadership
represents a return to the mold or womb of the Old Regime, adapted to modern
circumstances, especially to the special features of the style of political
authority: a baroque version of a classic style. Here, too, we find a sense of
distance between the leader and the led. The two military men, like the Radical
politician, were singularly unbending and ungregarious characters. But whereas
Mendès struggled somewhat against this sense, Pétain and de Gaulle have
cultivated it: Pétain by developing (and letting his sycophants develop) a
drooling cult of the idol who was "assuming" France's woes as a sacrificial
priest; de Gaulle by following rigorously the precepts so exaltingly laid down in
The Edge of the Sword. In both cases, there is the same repudiation of
familiarity, the cult of separateness from the herd, which reproduces somehow
the distance between the subjects and the King. Mendès wanted his popularity
to be based merely on respect for things well done, although his precarious
position obliged him to try whipping up respect with the drug of drama;
Pétain wanted from the French the dependent love and anxious trust of
children; and de Gaulle, cynical or contemptuous toward love, prefers consent
based less on reason than on awe. Mendès tried to mitigate a sense of personal
separateness and the budding personality cult that grew around him by stressing
his team. Pétain and de Gaulle have tried to associate personal distance, which
removes them from the crowd, with personal dips into the crowd or with
personal delegations from the crowd, thus paying homage to the requirement
of equalitarianism. But, as in the *bande* described by Pitts, "where all members
are equal in their common subordination to the leader," the result of that

apparent departure from the lofty practices of the Old Regime merely confirms the purely personal, uninstitutionalized nature of leadership and the abyss between Him and Them: it is paternalism on a grand scale. In a greatly homogenized community with rapid communications, such methods of personal command and contact accentuate the contrast between impersonal administration (including the anonymity of the ministers, *commis* who serve the Leader) and personal responsibility, between impersonal immobility and personal action. They recreate the situation that existed when *le bon peuple* cursed the King's aides, saved its love for the King, and lamented: *si le roi savait*.

The natural habitat of French heroic leadership has always been monarchic: the two Napoleons established Empires; Pétain transferred and transformed his 1917 technique of command by personal presence and appeal into a pseudo-monarchy with the cramped ceremonial of Vichy's *Hotel du Parc* and the pomp of provincial tours, masses in cathedrals, dedications of symbolic trees, pictures of the Leader in every home, school children's letters to and food packages from "le Maréchal." De Gaulle (who inclines toward Louise XIV rather than St. Louis) has the rites of the press conferences, the parades, receptions, and caravans. All of them have cultivated mystery and cunning, in the best imitation of *le secret du roi*. This half-instinctive, half-deliberate recreation of an old tradition shows once again that heroic leadership has two faces: the repudiation of a certain set of rules, on behalf of personality, and the framing of personal power into a reassuring alternate set of rules. Heroic leadership is original insofar as it accepts, develops, and exploits the plebiscitary implications that were latent in the Old Regime (a regime that was once engaged in a battle against the political power of the feudal elites, just as the heroic leaders battle the political power of "routine authorities"); it is the neglect and dessication of those plebiscitary possibilities which were largely responsible for the Old Regime's decline and overthrow. At the end, the Old Regime had become anti-equalitarian and too impersonal, just as routine Republican authority became too anonymous for crises: the thirst for personal rule, which produced the leadership of a Robespierre and a Napoleon, today breeds personality cults around every potential heroic leader, however unrewarding (Pinay), chilling (de Gaulle), unworthy (Pétain), or reluctant (Mendès) his personality. Certainly, the heroic leaders' approach to *la population* differs from the resolutely antiplebiscitarian "heroic leadership" of the Iberian peninsula. Yet it differs even more from totalitarian concepts of people or *Volk* (which require not just cheering spectators but structured, self-sacrificing slaves) and from the Republican notion of *le peuple* (unfortunately more a myth than an organized force). The heroic leader is neither the *peuple's* son (or rather the bourgeois' son) nor the gang leader or big brother of modern Europe's nightmares. He is a personalized King—without camaraderie or concentration camps.

A clue to the hold of the classical cast is provided by the two leaders' rhetorical style, which would also allow for a fine study of contrast with the far less self-conscious flow of Republican eloquence and with the delirium tremens and ideological gobbledygook of totalitarianism. Pétain (who rarely wrote the first drafts of his speeches) prescribed for himself a code-like simplicity and directness of style that seemed to dismiss all the impurities and excrescences grafted on the French language by the nineteenth and twentieth centuries; stark formulas worthy of medals and frontispieces were his form of eloquence—and, in a highly word-conscious nation, not the least of his appeals. De Gaulle's range is greater; whereas Pétain liked his sentences short and striking, de Gaulle indulges in long and complex phrases as if to display his incredible memory. Yet he too, so much addicted in other respects to Chateaubriand's precept of "leading the French through dreams," uses a style of eloquence closer to Corneille or Retz than Chateaubriand or Hugo: a certain fondness for archaic words, sentences that often seem translated from Latin give an early seventeenth century flavor to speeches that are (therefore) almost impossible to translate well. The fact that both men were educated by the Jesuits, steeped in classics, and collaborated on literary projects for a while is part of the explanation—but only part: de Gaulle's speeches as a statesman differ in style from his prewar writings; the older he has become, the heavier the classic patina.

However, the Old Regime is very much of the past: although imitative resurrection always finds a response in times of emergency—for the strait jacket state described by Richelieu is the natural refuge from and remedy for intolerable centrifugal forces—it would not suffice to bring solace to the led and support to the leader, even with the full flowering of plebiscitary seeds. The Old Regime, before the "age of the democratic revolution," could afford to be nonideological, and its Kings could be just statesmen (or weaklings surrounded by statesmen). As Louis XVI's brother discovered, there are limits to mere restoration. What modern heroic leadership needs is not only the techniques of undifferentiated unanimity, which are within the realm of means, but also a grandiose sense of purpose. The heroic leader, to use Weber's distinction, must be both statesman and prophet; here his dogmas serve him well, and if his dogmas are too sketchy or too dry, he must somehow wrap them in a vision. The classicism of the statesman must be wedded to a prophetic romanticism. The literary style, to be most effective, should convey all the allusions and associations of France's golden classic age; yet the modern heroic leader must rule by the romantic resonance of his language as well as by the weight of deeds. Even Mendès, the least romantic of men, communicated a vision of economic progress, social change, efficiency, and fraternal "concert" that, in the cesspool climate of 1954, attracted those perpetual seekers after romantic causes, the young and the intellectuals. Even Pétain, flayer of ideology and foe of romantic disorder, tried to be a quaint sort of prophet: the prophet of a return to *"une francité archaique,"* the reluctant awakener of a romanticism of youth camps, physical fitness, folkloric revival, imperial duty, and agrarian utopia. And what was wartime Gaullism if not the prophecy of resurrection, the romanticism of patriotic exploits, the adventure of the ragged Resistance risking French lives against a formidable foe in order to save French honor, the epic of the unknown leader "too poor to bend," spiting the Allies in order to save France's future? If the second coming of Gaullism has seen a marked prevalence of statecraft over prophecy, the prestige of the *Rex* of 1966 still rests fundamentally on the myth and mystique of the *Dux* of 1940, and de Gaulle's foreign policy remains a remarkable blend of machiavellian (or rather bismarckian) tactics at the service of a vision sufficiently sweeping and remote to be termed a prophecy. But here we move from style to substance.

THE SUBSTANCE OF HEROIC LEADERSHIP

Whereas our analysis of the style of heroic leadership aimed at elucidating such leadership's relations with the style of authority and the political system, a discussion of substance aims at adding the third variable—the nature and scope of tasks undertaken—as well as at evaluating the leaders' performances in accomplishing those tasks. . . .

Let us turn to domestic affairs. There are interesting lessons here about the interplay of the socioeconomic system with the political one. All three leaders have been concerned with transforming the socioeconomic system and two of them with overhauling the political; but their appeals and performances have been extraordinarily different.

The simplest case is that of Mendès-France. He came to power with a clear idea of economic reform as the key to all of France's difficulties; in his speeches he talked at least as much like a professor as a political leader. But the irony of his turbulent stay in power lies in the fact that he was never able to do more than begin. He never was the master of his time. He had been selected to cope with Indochina: this he did, and he was duly praised for it by the National Assembly. But his determination to be more than an emergency "effective leader" within the confines of "the system" proved his undoing. There was no stable majority behind his over-all program: he therefore had to try to realize it piecemeal, exploiting both different ad hoc alignments and his capital of support while it lasted. In order to get to what he saw as the core, he first had to try to get more urgent issues out of the way. Thus he spent most of his time on the foreign and colonial issues because they were altogether more pressing, even though they were ultimately dependent, in his eyes, on the economic *redressement* he was never allowed to launch. He had to hop from issue to issue instead of dealing with them according to his thread of economic reform and priority, thus giving a paradoxical impression of breathless discontinuity. This was bad enough, in that it allowed his foes to wonder "where he was going," but what was worse was that his handling of EDC and of North Africa cost him the votes he would have needed for his economic projects; with each vote of confidence forced upon him by the swelling ranks of his opponents, his majority, hence his effectiveness declined. To be sure, he was often clumsy in handling the deputies, yet no amount of clever cajoling would have been of much help, for he too wanted not only to accomplish certain substantive things (not so different from those his rival, minister, and successor E. Faure desired), but he also thought that the accomplishment would lose much of its worth and substance if it had to be squeezed out of the laborious, devious, and often humiliating devices of the system. Within the system, tasks could be performed in a certain way, but in the process, the performance was bound to take a frayed air and a dubious smell; yet within the system, the kind of performance heroic leadership seeks was impossible—only the style remained. To play according to the rules (as Faure did), issues had to be delayed, laminated or redefined until the cabinet's majority reached a consensus, usually at the expense of effectiveness. This is precisely what Mendès wanted to avoid; in his game, fluctuating majorities shaping issue after issue were the only tolerable alternative to the impossible ideal world in which problems could be taken up in order of intellectual importance. He thus exhausted his credit; but he got some issues settled. After him, Faure also got some issues settled; yet the way in which he did it made both the settlements and him look tarnished, and for all his skills he did not last much longer than Mendès.

Once out of power, Mendès-France's attempt to retain his charisma as a leader for times of trouble collapsed for three sets of related reasons. One, as I have indicated before, there was no room within the political system for the kind of renovated Radical party he belatedly tried to build: turning into a stern and programmatic opposition force an institution which was both a prize exhibit of "delinquent peer group" behavior and a machine for the occupation of power was a hopeless task. Two, in French society, intense hostility rose against a man whose ideas seemed to violate the French notion of change. This emanated from another tension in Mendès. On the one hand, in conformity with the idea that change is acceptable only when total, he presented his views in the most provocative and global fashion: "we are in 1788," and only a totally new approach to economic management was going to save France. On the other hand, if one looked at his more concrete suggestions, one saw that the apostle of budgetary transfers, tax reform, productive uses of resources, and colonial liberalism aimed not so much at moving France from one rather depressed plateau to a more exalted one where the hierarchy of statuses and the various strata's vested interests would be intact, but at demolishing some of those privileges and at overhauling the hierarchy. Precisely because of the nature of his plans, his stress on total change hurt rather than helped, for it sounded too much like "uneven" total change, rather than that harmonious massive shift of the whole which leaves relations among the parts intact. Anti-Semitism in France develops only against Jewish leaders who threaten "equilibrium:" Blum or Mendès, but not René Mayer. Among marginal producers—farmers or businessmen—and inefficient shopkeepers, as well as wealthy *colons*, Mendèsisme became a *bête noire*. Mendès' conception of his task clashed with the values of French society. Three, this would not have been fatal if the electoral base of Mendès had been solid, but here was the rub: at the intersection of the economic and social system and of the political one. There was in the electorate a large mass of voters who either were, in their dissatisfaction with the regime, floating from party to party, or were supporting conservative candidates without being so committed to the parliamentary regime that they preferred those candidates to the right kind of an anti-parliamentary "heroic leader," should one emerge. Yet Mendès could not count on too many of those votes, for most of this electorate was socially made of the very groups that felt threatened by him, and ideologically hostile to or skeptical of the orthodox left-wing ideology Mendès represented—for all his impatience with the "system." He was a man of the Left, and much of the floating vote or the vote that was only "conditionally Republican" was a vote of the Right. In the elections of January 1956, most of these men went to Poujade or stayed with the conservatives. Mendès' fraction was far smaller. The groups to whom Mendès appealed were largely committed to the established parties, and thereby ultimately lost to Mendès: the MRP was his enemy, Mollet's Socialists were false friends, and his own Radical candidates were, in most cases, traditional Radicals rather than faithful Mendèsistes. To sum up: what he wanted to accomplish in French society simply could not be done by a man of the Left within the French parliamentary system.

Marshal Pétain's domestic tasks were of two kinds: the establishment of a new political system and the creation of a new economic and social order. He failed on both counts, not only because of the external circumstances, nor because of the difficulty any heroic leader meets when he tries to institutionalize his personal power. There was a deeper reason: in both realms, Pétain violated some of the most important canons of the French style of authority. In the beginning, he enjoyed extraordinary advantages. He (by contrast with Mendès) could count on the support of all the forces of the Right that had become disenchanted with the Republic in the 1930s and, after many disappointments with pseudo-heroic figures, had been more or less impatiently waiting for their Godot. The collapse of left-wing parties—the suicide of the Republicans—left many of their supporters with no other resort than the old Marshal. Moreover, in two respects he was the man of the hour. At the level of ideas and values, what he proposed seemed to represent exactly the preferences of the bulk of French society, the nadir of the downward trend toward crumpled *repli* and shivering stagnation characteristic of the 1930s. His views about the right kind of social order—"only the soil does not lie"—read like the quintessence of the stalemate society: he was going to provide the magic that would prevent its dissolution by the evil forces of industry (labor and big capital), urbanization, or experimentation; he was going to freeze and embalm it both by organizing it at last for the sake of its own protection and by purging it of all the political and social forces of drastic change. His masochism of regenerative suffering was no more than the exaggeration of a theme often heard in the 1930s: only through a period of insulation and self-concentration could France avoid the disintegration of its cherished "equilibrium." On the level of emotions and symbols, Pétain's own appearance and speeches suggested the incarnation of a certain essence of France that had been submerged by the turmoils of the past century and a half: he was the Ancestor to whom one turned to escape from an unbearable present and a distasteful recent past, and whose appeals—of pathos and for solidarity—spread some warmth over schemes that were basically narrow, petty, and cold.

However, the dream of restoring and strengthening the stalemate society did indeed prove foolish. Pétain literally exceeded the limits which even heroic leadership has to observe. To be sure, his attempt at building a corporate society with rule-making powers in the hands of each functional body, his political system purged of politicians, fitted Crozier's model in that they intensified the distance between strata, provided each stratum with a higher authority to save its members from *le face-à-face*, and endowed each authority with impersonal rule-making attributes. However, there were three major violations of the unwritten rules. First, French authority patterns show a permanent resistance to arbitrariness. Now, especially in the setting up of Vichy's political system, Pétain gave revenge—purges, arrests, a mushrooming of political courts— *de facto* priority over the quest for unanimity and gave reprisals priority over the demand for impartiality. As a result, quick disenchantment, then hostility gripped his earlier supporters. All heroic leaders need support, for without it their aides find themselves working in a vacuum; but few leadership groups needed a vacuum less than the amateurs—admirals, generals, businessmen, local notables long discarded by universal suffrage—Pétain put into many of the positions from which the old political class was being expelled. Second, in the new political system as well as in the new social order, French equalitarianism was being trampled. As we have seen, it is particularly strong in the pattern of political authority; Pétain's paternally indiscriminate swims in the emotions of the crowds were not enough to compensate for a state that seemed almost exclusively reserved for members of the authoritarian elites: the *boursier* was out, only the men with *réserves* were in, except for a few *arrivistes* like the ex-labor leader Belin. In the social institutions created by Pétain, elitism was the rule (this became particularly visible in the industrial Organization Committees and in the Labor Charter); but in French affairs the hierarchy among strata accompanies a desire for equality in each stratum. Vichy seemed too much like the mere triumph of the former "parallel relations" for solving conflicts, the revenge of behind-the-counter.

Third, and most serious, in the economic and social sphere Vichy violated the desire for "balanced," if total change. Pétain and his advisers did not know how to distinguish between stopping the clock—as so many elements in France wanted—and turning it back. It soon became obvious that what the regime's ideologues were after, under the name of *"retour au réel,"* was a flight to the type of social order that existed in Balzac's days. The emphasis on the kind of decentralization that would have made sense when local issues or professional problems could be treated apart from national ones, the rehabilitation of the peasantry, the rural notables, and the small entrepreneurs, the glorification of the Catholic Church, the dislike for uprooted proletarians and adventurous businessmen and civil servants (except those at the top)—all these pointed to a somnambulistic belief in the reality of the unreal, next to which Mendès' faith in the "integral rationality of reality" appears positively sophisticated, and de Gaulle's assumption that *les réalités* are clear and simple to the unbiased mind seems self-evident.

Given those errors, Pétain's leadership could not escape from the following dilemma. He might set up the institutions (political and social) that his dreams required; but they would prove totally ineffective (cf. the Labor Charter, and many of his educational directives) unless they actually worked in a direction quite opposite from the one he envisaged. They would, in effect, prepare the stalemate society for the more dynamic and "concerted" experiences of the post-liberation era, instead of accentuating its static nature and its fragmentation. Instead of embalming it, they would revive its circulation. Or else, sensing the resistance of economic, social, and political realities to reactionary ruminations, he might try to extend the scope and intensity of his power; however, then not only would arbitrariness escalate, but his very ideal of a state that was authoritarian yet limited to the protection of a self-ruled society would be shattered: a totalitarian Vichy would have both increased resistance and violated its own precepts. The instruments Pétain selected, such as the Veterans' Legion and the youth movements, all conformed to the pattern of emotional mobilization without political organization—and to the model of delinquent peer groups, primarily concerned with reporting misdeeds to the police, or with in-fighting, or with the defense of their own interests. Too weak to be effective, they were cumbersome enough to be detrimental. Thus here, as in external policy, Pétain set himself an impossible task; and, here again, the performance of a bad role was execrable, marked by inconsistencies, tipsy twists and turns of men and measures, and an increasing sense of drift. The old Ancestor, the living incarnation of the metaphoric "tree," was a senile man only intermittently lucid; the tree looked impressive, but it was dead.

De Gaulle's domestic leadership falls into two very different periods. In the first, he set himself three main tasks: the unification of French resistance, the initiation of measures of economic and social change designed to restore French power, and finally the establishment of a political system allowing for effective leadership. There were tensions between those tasks. The first task he performed in a way which involved a mixture of intransigence (especially during the Giraud episode) and cunning (using the parties as a means of pressure against the resistance movements), and a masterful exploitation of what could have been a fatal flaw: his very outwardness. Not being connected with any organized political or social force made him a focal point instead of a nobody: a fact Roosevelt never grasped. He had to pay a price in order to succeed: he had to remain above all factions, without any organized support all his own, bring the Communists into power, allow the old parties to reemerge, and thus encourage the resistance movements to create parties in turn. This price contributed powerfully to his failure to carry out his third task. But there would have been no possibility of even thinking about the third, or of performing the second, had the first not been accomplished.

With the benefit of hindsight, we now see that the performance of the second task marked the beginning of the liquidation of the stalemate society's socioeconomic system and associational life. The reasons why the measures of 1944-45 could be taken are numerous. The old consensus on the social order had broken down: the Resistance forces, so largely composed of foes of or dissidents from the stalemate society, were unanimously for those measures. The social groups most likely to be the victims of the reforms (essentially the *patronat*) were resigned to accept change as a substitute for the far more radical kind of purges the Left and Extreme Left were talking about. In other words, de Gaulle (who remembered the lesson later) by his moderating presence gave a kind of "homeorhetic" cast to changes which, although they stopped short of social revolution, involved the creation of a permanently interventionist state (and not only intermittently, in emergencies): a state that would guide more than protect, one that could push France away from the structures and values of the traditional social system. Finally, the traditional style of authority was respected, insofar as the measures were taken from above, involved a minimum of *face-à-face*, were mostly impersonal, and maintained equalitarianism. Indeed, it is because in one important respect de Gaulle chose to be too noninterventionist, too traditional, that his objective—social and economic reform for power—was not fully attained; this happened when he opted for Pleven's laissez faire finances over Mendès' rigor.

The goal of institutional reform was not reached at all, precisely because the role de Gaulle had chosen in order to perform his other tasks made him impotent here. As "the symbol," the champion of unanimity, and the leader above factions, he could not impose his views: the parties he had boosted and the movements he had tried to weld filled the political vacuum left by Vichy. In a familiar swing of the pendulum, they reacted against the two simultaneous displays of heroic leadership—Pétain's and de Gaulle's—by establishing a political system that was designed to be a bulwark against heroes and turned out to be a barrage against leadership. De Gaulle, condemned to solitude, chose, in conformity with his conception of the hero, to get out before being thrown out or used up—for the hero who wastes his time hanging on where he can leave no mark is a fool.

De Gaulle's second exercise of power is a very different enterprise. The circumstances in which he came to power were quite different: more like Pétain in 1940, but better. Like Pétain, de Gaulle in 1958 could count on the electorate that had grown disaffected with the Republic—the mass of voters who had supported the conservatives or had swung from one party to the other and who were predominantly on the Right. But he also had the support of most of the parties: this made it both easier and almost necessary for him to play his favorite role of unifier, instead of threatening revenge and punishment. There was a large electorate available for a Gaullist party: he did not have to try, as in 1945-46, to rule above the vigilant heads of the "politicians." Nor did he at any time share Pétain's illusion that one could manage a political system exclusively with social elites: indeed, precisely because so many of those elites had been with Vichy, his own standing with and feelings for them were never very good. Also, he was able to make his various tasks consistent with one another, as they had not been in 1940-45, and to be at all points the master of his time. Now he could start with institutional reform; he handled the Algerian powder keg in a way that made it lose much of its explosiveness under the combined impact of political stability, economic expansion, and external successes, before he finally disposed of it.

If we look at his performance of what he set himself as his first task—establishing at last the political system he had had in mind for so long—we find that his statecraft has been quite ambiguous. On the one hand, by preserving public freedoms, letting parties operate, allowing his own followers to create a Gaullist party—and manipulating the electoral system as well as the Constitution—he has created an effective political system for his purposes. There is an opposition to him and his style, but no determined resistance either to the man or to the Constitution; there is a Gaullist political class that provides a transmission belt between the country and its leader—the kind of belt Pétain had been reluctant to create and de Gaulle in 1945 had been deterred from creating by his own definition of his task. On the other hand, the victory of the Gaullist forces is itself largely due to de Gaulle's constant attacks on the old parties, a fact that encourages them in their determination to avoid a perpetuation of

Gaullism after de Gaulle. The Gaullist party, which is invaluable in providing the Leader with a cooperative Parliament, is both held at arms' length by a man hostile to all parties, and devoid of any program other than following the leader. It thus tends to behave as the classic peer group, primarily concerned with being "in" and with keeping all others out—which raises the questions of the viability after de Gaulle of a party that is far from homogeneous and of a Presidency which de Gaulle has tried to keep tied only to the undifferentiated "people" and divorced from the party system. For as we have seen, if the Presidency stays thus divorced, it risks constitutional deadlock, yet if it becomes the plaything of parties anxious to return to routine authority, it risks debasement. Whereas in foreign affairs de Gaulle has chosen example over success, the success he has achieved in reforming the political system may prove to be unexemplary after him.

One may be tempted to resolve this ambiguity by turning to his second area of performance, the resumption of his second task of 1944-45: economic and social modernization for power. But here again we get a two-faced answer. The liquidation of the stalemate society has proceeded, and de Gaulle has neither hesitated to stress, in tones the prudent Fourth Republic had shunned, the imperatives of constant (not just cataclysmically occasional) change, the need for organized groups capable of cooperative action, and the duty of "public action to guide our economy," nor refrained from doing what he had failed to do in 1945: hurt "established situations" and privileges by drastic financial measures in December, 1958 and again less drastically in the 1964 stabilization plan. If he has succeeded in his role of modernizer, it is partly because the ground had been laid ever since 1945, and the wave of expansion, industrialization, urbanization had been advancing for some years when he returned to power; all he had to do was to maintain the pressures, so that there would be a continuing flow of benefits to help convert the skeptics to the virtues of growth and compensate the losers. But he has succeeded also for another set of reasons. Less rash than Mendes-France, he has been careful not to destroy the homeorhetic image. When he sings the praise of change, it is because the "old equilibrium" has become untenable, and only *orderly* change can lead to a *new* equilibrium: change is but the condition of permanence. There must be progress, but in stability; industrial growth, but in financial rigor and with balanced budgets: "In France, the revolution goes on regularly, day after day, because it is accepted by the public and inscribed in law." Thus the style of authority is preserved, separated from the stalemate society that had so long been its symbiotic partner. His handling of the Algerian crisis is a case in point. In order to convince a stuck and sizzling army to sacrifice the old *vested interests* of the nation overseas, of the settlers in Algeria, of the colonial army itself, he showed that an obstinate and futile pursuit of victory would actually wreck the new "equilibrium" of France; he showed that the

army could find in conversion to atomic defense a far more prestigious equivalent of its imperial glories: once again total change, but in orderly harmony,
was presented as the answer to both the irresistible pressure for change and
the fear of changes in the hierarchy of statuses.

What serves de Gaulle so well in this double performance is his indifference
to problems of class. He is not wedded to the old order, and he is ready to
throw his support to whatever group is most likely to serve his goal of power:
the workers in 1945, the public and private "technocrats" today. Yet his very
indifference allows him to combine the notion of change-for-power with that of
a harmonious hierarchy. The ambiguity in performance corresponds to a tension
in the man. His vision is one of "association," of a kind of cooperative concert
for growth and grandeur, very different indeed from the patterns and practices
of authority in the stalemate society; yet his methods respect the old style. The
State rules above the citizens, the associated groups are merely consulted, much
intellectual distance between strata persists, and the behavior of each stratum
toward authority still conforms to Crozier's model. Thus in France today, many
of the structures of the stalemate society and the values that referred to its
socioeconomic system are being abandoned, but the values that refer to authority—values which preceded the post-Revolutionary stalemate society—survive
and preserve many residues from it, just as they had conserved in it residues
of the feudal society.

Let us go back to the political sphere. To be sure, it reflects some of the
changes that mark French society. An increase, however moderate, in "dialogues," the homogenizing impact of industrialization on a formerly fragmented
economy and society, the soothing effects of economic growth and political
stability have muted apocalyptic thought, calmed revolutionary talk, tamed
ideological stances. This is felt throughout the political system, and it gives to
most political parties a startling similarity of programs. Yet it would take an
act of faith to proclaim that de Gaulle's exercise in heroic leadership will
succeed in providing France after him with that synthesis so often sought
between the two kinds of political systems and the two poles of authority
patterns. Among the encouraging signs, there may well be the presidential
elections of 1965, which tarnished de Gaulle's personal halo yet gave him an
institutional blessing, in a way routinizing an excessively "charismatic" rule.
Among the discouraging signs, there are the legislative elections of 1967. They
have weakened and strained the Gaullist forces; they have decimated yet preserved a strategically important center; they have given back to a reviving Left
that thirsts for blood its anti-Executive itch, which feeds on the Left's strength
in Parliament (once again the preferred arena for the Left's exploits), on the
Left's own divisions (which make pure negativism much the easiest tactic as
well as the most familiar) and on the provocations of an Executive that prefers
the risky exhilaration of whiplashing Parliament to the compromising attrition

of reasoning with it. Thus, suspense continues. The political system remains unsettled, in part because it has its own rules, different from those of the economic and social system, and, despite all reforms, still perversely favorable to fragmentation (due to the impact of the electoral system, the tendency of old parties neither to die nor to fade, the nonsubstantive yet crucial and complex issue of the fate of the UNR after de Gaulle, the role of memories and resentments in shaping alignments), in part because the style of political authority persists. Indeed, it has changed much less than patterns of authority in the rest of society; there is less participation, less willingness to compromise and cooperate constructively, less discipline even than in the economic system; and heroic leadership takes only too fond care of that style, thus making possible by its own behavior a return to routine authority as soon as the hero is gone and as his foes, resurgent and relieved, are able to express their joy of leaping from one extreme to the other.

THE IMPACT AND FUTURE OF HEROIC LEADERSHIP

Its importance has been stressed throughout this chapter. It is heroic leadership alone that can succeed in injecting massive doses of *innovation* into a national system that is highly suspicious of change and ordinarily combines tolerance for individual experimentation with social conformity. But since even heroic leadership must respect the rules of homeorhesis, and since the conversion to change requires a mobilization of national energies, a reawakening of the general will, a call to national identity, such leadership serves also as the *maintainer* of the system. When routine leaders can no longer preserve it or make change acceptable, heroic leadership saves the society by adapting it and perpetuates it by renewing it. Yet heroic leadership's importance should not conceal its disadvantages. The features of the national system which heroic leadership sustains may themselves deserve to be jettisoned, whether we think of a style of authority that impedes participation, delays, restrains, and twists economic and social progress, or of a style of behavior on the world stage that prolongs the game of national units proud of cultivating their differences. Even if one accepts these features, one cannot help noting the special flaws of heroic leadership in the French polity. First, the plague of impermanence, which drives heroic leaders into an endless and often reckless gamble for legitimacy; second, the rallying of support through magic rather than reason, the manipulation of frequently infantile needs for dependency, the creation of a civic culture in which mass hypnosis replaces organized citizenship; third, the tendency of a brand of leadership that represents one pole of a French style which juxtaposes the need for and the fear of authority, to slide into tyranny or to glide from the search for unanimity into the imposition of conformity—even if the French body politic produces its own antidotes.

Good democrats would like to celebrate at last the demise of French heroic leadership. Yet, *on ne détruit que ce qu'on remplace*. The new social system is not completed, the new style is still in limbo, the new political system is still in question. De Gaulle has written that when the traditional leadership of the old elites vanishes, the "man of character" becomes the only alternative to anonymity. Whether a "man of character" can be found every seven years, and not only in emergencies, or whether the anonymous elites of routine French politics will resume their role remains to be seen. De Gaulle's inner conflict between an aspiration to political institutionalization and concerted modernization, and his instinctive, temperamental grasp of prowess-leadership which shuns institutionalization and disdains concert reflects France's own state of suspense: between drastic changes in social structure and values, and striking continuity in the structures and values of authority relations, especially political, between the so-called requirements of an industrial society, and the residues of France's pre-industrial mold, there is bound to be battle. Will change defeat continuity? Will the residues prove so resilient that they will both limit the impact of industrialization and preserve the traditional oscillation in the political system? Will, as Crozier and others believe, industrialization and mass consumption bend the style of authority throughout the social and the political systems to their own need for better communications among and greater participation of all the people? Or will the old aristocratic concerns for prowess, prestige, and rank, the old clinging to independence and the fear of participation remain undefeated, at least in the political realm?

We can only raise the questions. We can also (as usual) point to some fine paradoxes. In an age in which economic progress has become a primary concern of the French, the leader who made of it the cornerstone of his program owes most of his diminished appeal to the memory of the spectacle he once gave. The leader most apparently concerned with stabilizing what he saw as the essence of France and with safeguarding the existence of the French, most adventurously strayed from what her "essence" allowed and her (if not their) existence required. The leader apparently most suspicious of dogmas, most "existentialistically" engaged in recurrent self-definition through action, without attachment to old forms of shibboleths or any other limits than the "realities" of the "situation," has been the one most aware of the unwritten rules even heroic leadership must respect to be successful. French heroic leadership is like French classical theater: it never ceases being dramatic, yet the drama must follow rules. Whether such leadership is closer to the august and candid characters of Corneille, or to the devious and driven characters of Racine, is up to the reader to decide.

18 GEORGE W. JONES

The Prime Minister's Power

Personality bears the burden of much contemporary writing about the office of the Prime Minister. Yet this position has only recently been held by men as different in character as Sir Winston Churchill, Clement Attlee, Sir Alec Douglas-Home and Harold Wilson. Such men come and go in Downing Street; the institutional features of the office persist. George Jones's review of these characteristics provides an unemotional and detailed account of the constraints that operate upon the Prime Minister of the day, whatever his personal characteristics.

It has become part of the conventional wisdom expressed by some academics and journalists that the position of the Prime Minister in the British system of government has altered significantly in recent years. No longer, they assert, is he merely *primus inter pares* or just the leading member of the Cabinet, but he has been transformed into something quite new, perhaps a quasi-President, or an elected monarch or even an autocrat. The Prime Minister's predominance, attained by Churchill during the Second World War, is said to have persisted in peace-time during the administrations of Attlee, Churchill again, Eden, Macmillan, Douglas-Home and now Wilson.

Reprinted from *Parliamentary Affairs* (Vol. XVIII, No. 2, 1965), pp. 167-185, by permission of *Parliamentary Affairs*. Footnotes omitted by the editors.

If this view is correct then Cabinet Government is a dignified façade behind which lurks the efficient secret of Prime Ministerial power.

It may not be possible to test the validity of these suppositions until the Cabinet papers are made available, fifty years after the events they refer to have taken place, and until the politicians and civil servants involved in the process have published their memoirs. But even with the scanty evidence at present before us, there are grounds to argue that the Prime Minister's power has been exaggerated and that the restraints on his ascendancy are as strong as ever, and in some ways even stronger. The aim of this paper is to consider the argument that the Prime Minister has become more powerful and to suggest some countervailing factors which seriously inhibit his freedom to initiate and manoeuvre.

The elevation of the Prime Minister is attributed to many trends. The extensions of the franchise, the growth of nation-wide mass parties and the development of the mass media of communications are said to have changed the nature of a General Election. From a number of separate constituency contests it has become almost a plebiscite, a gladiatorial contest between the party leaders. On them are concentrated the efforts of the party propagandists and the attentions of the press, radio and television. Their words and nuances of expression are carefully analysed to expose their parties' policies, which they are supposed to embody. This personalisation of political issues and allegiances is said to be essential if most of the electors, who are not very politically conscious, are to be reached, interested and won over. They may not understand or follow debates about policies, but they appreciate a clash of personalities. The leaders appear to be the only significant contestants during the campaign; neither the calibre nor the personal views of the other candidates count for much more than 1,000 votes, since the electoral swing over the whole country or at least regionally at a General Election is fairly uniform. Candidates seem to attract or repel voters solely on the basis of which leaders they will support in the House of Commons.

Thus the only mandate given by the electorate to an MP is to support his leader. The Prime Minister therefore can be sure that his party in the Commons will back him. Obedience to the Prime Minister, however, rests not just on the commands of the electors. Some commentators claim that the Prime Minister's power to obtain a dissolution of Parliament from the Crown deters his supporters from rebellion, since they wish to avoid a costly and arduous election campaign which may jeopardise their seats. Others stress that if MPs voted against their party in the House, their constituency parties would be likely not to readopt them as official candidates, and without party endorsement the former MPs would be defeated ignominiously, like Dr. Donald Johnson at Carlisle in October 1964. Party loyalty, feelings of personal attachment to a group of colleagues and fear of letting the other party either damage the standing of his own party or even gain office, are additional pressures on an MP to follow his party's line.

The party policy which the MP has to follow is most likely the Prime Minister's policy, rather than a collective party policy which all members have helped to form. A Prime Minister, whether Conservative or Labour, effectively controls his party and is not restrained by it, despite the differences in the formal constitutions of the parties. The limitations which the Labour Party's constitution places upon its leader fall away when he becomes Prime Minister, and are superseded by the conventions of the British Constitution, which put into his hands the power to choose his colleagues and decide policy. The powers of a Conservative and a Labour Prime Minister are identical: they have the freedom to choose whom they will to be members of their Governments. One appointment in particular is of special importance in sustaining the Prime Minister's sway over his Parliamentary colleagues, and that is the Chief Whip. As a Lord of the Treasury he is directly responsible to the Prime Minister for the performance of his duties. He lives at 12 Downing Street, close to the Prime Minister, with whom he can communicate unobtrusively whenever required. They have daily sessions together, called 'morning prayers', when they discuss the state of the Parliamentary party. The Chief Whip has to maintain discipline amongst its ranks, and he does this not just by bullying, but also by explaining and clarifying the Prime Minister's views to those who are anxious. He also assists the Prime Minister to dispense a host of honours, awards, decorations, knighthoods and peerages, and of particular significance for the MPs, Government offices. MPs are said now to have less scope to make reputations as mere backbenchers. They want Government office, and the easiest way for them to earn this reward is to give loyal service to the Prime Minister and not to appear to him or the Chief Whip as nuisances. Criticism of the Prime Minister will bring his disfavour which will block future prospects of advancement. The importance of the power of patronage has increased as the number of Government offices has grown. Conservatives have recently attacked Harold Wilson for enabling more MPs to hold Government offices, on the grounds that he is reducing the independence of the legislature, by packing it with placemen dependent on the executive and his will. Alarm has also been expressed that even Parliamentary Private Secretaries are being regarded as junior members of the Government, liable to lose their unpaid offices, if they oppose a Government decision. Promotion seems to depend on knuckling under to the Prime Minister's decisions. Thus the loyalty of the MPs is cemented to the Prime Minister because the Chief Whip, who maintains discipline and helps to bestow patronage, is a personal agent of the Prime Minister, and because the amount of patronage at the Prime Minister's disposal has increased.

Through his control of his party the Prime Minister can be certain that the Commons will support his Government and accept his measures. His will becomes an Act of Parliament, for the House of Lords is no obstruction to Commons' decisions and the Queen's assent is automatic. The Courts, too, will not resist a statute. Parliamentary Sovereignty means Prime Ministerial Sovereignty. It does not mean Cabinet Sovereignty, because the Prime Minister is said to dominate his Cabinet through his power to appoint and dismiss its members, to control its operations and even to bypass it altogether by the use of Cabinet Committees and informal conversations with individual Ministers.

The Prime Minister's power of patronage is said to enable him to master his Cabinet. Able to hire and fire, to demote and promote and to allocate particular offices to whomever he pleases, he holds the political future of his colleagues in his hands. He can advance the careers of those he favours and check those he dislikes according to the positions he gives them, for some offer the chance to make a good reputation, while others can bring the holder little esteem. Thus a Minister who wants to climb is dependent on the Prime Minister, and the easiest way to earn his gratitude is to serve him loyally. Ministers are not usually keen to retire. Since the Cabinet consists of a fairly formal hierarchy of Ministers, resignation would take a man out of the queue for higher office. Few want to lose their places, so they stay, often consoling themselves and others with the thought that they can be more influential on future policy inside rather than outside the Cabinet. If they do resign, they will be asked to explain why, and if the reason is a disagreement over policy, then the Opposition is given an opportunity to damage the party, which injures even more the reputations of those who resigned. The Prime Minister is strengthened because of his Ministers' reluctance to resign. Even when some important Ministers do resign, the Prime Minister can remain secure and laugh the episode off as a little local difficulty. He can dismiss a large part of his Cabinet and still stay secure. The famous purge of 12 July 1962, when Harold Macmillan sacked one third of his Cabinet, made twenty-four Governmental changes in all and brought eleven back-benchers into the Government, is said to indicate the great power of the Prime Minister and the dependence of his colleagues on his whims. He creates and destroys his Cabinet at his pleasure. When he retires, so do all his colleagues; his successor has a free hand in forming his own administration.

Once the Cabinet is chosen the Prime Minister is said to have a free hand in managing its operations. It meets in his house; its members wait outside the door of the Cabinet room until he is ready to start. He controls the agenda; his Ministers send their papers to the Cabinet office, whose Secretariat prepares the agenda, which the Prime Minister has to approve. He can therefore keep off the agenda anything he wishes, include what he wants and stop the circulation of any memoranda he objects to. No Minister, it is claimed, can get anything discussed at Cabinet which is not on the agenda. If he tries to raise such an item, the Prime Minister as Chairman can rule him out of order and even walk out, thus closing the meeting. During the proceedings he guides the discussion, naturally along the lines he wants, and when he is ready, he can end the discussion with his summary and assessment of the sense of the meeting. He may have listened to the Cabinet's advice, but the last word is his. Since no votes are normally taken, it is hard for opposition to his views to crystallise, and it is rare for his decision to be challenged.

It is often claimed that the Prime Minister has scant concern for his Cabinet, whose approval of his decisions is a mere formality, or which he can side-step completely. Through informal talks with individual Ministers, who are more amenable alone than in Cabinet, he can infiltrate his views, influence and even reshape the Minister's proposals. At his house, at Chequers, over meals, or through the network of private secretaries, he can arrange with Ministers the main outlines of what they will present to the Cabinet. Policy will have been settled before the Cabinet stage. The Prime Minister can set up Cabinet Committees, chaired by himself or a trusted colleague, to watch over certain topics or certain Ministers. Here issues can be thrashed out in a thorough discussion and policy proposals agreed. Members of the Cabinet not in on these discussions find it very difficult to raise objections in Cabinet when these matters arise. They lack knowledge about the problems involved; they would be unlikely to prevail and fear to make fools of themselves through their ill-informed contributions. The crucial policy decisions, it is said, are taken not in the Cabinet, but in inter-departmental Committees after consultation with the interests concerned, in Cabinet Committees, or in conversations between the Prime Minister and an individual Minister. This downgrading of the Cabinet is said to have been encouraged recently by some new methods introduced by Harold Wilson; working weekends at Chequers for the Ministers and officials concerned to discuss defence and economic policies, working dinners at 10 Downing Street for Vice-Chancellors and exporters, and the meetings between the Prime Minister and the heads of the aircraft industry. These developments show once again that the Prime Minister and not the Cabinet is the crucial element in the decision-making process.

Some commentators have said that an inner Cabinet has emerged, the efficient part, which really directs the formal Cabinet's activities. It is said to comprise the Prime Minister and a clique of his personal cronies. They take the important decisions and get them through the Cabinet or else avoid it. Churchill is said to have ruled in this manner; Attlee began the large-scale production of atomic weapons and Eden carried out his Suez policy by means of these techniques of government. The Cabinet as a whole and individual Ministers are kept very largely in ignorance; a Minister may find that a decision is taken concerning his own department without his being consulted. Thus the traditional concept of collective Cabinet responsibility applies no longer, or else applies in a new way. Ministers have the choice now if they disagree with the Prime Minister's decisions either of resigning or of accepting them. The concept of collective responsibility is used to muzzle the opponents of the Prime Minister in the Cabinet. The Cabinet has been transformed into a network of Committees and individuals, all subordinated to the Prime Minister who controls them. His personal policy is endorsed automatically as Cabinet policy.

The concept of individual Ministerial responsibility has also been transformed, since a Minister is said now to be the public relations man for his department and the errand boy for the Prime Minister. This change is supposed to have been revealed in 1962 by the Foreign Secretary (Lord Home) when he said in an interview. 'Every Cabinet Minister is in a sense the Prime Minister's agent—his assistant. There's no question about that. It is the Prime Minister's Cabinet, and he is the one person who is directly responsible to the Queen for what the Cabinet does.

'If the Cabinet discusses anything it is the Prime Minister who decides what the collective view of the Cabinet is. A Minister's job is to save the Prime Minister all the work he can. But no Minister could make a really important move without consulting the Prime Minister, and if the Prime Minister wanted to take a certain step the Cabinet Minister concerned would either have to agree, argue it out in Cabinet, or resign.'

The Civil Service is also said to be dominated by the Prime Minister. As Government has expanded its activities, there has been a growing need to centralise and co-ordinate the administration to ensure coherence of policy. Free of departmental entanglements the Prime Minister is able to survey the whole range of Government and to intervene where he likes. He is aided by the Cabinet office and his own private office, both of which act as his intelligence agencies. Through their work 10 Downing Street is said to be much better informed about the full spread of Government business than any other department, and this factor tends to set the Prime Minister apart from his colleagues. 'In the nervous system of Whitehall, the Prime Minister's office must be the ganglion.' His control over the Civil Service is achieved also by his close links with the Treasury. The personnel of the Civil Service are managed by the Establishment Division of the Treasury, whose Joint Permanent Secretary, the Head of the Home Civil Service, is directly responsible to the Prime Minister in his capacity as First Lord of the Treasury. He is, therefore, able to decide which Civil Servants will hold the most important positions in the departments. This patronage is said to enable his will to prevail in Whitehall.

Thus the Prime Minister controls his party, Parliament, the Cabinet, and the Civil Service. But he can also control to a great extent the succession to his position. If he retires in mid-term, he is strongly placed to pass on his office to the man of his choice. This is somewhat easier for a Conservative than a Labour Prime Minister to do, since the Labour Party's constitution lays down that the MPs shall elect a new leader, while the Conservative Party uses certain processes of consultation, which allow the outgoing Prime Minister great scope to gain support for his favourite. It seems that Harold Macmillan's activities helped Sir Alec Douglas-Home to succeed him. A Labour Prime Minister, however, can smooth the path of his choice and obstruct the course of another through his power to allocate Governmental offices. His candidate can be given a position from which to earn a good reputation, while the other can be landed with a difficult assignment unlikely to advance his career.

When the Prime Minister has finally to face the people at a General Election, he does not undergo a severe ordeal. He can decide when to appeal to the country within the statutory limit, and since opinion polls furnish him with a fairly accurate assessment of the likely result, he can pick a favourable time. For the actual campaign he has many advantages over the Leader of the Opposition. Publicity is showered on him as Prime Minister, wrestling with the nation's problems and speaking for the whole country. He can be depicted as more constructive and less partisan than his apparently party-minded and carping opponent. He can turn his whole term of office into a permanent election campaign, using the manipulative techniques of the advertisers and public relations men to create for him a favourable image in the eyes of the gullible public. Prime Ministers have rarely lost elections in the twentieth century. Sir Alec almost won, and might have succeeded if he had been able to stay on longer.

The Prime Minister, therefore, is in a position of unrivalled predominance, and one ex-Prime Minister has been prepared to admit this himself. Lord Avon has said, 'A Prime Minister is still nominally *primus inter pares*, but in fact his authority is stronger than that. The right to choose his colleagues, to ask for a dissolution of Parliament and, if he is a Conservative, to appoint the Chairman of the party organisation, add up to a formidable total of power. So powerful has he become that one journalist has advocated that he should give regular press conferences to let 'a window into the Prime Minister's mind'. Apparently he is the only individual who counts. His supremacy was shown in 1963 when the opening of the Commons session was delayed until Lord Home was made a commoner and an MP.

The arguments which have been outlined so far neglect many factors which restrain the Prime Minister in the exercise of his power. His actual position is not as predominant as has been presented.

Election studies and opinion poll data present no firm evidence for a categorical statement that people vote for or against party leaders. What can be said is that voters are greatly influenced by the images they have in their minds of the parties, and the image is not composed just of the leader but it is a compound, whose main component is the record and achievement of the party when it was in Government. The overall performance of the Government and not the activity of the Leader shapes the image of the party. Other less significant elements of the image consist of the main figures of the party, their views and attitudes, the ways they behave to each other, the history of the party, its traditional and present associations, its past and present policies and its broad ideals. These, however, are not as decisive as the conduct of the party when in office. This creates the impression of the party in the minds of most electors. Elections then are won or lost by Governments not by Oppositions, and not just by the leaders. If the role of the leaders were as important as some suggest, then it might be expected that the electoral swings in the constituencies where they stand would show significant variations from the regional and national swings. In fact no such divergencies can be shown. The leader is as much the prisoner of the image of his party as the other candidates. Although much of the propaganda of the parties concentrates on the leaders, there is no evidence that it is effective. Studies of the effects of television show that most people display a sturdy resistance to the blandishments of the manipulators. They seem to absorb from a programme only what fits in with their preconceived notions. Their previous attitudes are reinforced not overturned. The claims that advertisers and public relations men make for their techniques are exaggerated in the face of the dogged obstinacy of the public.

If the leader is not the individual whom the electors vote for or against, then there is no mandate on the MPs to support their leaders. Their obedience to their leader is not based on the wishes of the electorate, nor does it arise because of his ability to call for a dissolution when he likes. The cost of an election campaign is no burden to an MP, since his expenses are paid by his party. The campaign is not very arduous; for most MPs, a three weeks irritation at worst, while it is more arduous for the leader who is the leading campaigner, having to travel over the whole country. Since the bulk of Parliamentary seats, over two-thirds, are safe, few MPs worry that they will lose. Thus dissolution is not a very realistic threat against potential or actual rebels. Indeed, the individual who has most to lose from a dissolution is the Prime Minister himself, who may lose his Government office, his prestige, power and high salary. Further, since he wants to win, he is hardly likely to enter an election campaign wielding the weapon of dissolution against his own party, for the Opposition will make much capital out of the splits within his party. If dissolution is the potent device some suggest, then there should be a tendency for rebels to sit for safe seats, immune from the changes of electoral fortune. But there is no correlation between the tendency to rebel against the party leadership and the size of the MP's majority. Thus neither the actual use of nor the threat to use the power of dissolution are the means of enforcing discipline on MPs. They are kept in line by their constituency parties who may not readopt them. But local parties do not penalise their members for all acts of rebellion. MPs can expect trouble from their local parties if they go against their Parliamentary party over a period of time by taking up a position close to that of the Opposition party. A revolt to the centre will arouse the anger of the local parties far more than a revolt to the extreme wing, farthest from the position of the Opposition. A revolt therefore is not completely out of the question.

Parties are not the monoliths as depicted by some commentators. Neither inside nor outside Parliament are the parties tamely subservient to the will of the Prime Minister. They are riven with factions, divided over both short and long term policy objectives, the claims of various interests and local and regional issues. More commonly in the Labour than in the Conservative Party the alignment over one topic persists for a whole range of others, so that more permanent cleavages exist in the Labour Party than in the Conservative. The most important factions in both parties are those which coalesce around the main figures in the party. Each of the chief colleagues of the Prime Minister has a personal following which would prefer to see their man leader rather than the actual leader. There is no loyalty at the top because the Prime Minister's colleagues are his rivals, eager to replace him, and he is engaged in a constant battle to fend them off. Many attempts were made to displace Mr. Attlee, but they collapsed because his prima donna rivals failed to unite around a successor. Churchill, it seems, had to retire earlier than he wanted in order to please Sir Anthony Eden and his following. Even before the Suez venture there were serious rumblings against Eden, and if he had not retired through ill-health after the Suez affair, it is most likely that he would have been forced out. Mr. Macmillan had to fight hard to remain leader, and but for his operation he too might have been forced out. Sir Alec Douglas-Home became Prime Minister not because Mr. Macmillan or the Queen chose him but because his chief rivals tolerated him and led no revolt against him. It is significant that the Queen asked him at first only to try to form an administration. He kissed hands as Prime Minister twenty-four hours later. These were the crucial hours when he sought to win over Butler, Maudling and Hogg; it was during those hours that he was chosen as Prime Minister, by his colleagues. Today Harold Wilson is not secure; George Brown's reputation has risen considerably. Some commentators detect opposition to Wilson from within his own party. He has been described as tending 'to look more and more like a Labour Foreign Secretary, with Mr. Brown as Prime Minister'. The Prime Minister is only as strong as his colleagues let him be. Without their support he falls. To become and remain Prime Minister a man must work hard to retain the support of his main colleagues and not present them with an opportunity to remove him.

Television has enhanced the stature of the Prime Minister's rivals far more than his own standing. Gladstone and Disraeli, Asquith and Balfour, MacDonald and Baldwin were at the centre of the stage because of the office they held; their colleagues did not have the opportunities to display themselves to their party members and public which the colleagues of a post-war Prime Minister have. Today television brings into almost every home not just the Prime Minister, who cannot be on the screen all the time, but also the major Ministers, his chief colleagues. They have the chance to win, consolidate and encourage a personal following, which their pre-war counterparts never had. They have been strengthened in their relations *vis-à-vis* the Prime Minister. Thus the significance of the development of television is not that it has elevated the Prime Minister but that it has contributed to undermining his position. Maudling, Heath, Macleod, Brown and Callaghan are the men who have been helped by television. Even if the Prime Minister does receive considerable attention from television, it is not necessarily a one-sided blessing. Much depends on his telegenic qualities. Sir Alec Douglas-Home seemed to think that exposure together with Mr. Wilson would not help his cause in the 1964 election campaign. The standing of a Prime Minister can be damaged, if he gives a poor performance, and a skilful interviewer may make him seem very foolish. Thus the case that the Prime Minister has been strengthened by television is not proven.

The Prime Minister if he is to remain in office must carry his leading rivals with him. He might withstand a backbench revolt with their support, but if a backbench revolt found a spokesman of leadership calibre, who could win the backing of his other colleagues, then the Prime Minister would be in a very insecure position. To avoid this fate he must woo and coax his colleagues and party to support him and his policies. He is engaged in a continual dialogue with his party both inside and outside Parliament. The Whips act as his eyes and ears, conveying to him through the Chief Whip the feelings of the Parliamentary party. The Chief Whip's job is to tell the Prime Minister what the MPs will not stand; he restrains the Prime Minister as much as the MPs; he mediates between the two, explaining each to the other. The Whips are responsible for knowing thoroughly the views of certain groups of MPs divided into the geographical areas of their constituencies and they also attend the specialist party Committees in the House. Whenever any policy or tendency of the leadership is found to be creating displeasure then the Whips inform the Prime Minister and try to effect a reconciliation. The Whips should not be regarded as the bullying agents of the Prime Minister. By other means also he keeps in close touch with the feelings of his party, through individual trusted MPs, his private secretaries, his own personal contacts in the House, in its tea room, dining room, bar and corridors and through more formal meetings with back bench committees. It would be fatal for a Prime Minister to set himself apart from his Parliamentary party. It requires management. So too does the extra-Parliamentary party, especially the Labour Party which has less of a tradition of loyalty to the leadership than the Conservative Party. To keep the outside party conversant with the policy of the Parliamentarians, Ministers, since the Leyton by-election, are to explain their positions to area conferences of party members all over the country and a liaison Committee has been established to mediate between the Parliamentary Labour Party and the National Executive Committee. The leaders in Parliament recognise that the basis of their power would vanish if they alienated their party activists. Thus the Prime Minister is not the master of his party. Leaders can lose their parties' support and be toppled. They lead only with the sufferance and by the courtesy of their followers. A Prime Minister is only as strong as his party, and particularly his chief colleagues, lets him be.

The Prime Minister's power of patronage has been exaggerated as a means of keeping his supporters loyal. Careerists can argue with great force that the way to achieve top office is not to give loyal and silent service, but to build up a following, to gain a reputation of having expertise in a certain sphere and to make a nuisance of oneself. The Prime Minister will then be forced to give the man office to quiet down his attacks, to restrain his following and generally to keep the party contented. But once in Government office the man is not necessarily neutralised and muzzled. He will still maintain his following and keep open his informal contacts with them: indeed his stature amongst his faction may be enhanced by his performance in office. Thus he will be able to bring forceful pressure to bear on the Prime Minister whenever a policy is contemplated that he thinks undesirable. And if the opponent is a leading figure in the party with a significant following, the Prime Minister will be most reluctant to force the matter so far that he will be faced with a rebellion and resignation which will injure the reputation of his Government. The Prime Minister's power to offer office and promotion to backbenchers and Ministers is not a sure-proof device for obtaining their obedience to his wishes. He is seriously checked by his major colleagues who can rally other Ministerial and formidable backbench support against him. The MPs then are not mere 'lobby fodder' for the Prime Minister, nor is the House of Commons just a 'rubber stamp' or 'talking shop'. MPs can bring their views to the notice of the Prime Minister, individually or collectively, through discussion with the Whips, in the specialist Committees, and by approaching him themselves directly. Since he depends on their allegiance, he will try to accommodate his policies to their wishes.

The Prime Minister's influence over policy has been exaggerated. Government business has so increased and involves many technical and complex factors that no one man is able to survey the whole field. Policy initiatives come from many sources, not just from the Prime Minister, but from party policy, from the recommendations of Civil Servants who have worked out schemes with various interests often before the Prime Minister knows about them, from administrative necessity, from the sheer pressure of events at home and abroad and from the demands of public opinion channelled upwards in various ways. The House of Commons itself is no negligible factor and even the Opposition is influential. On some issues the arguments of the Opposition may gain favour with the electorate and then the Government party, especially if an election is imminent, will take over some of the Opposition's suggestions as its own, so as to blunt the force of its attack. Before the last election the Labour Party frequently claimed that its policies had been filched by the Government. Debates in the House of Commons, therefore, are not a meaningless charade; they can help shape the Government's policy. The Prime Minister has also to take into account the views of his own party both in and outside the House. Through their specialist Committees MPs have opportunities for gaining expertise in the work of particular departments and can therefore keep significant checks on the policy of the Government. The coming of Independent Television indicates that a specialist Committee can even impose its policy eventually on a reluctant Cabinet. Thus the Prime Minister is not necessarily able to initiate the policy he wants, nor shape policy as he desires. There are too many political pressures which he has to take account of.

A Prime Minister has a free hand constitutionally to form his own Cabinet, but politically he is limited. He has to include the leading figures in the Parliamentary party, and they may be so influential within the party and in the country that they may even dictate which office they will have. His Cabinet must represent a cross-section of opinion in the party and contain the main faction leaders. Harold Wilson before the election said that Sir Alec Douglas-Home's Cabinet was too large. It revealed, he said, the Prime Minister's weakness, because he had had to strike a large number of bargains. He promised to form a smaller Cabinet. In fact it was exactly the same size, again evidence of the number of powerful figures and interests the Prime Minister had to conciliate. Moreover, the actual offices to which he allocated the individuals showed very few surprises and suggested that he had not had much freedom to manoeuvre. Most went to offices to which they had already staked a claim, as members of the Shadow Cabinet, as front-bench spokesmen, and because they had some expertise or interest in the subject. Thus the Prime Minister has not a free hand in the choice of his colleagues or the allocation of their offices.

Nor has he a free hand in dismissing them. None of the Ministers who were dismissed or retired after disagreement with the Cabinet in the post-war years were men of sufficient standing in their parties to present a significant challenge to the Prime Ministers, with the exception perhaps of Aneurin Bevan. No Prime Minister threw out or forced the resignation of a man who had support enough to displace him. Even in the July purge of 1962 no serious contender for the leadership was removed. The Prime Minister took good care to keep in the Cabinet his main rivals. His display of butchery illustrated further the limitations on his freedom of action. It did not enhance his position, rather it damaged an already fading reputation. He appeared to be making scapegoats of Ministers who had served him loyally and carried out policies he had agreed with. He seemed to be sacrificing them to save his own skin. His actions did not increase confidence in his powers of judgment or timing. He made enemies inside the Parliamentary Party and inside the Conservative Party outside Parliament. He did not increase the popularity of the Government. He undermined his own position by his purge. The incident also illustrated the point that loyal service is not enough to bring a Minister promotion and to prevent dismissal. None of those axed had a reputation for being awkward or nuisances or opponents of the Prime Minister. They were removed because they were easy targets and appeared to have no significant following among the remaining leading Cabinet Ministers or the MPs generally. Thus the importance of the Prime Minister's powers of appointment and dismissal has been grossly overestimated, perhaps most of all by Harold Macmillan.

Although the proceedings of the Cabinet follow a formal protocol, the predominance of the Prime Minister suggested by the customs of Cabinet etiquette has been exaggerated. His control over the agenda is not as absolute as has been presented. He may temporarily be able to keep off the agenda an item he dislikes, but he would be unable to prevent permanently a group or even one of his major colleagues from bringing up a matter they wished to discuss. If he did try to obstruct them, he would be acting senselessly, stirring up their opposition and encouraging them to rally support amongst the rest of the Cabinet and the MPs against him. It would be very foolish for a Prime Minister to storm out of a Cabinet meeting when one of his leading colleagues brought up an issue which the bulk of the Cabinet wished to discuss. To walk out on such an occasion would seriously damage his reputation in their eyes. The actual drawing up of the agenda is not solely dictated by Prime Ministerial whim. Outside pressures are significant, from his colleagues, departments, the party in and out of Parliament, public opinion and events both domestic and external. Nor is he in command of the final verdict of the meeting. His summary and decision cannot go against the sense of the meeting. He cannot impose his own views on a reluctant session, especially if the chief figures in the Cabinet oppose him. He may see his ideas modified and even rejected in the give and take of discussion. To carry on as leader, the Prime Minister must retain the confidence of his Cabinet, which means that he cannot dictate to it. Just because there is little evidence of revolts against the Prime Minister within the Cabinet, does not indicate that its members are tamely subservient to him. Most likely it shows that the final decisions are agreed ones, reached after discussion and compromise. Harmony implies not so much obedience to the Prime Minister's will as general agreement amongst the Cabinet members, including the Prime Minister.

The charge that the Prime Minister bypasses the Cabinet through conversations with individual Ministers, cronies, Cabinet Committees, and experts outside Government, loses sight of the important fact that any major decisions, which such meetings come to, have to pass through the Cabinet before they can be implemented. Any participant in such sessions with the Prime Minister, who objects to any decision, can get it discussed and decided at Cabinet level, and any member of the Cabinet can query any decision of such sessions, get a discussion started and a Cabinet decision taken. The doctrine of collective responsibility is still meaningful. By it, Ministers are encouraged to take an interest in the work of other departments than their own. It is a myth that a Minister is so completely absorbed in the work of his own department that he neglects the other aspects of Government policy. Ministers are still members of the House of Commons and members of their Party. They have to defend the whole range of Government policy and not just that of their department. Moreover, they are usually keen on promotion, and thus do not immerse themselves in a single subject to the exclusion of other topics.

It is only sensible for the Prime Minister to keep on specially close terms with his chief colleagues and major rivals. These are the men with most weight in the Cabinet; to square them would be the first stage in getting a policy through the Cabinet. This inner Cabinet has no formal structure, nor is it a collection of the Prime Minister's personal friends. He consults them not because he likes their company but because they are the most powerful men in his Government. This kind of grouping is quite different from those meetings which Churchill used to hold late at night with some cronies. These were his personal friends with whom he enjoyed discussing matters, using their ideas to stimulate and sharpen his own. The chief men in his Cabinet were a different set. The former had not the real influence in Government which the latter had, who could block some of Churchill's own objectives.

Harold Wilson's meetings with Ministers and officials to discuss particular topics are not innovations. Other Prime Ministers have had such meetings, and dinners with experts; what is new is the publicity given to them. This is part of the technique of government, creating the impression that the Government is active.

The two instances always quoted to show the great scope of Prime Ministerial power, the decisions to produce atomic weapons and to carry out the Suez venture, have been presented in a very biased way. The decision to produce atomic weapons was taken after thorough discussion in the Defence Committee of the Cabinet; it was circulated in the Cabinet agenda, but not discussed in Cabinet because the decision was accepted by the Cabinet Ministers; the decision was also announced to Parliament, and again no discussion took place because at that time in 1948 there was no significant opposition to the manufacture by Britain of such weapons. The Suez affair was not the personal policy of the Prime Minister. The policy was discussed and initiated in a Committee of the Cabinet, comprising the chief men in the Cabinet; the full Cabinet was kept informed about the Committee's decisions, and objections seem to have been raised by a few members; but clearly the majority of the Cabinet was behind the policy of the Committee. Thus in neither case were these decisions taken solely by the Prime Minister. He had to carry with him his chief Colleagues and the majority of the Cabinet.

The standing of the individual Minister has not been so depressed as some have suggested. The quotation from Lord Home, as he then was, has been overrated. It may tell us something about his relations with the Prime Minister, but nothing about Harold Macmillan's relations with other Ministers. Some said that Lord Home was appointed Foreign Secretary because Macmillan wanted a man who would agree with him, performing much the same role as Selwyn Lloyd. In any case it has long been the custom for the Prime Minister to be virtually his own Foreign Minister. Only Austen Chamberlain and Ernest Bevin since 1919 were allowed a significant measure of independence by their Prime Ministers. The Foreign Office has often succumbed to Prime Ministerial intervention. Thus, since the relations between the Prime Minister and the Foreign Secretary are of a special character, any statement about their relations is not a general statement about the Prime Minister's relations with other Ministers. A more apt quotation by a Minister about Harold Macmillan's practices comes from Iain Macleod, 'Mr. Macmillan set a new standard of competence in the business of forming, controlling and guiding a Cabinet. He knew how to delegate to individual Ministers and to leave them alone. It was because the whole Cabinet worked so well and so smoothly that people formed the impression of an absolute personal ascendancy, and the notion grew up that we were changing from a Cabinet to a Presidential system of Government. In fact the reverse was happening. Mr Macmillan by his skill, restored a great deal of vitality to the Cabinet as a body.' And Sir Alec Douglas-Home in a later interview in the *Observer*, when he was Prime Minister, said, 'A good Prime Minister, once he had selected his Ministers and made it plain to them he was always accessible "for comment or advice", should interfere with their departmental business as little as possible. Harold Wilson has described the task of a Prime Minister as 'conducting an orchestra and not playing the instruments oneself'. The only post-war Prime Minister who claimed that he was more than *primus inter pares* and acted as such by for example interfering and fussing with Ministers and their Departments was Sir Anthony Eden. His activities did not gain him the support of his colleagues, and he can hardly be called one of the more successful Prime Ministers of Britain.

The Prime Minister is at a serious disadvantage with his colleagues. Unlike most of them he has no department to keep him informed and to brief him. He is not able to check the information flowing to him from the departments and their Ministers. Without alternative sources of information he cannot easily evaluate their advice. He is especially weak in that he cannot involve himself in the 'germinating stage' of a policy, when the Civil Servants and Ministers are mulling over some proposals. He is most likely brought in when discussions are completed, and opinions have solidified. His private office and

Cabinet office are not comparable to the departments behind his Ministers, nor do they approach the large number and expertise of the advisers of the American President. Harold Wilson, before becoming Prime Minister, expressed the view that the Prime Minister needed to be served by a briefing agency to ensure that he was as fully informed as a departmental Minister, and that the Prime Minister should come in on policy discussions at an early stage. Harold Wilson's sessions at Chequers, which he claims are a return to the methods of Churchill and Attlee, are attempts to bring the Prime Minister into this early stage, and his attaching to the Cabinet office of certain academics and civil servants, economists, scientists and technologists in particular, is an attempt to provide himself with new sources of information and advice. He has not added them to his private office, which has remained very much the same as before, but to the Cabinet office. It is, however, not just the servant of the Prime Minister; it has a collective loyalty to the Cabinet and its prime function is to serve that body not a single man. Indeed Wilson's refusal to turn his private office into a strong central intelligence service for himself indicates some limits on his power. If he had done so he would have irritated his Ministers and civil servants. To avoid their displeasure he had to strengthen the Cabinet office. But far from enhancing the position of the Prime Minister above his colleagues the Cabinet office has served to sustain the doctrine of collective responsibility, since it has been loyal to its function of serving the Cabinet as a whole.

Even if he had established a stronger private office, it is unlikely that it would have prevailed against older and larger departments. They have usually triumphed over small *ad hoc* teams of civil servants attached to new fangled Ministries with lofty aims and no traditional establishment. Non-departmental Ministers and Prime Ministers have had little success when fighting the entrenched departments, who remain impervious to take-over bids. The civil service consists of a number of departments, each possessing a strong *esprit de corps*. It is not as centralised and monolithic as some have suggested and therefore not so easily amenable to Prime Ministerial control. His power over appointments is not such that he can put exactly whom he wants in any position he likes. He has to defer to the advice of the Joint Permanent Secretary to the Treasury and the consensus amongst the top echelons of the civil service about who should fill the major posts. Even if a personal choice is put in charge, there is no guarantee that he will remain a loyal servant of the Prime Minister. He will most likely become the spokesman of his department's view, defending its interests against all comers.

It is hard for an individual Minister to know all that is going on in his own department, and therefore even harder for a Prime Minister to know all that is going on in the whole machine of Government. If on one item he does exert himself to influence the course of a decision, he will have to expend much energy and effort, and in so doing will naturally neglect other aspects of policy.

If he does prevail in one area, he fails in others, because he cannot influence everything at once.

The Prime Minister has no executive powers vested in him. To achieve anything he must work with and through his Ministers who have executive power vested in them. These men have powerful and independent departments to brief them and possess significant followings in their party who hope to see their man one day leader. To become and remain Prime Minister a man must carry these major colleagues, who are his rivals, with him. He cannot dictate to them, but must co-operate, consult and negotiate with them and even at times defer to them. Cabinet Government and collective responsibility are not defunct notions. Shared responsibility is still meaningful, for a Prime Minister has to gain the support of the bulk of his Cabinet to carry out his policies. He has to persuade it and convince it that he is right. Its meetings do not merely follow his direction. Debate and conflict are frequent. It cannot be bypassed and he cannot be an autocrat. To attempt to become one presages his political suicide.

The Prime Minister is the leading figure in the Cabinet whose voice carries most weight. But he is not the all powerful individual which many have recently claimed him to be. His office has great potentialities, but the use made of them depends on many variables, the personality, temperament, and ability of the Prime Minister, what he wants to achieve and the methods he uses. It depends also on his colleagues, their personalities, temperaments and abilities, what they want to do and their methods. A Prime Minister who can carry his colleagues with him can be in a very powerful position, but he is only as strong as they let him be.

19 ALFRED GROSSER

The Evolution of European Parliaments

THE POLITICAL CONTEXT

Whether institutions function well or badly does not depend only on their machinery or on the value of each institution in itself. The ideological orientation of a given political regime and its legitimacy are often the determining factors. By legitimacy I mean a consensus of the citizens to accept the existing institutions as the normal framework in which to deal with their differences. Belgian institutions did not change between 1930 and 1945, or between 1945 and 1960, or even in recent years, but the "royal question" and, today, the intensification of the language conflict have put the institutional system itself in a precarious position.

Why has the West German Federal Republic existed from the beginning in an atmosphere of political calm, envied by many Frenchmen and Belgians, in contrast to the Weimar Republic, which was virtually never free from troubling disorder? Is it the value of the institutions—particularly parliament—as such, that is in question? Not at all. The real reasons are quite different. One is that the words "republic" and "democracy," synonomous in the

Reprinted from *Daedalus* (Vol. 93, No. 4), pp. 153-160, 161-172, 176-177, by permission of *Daedalus*, Journal of the American Academy of Arts and Sciences, Boston, Mass. Footnotes omitted by the editors.

1920's with defeat, humiliation and misery, have acquired the connotation—even if they are not synonomous—of "escape from chaos" and "economic and diplomatic rehabilitation." The regime and its institutions have been reinforced, legitimized. The second reason is that the Weimar Republic was ideologically torn apart. The Communist extreme left was only a minority in the parliament, but it constituted a force of opposition to the regime. On the right and extreme right, the republic in its liberal form was vilified and attacked. Today, the Federal Republic is unanimously anti-Communist and the anti-liberal extreme right has practically disappeared. Since it had no colonies, West Germany has been spared the conflicts over legitimacy caused by decolonization. It has also up to now been able to make its institutions work on a basis of ideological unity very favorable to the regular functioning of a pluralist democracy. Parliament can discuss the most difficult questions without disrupting a kind of fundamental unanimity which affects even the most essential national interest, because the overwhelming majority of citizens prefer the continued division of Germany to any form of reunification that would not insure its protection from Communist influence.

In France, on the contrary, disputes over legitimacy have not ceased to hamper the effective operation of its institutions. In my opinion, the poor functioning of the parliamentary regime was only an accessory cause of the decline of the Fourth Republic. Its essential cause was the internal schism in France, reflecting the divisions of the contemporary world as a whole: anti-Communists against Communists, old states against new nationalisms. Italy has experienced the first conflict, Great Britain and Belgium the second. Only France has had the legitimacy of a regime established by majority vote challenged in both ways at once. There was also the challenge of European supra-nationalism.

Between 1947 and 1958 the Communists challenged the majority decisions in the name of peace, and the Gaullists waged a campaign against the European treaties in the name of a national legitimacy above the will of the majority. There was a moral dispute over Indochina and Algeria: a regime which violated its own principles in opposing the liberty of other peoples was thought by some to have lost its legitimacy even if the administrations were elected by a majority of the electorate. At the same time there was another opinion that could be called the national type of establishment of legitimacy whereas the precedent type was in the ethical sphere: no government, no parliamentary majority, has the right to abandon a part of the nation's patrimony or to accept a decrease in territory—notably in Algeria—or to permit the expulsion from the national community of men desiring to live in it—as was the case with many Algerian Moslems. The *coup de force* of May, 1958 that brought de Gaulle to power, and later the abortive uprisings against de Gaulle in January, 1960 and April, 1961 were inspired by this feeling.

Today quarrels over legitimacy continue; the question of a successor to Chancellor Adenauer involves merely an individual, the question of a successor to General de Gaulle involves a regime. French debates over institutions and especially over relations between the parliament and the executive are continually falsified by conflicts where what is at stake is above and beyond the level of institutions. The specific debate over the Fifth Republic and General de Gaulle should not, however, obscure the ameliorating factors that have already or soon will have manifested themselves: the absence of colonies reduces conflicts arising from decolonization, and the evolution of the Communist party transforms its doctrinaire hostility of 1947-1954 into acceptance, albeit an acceptance qualified by combativeness. For reasons deriving from changes in France and outside, the French Communist party no longer has the goal of hindering the operation of institutions as it did at the height of the cold war, and it is accepted more and more by others as a participant in the political game. This is normal in a period of rapprochement between Khrushchev and Kennedy and of alliances within France against the "personal power" of General de Gaulle. In the immediate future, it is in Belgium rather than in France that the most violent troubles arising from a conflict over legitimacy seem likely to occur. It is nonetheless true that the presence of strong Communist parties in Italy and France will for a long time yet be a decisive factor in institutional life, quite independent of the text of the constitution and of the nature of parliamentary operation.

Disputes over legitimacy are all the more important in France because the will of the majority has traditionally been considered to stand above the constitution. Constitutions are of two kinds, illustrated by a comparison between France and the United States. In France, the constitution has long been thought to be a method of operation, a technique, supposed to implement a political system founded in any case on the will of the majority. Article 91 of the Constitution of 1946 said, "the Constitutional Committee examines [the question] whether the laws voted by the National Assembly assume a revision of the Constitution." On November 6, 1962, the Conseil Constitutionnel of the Fifth Republic declared that it had no jurisdiction in the case of laws "which, adopted by the people as the result of a referendum, constitute the direct expression of the national sovereignty." In both cases, the superiority of the will of the majority over the text of the constitution is clearly affirmed.

In the United States on the other hand, the Constitution is considered the sacrosanct charter of the national life, quite literally the "fundamental law." The expression used by the framers of the Bonn Constitution show that they were referring to the American concept. Respect for the charter should be so thoroughly imposed on all the machinery of the state that the chief of state himself will be its servant and not its guardian. This latter function belongs to the judiciary. Its task is not only to declare the law. When the United States Supreme Court hands down a decision on segregation or when the Tribunal of Karlsruhe issues definitions in regard to liberty of information, it is not simply a matter of judicial interpretation of the constitution, it is a matter of rendering precise and explicit the ethic, the moral code which the national community holds as its standard.

It is partly the limited extent of a common ethical standard in France which has prevented such a charter-constitution (and a constitutional court worthy of the name) from materializing in that country. Instead, the great decisions of principle have been referred to majority opinion in parliament, and since 1958 to popular opinion through referenda, but the same lack of consensus has prevented the decisions thus reached from being really accepted by all.

Such a situation is not confined to France, however. Relations between Walloons and Flemish are not regulated by a simple majority vote but by a compromise which can only be rejected by the extremists of both camps. The Oder-Neisse line will be recognized as definitive only by a majority which would include at least the two major parties in West Germany, that is, the delegates of four fifths of the electoral body. The effectiveness of majority decisions adopted by the parliaments depends on the type of problem involved. In order to make any predictions about their effectiveness in the future, it would be necessary to make an inventory of the questions pending or possibly pending which lie outside the usual institutional or constitutional arena.

Within the constitutional systems the place of parliament depends on how popular sovereignty is exercised. All the constitutions affirm forcefully that sovereignty lies in the people, without giving this affirmation a really precise meaning. When we read in the fundamental law of Bonn (Article 20, Number 2), "All power comes from the people, who exercise it through election and through the intermediary organs of legislative power, executive power and judicial power," we see at once that the parliament in West Germany has a lesser place than under the Fourth Republic in France. Did not Article 3 of the Constitution of 1946 say, "National sovereignty belongs to the French people . . . the people exercise it in constitutional matters through the votes of their representatives and through referenda. In all other matters, they exercise it through their deputies in the National Assembly"?

The order of chapters or subdivisions in the various European constitutions is very significant in this respect. In Italy the order is as follows: I Parliament, II the President of the Republic, III the Cabinet, IV the Judiciary, V Regions, Provinces, Communes. In the Fourth Republic in France: I Sovereignty, II Parliament, III Economic Council, IV Diplomatic Treaties, V the President of the Republic, VI the Council of Ministers. In the Fifth Republic: I Sovereignty, II the President of the Republic, III the Cabinet, IV Parliament. The order of subdivisions in the West German Constitution is Bund and Länder, Bundestag,

Bundesrat, the Federal President, the Federal Government. These comparative lists show us the relative importance of the different aspects of government as the framers of the constitutions conceived them. We shall have to consider whether it corresponds to the reality. In any case two observations should be made.

First, the nature of the national legislature is a function of the structure of the state, centralized or federal. The German bicameral system is justified in ways similar to bicameralism in the United States or Switzerland. The sovereignty of the people is supposed to express itself through two channels because the national collectivity rests on a double notion of equality and each must find its own means of expression. There is the equality between the citizens and there is the equality (or near equality) of the territorial collectivities. In the House of Representatives the idea of equality between American citizens is expressed, while the Senate expresses equality between states, even though they are very unequal in population. The composition of the Italian Senate reflects a much less clear-cut situation in this respect. In France, the way in which the Senate is chosen strengthens the small communes at the expense of the large ones. It does not appear to us certain that the utility of this double representation will in the long run be sufficient to justify the existence of a separate legislative chamber.

Since the upper houses based on privileged personal status, like the House of Lords, will not come back in favor, the domination of assemblies elected by direct universal suffrage will become greater unless one or the other of two possible developments takes place: either the formation of a federated Europe can revive respect for federalism and give birth to a doubly federal structure, both within the nation-state and above it; or the constantly increasing role of pressure groups (including the regional ones) will lead to the development of legislative assemblies reflecting economic and social pressure groups. We shall return to this point later.

The second necessary observation is that what is meant by parliamentary representation is not defined in the constitutions. Immediately after World War I, André Maurois could write with irony in *Les Silences du Colonel Bramble*:

> So you condemn us, Doctor, to oscillate continually between brawls and coups d'état?
>
> No, because the English people, who have already given to the world Stilton cheese and comfortable arm-chairs, have invented for our welfare the parliamentary safety-valve. Our elected champions now enact the brawls and the coups d'état in the House, which gives the rest of the nation leisure to play cricket. The press puts the finishing touch on the system by letting us take part in these clashes vicariously. All this is a part of modern comfort and in a hundred years every man, white, yellow,

red or black, will refuse to live in an apartment without running water or in a country without a parliament.

This notion of the parliament as the real center of political life, with citizen-spectators and power to govern delegated by the representative assembly, already disputable at the time, is today in the process of disappearing because of the changed relations between parliament and administration that we shall analyze subsequently—and because of recent social changes. As it is not possible here to present a kind of sociology of Europe serving as a basis for institutional change, I shall confine myself to one example, which, in my opinion, is particularly important because it relates to one of the most important functions of parliament—even if this function is not spelled out in the text of the constitution—to wit, parliament's role as a transmission-belt of political information.

How does an administration proceed when it wants to inform the citizens about policy or has important news to communicate? The tradition of the parliamentary regimes gives a clear answer: a representative of the cabinet makes a statement in parliament or answers questions from the members. Subsequently the information is promulgated in two ways: the press reports the parliamentary sessions and the members, returned to their constituencies, explain to important groups and individuals how the administration statement should be interpreted.

Today this model no longer holds. This is because, first, the powerful organization of the parties often leads the administration to use the channel of the majority party, and second, and above all, because the development of the mass media (everywhere to some extent) has brought about a diminution of the role of parliament both as the representative of public opinion and as the intermediary between administration and the citizens. Radio and television permit direct contact between the governing and the governed that calls into question the very essence of representative democracy. As in other matters, General de Gaulle has simply carried to extremes a tendency discernible almost everywhere.

The American example seems to me particularly striking. Nowhere—as I hope to show—does the legislature hold a more important position or have a greater real influence on national policy or control the administration more directly; but, in the realm of information, the political system of the United States has a real institution unforeseen in the Constitution: the presidential press conference. The importance of the press conference as a test of the American Chief Executive has often been noted. It should be emphasized that the institution of the press conference makes the press the representative of public opinion and gives to the press the role of intermediary between the citizens and their government which classic theory reserved to the legislature.

It is characteristic that American senators and representatives often put their questions to the President by getting friendly or sympathetic reporters to ask certain questions at a presidential press conference.

Of course, the American presidential system, with the separation of powers, virtual direct election of the President and his nonparticipation in congressional debates, facilitates this recourse to a means of disseminating information that bypasses the legislature; but the situation is a phenomenon of modern civilization and not of the institutional machinery. "The President from time to time shall report to Congress on the State of the Union." The Founding Fathers certainly did not intend this to mean only the annual message to Congress. In the Cuban crisis of October, 1962, a statement to Congress would have corresponded to the text of the Constitution, rather than a televised talk to the nation. In Europe, outside of France, the technique of radio and television statements, of press conferences and interviews has not yet been developed sufficiently to eliminate parliament as a means of disseminating information, but it seems to me that the tendency is increasingly in that direction.

In the other direction, of the government informing itself on the state of opinion, the situation is slightly different. Here there are two rivals to the legislatures as intermediaries or representatives, the press and the public opinion polls. Government depends less and less on members of parliament for information about the state of public opinion. Instead, it increasingly depends on the press, and unfortunately, in my opinion, on polls, because passive citizens, who must be sought out and then interrogated, are thus equated with active citizens who show their positions. The government uses the opinion polls to know how to conduct itself, what to say and also how to act. At the same time, especially in countries with single-member constituencies, the deputy often succeeds in maintaining his own role because he is in a position to be in contact with a psychological reality that often is not accessible to the executive branch, the other source of official information. . . .

LEGISLATION AND THE BUDGET

The legislature makes laws; the executive carries out the laws. Reality does not any longer correspond at all to this official statement. Everywhere the legislative initiative has passed into the hands of the administrations. The legislatures sometimes amend, rarely reject, usually ratify. Their members continue, indeed, to call themselves collectively "the Legislative Power" in the law books, but in most cases they merely participate in a procedure of registration. Here, for example, is the summary of twelve years' legislation in Bonn:

	1949-1953		1953-1957		1957-1961	
	Bills Submitted	Number Enacted	Bills Submitted	Number Enacted	Bills Submitted	Number Enacted
By the Cabinet	472	392	446	368	401	348
By the Bundestag	301	141	414	132	207	74
By the Bundesrat	32	12	17	7	5	2

The reality is both a little less and much more serious, from the point of view of parliament, than the figures suggest. On the one hand, the federal organization of the German state does after all permit the Landtage to play a certain legislative role, although even at the level of the Land, the administration predominates. On the other hand, the administration can bypass the assemblies to a considerable extent by issuing directives. As in other spheres, the Fifth French Republic has pushed to extreme limits a tendency that is general but less pronounced elsewhere. While tradition reserves to parliament whatever is not specifically designated to the administration, the Constitution of 1958 describes the domain of the law in a limiting way, after having stipulated that "laws are voted by Parliament."

Why is the legislative function of the parliaments in decline? There seem to me three competing ways of explaining this phenomenon:

1. The nature of the law has changed. With rare exceptions, laws, which used to be few, formerly served to make more explicit the rights and duties of citizens or the organization of society, conceived as a stable whole. Civil law, criminal law and administrative law belonged in the legislative assemblies. The administration was there to direct, to administer. Except in the international sphere, did the administration even need to have a policy? It is not by chance that the constitutions framed since World War II no longer define the administration as an executive but as an initiator of policy. Administrative action is destined to transform society, and the law is the privileged instrument of this transformation, but if the legislative assembly expresses its adherence to a policy in instituting an administration, does not the administration have the right to claim the means to carry out the policy? Or in other words to demand that laws be passed to provide the means?

2. The epoch of the "representative of the people" is largely over. The existence of organized parties, whenever one of them is in a dominant situation, involves a relative dispossession of the members of the legislature. Should the members of a majority party in a parliament criticize an administration proposition—or should they, on the contrary, defend it against opposition attacks?

3. The technical complexity of economic and social legislation is such that the administration, using its bureaucracy and its experts, is able to impose it on the legislature. It is no longer enough, as in the nineteenth century, to be a good speaker and well versed in the law to be an impressive legislator.

We shall see why this point is even less applicable to the United States than the previous points.

Even if parliamentary resistance were strong, the administrations often have effective means of constraint at their disposal. The vote of confidence is to parliamentary life what the referendum is to the political life of the French Fifth Republic. It might be phrased, "Even if you do not like this particular text, vote yes, or you will oblige me to resign, which you do not want either."

The Constitution of 1958 has brought to fruition an inheritance from its two predecessors. In France, as it does still in the other countries, it used to require a positive vote to enact a law. Today, all that is necessary is for the prime minister to indicate that the administration is committed to a given text. "In such a case," says Article 49, "the text is considered as enacted unless a motion of censure . . . is passed." This is how, for example, the nuclear striking force, an essential element in French foreign policy, came into being without being approved by a parliamentary majority. At the end of the parliamentary session where the motion of censure was being voted upon, the chairman said:

> Here is the result of the vote on the motion of censure. Two hundred and seventy-seven votes are required for adoption.
>
> For adoption, 214 (applause on the Right and Extreme Left)
>
> Since the necessary majority was not reached, the motion of censure is not adopted (applause on Left and Center).
>
> As a result, the law establishing the program for certain military installations is considered to be adopted . . .

The Magna Carta imposed on King John in 1215 said, "No scutage nor aid shall be established in our kingdom without the consent of the common council of our Kingdom." Since then the power of the purse, or exclusive right to tax, has constituted an essential prerogative of parliament. But is this not also more a matter of form than of substance? There are, in any case, several phenomena which suggest that this is so.

1. National budgets have become monstrously complex. What member of a legislature, in spite of simplified versions prepared to help him, can find his way in such a jungle of chapters and provisions? Furthermore, at a certain level of importance, figures lose their meaning. The famous meeting of an administrative council described by Parkinson could be reproduced in a parliamentary assembly. At this meeting it was decided to authorize fantastic expenditure for the construction of an atomic reactor, but the cost of installing a bicycle rack was considered too high. In the same way, the average deputy will dispute the subsidy accorded to a small private association but will allow tremendous military expenses to pass without much discussion.

2. The limitation of the budget to one year and the annual debates on the budget do not fit the conditions necessary for good policy or efficient administration. In practice, the basic funds are granted once and for all and are not later called into question. Other items, especially in countries which tend to long-range planning, cannot safely be changed in less than several years. What a relief it would be for the President of the United States—and for the countries receiving United States aid—if foreign aid could be granted clearly and with carefully worked out detail for a period of four or five years. Things are moving in this direction. In Europe, programs for disposition of land, industrial development and the transformation of agriculture make it increasingly necessary for budgetary commitments to be made for longer periods.

3. Pressures put on members of legislatures do not cause them to call into question the main lines of the budget, but they do cause them to quarrel among themselves over particular points. Pressure groups bring pressure either on the government or on party leaders rather than on individual deputies. The real struggle often takes place before the budget is presented to the parliament. In a hierarchy of western legislatures based on the criterion of budgetary control, the Congress of the United States would be at the top: Congress is almost as much of a force to be reckoned with by the administration after the budget has been voted as before. At the bottom of the ladder would be the House of Commons, whose lack of power is striking once the Chancellor of the Exchequer has revealed "his" budget to the public.

CONTROL

The third function of the parliaments, after legislation and consent to taxation, is the control of executive action. This is a less well defined area than the others. First, what *is* the legislature in relation to the administration? Or what is the cabinet's relation to the assembly? The physical arrangements are very revealing of the political or psychological situation. In Westminster, the Government, or cabinet, is not separated from the parliamentary group. The arrangements anticipate an exchange between a majority and a minority rather than a confrontation between the administration and Parliament. At the Palais-Bourbon, the cabinet sits in the front row of the members, facing the speaker and the chairman. Is the cabinet not an emanation of the assembly and do not persons speaking from the rostrum—even members of the ruling majority—address the cabinet at the same time (and even more) as the other members? At least this was the case under the Third and Fourth Republics. Since 1958 it would have been more appropriate to adopt the arrangements of the Bundeshaus in Bonn: the government bench, a long raised table, is placed beside the presidential armchair, slightly behind the rostrum, facing the deputies. This gives the government the air of attending as a spectator the parliamentary game it dominates.

In Europe, it is rare for a parliament to control the administration by acting as a whole. The hearings of ministers before committees cannot be compared to the hostile grilling to which administration leaders are subjected by congressional committees in the United States. The West German Federal Republic has developed an interesting technique as a result of a delicate and controversial problem. Article 45 b of the fundamental law, passed in March, 1956, anticipates the establishment of a *Wehrbeauftragter des Bundestages* "for protection of fundamental rights and as an auxiliary organ to the Bundestag in the exercise of parliamentary control." This permanent commissioner of the assembly, chosen jointly by the opposition and by the majority, received in the year 1961 alone 4380 complaints, of which 1330 were found to be entirely justified, and 296 partly justified. The annual reports of the commissioner to the assembly show the extent to which he has become a kind of parliamentary control on the military administration.

In a more general way, administrative action is controlled by means of questions posed by individual deputies. The two most usual methods at the present time are those of the written question and of the so-called oral question, which is submitted in writing but answered orally. Two points are important here:

1. In a highly centralized country like France, where, moreover, the deputy is traditionally considered to be the representative of his constituents in the sense that a traveling salesman represents his employer, a member of parliament does not ordinarily use the procedure of written or oral questions to control the administration, or more precisely to bring his weight to bear on its decisions. The French member of parliament spends a considerable part of his time writing directly to ministers in various departments of the administration or in taking steps to hasten an administrative decision. We must remember that the financing of the construction of a village street by a savings bank in the neighboring town cannot be arranged in France until all the relevant documents have been to Paris and back.

2. In London, Bonn or Paris, if the oral question is usually a method of controlling executive management or efficiency, it can also be easily trans-formed—in the first two capitals—into a method of exerting political control. When M. Debré was drawing up the constitution of the Fifth Republic, he hoped to achieve the same sort of relation between the administration and parliament in France. The result has not fulfilled his intention. In vain would one search for examples of a real political dialogue arising from an administrative response to an oral question in French parliamentary life since 1959. It is true that the rules of the French parliament do not permit further debate by other members, while in Bonn the debate on the Spiegel affair in December, 1962, grew to great importance because the minister (administration spokes-man) had to undergo a real crossfire of related questions and was forced

to admit that he had lied in an earlier part of the discussion. From that moment his resignation seemed probable.

It is important to note that Mr. Franz-Josef Strauss had to resign because he agreed to submit himself to questions and also because the chairman of the Bundestag conducted the debate with total impartiality. The Spiegel affair proved the reality of parliamentary control in the Federal Republic, a control made possible because the minority can oblige the government to discuss a point seriously. We cannot overemphasize the point, because from the exchange or dialogue arises a political reality which is not defined in any constitutional text or regulation. At the end of a clash with the opposition the government can sometimes no longer maintain a certain decision, or it is compelled to modify a certain stand. No vote has forced the government into a change of position, however; it is a matter of purely moral constraint. For such a force to exist, the necessary and sufficient condition is that the cabinet and the majority party accept the fundamental idea of pluralist democracy: respect for the minority.

A supplementary condition should also be fulfilled. The minority must follow the rules of the game also. The French deputies in the Fifth Republic are not used to debates except those which threaten to bring down the government. Between 1875 and 1958 the principal means of political control of the executive by parliament consisted of attempts, often successful, to overthrow the government by the technique of what the Germans call *Grosse Anfragen*, although other means were also used.

In France there was and still is a long debate to determine how efficient executive control could be obtained by the legislature without constantly calling into question the existence of the administration. I cannot go into the details of this debate here, all the more because the remedies proposed were extremely varied—(the establishment of an American-style regime, for instance, with a president directly elected and not responsible to the assembly and without power of dissolution; automatic dissolution of the assembly when it voted against the administration, etc.) It must suffice to re-emphasize the extent to which the situation of the Fifth Republic is unique and does not allow one to make predictions: The government is stable and parliamentary control limited because General de Gaulle, the chief of state, is so popular. In other words, if he threatens to dissolve the Assembly it gives in because the voters would choose the general rather than the majority deputies. This is what happened in 1962. With another president one might find the reverse situation: The president would not dare to dissolve the Assembly because the nation would rally to the support of the anti-administration majority. Furthermore, as we shall see later, the system of parties is undermined by the fact that the present dominant party derives its strength from the personality of the chief of state.

METHODS OF OPERATION

In the European parliaments great debates have become rare. Everywhere one hears complaints about the absenteeism of deputies from the plenary sessions. In Germany the televising of these sessions was stopped largely because of the unfavorable impression the sight of the empty seats made on the viewers. No system of coercion has so far remedied this situation, although in France theoretically deputies may not vote by proxy and in West Germany absent members are fined. The causes of this situation are profound: lack of interest or lack of professional conscience on the part of the deputies are only a part of the explanation, and not the most important part. The basic work of parliament takes place in committees. Committees listen to the members of the administration, even if they cannot summon them as do congressional committees in Washington. The committees of the Bundestag, unlike French committees, can organize hearings, and the members are quite well informed about questions under their jurisdiction. They often have the services of a staff which assembles the necessary information. Why should the other deputies come to plenary sessions if they have confidence in the specialists of their own political group? Each group has its experts on agricultural and on social questions, and they are the ones who attend the plenary sessions, having already discussed the matter in committee. Would it not be better to give the committees the power to draw up laws or at least to reserve to them the right to amend laws, leaving the prerogative of the final vote to the full assembly? This method has been proposed and some concrete suggestions in this direction are being made.

There is another possible remedy for absenteeism—to reduce the number of deputies while paying them more. Indeed, why is the United States congressman an important personage? Because he is not subject to group discipline, but also because there are few congressmen and because the considerable sums they get as perquisites and for secretarial service permit them to have a personal staff. The European deputy is not so well off, and a member of Parliament in Great Britain, in particular, is badly paid. Even the deputies of the French Fifth Republic, who have relatively good salaries, cannot afford to engage young economists or political scientists as research assistants. Furthermore, the collection of documents and sources at the disposal of the European parliaments are laughable in comparison with the resources of Congress. The result is the incompetence mentioned above. In these unfavorable conditions the European parliamentarian has only three sources of information—and each shows his subordination to an outside force: administration and cabinet, the political party, and the pressure groups who wish to enlist his aid. We must examine these dependencies more closely.

PARLIAMENT, PARTIES AND PRESSURE GROUPS

What is the Administration?

The European regimes are theoretically parliamentary, that is, the administrations are responsible to the parliaments; but what is the administration? It is possible to give a variety of very different answers.

In the France of the Fifth Republic the government, in contrast to what the constitution says, is in fact a group. The administration is a group of ministers, some of whom are direct collaborators of the president of the republic, an executive head who is not responsible to parliament, while others work under the prime minister, himself a sort of chief of staff of the president.

In the Fourth French Republic, the administration was a kind of executive committee of the parliamentary majority, although the scattered nature of the groups permitted the president of the republic to exercise initiative in the choice of the président du conseil or premier, as in the case of Antoine Pinay in 1952. Although the framers of the constitution wanted to make the government a team of ministers under a head who was exclusively responsible for cabinet policy, in reality the ministers were transformed into delegates of their respective parties. In 1954 the Socialist party did not take part in the cabinet of Mendès-France, largely because its secretary-general, M. Guy Mollet, had refused to allow the premier to exercise his constitutional prerogative to choose his own ministers. Mollet took the position that the premier should take as ministers those whom the party considered worthy—or there would be no Socialists in the administration.

In Italy, the power to make and unmake cabinets does not belong to parliament, but to the Christian Democratic party. Only De Gasperi's eighth cabinet (1953) and Fanfani's second cabinet (January, 1959) fell as a result of parliamentary action. The fate of the others was determined by the internal struggles of the Christian Democratic party.

Curiously, the much discussed Article 67 of the West German fundamental law arranges for administrative succession between two elections by means of a crisis within the coalition. Established in anticipation of preventing the negative majorities that had blocked the parliamentary system in the death-throes of the Weimar Republic, the mechanism of the constructive no-confidence motion can only function in the Federal Republic if there is a coalition government and if one of the member parties of the coalition changes sides. Up to now Article 67, or more precisely its imitation, Article 61 of the Constitution of North Rhineland-Westphalia, has only been used once, when in February, 1956, the Liberals (in Düsseldorf) left the Christian Democrats in order to form a new majority with the Socialists. Can one really say that parliament overturned the cabinet of Arnold and established that of Steinhoff?

How does one explain the fact that Adenauer's third cabinet (1957-1961) experienced no change in its entire period in office while his second cabinet (1953-1957) had internal difficulties in 1955 and 1956, and his fourth cabinet had great difficulty coming into existence in 1961 and underwent a serious crisis a year later? The answer is simply that the Christian Democrats having obtained an absolute majority in the election of 1957, the third cabinet did not depend on negotiations between parties. After the elections of 1961, on the other hand, Adenauer was forced to sign a "charter of coalition" with the Liberals, which was deeply contradictory to the spirit of the constitution. If that charter had been followed, legislative action and the general policy of the administration would have been put under the control of a special committee designated equally by the two parties.

The existence of an electoral plurality law would have been sufficient to eliminate the third party, just as the introduction of a proportional system would have allowed British cabinets, from 1932 to 1935 and since 1950, to be the expression of a coalition of parties. It is not the electoral law that matters here, but the transformation that the change would have made in the nature of representation. In my opinion this is a fundamental matter.

In most of the parliamentary regimes the cabinet is no longer an outgrowth of the legislative assembly. The citizens, in voting for this or that party, understand that they are taking a hand in the selection of the executive. In Great Britain, in Belgium and in Germany one votes for or against the outgoing administration. Under the Fourth French Republic—as in the Weimar Republic—the rise and fall of coalitions forced the citizen to give a blank check to his party without knowing what cabinet the party would accept or overthrow and without having the power to pass judgment on the administrative action of the past cabinet at the following elections, because his party was sometimes in power (and never alone) and sometimes in the opposition. One of the major causes of the alienation of the French people from politics, one of the chief reasons they have several times given a plebiscite to de Gaulle and voted for the UNR in 1962, is that they had formerly disliked feeling themselves dispossessed by the parties and they are now pleased to be asked their opinion about the administration.

Parliamentary democracy thus seems to me to have changed. One of the chief functions of parliament used to be that it constituted the source of executive power. Today one might say, with hardly any exaggeration, that the freedom of the members of the legislature to choose the administration—in regimes which function well—is not much greater than that of the American electoral college in a presidential election.

The Legislator and His Party

In theory, a member of a legislature is responsible only to his conscience and his constituents. The reality is shown in the following figures. According to an analysis of the 288 roll-call votes taken in the Bundestag in the first two legislatures, between 1949 and 1957, deputies were overwhelmingly loyal to the decision of their parties: Social Democrats, 99.8 per cent; Christian Democrats, 94.5 per cent; Liberals, 90.5 per cent. The concept of the deputy as an individual has given way to the concept of the deputy as a member of a parliamentary group which itself depends on a political party.

The mechanisms of decision in parliamentary groups have not yet been sufficiently studied. We know only that sometimes the party dominates the group, sometimes the group enjoys great freedom, and sometimes the party ministers, arising from the group, dominate the party. In France the Socialist party, the Radical party, and the Mouvement Republicain Populaire represent these three possible models of the relations of power. In Italy, Article 84 of the statutes of the Christian Democratic party says: "In all questions of a political nature the Parliamentary groups should respect the general lines fixed by the Congress [of the party] and the directives of the National Council and the Governing Board which interpret and apply the said orientation." The domination of members of parliament by the party in Italy is so real that breaches of party discipline do not occur in votes of confidence (by roll-call) but in the ordinary votes, which are secret. Immediately following the elections of 1963 the political game depends even more on the relative strength of factions within the Christian-Democratic party. It is up to the dominant party to make the essential choice concerning the future orientation. But a second element has intervened: the struggle within the Socialist party in which Pietro Nenni was outvoted by the "leftists," who would have nothing to do with a pact with the Christian Democratic party. The Italian example clearly shows the transformation of the political system: the elections furnish the brute facts, that is, the numerical composition of the assembly, but this raw material is manipulated outside the assembly.

The dependence of members of parliament on the party can sometimes be explained in financial terms, especially in socialist parties, where a good many of those elected are officers of the party; but above all it stems from the simple fact that the party machinery fairly generally plays a decisive role in the designation of candidates in the elections. The voter votes for a party rather than for a man. The electoral system does not influence this phenomenon. If Macmillan were to leave the Conservative party tomorrow and present himself in his constituency against a Labour candidate, a Liberal and an unknown Smith or Jones chosen by the Conservative party, he would have only a feeble chance of retaining his seat. In France, the elections of 1962 as a whole confirmed the triumph of the label over the personality. Certain electoral systems can reinforce the deputy's dependence still further. In the West German Federal Republic, for example, half the members of the Bundestag are not really elected in the true sense of the word. In fact, the parties have a right, according to the number of votes received, to a certain number of "places on the list"; the voters do not know even the names that are on the lists. . . .

CONCLUSION

If one defines as "parliamentary" no longer a political system where the administration is responsible to the legislature, but a system where parliament as an institution exercises an important influence on political decisions, everything I have said leads me to conclude that the European governments are clearly less "parliamentary" than the government of the United States.

The indisputable decline of the European legislatures, their dispossession by the administrations on the one hand and by the parties on the other, should not be exaggerated. Their functions are still often important. To be a member of the legislature is not futile, even for the back-benchers. The dominant political ideology in western Europe has made the existence of a freely elected parliament so clearly the touchstone of democracy that the institution is in no danger of disappearing.

Nevertheless, the European parliaments are definitely in a state of crisis—precisely because the nature of the institution is at stake. Formerly, the institutionalized political power of a nation meant the legislative power and the executive power. Today, when one speaks of the government in Europe one means the administration, meaning only the former executive; whereas in the United States the word *government* continues to designate the political institutions as a group, Congress included. In Europe, the legislature has, to a great extent, become the intermediary body between the citizens and the administration, with greater legitimacy and tighter institutional structure than the pressure groups or the parties, but not necessarily more useful or more efficient in the eyes of the citizens. In Great Britain, Germany and Italy the parties have a tendency to displace the parliament as the intermediary between the citizens and the government, whereas in France it is the pressure groups that do this. Everywhere the original model of a parliamentary regime is to some extent in the process of disappearing.

Those who value the institution of parliament—like me—wish that men in public life and political scientists would investigate these changes further and ask themselves what remedies exist, if it is desirable to change the present trend.

20 SAMUEL H. BEER

The British Legislature and the Problem of Mobilizing Consent

The tasks of legislatures change with the times. One of the newer and more important of these tasks, and one to which not nearly enough attention has been paid, is the function of mobilizing consent. Modern governments impose vast and increasing burdens on their citizens, not only in the form of deprivations in terms of money, time, effort, and so on—as in the payment of taxes or performance of military service—but, even more important in these days of the welfare state and managed economy, in the form of requirements of certain often intricate patterns of behavior—such as conformity to wage and price "guidelines."

Yet the reasons for these impositions are usually technical, complex, and hard for the ordinary man to understand and make part of his personal motivation. If a government is to rule effectively, therefore, and since it cannot depend solely upon force, it must continuously mobilize consent and win acceptance for its policies. The legislature is one of the agencies that helps perform this task.

Reprinted from Samuel H. Beer, "The British Legislature and the Problem of Mobilizing Consent," in Elke Frank, ed., *Lawmakers in a Changing World*, © 1966, by permission of Prentice-Hall, Inc., Englewood Cliffs, New Jersey. Footnotes omitted by the editors.

THE PARADOX OF POWER

This function of mobilizing consent, I wish to emphasize, is not one of the traditional functions of the legislature. It is certainly not the representative function by which in greater or lesser degree the legislature brings the grievances and wishes of the people to bear upon policy-making. It does not refer primarily to the kind of consent that is involved when the voters at an election give their approval to a certain body of men and/or to a certain program of proposals. On the contrary, it is especially the consent that must be won insofar as the voters did not originate or mandate the policies being imposed upon them.

British experience in recent years illustrates vividly this new necessity of modern government. On the one hand, we find there a governmental system that might seem to satisfy all the conditions for decisional effectiveness. "Of all governments of countries with free political institutions," Professor Bernard Crick has written, "British government exhibits the greatest concentration of power and authority. Nowhere else is a Government normally as free to act decisively, so unfettered by formal restraints of Constitutional Law, by any Federal divisions of power, by any practice of strong and active local government, or by any likelihood of defeat in the Parliament."

Yet in recent years, according to many British critics, this powerful system has performed weakly. The burden of their complaint is not that it has been illiberal or undemocratic, but that it has been ineffective—in particular, ineffective in meeting the great but surely not unmanageable problems of the British economy. Here is a country that was once the workshop of the world. Yet year after year it has lagged behind the other economies of the free world. . . . The question now is: Has Parliament a role in helping Britain overcome these essentially political difficulties?

It may help us see the possibilities if we briefly consider some of the conventional views of the functions of legislatures in general and of Parliament in particular. I will take these in the chronological order in which they have flourished, but I want to emphasize that in greater or lesser degree they still give us insight into what actually goes on today.

One of the oldest conceptions of the role of Parliament is that of controlling and restraining the executive. An acute Tory thinker of the last generation claimed that throughout British history, from the origins of the constitution in the Middle Ages, this had been the essential function of Parliament. In the view of L. S. Amery, there are and always have been two main elements in British government: one is the central, initiating, energizing element—formerly the monarchy, today the cabinet—while the other is the checking, criticizing, controlling element—the Parliament, and nowadays especially the Opposition. The task of the Government is to govern; the task of Parliament is to criticize and control—that is, to present grievances and to let the ministers and bureaucrats know what the people will not stand.

This bipolar model still tells us a great deal about British government. It provides, for instance, an illuminating rationale for much of the procedure of the House of Commons. As stated in Standing Orders and in long-honored conventions, the rules of the House presuppose on one side a Government—that is, not merely a number of ministers, but a unified ministerial body which has a program of business that it will put before the House—and on the other side, an Opposition similarly organized and ready to act. Within this framework, the activity of the House is organized under various formal headings. One authoritative classification, for instance, relates the forms of procedure to the following functions of the House: (1) control of finance; (2) formulation and control of policy; and (3) legislation. This is a helpful scheme, but when we examine how the procedural forms under these headings are actually used, they usually turn out to constitute criticism and control. The nominal function of a procedural form is usually not its real function. In a debate on an adjournment motion, for example, one does not discuss whether or not to adjourn. In the debates on the estimates, the House rarely discusses the amount to be appropriated, but rather some aspect of departmental policy which the Opposition has chosen to attack. Whatever their nominal content, the forms of procedure of the House are used very much in accord with the bipolar model. The Government governs, but subject to a continuous flow of criticism varying in scope, timing, specificity, and so on.

The opportunities for criticism are clear enough, but may one also speak of them as a means of control? To be sure, in these days of monolithic majorities, such criticism is not expected to result in defeats for the Government—not, at any rate, in defeats serious enough to cause a resignation or dissolution. Yet such criticism is not without influence. By building up points in these debates, the Opposition may hope to sway voters when they next go to the polls. Moreover, one cannot neglect the real though immeasurable influence that criticism may have without reference to electoral consequences. The House itself is a community with its own standards of excellence in the light of which, quite apart from party considerations, reputations are made and lost. Furthermore, this community blends with a special public linked by communication centers such as the clubs of Pall Mall, university common rooms, and the editorial offices of the better daily newspapers and weekly political journals. No self-respecting minister or civil servant can enjoy having acts of injustice or stupidity for which he is responsible exposed to the scrutiny and comment of such circles in the House and adjacent to it. In trying to understand what influences British Governments and politicians, it is certainly a mistake to neglect the sanctions of these critics and to consider only those of the electorate. To be sure, only the voters can ultimately withdraw or confer power. But not the least of the sweets of power is to use it in such a way as to earn the praise of a discriminating public. Otherwise, one may have power without glory.

This criticizing and controlling function of Parliament, although perhaps its most ancient task, is still important today. Another function, that first became prominent in a later historical period, however, gives the legislature a more positive role. In the light of this function, the essential task of the legislature is to legislate, to make laws—in a fundamental sense, to lay down the lines along which the country will be governed. Two major historical views that attribute this function to Parliament are the Liberal and the Radical. The Liberal conceived of Parliament as performing this lawmaking function under the guidance of its own sense of what was right and prudent without regard to pressure from the outside. In short, he took Parliament to be a deliberative body, making its determinations in response to reasons and forces arising within it. According to the Radical democrat, Parliament was also to be the chief lawmaker, but with the important proviso that it express the will of the people. In some versions, this relationship was to be secured by means of a party program approved by the voters at a general election and conceived as giving the Government a "mandate" to carry out what was promised.

Today, of course, Parliament is not the chief lawmaker, if by that we mean that it lays down a set of general rules which so far control the actions of administrators that they need merely apply them by deduction to particular cases. As we have previously observed, a continually larger proportion of government action consists of managerial decisions governed only broadly by statutory authority and formulated in many cases by the *ad hoc* bargaining of public and private bureaucrats. Moreover, even those broad statutory grants of power to the executive have not originated with the rank and file of the legislature. The initiative in legislation, as in other policy-making, is exercised almost exclusively by the executive. If we want to know what laws will be debated in a coming session of Parliament, we do not take a poll of MPs. We look rather at the Speech from the Throne in which ministers state the objects for which they will seek legislation. Indeed, not only does the Government largely monopolize the initiative in drafting and proposing bills to Parliament, it also gets substantially all legislation for which it asks. Under modern conditions of cabinet and party government, it would be misleading to picture Parliament as the law-making power.

Yet, again speaking in terms of realities, we cannot neglect the influence of the legislature, in particular the parliamentary party upon which the Government depends for its "mechanical majorities." When the governing party went to the country, it took a position on many public questions. It may have presented a detailed program; at the least, it gave an impression of its broad approach to problems. This public stance in part reflects and in part creates a body of ideas and sentiments among the party's MPs which the Government cannot easily disregard. "Collectively and individually," D. N. Chester has recently written, "Ministers cannot get far out of line with the views of their supporters in the House. The electoral campaign and Party manifestoes, the basic attitudes of active Party members, are as much part of the heritage of the Government as of their supporters and almost as compulsive on their actions."

An ancient task of the party whips is to keep leaders informed of feeling among the rank and file and of whether the limits of their loyalty are being approached. A more modern instrument for taking such soundings and for enabling leaders to anticipate disaffection is provided by the elaborate organization of back-benchers that has grown up in both parties in the past fifty years and especially since World War II. In both parties there are regular weekly meetings of what we would call the party caucus; in addition there are many specialized committees roughly corresponding in their subjects of concern with the main departments of state. In both parties leaders keep in touch with these meetings, and discussion at them can be fierce when the party is divided over some question of policy or leadership. Indeed, it is sometimes said that the most interesting debates in the Palace of Westminster take place not on the floor of the House, but in the rooms where the party meetings are held. If the ancient function of criticism is nowadays performed especially by the Opposition, the more modern function of keeping the actions of government in line with its electoral commitments depends in no small degree upon such pressures from the back-benchers of the governing party.

As a model of what actually goes on, the notion of Parliament as chief lawmaker, whether in its Liberal or Radical versions, is a gross distortion—a common fate of models. Yet it does give us a systematic insight into a function of the legislature that is a necessary supplement to the view that Parliament's role is to criticize and control. At times Parliament does behave as a deliberative body—for instance, when amending bills in the less partisan atmosphere of standing committee where the special knowledge of members has a chance of being attended to by civil servants, ministers, and other MPs.

Moreover, although pure mandate theory is an exaggeration, Parliament performs its criticizing and controlling function in the context of a lively system of democratic and party politics. It is the principal forum from which the parties appeal to voters for their support in the next general election. "Governing," writes Professor Crick, "has now become a prolonged election campaign." "Parliament," he goes on to observe, "is still the agreed arena in which most of the continuous election campaign is fought," and the principal device by which "the Parties obtain something like equal access to the ear of the electorate in the long formative period between the official campaigns." One must not exaggerate the attention given to Parliament. Those newspapers that carry reasonably full reports of parliamentary debates are read by only 11 per cent of the population—that is, rather more than 5 million persons. About the same number (though not necessarily the same people) have been identified as the "serious public" who declare themselves to be "very interested" in political affairs and who follow them between elections. These people are only a fraction of the total electorate, but as opinion leaders they play an important role in the formation of the opinion that is expressed at elections.

TO MOBILIZE CONSENT

There are two aspects of this opinion that are of interest to us. On the one hand, it includes those "electoral commitments" which were made by the leadership of the winning party and will be in some degree pressed on that leadership by their parliamentary followers. This aspect of the electoral process is a primary concern of traditional democratic theory which emphasizes the flow of public will into governmental action by means of such commitments. In this view, voters use elections to oblige government to follow their wishes.

For the purposes of this paper, however, another aspect of the electoral process is more important. This is the fact that these "electoral commitments," so to speak, commit not only the Government, but also the voters. They constitute a set of expectations—some specific, most rather vague—about the future course of government policy which the voters in substantial numbers have shown themselves to share. These expectations originated with the public itself probably in only a few instances and in a very distant sense. As our previous discussion suggested, they may well have been initially communicated to the electorate by means of the party battle in Parliament. The important point is that the expectations, however they originated, have laid a foundation of consent and acceptance for relevant government programs in the future. A first step in mobilizing consent has been taken.

With some stretching of democratic theory, we may say that this process is one way in which the legislature fulfills its representative function. The voters did not originate the commitments and there was perhaps some "dependence effect" in the way they were brought to accept them. Still, the electorate made the choice and the legislature, more or less faithfully, carries out its will. It is immediately clear, however, that such an expression of popular will—such a set of commitments and expectations—can realistically control the course of government in only the most limited sense. Many—and quite possibly the most painful—decisions will have to be taken after the election.

How to legitimize these decisions may be a problem for democratic theory. Our concern here is to point out that winning consent for them among the people they affect will certainly be a problem for the government. For modern government cannot and does not rely solely upon the legitimizing effects of periodic elections. It must make continuous efforts to create consent for new programs and to sustain consent for old ones. *It must mobilize consent between as well as at elections.*

In so mobilizing consent, various elements of British government make a contribution. The "exhortations" to which ministers resort from time to time in an effort to win voluntary cooperation with some painful policy have not been uniformly successful. Still, the kind of leadership ministers provide, and especially the confidence the prime minister is able to arouse, are vitally important. Likewise, the spirit and the incentives that government imparts to the bargaining process can make a difference. My concern here, however, is briefly to suggest the possibilities of an enlarged role for Parliament.

I do not know of a theoretical exploration of this function by a political scientist. It has, however, been recognized as an important function of the American Congress by one of the most effective and scholarly of the new generation in the United States House of Representatives. Writing of "the emerging role of Congress," John Brademas has isolated and described an important aspect of the modern legislator's relationship with his constituents. Referring specifically to the recently enacted education, anti-poverty, and medicare programs, he reports that as he traveled around his district, he was constantly questioned by "state and local authorities, officials of private organizations and individuals on how the programs work."

> It is more than a question of red tape and filling out applications, [he writes.] Many local leaders may not understand the purposes of the legislation or see its relevance to their communities. The Congressman or Senator, by organizing community conferences, mailing materials and in other ways, can supply important information, interpretation, justification and leadership to his constituency. . . . These activities of explaining, justifying, interpreting, interceding, all help, normally, to build acceptance for government policy, an essential process in democratic government. . . .

When Congressman Brademas writes of how the legislator can "build acceptance for government policy" he means exactly what in this paper has been called mobilizing consent. In his illustration he refers to programs which have already been enacted into law, but which are not understood or fully accepted even among those whom they benefit. That he sees the necessity to "build acceptance" for these particular programs is especially interesting, as they are concerned with direct "welfare" benefits rather than more remote objectives, such as economic growth. Yet even in the case of such "popular" programs and among people who stand to benefit from them, he finds a need to "build acceptance."

The welfare state and the managed economy bring many benefits, but inevitably they also impose many new and complex coercions—often in the very process of conferring benefits. A great deal is expected of the citizen in the form of new necessities that oblige him to conform his behavior to the complex requirements of economic and social policy. On the one hand, the burdens that government imposes on citizens are very demanding and, on the other hand, the reasons for these impositions are often highly complex and technical. To win both the mind and the heart of the citizen to an acceptance of these coercions is a major necessity, and a severe problem. And if, as Congressman Brademas shows, this problem is substantial in our own country, it is far more acute in Britain where welfarism and economic management have become more comprehensive and elaborate.

The democratic process, focused by the legislature upon periodic elections, can do a great deal to meet this problem. Yet much more is required—a more continuous, intimate interchange between authority and those subject to authority. The process of policy-making itself, insofar as it is carried out in public, can be shaped as a means of winning consent to the very coercions then being explained, defended, and attacked. If I may again quote Professor Crick: "The truth is that if anything useful and significant is to be done in a free society, it must be done publicly and in such a way as to consult, involve and carry with it those affected." *Consent in this instance does not spring from some previous interaction of government and voter at a general election, but is the constantly renewed product of a continual exchange of communications.*

In performing the function of winning consent in either of these modes, Parliament displays glaring inadequacies and as one goes through the current literature advocating reform of Parliament, one can catch many glimpses of how these inadequacies might be remedied. I refer those interested in the detail of these proposals to Professor Crick's excellent little book, *The Reform of Parliament.* Here I shall simply bring out a few main points.

In the first place, the level of secrecy should be reduced. It is not plausible to expect people to identify with the output of the governmental process when only the product and not the process itself is revealed to the public gaze. Defense matters no doubt require much secrecy. So also in Britain does the system of party government and cabinet responsibility by which sharp conflicts within a party, a Cabinet, or the civil service are removed from public knowledge and scrutiny. Too much public scrutiny could—as the example of Washington, D.C., warns us—exacerbate personal relations and abrade the channels of communication and decision within the Whitehall machine.

Yet it is nevertheless clear to the growing body of British critics that the level of secrecy in British government is excessively high. The reporting of parliamentary news is faulty. Party leaders in office and in opposition hold too few press conferences. The restraints on reporters at Westminster are too strict. Another area in which the veil of secrecy could be lifted is the parliamentary party. Already the debates in meetings of the parliamentary parties seep out, often in distorted form. It would add greatly to the vitality of British government if the press were admitted on a regular basis to these debates.

If the public is to be given a greater sense of participation, not only must secrecy be reduced, but MPs must be given better instruments for understanding, explaining, and—inevitably—criticizing what the government is doing. A major reform toward this end would be to substitute for the present non-specialized committees of the House, a system of committees, each with a sphere of competence parallel to one or more ministries. Such committees would take the committee stage of bills, but more important they would have some of the functions of reviewing administration—"legislative oversight"—that the specialized committees of Congress perform. The essential point is that such a committee system would not only enable MPs themselves to gain some competence in a substantive field of government, but would also provide a focus for public attention upon government action in these fields. For the same general purpose, MPs need much more expert staff assistance. The specialist committees should have such staff and the House Library should be expanded.

A government today is strong for any purpose—economic, social, or military—only so far as it can mobilize consent among its citizens. As events of recent decades have shown, democratic governments are more likely to have this power than non-democratic governments. A leading instance is the comparative war effort of democratic Britain and Nazi Germany. Although it started far behind Germany in mobilizing its resources for war, Britain was much more successful in total mobilization. After the war, the German Minister for War Economy, Albert Speer, said: "You won because you made total war and we did not."

Today Britain confronts the political problem of breaking through the politics of stalemate and at once releasing and concerting untapped energies among her people. There is no simple solution to this problem and no single agency of government or politics can be expected to cope with it. It is, however, essentially a task of mobilizing consent in which the legislature could be given a much more important role.

21 ALFRED DIAMANT

Tradition and Innovation in French Administration

Some years ago I suggested that in the presence of a weak political sector, one in which the decision-making process is stalemated as the result of sharply divergent interest group conflicts, the public bureaucracy will govern the country by default. It seemed to me then that when parliament and cabinet are unable to act, the *grands commis* will do what the political sector fails to do. But a strong, determined, and public-interest-oriented higher bureaucracy is not the necessary consequence of a weak or paralyzed political system. There is no necessary connection between these two phenomena, and the French experience would indicate that, in fact, during periods of political indecision the *grands corps* do not really govern the country, they simply continue routine operations, maintain the status quo, and protect their own interests. It would seem, particularly from the experience of the Fourth Republic, that under then prevailing conditions the administration could carry on from day to day, but it could not carry through

Reprinted from "Tradition and Innovation in French Administration" by Alfred Diamant, *Comparative Political Studies*, Vol. 1, No. 2, pp. 255-273, by permission of the publisher, Sage Publications, Inc. Footnotes omitted by the editors.

radical innovations. There was no lack of ideas, plans, proposals, but in the absence of a determined political will these plans remained dormant.

This is not meant to deny the influence which the French higher bureaucracy, like its counterparts in Great Britain and West Germany, wields over public policy. It has always exercised such influence and will continue to do so; but for anything more than routine adjustments and especially for far-reaching innovation, the French bureaucracy has always had to become identified with a determined political master.

The administration is not the only source of innovation in France. Extra-administrative sources include, first of all, those sectors of society with which the higher bureaucracy is closely identified. These are the faculties of the institutions in which the future administrators are educated and trained. Here the influence of the law faculties is great and pervasive. The connections between the higher bureaucracy and the professors of law are particularly close. For a long time there has been almost a monopoly of influence exercised by the professors of administrative law, though very recently other social scientists have begun to be heard. Administrative law is still the dominant orientation in the professional preparation and outlook of the French bureaucracy, even though some changes are visible.

The political sectors, parties, parliament, politicians, have been sources of renewal of French administration. However, often the men in these sectors who have been innovators in administration have been those whose careers began in the high administration, because that was the only road to financial security for young men from the middle class. The combined administrative-political career so common in the French higher civil service leads observers to conclude that men in the political sector have considerably more sophistication about the problems of the bureaucracy than in Great Britain and the United States. On examination, it turns out that men like those mentioned above spent a good part of their formative years in the higher civil service. Their role as innovators was facilitated by their shift into a political career, but the reform ideas themselves grew out of their earlier administrative background.

The influence of the private economic sector and of such disciplines as business management, organization theory, etc., is a recent development. This does not suggest that in the past members of the higher bureaucracy did not share the conservative, private-enterprise views of the social strata from which they came. Even a cursory examination of the trends of the decisions of the *Conseil d'Etat* in economic and social questions between 1870 and 1940 reveals a consistent commitment to a sort of minimal *laissez-faire* economic system, tempered only by concessions to a persistently corporative trend in French nineteenth-century thought and practice. But on the whole, the methods, structures, and processes of public administration were influenced little by developments in the private sector.

All this has changed radically since 1945. It was in the remarkable identity of ideas between certain men of Vichy and of the Resistance, in the war years, on the need for renewing French society, that the foundations were laid for the modernized, industrialized, welfare state now emerging in France. The foundations for this new France were the nationalizations following World War II and the comprehensive economic planning system developed by Jean Monnet and his successors. As a result of increased blurring of the public-private distinction in the economic sector, there now exist intimate contacts between the classic public administration sector and the private economy. In administrative organization, budgeting, decision-making patterns and data-processing methods, public administration and the public sector, on the one hand, and the private and semi-private economy, on the other, have moved closer to each other.

In its dysfunctional conception, the term *bureaucracy* is identified with slowness, ponderousness, routine, complication of procedures, maladapted responses, and frustration. In such a view, the assumption that a bureaucracy could be capable of innovation simply has no place. This, however, flies in the face of the French evidence since World War II. It is true that, without the support of a strong political executive, the bureaucracy would have been unable (perhaps also unwilling) to venture beyond the routine of day-to-day administration. However, even before 1958 there is a respectable record, at least in the economic field. Certainly since 1958—and during the gestation of ideas and plans well before that time—the bureaucracy has been an important source of new ideas as well as an executing organ for plans originated elsewhere. Ordinarily, one might not expect a well-established bureaucracy, like the French, to originate or willingly execute plans that would destroy or alter radically the "Establishment" of which it is a part. Nevertheless, during the last decades important ideas have come from the French bureaucracy, especially from its higher service.

Three caveats are in order. First, this tendency toward rule and renewal by the higher bureaucracy is not without difficulties, as was demonstrated by the Vichy episode and the need for a subsequent housecleaning in the higher bureaucracy. Secondly, the innovative group is a small elite at the top of a hierarchical public service, and the material and prestige benefits that result from this activity are generally limited to this elite. One might say that the system is arranged in such a way that only this top group finds the public service attractive, while down the line dissatisfaction and alienation are the rule. Finally, no answer is possible, in the present context, to the question whether the price to be paid for this creative and innovative elite is too high for the remainder of the public service and for French society. Since 1958, at least, French society seems to have been willing to pay whatever price was necessary to obtain stability and material prosperity. This has included the assignment of a major role in initiation and execution of public policy to this bureaucratic elite. So far the French, when consulted through the peculiar plebiscitary machinery of the Fifth Republic, have indicated that the price was not excessive, though in the presidential elections of 1965 some doubts began to appear which deepened in the legislative elections of 1967 and found their most clamorous expression "on the barricades" in May and June 1968. De Gaulle's backlash victory in the legislative elections of June 1968 cannot really be said to have settled French doubts about the validity of a plebiscitary autocracy supported by an elite bureaucracy.

Though the two cases studied deal primarily with how the administration goes about its business, they nevertheless throw considerable light on the interplay between tradition and innovation and on some aspects of national policy.

The first case, "Regional Administration and Economic Planning," goes beyond the details of structural administrative arrangements and touches on problems of the economic, social, and ecological balance in French life. The material marshalled for this survey also demonstrates how, in the conflict between traditional and modernizing corps of bureaucrats, conflicting concepts of "law and order" vs. "welfare" work themselves out in French society. Given the weakness of parties and parliament in the present regime, socio-political conflicts may well have to be fought and resolved on the level of major bureaucratic corps. As already suggested, it might be that the French are beginning to lose patience with this sort of decision-making pattern.

The second case, "Personnel of the Higher Service," examines the political and social composition of the present and future senior policymakers, and thus touches on the shape and content of French public policy. The fact that this study finds the balance to be tipping in favor of tradition over innovation suggests the likelihood of sharp limitations on innovation in national policy. For radical departures in policy can seldom be initiated and completed successfully with personnel who are identified with and have a stake in the status quo. Thus both case studies provide some insight into crucial issues of French national policymaking.

REGIONAL ADMINISTRATION AND ECONOMIC PLANNING

One of the most clearly innovative administrative developments has been concerned with regional planning and administration. France has remained the classic case of a highly centralized government and administration. With few exceptions, the role of the central authorities in this system has not been changed radically in the post-war years. Certainly, the military administrative structure was unified, and new ministries and other agencies were created for new functions. But not even the series of nationalization measures which were carried through after the war resulted in radically new administrative structures.

The problem of economic development led to a sweeping reconsideration of the structure of government and administration in the early 1960's. About the same time that the Soviet Union was experimenting with regional economic councils, France began to realize that the existing highly centralized administrative structure was a bar to its further economic development. Only if the tasks of development could effectively be decentralized or regionalized would it be possible to overcome the socio-economic weakness of certain of France's geographic regions.

The existing arrangements had two weaknesses. First, the ninety *départements* of metropolitan France were simply too small for most purposes of modern government. Though there had been considerable discussion and tinkering with that pattern, no genuinely new ideas had been brought to bear on this problem. The other weakness was the increasing difficulties the prefects faced in their efforts to coordinate the rapidly growing field services of the central ministries and in their relationship to the planning process.

The proposals for change, which emerged chiefly from the Ministry of the Interior, from the ranks of the younger prefects, and from the *Commisariat général du Plan*, centered on the creation of new regional government, but these ideas had nothing to do with the old regional ideology which was a favorite plaything of Vichy, nor with Rousseauist notions of small independent republics. The key word in these plans was not *regionalisme* but *regionalisation*—translated imperfectly as "not regional self-government, but regionalization of central functions." There was no thought of strengthening grass-roots participation, but simply of creating regional authorities for the effective execution of centrally-conceived economic development. This spirit is not far removed from the essentially anti-democratic ideas behind much of the regional ideology which has issued from the French right in the past.

Leaving aside the ideological parentage of plans for regional administration, one must recognize that future economic development in France depends in part on creating a better balance, first, between the "East" and the "West"; next, between Paris and the remainder of the country; and finally, between the urban and the rural components of French life. It has almost become a cliché to recite the facts concerning the imbalance of French life: the chronic under-development of the Southwest, the dominant position of Paris, and the general decline of rural life. In the past the rates and patterns of growth have always favored Paris, which today has 19% of the total population and 29% of the total urban population. Between 1850 and 1939, the population of Paris increased 300%, but that of the other major urban centers only 14%. But since 1950, the population growth rate of Paris is only twenty-third among cities of

100,000; the spectacular growth of the 1960's is taking place in such areas as Rhone-Alpes and Provence-Côte d'Azure.

The current (Fifth) Plan is devoted to curing these imbalances. It proposes to do this, first, by fostering the growth of eight other major-area capital centers to create a better balance between Paris and the rest of the country; secondly, by improving the West-East balance through such measures as industrial location, relocation and reconversion; and finally, the plan looks to a restructuring of French agriculture within the Common Market framework.

The machinery and structure to realize balanced regional development partly consisted of the establishment of twenty regions (into which existing *départements* would be subsumed) with regional prefects, and a Paris regional government with institutions reflecting the special needs of the capital region. In each of these twenty-one regions there would be a prefect who, for the first time, would not be simply *primus inter pares* in relation to the other prefects in the region, but a chief administrator assisted by a planning staff (*état-major régional*), a *conférence administrative régionale*, an advisory body consisting of the prefects and the principal field service officers of the region, and a committee of regional "notables" (*Commission de développement économique régional*), also in an advisory capacity. At the same time, in the existing *départements*, the prefect became a real chief administrative officer. It is interesting to note that in at least one "official" source it is blandly asserted that the functions of the regional prefect are simply to stimulate and coordinate, and only in matters of areal reorganization and economic development; and furthermore, that the powers and functions of the existing *départements* and local governments are not to be curtailed by these measures. One wonders whether the commentator was trying to characterize these measures as a radical revamping of territorial administration which, however, would leave the position of local governments and other interests untouched?

The genuine potential for innovation through regional administration and planning lies not in the simple reshuffling of territorial administrative organizations but in replacing an administrative apparatus built around concerns for "law and order" with one for "welfare and development."

The "law and order" system has traditionally centered in the ministry of the interior with its responsibility for internal security and its control over police forces and the prefectoral system. The prefects, as representatives of the central power, were to maintain order not only in the "law and order" sense, but also in the political sense—for many decades prefects were expected to "manage" elections on behalf of their Paris masters. Prefects also were to supervise the growing number of field services of the central ministries, a task for which they became less competent as the technical nature and complexity of the various agencies increased sharply. The technicians, in turn, found that the prefects had little understanding for the technical requisites of their work, and thus tended to bypass them whenever possible. Periodic re-assertion of the prefects' role as the sole representatives of the central government did little to alter this growing administrative pluralism—or anarchy, as some would have it.

With the development of regional administration and economic planning, a genuine alternative to the prefectoral system has come into being; what Professor Debbasch has called "l'administration parallèle." This new system, firstly, eclipses the *département*, the traditional stronghold of the prefectoral system, and replaces it with the region, whose principal function is economic development. Secondly, at the center in Paris the crucial instrument for exercising control is no longer the Ministry of the Interior but the various economic ministries. Their structure and titles have changed from time to time, but significantly it is the economic planning, investment, and development experts directly related to these ministries who hold the center of the stage, rather than the prefects.

Certainly, the regional prefect plays a major role in this new scheme, as do some other members of the prefectoral corps. But these are the very ones whose personal orientation has changed from "law and order" to "welfare and development"; they are the "Young Turks" of the prefectoral corps who, together with some of the senior men who have reoriented themselves, represent the wave of the future. At the same time, the classical administration has not been eliminated, for it remains essential for daily routine. But important broad policy decisions involving welfare and economic development have shifted to these new economic and planning agencies and to the "new men" on their staffs. If the conflict between "law and order" and "welfare and development" has to be fought at the level of rival bureaucratic contenders—this is likely, given the current weakness of the traditional political sectors—then one might suspect that "welfare and development" stands a good chance of winning, perhaps for the first time in recent French history.

Creating a regional government for Paris posed especially difficult problems. Here it was not sufficient to group existing *départements* into a new region: account had to be taken of the spectacular population growth of the suburban fringe. The problem was tackled in three stages, beginning in 1961 with the creation of the Paris region, headed by a "delegate" who was assisted by an administrative council and an economic chief of staff. This was followed by legislation in 1964 which redrew the lines of the *départements* around Paris. Finally, in 1966, the position of prefect for the Paris region was created, and powers from the Prime Minister's office and the ministries of Interior and Economics and Finance were delegated to it. Like other regional prefects, the Paris officer's principal functions were to be those of chief planner and capital investment and economic development officer. Even here, however, the innovation stopped short of some of the great administrative power centers of France, such as that dealing with education.

The current transition period in the Paris region best shows the strains created by administrative innovation and the chances for success of the new structures. For example, the new *département* Hauts-de-Seine has been partly carved from the old *Préfecture de la Seine* which together with the old *Préfecture de Police*, carried out both municipal functions and those of a *département*. In addition, the relations between the old Seine prefecture and the central ministries were unlike those of any other *département*, because the ministries dealt with it not through their field services but directly through their central bureaus. Since the Seine prefecture included both the city of Paris and suburban areas, what share of the funds, of the work, and of the staff should be credited to the suburban areas and thus to the new Hauts-de-Seine *département*? If the prefect of the new *département* was to be responsible for the field services in his domain, how were the various ministries to carve up their existing field services to give the new *département* its fair share? Of course, the area of the new *département* was already cared for by the various ministries. The problem was for the prefect to get the attention of these field services or of the appropriate central bureaus which were located not in or around the prefecture administrative center but elsewhere in the sprawling Paris suburban complex. Field service officers had to be "invited" by the prefect of the new *département* to "visit" him in his temporary administrative headquarters. But while prefects of these new Paris region *départements* were struggling to establish their authority, the creation of the Paris regional prefect subordinated them to this new regional authority in certain crucial economic and developmental matters.

The most interesting and profitable time to assess innovation is the very time when the innovative processes are still at work. But at this stage, only tentative answers can be given. In matters of regional administration and planning, one can say that a group of people, mostly in the higher service or with their roots in that service, though now ostensibly part of the political sector, have tackled the problem of innovation with imagination. They have developed new concepts, made them operational, and attempted to translate them into action. Given the political system of the Fifth Republic, they have done so largely without the effective legitimation of the elected representatives of the people. But in our day, government by brilliant, conscientious, and, in their own light, public-spirited experts, though increasingly fashionable in a steadily more specialist world, ought to trouble the political scientist who operates from democratic premises. No amount of fascination with the glamour of innovation nor with the manner in which the Fifth Republic manages to cut through problems which had paralyzed its predecessor Republic should blind the democratic political scientist to the fact that in France change and innovation are the work of an administrative elite whose actions are legitimized by a plebiscitary ruler. As has been suggested above, the present analysis will not attempt to assess the costs to French democracy of buying innovation and change at the sort of price suggested here. But in our admiration for this innovative achievement, we should not forget to pose the question.

PERSONNEL OF THE HIGHER SERVICE

The ability of French public administration to overcome tradition and to strike out for new ground has been considerably less in matters of personnel than in regional administration and planning. Informed observers of the higher service are likely to complain that the personnel and structure of the service no longer meet the needs of the modern state, and that the service lacks uniformity because of recruitment practices which vary from agency to agency; that there is little post-entry training; that there is excessive specialization and compartmentalization in the higher service; and that often young officers entering the service are assigned tasks far below their competence. Actually, all these statements date from 1945 and were part of the argument for the creation of a new school of administration and of a unified corps of higher administrators. Indeed, the *École Nationale d'Administration* and the corps of general administrators, the *administrateurs civils*, were created during the post-war reconstruction. Today, after twenty years of E.N.A. operation, many of the same criticisms are still made with considerable justification, for although the lower and middle ranges of the higher service (and even some of the top positions) are now filled with E.N.A. graduates, the *grands corps* have lost none of their ability to put a stamp on the young officers who join them after graduation. And those graduates who go as *administrateurs civils* into one of the important ministries, quickly orient their life around that ministry and have little feeling for their membership in a common administrative corps. The fragmentation of the higher ministerial service is so far advanced that when the defense ministry recently wanted to unify the three disparate groups of *administrateurs civils* in the army, navy, and air force ministries into a single defense ministry corps, the necessary steps could not be taken legally because the three groups were "legally" not separate at all.

The E.N.A., far from being a single source of the higher service, serves chiefly as a training school for initial appointees to the *grands corps* and for a very few of the ministries. Of approximately 1,300 E.N.A. graduates to 1963, 99 now serve in the Council of State, 101 in the Court of Accounts, 130 in the Foreign Ministry, 250 in the Ministry of Finance, and 114 in Interior; that is to say, well over half the graduates are absorbed by the *grands corps* and the ministries controlled by these elite corps. By contrast, there are 16 E.N.A. graduates in the higher service of the Ministry of Agriculture, 2 in the postal service (which recruits its own *administrateurs civils*), 4 in Veterans Affairs, and 1 in the Ministry of Justice—and *he* works with the Council of State.

A fuller picture of the way E.N.A. supplies the personnel needs of the higher service emerges from the assignment list of the 1964 graduating class, a class which differs little from its predecessors or successors. At graduation all members of a class are ranked in transitive order, and this determines the assignment of the graduates to the various agencies. The class of 1964 had 112 members; of those graduating in the top decile, six went to the Council of State, four to the Finance Inspectorate, and one to the Foreign Service. Of those in the second decile, eight went to the Court of Accounts, and one each to the Council of State, the Finance Inspectorate, and the Foreign Service. By contrast, the last decile found assignment in such agencies as Social Welfare, Defense, Supply, and Social Security; and in the fifth decile the Prime Minister's office, Economics and Finance, and Foreign Affairs were the agencies drawing on the class. What emerges clearly is the essentially traditional character of the educational practices of E.N.A., with its transitive rankings, and the reliance of appointing agencies on these rankings. To this should be added the informal but effective way in which the prospective higher civil servants learn about the prestige hierarchy of agencies and reveal this in their preferential listings of agencies. Thus, the *grands corps* and a handful of prestigious ministries are able to draw at will from the top graduates. The question remains, however, whether these top graduates are indeed the best the higher service can hope to attract and whether high marks given through the present system of E.N.A. education are indeed the most reliable indicator of top performance in the higher service. Do the best young people of the current age groups no longer consider careers in the public service? Does the system of selection, training, and post-E.N.A. appointment produce a steady supply of conscientious, skilled, and intelligent young people who have already given substantial evidence that they can fit themselves into an "establishment," but few, if any, creative innovators? There is little indication so far, that the service has asked these questions, still less that data are available to sustain or deny the critical questions raised here.

Although there seem to be no difficulties, as yet, in recruiting for the higher services, we know that recruitment for the levels immediately below has run into serious difficulties. For the levels below that of the *administrateur civil*, namely *attaché d'administration* or *attaché de préfecture*, which are not recruited through E.N.A., but for which a university education is still required, the figures for the last decade are rather grim. For the first type of position there were 217 applicants in 1957 and 57 in 1964 and, in the latter year, only 17 were actually appointed. For the *attaché de préfecture* positions, the number of applicants fell from 56 in 1958 to 4 in 1963. Reforms were instituted in 1963, which include scholarships for those who would combine university study and preparation for a unified examination to be used by all agencies wanting to make appointment at the attaché level. Given the continued dominance of the service by the higher bureaucracy, it is doubtful whether the reforms will have any effect in shoring up the attractiveness of the lower levels of the public service. The situation at the clerical level seems even more hopeless, judging from the critical analysis of a number of clerical agencies made by Crozier.

The persistence of traditional patterns of French public personnel policies is also revealed in the lack of change in the social composition of the higher service and the unchanging political and ideological alignments of public servants, including professors and teachers—who must be considered part of the public service, in law as well as in practice.

It remains true that the lower and middle ranks of the public service are politically left, while the higher service tends to stand to the right. Traditional political identifications such as the officer corps being on the right and the educational bureaucracy on the left still hold. Sometimes there are political divisions within the same agency. In the Ministry of Public Health and Population, the public health services are generally identified as "Masonic" while the population-oriented sections are pro-Catholic. The ministries of education and interior were always "laic" or anti-clerical strongholds, even though the prefects as a group bear a center and right stamp. But the new sous-préfets coming from E.N.A. try to avoid political identification altogether. It is said that the Quay d'Orsay continues to have a "Catholic" and a "Protestant" party, and that while the military academy, St. Cyr, is obviously a bastion of the right, the *École normale supérieure* is said to be definitely on the left, with the French Communist party considering the Rue d'Ulm one of its strongholds.

How valid some of these generalizations still are can be seen by an examination of the political identification of bureaucrats and teachers of various sorts elected to the National Assembly in 1962 and by a comparison of the professional make-up of the public service sector of the last three legislatures. Table 1 shows the increasing number of higher civil servants elected to successive legislatures since 1956 and the decline in the number of teachers at all levels. The explanation is the general decline of left and left-center

Table 1

Public Servants in National Assembly 1956-1962

	1956	1958	1962
Primary school teachers	35	10	15
Secondary and university teachers	46	36	28
Higher civil servants	21	37	44

Table 2

Public Servants in the National Assembly by Party 1962

Political Party	Higher Education Teachers		Secondary Education Teachers		Primary Education Teachers		Higher Bureau-crats		Other Bureau-crats	
	N	%	N	%	N	%	N	%	N	%
P.C.F.	—	—	1	4	7	47	—	—	1	7
S.F.I.O.	—	—	9	36	8	53	6	14	5	36
U.N.R.	3	75	7	28	—	—	22	50	7	50
Others	1	25	7	28	—	—	16	36	1	7
Total	4	100	24	100	15	100	44	100	14	100

parties in French parliaments since the end of the Fourth Republic. It seems that the "republic of professors" has been replaced by the "republic of technocrats."

The breakdown for the 1962 legislature in Table 2 shows, firstly, that about one-fifth of the seats are held by public servants.

The distribution shows the anti-clerical left orientation of the primary school teachers, the *instituteurs*. By contrast, the political alignment of secondary school teachers is much less leftist, and the university professors, who have suffered a decline in absolute numbers since the 1956 legislature, are now represented only by men not identified with the left. In 1962, both categories of civil servants centered on the Gaullist party, with the higher bureaucrats showing the weakest left orientation of any group of public servants. A check of civil service representation in the various smaller parties shows that they are more strongly represented in left-center rather than in right-center groups. But with all that, the traditional political orientation of the public service, including the teaching profession, survives into the present day with only small modifications.

A clue to the social composition of the higher service is the position occupied by the family of the present generation of officials. Table 3 is a breakdown of the occupation of the parents of E.N.A. graduates from the years 1953 to 1963 who now serve in the four *grands corps*. The most striking feature of this distribution is that 40% of the current higher service are from "public service" families, with only little variation between the four corps. A further breakdown would have shown that, of the 103 who come from such families, the father was also a member of the higher service in 90% of the cases.

Table 3

Family Background of E.N.A. Graduates 1953-1963 Serving in 4 Grands Corps

Occupation of Father	Council of State		Finance Inspec- torate		Court of Accounts		Foreign Service		Total	
	N	%	N	%	N	%	N	%	N	%
Civil Servants	23	40	31	38	26	43	23	42	103	41
Craftsmen, Merchants	6	11	12	14	5	9	4	8	27	11
Heads of industrial enterprises	—	—	5	6	6	10	5	10	16	6
Commercial and industrial managers	13	23	14	17	11	18	10	19	48	19
Industrial and com- mercial employees	2	4	3	4	1	2	3	6	9	4
Free professions	9	16	9	11	11	18	7	13	36	14
No occupation	1	2	1	1	—	—	—	—	2	1
Agriculturists	1	2	6	7	1	2	2	4	10	4
Workers	2	4	—	—	—	—	—	—	2	1
Total	57	*	81	*	51	*	54	*	253	*

*Does not add up to 100 because of rounding.

It seems that there is little upward movement in civil service families; that is to say, children from families where a parent serves in the middle and lower ranks hardly ever aspire to membership in the higher service. Quite apart from possible inequalities of educational opportunities, might this not indicate a deep cleavage between the higher service and the other ranks, a cleavage so deep that the children from families of the middle and lower service simply want no part of public service from then on? Such a high percentage of public service back-grounds, particularly when laid against the fact that the next highest social category furnishes less than one-half the number of higher civil servants than do all civil service families put together, lends support to Brian Chapman's characterization of the European higher public service as something of a self-governing corporation with a life of its own; a life in which it is natural for the son to follow the father and not to consider other vocational and employ-ment possibilities.

The other features of this distribution confirm the conventional wisdom about the higher civil service. Children of unskilled workers continue to furnish an insignificant part of the elite corps, children from agricultural, industrial, and commercial families do little better. At the other end of the scale, the children of heads of industrial enterprise are equally poorly represented, though they show up much better in relation to the share of such families in the national totals. Children from families of commercial and industrial managers, though only one-half as numerous as civil service children, nevertheless furnish one-fifth of the total group under investigation. Apart from the over-representation of higher civil service families, one can say that, following a common pattern, under-representation of social groups in the higher service increases as one descends the social scale.

Data from other sources suggest that some changes are taking place, nevertheless. For example, primary school teaching has become a monopoly of women. In the old Seine *departement*, women now furnish three-fourths of primary school teachers—a considerable increase over the figure of 50% in 1906 and 66% in 1954. One consequence of this shift is the muting of the anti-clerical bias of the public school teachers. A recent survey concerning anti-clerical attitudes revealed that while 23% of the men considered themselves militantly atheist, only 9% of the women did so.

A most significant shift in the social origins of one of the *grands corps*, the Finance Inspectorate, was reported recently. A comparison of a group of inspectors of pre-E.N.A. origins with a group who entered the inspectorate after graduation from E.N.A. showed that the democratization of the higher service which E.N.A. was to bring about had succeeded, but only in part. The children of the lowest social strata continued to be excluded from the inspectorate, but the children of the lower middle class had made sharp advances, mostly at the expense of the top social strata for whom public service no longer seemed a sufficiently prestigious career.

Another shift in the socio-political configuration of the higher public service can be seen in the important role certain clubs play in the life of the higher service. Though the number of civil servants in the national legislature has increased steadily in the last decade, there is evidence that the bulk of the higher civil service increasingly turn away from conventional political partisan activity and toward such organizations as the Club Jean Moulin, which has come to be identified as a center of technocratic thought and activity. It seems, in contrast, that in the last few years this club has attracted fewer higher civil servants and more engineers and doctors and others with a syndicalist outlook. For Catholic-oriented young bureaucrats, there is now also *l'association Jeunes Cardres*, the civil service counterpart to *Jeunes Patrons* and *Jeunes Agriculteurs*. These and other clubs have a double significance. First, they reflect

332   Politics in Western European Democracies: Patterns and Problems

the trend of increasing professional contacts between the higher service and the so-called private sector. Secondly, the clubs are signs of the increasing dis-enchantment, especially of the younger E.N.A. graduates in the public service, with traditional party politics. These two features, the blurring of public and private sector boundaries and a turning away from partisan political activity, are the very characteristics of what is considered the *avant garde* of the higher service.

Lastly, changes in the social composition and the status of the higher service are reflected in the ebb and flow of the phenomenon called *pantouflage*— the departure from the public service for the private sector of civil servants in mid-career. Firm data are hard to come by, but the prevailing conventional wisdom is that the higher service, in addition to attracting fewer good people, is losing those it still has.

The study of the finance inspectorate by Lalumière cited above reports on this phenomenon. To begin with, *pantouflage* is not a new phenomenon, certainly as far as the Finance Inspectorate is concerned. Data going back to 1870 show an ebb and flow which can, in most cases, be linked directly to general economic conditions: high outflow from the public service in times of prosperity, very little shift in times of economic contraction. There is also evidence that *pantouflage* is not a purely economic act. Lalumière found that what he calls "career" reasons play a major role in the decision. At least, in the Finance Inspectorate, career patterns are sufficiently defined that one can know with some certainty after ten to fifteen years of service whether one has a realistic chance at the top position in the service. Finally, Lalumière found that a disproportionate share of those resigning in mid-career were the sons of upper-class families who, apparently, were using the training and experience provided by the Inspectorate for the future benefit of the family business.

It is, of course, not possible to generalize for the entire higher service from the very special situation of the Finance Inspectorate. But the findings suggest first, that *pantouflage* is not a new phenomenon either in character or scope; secondly, that it has other than purely economic causes; and finally, that in a rigid career system like the French, which provides for almost no lateral entry, the lateral exit of *pantouflage* provides for some cross-fertilization between public and the private sector.

In the light of this situation, what changes and innovations have been proposed in recent years which can compare with the body of reform proposals in functional and areal organization? Here the proposals are far less sweeping and will hardly alter radically the personnel structure of the higher service. The principal aims of recent reforms were the increased unification and mobility of the *administrateurs civils* group and further rationalization of the prefectoral career. A renewed effort is being made to pull together all the *administrateurs civils* into a single corps directly in the Prime Minister's office, and to use this central control to institute certain minimum forms of mobility by requiring everybody to spend at least two years away from his home service from time to time. These years can be spent in the field service of the home agency, abroad in technical assistance work, in local government, a public enterprise, or even an international agency.

The adjustments made in the regulations governing the prefectoral corps do not touch on basic issues at all. An attempt is made to restrict the number of persons bearing the title "prefect" by requiring that any new nominations must be for territorial posts. In addition, age limits of several kinds were eliminated, and some of the rules governing the appointments of "outsiders" as prefects were modified. As it is now, the government makes little use of that power, and what "outsiders" it appoints are usually civil servants from other corps or agencies. Altogether, then, the boldness that characterizes the innovative sweep of regional administration and planning is missing here.

At the outset a number of questions were posed concerning the general nature, the sources, and the conditions of innovation in organizations. What does the French experience with administrative innovation contribute to a meaningful answer to these questions?

In the light of the French experience, the rather precise answer advanced by March and Simon to the question "What is innovation?" proved to be too dogmatic and not easily applicable to the conditions we encountered. It is likely that a careful search of the record of French administrative development would have shown that many of the administrative innovations developed since 1945 had indeed been part of the "organization's repertory"—defining "organization" here as the entire French national public administrative apparatus. Perhaps a more commonsense approach to the question would be more fruitful. Such an approach would have us look, case by case, for radical departures from previous practices and ideas. It would then suggest that we determine whether this new departure was indeed carried through successfully. On this basis we must report that there took place considerable administrative innovation with regard to regional administration and planning, but that there was much less success in matters of the personnel system and structure of the French higher bureaucracy.

The answer to the question "Who are the innovators?" is fairly clear. The administrative innovators are found chiefly in the higher service, especially the members of the *grands corps*; quite often they are the younger men of the service, more strongly attuned to "welfare and development" needs than their older superiors. To this group must be added a number of "politicians" whose own careers began in the bureaucracy but who are now in a position to use their political power and influence to sponsor and support administrative innovation.

The answer to the question "What are the proper conditions for innovation in any organization?" is much less easily given. Firstly, there is some evidence to verify LaPalombara's suggestion that no program for administrative innovation will succeed if, as a result of it, the position, power, wealth, and symbolic significance of the administrators themselves would be threatened or destroyed. Such innovation would have to be imposed on administrators from the outside. The French experience leaves little doubt that innovation faltered, or simply was not seriously tried recently, in personnel policy. The reasons for this failure might well be those advanced by LaPalombara. Second, the evidence suggests that innovation is more likely to occur in newly-created agencies which face new or rapidly-changing demands. The willingness of an agency to innovate early in its life, followed by rigidity and unwillingness to change in the late stages, and the ultimate ossification and/or destruction of the agency for failure to function effectively, are the major states in the life-cycle of an administrative agency which Anthony Downs has specified in his recent bureaucratic model. The case of innovation in regional planning and administration partly fits these conditions. Third, conditions favorable to innovation in French administration also require the support of the innovative goals by a political master who can manipulate public opinion and political parties to obtain approval and resources. It seems that the picture of the French bureaucracy proceeding toward goals of its own choosing without help or hindrance from political forces is quite misleading.

Finally, no genuine answer is possible to the question "Innovation for what?" in the context of the present report. As was suggested in the opening section, the purposes of innovation are manifold, and no attempt was made here to identify examples from all possible categories of purposes or goals of innovation. Both case studies have dealt not with innovation in substantive policy directly, but with innovative arrangements which enable the higher public service at or near policy-making levels to carry on its work. Though civil servants proved to be reluctant to innovate in matters that would disturb the civil service status quo, it should be recognized that innovation in regional administration and planning, favored by the "Young Turks" in the civil service, did indeed involve considerable upheaval in the bureaucratic status quo.

It would be foolhardy to venture any generalizations about innovation from such limited evidence. I have simply tried to demonstrate how major aspects of the innovative process came into play in the case of two issues faced by French national policy-makers. If I were to try to draw some lessons, I would put them under three headings: (1) French senior civil servants are cautious innovators, at best—much conventional wisdom suggests that they share this trait with innumerable other national civil services. (2) Service traditions and social background help to account for much of this caution. (3) Successful innovation requires not only the threat of severe crises, as Crozier has suggested, but also the patronage (in the broadest sense) of a political chief. In a personal regime, like the present French one, senior civil servants and technocrats seem to play important policy roles, but I would suggest that their "glory" is chiefly a reflection of the "personal" leader; without him their scope would be severely limited. French administrators might well be able to pursue innovative programs for many years under conditions of political instability as during the Fourth Republic, but they require a reasonably unified political will to be successful innovators.

22 A. H. HANSON

Planning and the Politicians: Some Reflections on Economic Planning in Western Europe

It is now generally agreed that economic planning is too important a subject to be left to the economists. One may readily admit that, to plan effectively, one's economic objectives must be mutually consistent and based upon the best statistical and other data that one can find or mobilize. One may also recognize the great value of econometric models, input-output tables and the like, particularly for those countries that can build into them information sufficiently realistic and abundant to produce answers with genuinely operational significance. As Mr Maurice Zinkin has said, there are some things

Reprinted from A. H. Hanson, "Planning and the Politicians: Some Reflections on Economic Planning in Western Europe," from *International Review of Administrative Sciences*, (Vol. XXXII, No. 4, 1966), pp. 127-142, by permission of the International Review of Administrative Sciences. Footnotes omitted by the editors.

that economists can do very much better than the rest of us. 'Economists really are better at extrapolating demand or working out the input content of a given output or calculating the capital-output ratio of a given investment.' In the last resort, however, the effectiveness of planning depends upon a combination of political will and administrative competence. It is for the politicians, in consultation with the administrators, to take 'the serious decisions like what levels of tax will produce a riot or whether the public would rather have a school or a hospital, jam today or jam tomorrow'. It is for administrators, in consultation with the politicians, to devise the machinery and to formulate the rules and regulations whereby the broad objectives of the plan may be translated into detailed and mutually consistent decisions. This is my justification, as a political scientist with a special interest in public administration, for entering a field which economists until comparatively recently have regarded as exclusively their own.

THE ADVENT OF PLANNING

Although economic planning has been practised in the communist countries since the late 1920s, and has more recently been adopted by developing countries throughout the world irrespective of their political systems and ideological preconceptions, it is still not universally accepted as essential to the promotion of economic growth. In Western Europe, although the English and the French are now fully committed to it, the Germans, the Dutch, and the Italians as well as others still have their doubts. Indeed the question is still open whether state guidance of the economy in the light of long-term and medium-term objectives (which is the essence of economic planning in non-communist countries) constitutes the best method of growth promotion—or even whether it has any relevance to economic growth as such. Basically, the issue is that of who takes the initiative in economic policy formation—the public sector or the private. If the former is chosen, then the private sector has to be guided towards the achievement of objectives which (although it may have participated in their formulation) are not necessarily its own. (Indeed, where a measure of free competition prevails it is difficult to ascribe any objectives to the private sector as a whole, apart from self-preservation.) If the initiative is with the private sector, then the role of the state is largely confined to the removing of obstacles to a more or less spontaneous economic development and the taking of such measures (such as the redistribution of income and the maintenance of full employment) as are regarded as necessary to make a private enterprise economy politically and socially acceptable.

The above contrast presents two extremes which are not exemplified in a 'pure' form in any country, European or non-European. They are in fact 'ideal types', representing two ends of the spectrum the middle of which is occupied with an interesting variety of colours. It may, nevertheless, be argued that in most countries there is a uni-directional movement towards the fully state-planned economy. The reasons for this are threefold. Firstly, it is now generally recognized that *ad hoc* 'interferences' in economic life logically lead towards and in some cases actually demand the formulation of medium-term and long-term objectives, insofar as such objectives are necessary if acts of intervention are to be more rational and more timely and less improvised and less sporadic. This has been illustrated by Mr Angus Maddison by reference to the well known deficiencies in the fiscal policies of many Western European countries in the 1950s. 'Fiscal policy', he writes, 'is mainly and necessarily concerned with short-term problems, but a better idea of the longer-term perspective of investment demand, spending on consumer durables, or the level of exports required would probably help orient the choice between different policy decisions.' Second, one must remember that state intervention possesses a dynamism of its own. The state in fact is under a strong temptation to use more and more vigorously the means of intervention which it possesses—and the states of Western Europe are now for the most part excellently equipped with such means. Not only do they possess a large, widely-ramified and increasingly specialized administrative apparatus; they enjoy the advantage of access to an ever-increasing body of statistical and other information relating to the economy. Public opinion can hardly fail to demand that they should use both with all the vigour that may be required when there are economic problems that require solution. Third, and most important, there is the overwhelming fact that the public sector (as measured by the proportion of the gross national product which passes through the hands of the state or by the proportion of national investment for which the state is directly or indirectly responsible) has reached a size where the state, whether it likes it or not, is in the last resort responsible for determining the over-all pattern of economic development. In most Western European countries today, taxation absorbs between one-quarter and one-third of the G.N.P. while between 40% and 60% of total investment activity is directly state controlled. This means, indeed, that the old spontaneous trade cycle as we know it in the 1930s has virtually disappeared, probably never to return. As Maddison said of the 1950s:

> Although the basic elements of private demand—durable and non-durable consumption, fixed productive investment, exports, inventories and house construction—remained volatile, the basic rhythm of activity was set by government. The fluctuations in 1952 and 1958 and the boom of 1955 to 1956 were not business cycles in the spontaneous or self-generating sense but were policy determined. Both of the 'recessions' were due to policy restraints and a good deal of the boom was due to special investments stimuli. The business cycle in the classical sense has virtually disappeared in Europe.

FRENCH, GERMANS, AND ITALIANS

For these reasons, the idea of planning (in the sense of formulating long-term and medium-term objectives, arranging priorities and taking steps calculated to secure their realization) has become increasingly accepted in Western Europe. The French, of course, are the great pioneers in this field. Having accepted the necessity of economic planning, they have pursued it with a vigour and a logic unexampled elsewhere. In this they have been assisted, as is well known, by certain peculiarities of their economy and—more especially—by the type of relationship prevailing in France between the state administrator and the private entrepreneur, a relationship of mutual trust and understanding far stronger than that which prevails in most other countries. These advantages, however, are not a necessary condition for successful economic planning, and hence the apparently favourable results of the French experiment have evoked not only widespread admiration, but a certain amount of imitation. It would obviously be going too far to say that economic planning is now generally accepted in other Western European countries, but it is true to say that even those countries formerly most hostile to the idea are now making tentative moves in the 'French' direction.

Among the many examples of this trend, one may mention the establishment in 1964 by the Federal Republic of Germany of a Council of Economic Experts. This body produces an annual report for the guidance of the government and is also engaged in a number of long-term 'trend' studies. Admittedly, its functions are no more than advisory and, for this reason alone, one cannot justifiably present its creation as a clandestine introduction of French-type planning machinery into the predominantly free market economy of Western Germany. It is nevertheless true, as Mr Andrew Shonfield says, that the Council of Economic Experts belongs to 'the same family as the planning organs that have been set up elsewhere in Western Europe since the war'.

In Italy too, there are signs of change. In that country, progress towards planning was at one time inhibited, not, as in Germany, by the wide acceptance of 'free market' doctrines, but by political factors. Important among these was the presence in the ranks of the Liberals and Christian Democrats of a number of very determined and dogmatic *laissez-faire* theorists. So long as the Socialists remained allied with the Communists, there was no possibility of forming a government of the moderate left in which 'statist' views would necessarily have greater weight. It was for this reason, more than any other, that the Vannoni plan of 1955 was virtually stillborn. With the formation of Aldo Moro's government, however, the situation changed and the new political alignments lend to the recently appointed Economic Programming Commission an interest which it would not otherwise have possessed. Potentially, this Commission, which is under the chairmanship of the Budget Minister, has considerable importance. As Edelman and Fleming say:

Its V.I.P. membership and the fact that it represents diverse shades of public opinion suggest that its major function may be to help win acceptance for plans formulated in governmental ministries rather than to formulate them itself. On the other hand some members of its staff are among the most authoritative and ardent exponents of programming in the country.

Germany and Italy, therefore, would seem to be moving toward those more comprehensive and long-term forms of state intervention in economic life that we call planning. But the reason for this development, it is important to note, is not that these countries have been unsuccessful or insufficiently successful as economic developers. On the contrary, it is, contradictorily enough, their very success in achieving economic growth which is now turning them towards planning. Their post-war reconstruction has been completed long ago, and today Germany has achieved the 'affluent society' and Italy is moving towards it, albeit somewhat unevenly. Under these circumstances, they find themselves confronted with economic issues which, in the opinion of many, can only be answered coherently and consistently if both public and private sectors are working to a plan. Among these are the distribution of income as between classes and regions, the rival claims of income and leisure, and the relative degrees of emphasis to be placed on consumption via social benefits and consumption through the mechanism of the market. Over and above these issues, however, there are two others which seem to be of even greater immediate importance. There is the issue of providing the entrepreneur with some guarantee that the future development of the economy as a whole will not differ too radically from the kind of development on which he is counting when he makes his major investment decisions. (It is the attempt of the French planning system to provide the entrepreneur with this kind of guarantee that has given him a degree of enthusiasm for planning that he would not otherwise have possessed.) Second, there is the issue of achieving steady and preferably rapid economic growth without inflation—an ideal which can only be realized in modern circumstances if the state is capable of devising and implementing an 'incomes policy'. These, one may say without fear of contradiction, are the issues which are causing the *successful* economic developers to move away from policies of sporadic and *ad hoc* government interventions and towards various kinds of medium and long-term planning.

PLANNING IN GREAT BRITAIN

In Great Britain we are confronted with a very different situation. This country shares with Belgium the unenviable distinction of the lowest rate of development among all the major Western European countries during the post-war period. Britain's development, moreover, has been sporadic, uneven, and beset by severe inflationary problems and periodical foreign exchange crises. If Britain needs to plan her economy, therefore, it is for reasons which are, at least in certain fundamental respects, different from those responsible for planning in France and the current moves towards planning in Germany and Italy.

The history of Britain's attempts to plan her economy is a curiously chequered one. The immediate post-war Labour government lacked clear-cut ideas about economic planning and was compelled by the severe difficulties of Britain's economic situation to live a more or less hand-to-mouth existence so far as economic policies were concerned. It nevertheless talked a great deal about planning and thereby unwittingly succeeded in convincing a large number of people that planning was to be identified with physical controls, regimentation, and austerity. Not surprisingly, the Conservatives succeeded in winning both popularity and elections with their slogan, 'Set the people free'. What is perhaps more surprising is that they themselves seemed to take this election slogan seriously; for the initial period of Conservative rule in the 1950s was one of anti-planning, when even the somewhat rudimentary planning apparatus devised by the Labour government was dismantled. It was also a period of inadequate growth, 'stop-go', and mounting foreign exchange difficulties. By the late 1950s it had become obvious that the *ad hoc* fiscal and financial controls upon which the Conservatives relied were by themselves insufficient to cope with a problem that was becoming critical. Hence, in 1960, the Conservatives effected a veritable volte-face in economic policy—nothing less than a return to planning. The National Economic Development Council was created, and the Treasury, which had developed a bad reputation for lack of economic prescience, was fundamentally reorganized. The Labour Party, on its return to office in 1964, carried the process further by concentrating planning responsibilities in the hands of a Ministry of Economic Affairs, with a senior minister in charge of it, and also by bringing two other new ministries into existence, *viz.* Technology and Land & Natural Resources. Both Conservative and Labour were now placing their faith in planning to enable the country to cope, not with the problems produced by rapid economic growth, but with those produced by the relative stagnation from which it had been suffering and from which it continued to suffer. Significantly, the first chapter of the national plan was entitled 'Planning for Growth'.

This is a plan [said its authors] to provide the basis for greater economic growth. An essential part of the plan is a solution to Britain's balance of payments problem: for growth cannot be maintained unless we pay our way in the world. For too long the United Kingdom has suffered from a weak balance of payments, periodical crises have lead to sharp checks to economic expansion and productive investment; these in turn have left us vulnerable to further balance of payments difficulties when expansion was resumed. It is the government's aim to break out of this vicious circle and to introduce and maintain policies which will enable us to enjoy more rapid and more sustained economic growth.

Planning, therefore, was being tried because non-planning had failed. There was no other solution available, apart from the politically unacceptable and almost certainly unrealistic policies of extreme *laissez-faire*, as advocated by the most eccentric if also the most intellectually distinguished of Conservative leaders, Mr Enoch Powell. The only question to be asked therefore, was 'What kind of planning?' The answer, in general, was 'Planning via the price mechanism', because this kind of planning, as everybody knew, was the only kind permanently compatible with a predominantly free-enterprise economy. The use of physical controls (e.g. over building and imports) was not, however, dogmatically ruled out, particularly as a temporary expedient. If there was a planning model, it was that provided by France; indeed the construction of the British planning machine involved a considerable imitation of French institutions. The National Economic Development Council might be compared with the Higher Planning Council in France. The staff attached first to N.E.D.C. and then to the Ministry of Economic Affairs bore striking resemblance to the French Commissariat du Plan; the 'little Neddies' formed to deal with individual industries and branches of the economy were obviously patterned after the French Commissions de Modernisation. There was even an attempt, as in France, to divide the plan into regional sectors and to establish effective regional planning machinery.

DIFFERENCES OF APPROACH

Britain, then, had decided to follow the French pattern rather than the German or Italian patterns—but was she likely to be as successful as France in her planning endeavours? So far the answer would seem to be unfavourable to Britain; but judgment is difficult, because the formulation of the National Plan was almost immediately followed by a series of severe economic crises which rendered it unrealistic or irrelevant. The situation for long-term planning will no doubt improve if and when these crises are successfully overcome. Nevertheless, one has to admit that some of the conditions which appear to have facilitated the success of planning in France do not exist or do not exist to the same extent in England. These are so important that the differences between England and France in respect of what might be described as the pre-conditions for planning must be made specific.

First, one must refer once again to the time-honoured cry of 'France one and indivisible'. For all the deep conflicts which have characterized her political history, making the establishment of the democratic consensus far more difficult than in England, France is a country in which the Rousseauan concept of the 'general will' has struck profound roots. The idea that government, in guiding the development of the economy, is expressing a consensus superior to the separate interests of different groups has been familiar to Frenchmen for a very long time; so is it also with the belief that government should play a leading role in the economic life of the country. The *étatiste* tradition, in fact, goes back at least to Colbert in the seventeenth century. Britain's traditions as regards government economic initiatives are profoundly different. She has been enormously successful in the arts of compromise and in the creation of a political culture far more unified than that of France; the nature of her economic development, however, has bred in her people a suspicion of the state in its role of economic initiator and guide.

Mr Andrew Shonfield expresses these differences of approach very percipiently in the following words:

> In the history of capitalism Britain and France supply the convenience of sustained polarity. It is remarkable how two nations geographically so close, so interested in their neighbour's ways of doing things, so proud of their capacity to learn from outsiders, should yet have been so little influenced by each other's experiences. The sharp contrast in national style and practice is not noticeably modified over the centuries. The essential French view, which goes back well before the Revolution of 1789, is that the effective conduct of the nation's economic life must depend on the concentration of power in the hands of a small number of exceptionally able people exercising foresight of a kind not possessed by the average successful man of business. The long view and the wide experience systematically analysed by persons of authority are the intellectual foundations of the system. The design and efficiency of the machine of government then determine the degree of practical success achieved.

These differences of approach are necessarily reflected in differences of attitude towards the public service. The French Civil Service possesses a prestige of a kind that its British counterpart certainly does not have. Admittedly both services, particularly at their top levels, are endowed with high intellectual powers; but whereas these are admired in France, they tend to be regarded with a certain suspicion in Britain, a country which distrusts 'cleverness' in both its politicians and its administrators. Top-level public servants in France, moreover, are also more varied in the talents that they have acquired and tend to be more highly and more systematically trained for the tasks they are called upon to perform. There is no equivalent in Britain of the *École des Mines*, the *École des Ponts et Chaussées*, the *École Polytechnique*, still less of the *École Nationale d'Administration*. The combination of prestige, intelligence, variety of talents, and systematic training within the framework of an *etatiste* tradition has meant that the French civil servant entirely lacks any inferiority complex, *vis-à-vis* the businessman, or any doubt about his own capacity, in association with his many-talented fellows, to plan the economy. Furthermore, the civil servant and the businessman in France have a remarkable degree, perhaps a unique degree, of mutual understanding. They tend to share the same background of education and training, and in very many cases have remarkably similar career experiences, since movement from the civil service into business and vice versa is much easier and commoner in France than it is in Britain. So important are these considerations that Professor Granick has gone so far as to say that 'the key fact in French planning is that the same type of men are sitting on both the management and civil service posts in the Cartel.'

In England, on the other hand, the civil servant (like the government he serves) tends to act much more as an umpire or referee policing the game played by rival interest groups. There is an assumption that businessmen best understand the needs of business, that trade unionists best understand the needs of labour, and that the main job of government is simply to bring them together round the conference table and hammer out some kind of compromise. This idea, in fact, has found expression in the *modus operandi* of the new planning machinery itself. N.E.D.C. is essentially a forum where leading businessmen and leading trade unionists come together, in the presence of representatives of the various economic ministries as adjudicators and advisers, to try to arrive at some compromise between their different views about what is desirable economic policy. Such agreement, if reached, can be embodied in general directives to be remitted to the economic planning staff for 'technical processing'. Originally at least, the economic planning staff was not conceived of as playing a leading role in policy formation like the *Commissariat du Plan* in France. Likewise the 'little Neddies' bore—and indeed still bear—little real resemblance to the French *Commissions de Modernisation.* They were not even brought into existence until two years after the creation of N.E.D.C. and are still regarded primarily as theatres of bargaining where government representatives play secretarial and advisory roles. As Andrew Shonfield puts it: 'Under this scheme the individual official brought in to represent the government department with an interest in the industry concerned was likely to feel that he had a junior status in a bargaining act where others made the running.'

Mr Shonfield goes on to point out that the contrast with French practice in this respect is striking. In France civil servants play key roles in the various commissions. 'They provide either the chairman or the vice-chairman for all twenty-seven of them and usually also the Rapporteur.' These men, far from regarding themselves as umpires or referees, assume the responsibility for directing the work of the commissions and seeing that they arrive at the 'right' conclusions.

It must be admitted, however, that important changes have taken place in the British planning system of recent years, particularly since the accession of the Labour Party to office in 1964. Government has begun to play a more positive and creative role. This change of emphasis was both reflected in, and facilitated by, the creation of the Department of Economic Affairs—a new ministry to which has been confided those tasks of economic leadership which the Treasury, preoccupied with its traditional function of guarding the public purse, was felt to be incapable of exercising. There has also been a strengthening of official representation on planning bodies, together with the appointment to such bodies of officials very different in type and outlook from their predecessors. Many have been recruited on a temporary basis from other walks of life as members of something which bears at least a faint resemblance to a 'ministerial cabinet' of the French type. Some of these men are socialists; others belong to what Shonfield describes as 'the new generation of radical industrialists'—men who, although lacking any interest in socialist ideology, show none of the 'traditional prejudice of the right wing in politics against the active use of public power to re-shape the private sector of the economy'.

It is as yet uncertain whether there are a sufficient number of these swallows to constitute a summer. A national style—particularly one as established as the British—cannot be quickly changed. Despite what has happened during the last few years, the contrast between the British and French approaches to planning remains and Britain does not yet know whether by imitating the French system, with the necessary national adaptations, she can emulate the French rate of economic growth in the 1950s and early 1960s. Shonfield considers, rightly in my view, that 'one essential element in the outcome is the issue of the struggle between an old and a new civil service style'. To this he adds, by way of warning: 'The old remains very powerful and very entrenched; the exponents of the new are still comparatively few in number and mostly temporary.' That changes in civil service 'style' have become overdue is, however, now almost universally admitted.

THE DUTCH SYSTEM

What is, perhaps, surprising is that Britain has taken far more interest in the French system of planning than in the Dutch system, for the latter would appear, *prima facie*, to be more relevant than the former to Britain's needs, insofar as Holland is a successful economic developer whose political culture bears a closer resemblance to the British than does the French.

Holland, in fact, has been engaged in economic planning for an even longer period than France has—since the creation of the Central Planning Bureau in 1945. The Dutch approach to planning, however, differs from the French in several fundamental respects. The Dutch organization for economic planning is far less elaborate, and the purely advisory role of the Central Planning Bureau is very heavily stressed. The Bureau is not expected to get itself mixed up either in top-level decision-taking or in the details of economic administration; its main task is to draw up annual forecasts into which are built various alternative public policy measures and thus to assist the government in envisaging the likely overall effect of its proposed interventions. For this purpose the Bureau makes use of an econometric model which over the years has been developed to a very high level of sophistication. As for the means of plan implementation used by the Dutch, these have hitherto been almost without parallel in other Western European countries—none other than the statutory control of wages and prices.

Two tendencies in the Dutch system have been recently observable. The first is an increase in the time span of the economic forecasts produced by the Central Planning Bureau. Since 1963 this body, in addition to its annual forecasts, has been producing what are termed 'medium-term plans', which attempt to look five years ahead. OECD reported in 1964 that 'both employers and wage-earners seemed more and more convinced' of the usefulness of such forecasting, 'especially to guide investment decisions and wage negotiations'. This development, of course, is in line with a general Western European tendency the reasons for which we have already noted. Second, and more serious, the statutory wage control on which the Dutch rely to such a large extent for the implementation of their plans has very largely broken down, and with its disappearance the retention of its counterpart, statutory price control, also becomes impossible. Among Dutch economic experts there is now a predisposition to accept the jettisoning of these controls as inevitable. Indeed, there are some who doubt whether the statutory control of prices has ever made any major contribution to economic stability. Even those who are of the contrary view believe that the time has now come to rely on monetary and budgetary policies to *influence* the price level rather than on statutory powers to 'hold the line'.

Oddly enough, Britain and Holland appear to be moving in contrary directions as far as wage and price policies are concerned. It may be that as a result of these opposite trends the two countries may eventually arrive at approximately the same point. Britain, which has hitherto relied on collective bargaining plus government exhortation to determine wages, and on monetary and budgetary policies to determine prices, is now in the course of adopting what purports to be a coherent wages and prices policy, the advent of which has been signalized by the appointment of a Prices and Incomes Board. Although statutory powers have been recently acquired, the effectiveness of this policy depends in the last resort on the government's ability to obtain the co-operation of both employers and employed. Holland, which has had a wages and prices policy enforced by the law, is moving towards one which, like that which the British are attempting to operate, is sanctioned by agreement. Moreover, as both countries are now thinking in terms of medium-range planning (mainly although not exclusively through a combination of public investment with incentives to those forms of private investment deemed most worthy of encouragement), it would appear that they have a great deal to learn from each other.

THE IMPORTANCE OF CONSENSUS

What is certainly true of all Western European countries is that, in vital areas such as wages and prices, statutory powers are in the last resort irrelevant or ineffective. The *sine qua non* is to obtain and retain the co-operation of the major interest groups. The methods used for this purpose are predominantly informal, although they may be usefully supplemented by the establishment of formal machinery, such as the *Conseil Economique et Social* in France, the Economic and Social Council in the Netherlands, and the National Economic Development Council in Great Britain. Statutory requirements are no substitute for such co-operation, although in some cases they may make agreement easier, and increase the chances of holding the various parties to the terms they have in the first instance voluntarily accepted. (It should be remarked, however, that in other cases such requirements may have exactly the opposite effect.) The enforceability of statutory wage-price policy in Holland was due not to its specifically statutory character, but to the fact that both employers and employed were agreed upon its necessity. As Edelman and Fleming say:

> Post war price policy in Holland has always in the eyes of the Dutch rested primarily on acceptance by the group concerned and there are a number of reasons despite irritation and resistance why there was often an inclination to co-operate in price controls. (All parties were more or less convinced that they were essential to economic expansion.) Also there is a disposition towards conformity among the Dutch and a sense of discipline which inclines them towards the advice of their employer federations. Irresponsible price increases might damage the business community as well as the general public. The Common Market increasingly exposes Dutch business men to the pressures of competition. In this connection many employers recognized that wage and price controls were logical corollaries and that one could not expect wage controls without a significant gesture in the direction of price controls.

To obtain a consensus of this kind is obviously easier in some countries than it is in others. The factors upon which it depends are complex. Important among them is the degree of far-sighted intelligence that the various groups concerned are capable of displaying. In this respect, the contrast between England and Holland has been quite sharp. Without deliberate self-restraint on the part of both employers and trade unions, the Dutch version of the economic miracle would have been impossible; but in Britain such self-restraint would appear to have been sporadic rather than continuous. In the past, British employers and

British trade unionists have favoured policies for economic growth only to the extent that these have not adversely effected their own immediate 'interests' (e.g. maximum profits and maximum wages, both in terms of current money values). A second factor is the relative degrees of power which the various groups have been able to exert. Where capital accumulation through the private sector is a vital determinant of the rate of economic growth (as has been the case with most of the post-war European economies), a relative weakness of the trade-union group has up to a point been an advantage. Such weakness has been the product of a divided and comparatively small trade-union movement in Italy, a divided and excessively politically-oriented one in France, and in Germany a movement lacking self-confidence and militancy. In all countries, however, the strength of trade unionism as a bargaining agency has been greatly enhanced by comparatively full employment. This gives a new urgency to the task of eliciting agreement from the worker's side. A third factor is the degree of prestige enjoyed by the public power—by which we mean not the government as such but the 'state' and its agents, the administrators. Such prestige is found at its highest in France, and here it has undoubtedly facilitated the development of a type of economic planning which, in many other countries, would be regarded as intolerable by the various interests whose co-operation has to be obtained. This, as we have already suggested, tends to limit the exportability or imitability of the French planning system, for all the attractions it may be considered to possess. Fourth and last, there is the degree to which economic growth is regarded by public opinion as having an urgency that demands its being given the highest priority. Such a sense of urgency was at its strongest in the war-damaged countries, where it gave rise to a readiness to co-operate in the adoption of whatever methods (whether or not they were given the name of 'economic planning') seemed likely to bring about the most rapid restoration of the fabric of economic and social life. Such a spirit became particularly evident during the post-war years in both the Netherlands and Germany—but it was certainly not entirely lacking in France and Italy either. In Britain, however, it was comparatively weak, for reasons which are not difficult to discover. Despite the destruction of many city centres by bombing, war damage was comparatively superficial. More important, the undermining of Britain's former economic position was very largely concealed from view, since the working class (mainly as a result of full employment) was in many respects better off at the end of the war than at the beginning, while the employing class could make easy profits out of apparently limitless demand. These, then, are some of the factors which have influenced the possibility of obtaining consensus on policies designed to stimulate economic growth.

In using the word 'consensus' in this context, one must clearly distinguish it from mere compromise. The achievement of consensus, in the sense that we have used the word, implies more than discovery by the government of a *via media* that satisfies all parties because it gives 'something to everybody'. In a democratic society governments are under strong temptation to take this road; but those that are serious about economic growth must obviously resist it. As we have seen, the sheer size of public sector expenditure means that a government cannot avoid influencing the speed and direction of economic growth, consequently it needs to develop ideas about the objectives of such growth which are at least as clear as those held by the various interest groups with which it is negotiating. Furthermore, once a substantial measure of agreement about these objectives has been reached, it must not hesitate to adopt the most effective means of implementation, even at the expense of giving offence to certain groups and at times provoking a general outcry; for a democratic government is, after all, supposed to represent an overriding public interest which transcends the separate interests of the groups with which it is attempting to co-operate.

PLANNING AND THE MARKET

The government which appears to have walked this tight-rope most successfully is the French, but it must be admitted that the appearance has some element of deception. There is in fact less contrast than is sometimes imagined between France and Germany and France and Italy in respect of the government's economic role. Germany, for instance, is by no means that which she has sometimes pretended to be—the home of a *laissez-faire* market economy. Her economic system is, in reality, a highly disciplined one, tightly and coherently organized by the banks, which play their traditional tutelary role, and by the Federation of German Industry, which acts as the apex of a hierarchy of well-organized industrial associations. (One may note, in passing, that many of their associations provide their members with a forecasting service similar to that provided by the *Commissions de Modernisation* in France.) Moreover, the role of government in the process of German reconstruction and recovery has been important and, in some fields, decisive. Public institutions such as the Reconstruction Loan Corporation have been used vigorously to widen investment bottlenecks. Company taxation has discriminated between those industries making a high contribution to economic growth and those making a comparatively low one. Indeed, as Maddison has said, Germany's fiscal policies 'provided stronger investment incentives than in most countries'. There have also been massive subsidies to agriculture. Most important of all, there is the insufficiently known fact that the state's contribution to capital formation has been on a large scale. According to Professor Roskamp's calculations, public funds financed in one way or another about one-half of Germany's net domestic investments and one-third of her gross investments over a period of many years. As Shonfield has put it with slight but pardonable exaggeration: 'Erhard's interest is not in the market as an institution but as a process. If the real life market does not behave as markets should then non-market forces must be brought in to do the job for it.' His 'ideal market' bears as little relation to the real market 'as Rousseau's General Will, which was supposed to express the true wishes of the people, bore to the apparent will of the majority of voters'.

It is well known that an even stronger case for the importance of government economic initiations can be made out for Italy, with particular reference to the role played in economic growth by 'quasi-governmental' agencies such as the I.R.I. and E.N.I.

There is no real alternative therefore, between planning and the free market. Nowhere is the market really free and everywhere the public authorities are compelled to guide the development of the economy. The uniqueness of France is not that she has engaged in more vigorous and pervasive forms of guidance, but that she has attempted to 'guide the guiders' through the formulation of precise medium-term and somewhat less precise long-term objectives, the product of a carefully devised planning system. This has not, admittedly, given her any decisive advantage over her neighbours, for other countries have achieved an equally high and even higher growth rate without the help of a planning mechanism as elaborate as the French and in some cases without any clearly recognizable planning mechanism at all. For reasons already given, however, planned economic intervention, as distinct from a series of unplanned *ad hoc* interventions, is growing in popularity everywhere. Furthermore, improvements both in the techniques of forecasting and in the sensitivity of the apparatus of economic control (both of which have been notably assisted by better statistical coverage of the economy and the increasing use of computers) have made planning more of a practical and less of an academic exercise. These considerations apply both to countries with a satisfactory growth rate and to those with an inadequate one. The former look to planning to maintain the rate and in some cases to ensure that more attention shall be paid to social priorities than in the past; the latter hope that with its help they may raise their rates of capital formation and bring down their costs of production. In general, the balance between public and private economic power has, during the war and post-war years, decisively changed in favour of the former. This has become increasingly recognized, and to the degree that it is recognized, the need for planning of one kind or another is accepted by all concerned.

The Challenge of the Future: Some Problems and Prospects

It is a difficult and rather pretentious enterprise to single out a few specific issues as being particularly central to the future development of Western Europe. There are, however, three general issue areas whose prominence in the media and on the agendas of diplomatic dialogues qualify them as points of major importance. The first concerns the capacity of the European nations to meet the technological and managerial requirements associated with economic leadership in today's world. The second group of issues revolves around the matter of providing for the military security of the continental countries. The third encompasses those questions bearing on the actual and potential unification of the major Western European nations into an economic and political community.

In recent years such phrases as "technological gap" and "brain drain" have enjoyed repeated appearances in the European press and in the statements of continental industrialists and governmental leaders. In their common usage, these phrases represent shorthand references to the consequences of an asserted superiority which the products and methods of American firms enjoy vis-à-vis those of their European counterparts. It is uncertain just who first sounded the alarm. According to Robert Gilpin, whose article on the "technology gap" leads off this section, President de Gaulle was

351

alert to the problem as early as 1964. With the publication in 1967 of J.-J. Servan-Schreiber's work, *Le Defi Americain* (*The American Challenge*), the possibility of Western Europe's economic "enslavement" to American capital and know-how achieved the continental status of a public nightmare.

Subsequent debates have followed on a variety of levels. Not surprisingly, some have been characterized by highly emotional overtones. In the arena of partisan politics, parties of the far left seized on the issue, making it a vehicle for their efforts to discredit the American presence in Europe. Assorted European businessmen, pleading danger of extinction, have sought greater government aid and protection for their products. Prior to his retreat from political life, Charles de Gaulle regularly pictured the American technological menace as a dire threat to the national autonomy of France.

Amidst the flurry of invective, a number of experts have sought to cast the light of objective analysis on the problem. The articles by Robert Gilpin and Theodore Levitt qualify as sober investigations into this very problematical dimension of Western Europe's confrontation with the future. Gilpin cuts directly to the heart of the dilemma in asking: "What is to be the role of Europe in a world where scientific research and massive technologies have become the bases of economic and political power?" Both Gilpin and Levitt agree that the continental democracies are encountering an uphill struggle in their efforts to narrow the industrial lead held by the United States. Yet in a manner symptomatic of the problem's intricacy, they diverge when identifying the main causes for the lag. As a result, the two reach somewhat different conclusions as to where corrective emphasis should be placed.

Along with the concern many Europeans have shown for securing a more equitable and independent position in the economic competition with the United States, an increasing amount of interest has been directed toward the role the United States plays in continental defense arrangements.

At the end of the Second World War, when the weakened nations of Western Europe appeared vulnerable to Communist aggression from the East, their reliance on American military strength was considered a foregone and not wholly unwelcome necessity. To this end, a protective guarantee was institutionalized in the form of the North Atlantic Treaty Organization which provided for an integrated Atlantic defense arrangement with its heart being the American nuclear capability. For many years, the debates which swirled around NATO focused on such issues as the strategic aspects of nuclear and non-nuclear responses to Soviet provocation and whether the members were willing and able to honor in practice the troop commitments they had made in principal. While these questions still invoke debate, they have been joined by queries concerning the continued relevance of the NATO alliance itself, at least in its present form.

It is frequently argued, for example, that the likelihood of a Soviet invasion of Western Europe has become so remote as to render the maintenance of an elaborate security mechanism economically and politically disadvantageous. Even many of those who find a coordinated Atlantic defense necessary question whether the prevailing balance of influence within NATO, which leans heavily to the American side, adequately represents the changed position of a resurgent Western Europe. It is certainly no secret that the major European members of NATO have from time to time complained about a situation which finds their ultimate security so firmly vested in the hands of their American ally. The decision by former French President de Gaulle to withdraw French troops from NATO command was motivated in part by an unwillingness to accept the dominance of the United States in affairs which he considered vital to French national security. In 1969 there was a good deal of speculation over whether any of the member nations would utilize the twentieth anniversary of the Alliance to announce their intention to leave NATO altogether. As yet, none have chosen to do so.

The future of NATO is the subject taken up in the selection by Klaus Knorr. In a straightforward manner Professor Knorr points out that the utility of the NATO organization is not a fixed item. Its existence or demise is contingent upon the availability of alternative peace-keeping arrangements and upon the prevailing balance between the burdens imposed on its membership and the benefits that the participating nations derive. The "market values" of these factors are subject to change in response to international and domestic events. It was evident, for example, that the Russian invasion of Czechoslovakia contributed added luster to the protective services offered by NATO, just as the relative quiescence of the Kremlin in the mid-1960's had acted to devalue the perceived importance of contributing to a collective defense mechanism. At the present time, there is also renewed interest in convening a European security conference that would seek to hammer out a cold war settlement. Such an agreement might include the dissolution of NATO and its communist counterpart, the Warsaw Pact Alliance.

Knorr tends to see the success of NATO in deterring military aggression as an argument in favor of its retention. Pierre Hassner begins from the assumption that the time when all parties feel relatively safe is an auspicious one for pursuing innovational responses to European security needs. In part, this is based on Hassner's belief that the current stability is not likely to last unless changes are made. Equally important are the possibilities which military detente open for political accommodations. "Precisely because we no longer fear war," he writes, "we should start thinking about peace."

Perhaps the central point to be derived from Hassner's piece is the extent to which military security in Europe is linked with the resolution of long-standing political questions. Chief among these is the German problem. It is difficult to imagine any significant grand design for insuring European security that does not include or proceed from a set of mutual understandings about the future of the two Germanies. It is widely assumed that Chancellor Willy Brandt's *Ostpolitik*, which to this point has produced historic treaties with the Soviet Union and Poland, has as one of its goals the easing of those tensions that have until now precluded genuine dialogues aimed at solving the German dilemma.

Attempts at evaluating West Germany's fascination with the East and efforts which may be forthcoming to reconcile the divided German nation must take into consideration how these events might affect progress made toward Western European cooperation in the economic sphere. Certainly, the grandest scheme for changing the face of Western Europe to come out of the postwar years has been the campaign to unite the major European nations into a tightly knit economic community. From the outset, it was a plan with both practical and idealistic dimensions. The coordination and consolidation of resources promised to aid economic recovery and growth by increasing the productive capacity of West European industry and greatly expanding the consumer market. In the early years, the United States served as an important stimulus to the integrative process by insisting upon the development of cooperative institutions to allocate and administer Marshall Plan funds. Later, the economic challenge presented by American industry gave additional impetus to efforts at streamlining and rationalizing the often small and scattered productive units of the continent.

By most measures, the efforts at economic integration have borne impressive fruit. For example, the European Economic Community (EEC), frequently called the Common Market, today encompasses all of the larger Western European democracies except Great Britain. Prolonged and hardheaded bargaining has often been required to resolve Common Market problems, but the present result is an economic entity with a common external tariff structure and a relatively free flow of goods, labor and capital within. And at the time of this writing negotiations are once again in progress to expand the scope of the EEC by bringing Britain and the small nations of Denmark, Ireland, and Norway into the fold.

There were those who from the beginning saw economic integration as merely a stepping stone to a more ambitious ideal—the political unification of Western Europe. During the 1950's the idea of a United States of Europe, or some similar formulation, gained widespread attention. A host of European and American observers were proclaiming and accepting theories that envisaged a more or less automatic evolution from economic unification to the rise of a supranational political community. Most of these projections assumed an extreme functional interdependence between economic and political processes. According to this conceptualization, successful experiences with unification in the transnational economic realm would "spill-over"—to use a term popularized by Ernst B. Haas in his influential book, *The Uniting of Europe*—into the governmental domain, producing integrative consequences there as well.

By way of contrast, the 1960's were for the most part devoid of such confident prophecies. The two articles that conclude this final section of the reader are representative of the more realistic and subdued spirit in which the problem of European integration is currently being approached.

The selection by Professor Haas is of particular interest in that it represents a rethinking of his earlier ideas. He is most candid in admitting that his assumptions regarding the progression from lower stages of integration to more advanced forms underestimated constraining elements lurking in the background. Haas singles out the appearance of Charles de Gaulle as an example of how an event, largely unpredictable by any scientific means, can upset even the most carefully devised formulation. In the end, the advance of supranational ties based on pragmatic calculations of mutual advantage (primarily economic) could not stand up to the determined resistance mounted by a highly committed opponent with de Gaulle's stature and authority.

Despite the acknowledgment of reversals, Haas appears to remain convinced of the logic in the spill-over theory. David P. Calleo takes a more skeptical view. While paying homage to the restrictive prowess of President de Gaulle, who was still in office when the excerpt was written, Calleo obviously felt that there was more standing in the way of building a politically unified Europe than France's recalcitrant leader. After subjecting the tenets of functionalism to investigation, he concludes that "it is difficult to accept the thesis that the success of the Common Market as a federal government is assured by an inherent, autonomous logic of economic integration."

At the moment, the future course of Western European integration is uncertain. Most interested parties would agree that even in the face of widespread good intentions the concept of national sovereignty is apt to prove highly durable. Still, the supporters of political unification are abundant and vocal, and the momentum for supranational cooperation has not been lost altogether. A politically united Europe may yet prove the long-range solution to the continent's search for identity.

23 ROBERT GILPIN

European Disunion and the Technology Gap

In late 1964, President Charles de Gaulle of France circulated to the members of his government a study which warned that France, and indeed all of western Europe, must either adapt to the contemporary scientific-technological revolution or risk economic and political subjugation by the world's foremost scientific power, the United States. The independence of France, de Gaulle warned, was being threatened by the technological gap between the United States and western Europe. He declared that, unless France took appropriate steps to meet this challenge, she would become a relatively underdeveloped nation in a world dominated by scientific superpowers.

In the three years since de Gaulle's warning, the issue of the technological gap has become a sore point in American-European relations and a rallying cry among the Europeans. Europeans are almost unanimous in their opinion that the technological gap is real, is threatening to their long-term well being, and is widening. It was in response to this generally shared European concern that

Reprinted from *The Public Interest* No. 10 (Winter, 1968), pp. 43-54, by permission of the author and National Affairs, Inc. © 1968.

Prime Minister Harold Wilson declared that Europe is threatened by an "industrial helotry" and that Europe needs Britain's scientific and technical capabilities if it is to meet the American challenge.

For Washington, on the other hand, the technological gap is an official nonissue. When Europeans bring it up, which they frequently do, American responses normally take one of several forms. The usual official American response is to reply that the problem is not really a technological gap but a managerial gap or an organizational gap—or, as former Commerce Secretary John Connor put it, an "industrial disparity." On other occasions, American officials will grant that a technological gap of some sort exists, but then go on to point out to the Europeans that it is their problems, not ours. Most ingenious of all is a response which goes like this: "Look! You Europeans do what you're good at, and we'll do what we're good at. You French stick to your wine-making and perfumes; leave the computers and high-performance aircraft to us." American academic economists, who tend to share the official position on the technological gap, phrase this in more sophisticated terms. Committed to the doctrine of free trade and the principle of comparative advantage, these American economists point out that the technological gap represents a rational division of labor among the members of an emerging Atlantic economic system.

ANXIETIES AND ISSUES

Actually the expression "technological gap" symbolizes many things which trouble Europeans. In the first place, it symbolizes American leadership in basic scientific research. Another element is the European dependence on the United States for advanced technologies and especially those technologies of military significance: computers, electronics, atomic energy, and aerospace. A third aspect is the "brain drain" of European engineers and scientists to the United States. And fourth, the expression "technological gap" is a shorthand for all the European concern about the invasion of western Europe by large American corporations whose financial and managerial resources are seen to be far greater than those of their European competitors.

Imbedded in these European anxieties are many practical and theoretical issues to which economists and political scientists have no clear answers. For example, does a strong, national capability in basic research confer an advantage in technological innovation, or do the findings of basic research become a free good equally available to all? Second, what is the role of technological innovation in economic competitiveness? Is innovation displacing price as a factor in economic competition, as the French believe? Or third, what is the effect on western Europe of the movement of European scientists westward and of American corporations eastward?

No clear assessment of the significance of the technological gap seems possible without extensive analyses of these and related issues. Perhaps such analyses, which have only begun, will prove that the concerns of the Europeans are unfounded. However, without more evidence to the contrary, there is good reason to accept as valid the challenge facing Europeans as expressed in the following statement to the Conference on European Cooperation in Advanced Technology which was held in July 1965:

> Modern industrial research programmes call for material and human resources hitherto undreamed of, and resources which are beyond the capacity of even the leading European nations, with populations of fifty millions or so. The conclusion forced upon us is that the European countries must pool their efforts if they wish to play a continuing part in world economic development. Otherwise, it will not be many years before they are so far behind the United States and the Soviet Union in advanced industrial fields that, relatively, they will have fallen to the level of underdeveloped countries.

While the economic concerns of the Europeans are real and pressing, the basic issue posed by the technological gap, as the Europeans themselves see it, is their political future. What is to be the role of Europe in a world where scientific research and massive technologies have become the basis of economic and political power? If one accepts the assumption that European nations are too small to master the technologies to which modern science is giving rise, what are the prospects for a European solution to the technological gap?

PREREQUISITES FOR A EUROPEAN SCIENCE POLICY

When one speaks of European cooperation in science and technology, there is a large number of things he could have in mind. There is first of all the Concorde Project—the bilateral effort of Great Britain and France to produce a supersonic commercial transport. Second, there is the European Launcher Development Organization (ELDO) composed of seventeen European nations and Australia. Or one might have in mind the Center of European Nuclear Research (CERN), which again is a multi-national effort, but in basic research. Another is EURATOM, which is composed of the six nations of the European Economic Community, or Common Market, and has for its responsibility the development of nuclear power for peaceful purposes. One could add to the list.

With the exception of the European Center of Nuclear Research, it is difficult to give high praise to any of these efforts. The Concorde Project promises to bring great financial losses to both French and the British. EURATOM is rent by extreme national conflicts, and its future is in doubt. ELDO must overcome rising doubts with respect to its value. (Why spend millions of dollars to build a rocket launcher when Europe has no long-term space program and nothing of significance to launch?) The reasons for the difficulties in these and other cooperative efforts can be seen if one looks at the requirements for a successful European science policy—an objective being pushed by the French as a means to develop a common front vis-à-vis the United States.

To be successful, a European science policy must go beyond mere short-range, bilateral cooperation and must fulfill certain functions. In the first place, sustained cooperation in science and technology would necessitate a common institutional framework in the governmental, economic, and academic spheres. Second, there must be a willingness on the part of the Europeans to concentrate their limited resources and to develop a division of labor which fosters specialization, the elimination of unnecessary duplication of effort, and the efficient utilization of resources. Third, as a prerequisite to the achievement of these first two requirements, there must be agreed upon economic, military, and political goals and policies.

Unfortunately, the attractiveness to Europeans of cooperation with the United States and the conflicts of interest and perspective which continue to divide the Europeans among themselves tend to overbalance these three requirements.

ABSENCE OF AN INSTITUTIONAL FRAMEWORK

Twenty years of talk of European unification have obfuscated the profound cleavages among political, economic, and educational institutions which nevertheless continue to make the articulation of a common policy toward science and technology nearly an impossibility. From the political level to university research and teaching, the development of common institutions within Europe is as yet in its infancy.

The separation which has existed between the efforts of one European nation and those of its neighbors in research and education can be illustrated in many ways. For example, prior to the founding of CERN in 1952, there were no European centers for basic research. Fundamental research is organized primarily, and supported only, on a national basis. The establishment of CERN, the initiation of a European Center for Molecular Biology, and the founding of the International Center for Cancer Research are important beginnings of cooperative research. But the larger and more significant effort required is the creation of what the French Minister for Science has called "a common market for brains." If Europeans are to build strong centers of research on the many frontiers of modern science, then they must pool their scattered manpower and financial resources. Scientific research today increasingly necessitates the coming together of a "critical mass" of costly equipment, a multitude of disciplines, and a supporting cast of technicians which no individual European nation can support in all, or even many, of the promising areas of research.

Though specialized organizations such as CERN are an important step forward, the barriers to the free flow of scientists and ideas must come down and a framework for European collaboration on a broader basis must be established. "Among these barriers," a recent OECD Conference of Ministries of Science brought out, "are rigid structures in universities, poor interchange between universities and industries, lack of equivalence between various countries' pay scales and university degrees, and lack of provision for travel and post doctoral fellowships." In short, effective cooperation in basic research may very well necessitate the creation of a truly European system of higher education.

In industrial research and development on a European scale, one witnesses the same pattern of institutional fragmentation. Though there are the shaky but nevertheless "successful" efforts such as Euratom, ELDO, and the Concorde project, in the long run and across the broad front of technology the type of technical collaboration required is that which can only be provided by existing industrial firms (whether private or government-owned). Here, the elaboration of a European science policy faces a double obstacle. In the first place, Great Britain, which has the most to contribute to a united European effort in the areas of advanced technologies—aviation, computers, reactors, space, etc.—is outside the framework of the emerging European economic community. Second, among the Six themselves the economic and political foundations for extensive scientific and technical cooperation have not been developed and may be actually eroding.

UNANTICIPATED CONSEQUENCES OF THE COMMON MARKET

One train of reasoning which has provided a basis for the European Economic Community has been the belief that a common market would lead logically to the formation of European corporations jointly owned and controlled by Europeans of different nationalities. This merger of corporations across national boundaries was expected by some to eliminate national economic rivalries and create binding, transnational economic interests. It followed that the growth and meshing of these many vested interests would slowly erode the significance of national borders, and political unification would evolve on the basis of common economic interests.

This expectation that a European common market would lead to European ownership of industry has not borne fruit. On the contrary, the forces set into motion by the Common Market appear to be moving Europe in a direction not foreseen by the signers of the Treaty of Rome. For a number of reasons, the rationalization of the European economic system is taking place along national *and* Atlantic lines, not European. The corporate merger movement in Western Europe is taking place almost entirely either within national boundaries or else between European and American firms. In contrast to the flood tide of mergers within individual European countries and the growth of American-European ties, by 1968 there had been only one major corporate merger across European frontiers, and it was only a partial one.

As a consequence of this situation, the only international corporations operating in Europe tend to be American. Through the establishment of new subsidiaries throughout Europe, mergers with European firms, and outright purchase of European firms, American companies are rationalizing and integrating the European economy. In the words of Charles Kindleberger, "It looks as though the international corporation, typically that with headquarters in the United States, is the leading prospect for the effective instrument of European integration." As Pierre Drouin cynically observed in *Le Monde*, "Actually the Common Market benefits American industry more than European" because only the Americans have the resources and managerial experience to take advantage of it.

What appears to be happening is that the economic forces being set into motion by the Common Market run counter to the reorganization of the European economy on the basis of European corporations. The lowering of tariff barriers among the Six has encouraged the rush into Europe of American corporations eager to gain a foothold in the vast continental market which is rapidly coming into existence. In response to this American corporate "invasion," European corporations are either linking up with the invaders or else are mobilizing to meet the challenge on a national basis rather than through the pooling of their scattered resources and talents in large Europe-based corporations. The French even have prevented the merger of French and other European firms; the French, it would seem, are less interested in having their firms controlled by other large European firms than they are concerned over American domination.

The reasons for the absence of a "European" response to the challenge posed by the Common Market and the American corporate offensive are many: the absence of a European legal framework within which mergers can take place, the weakness of the European capital market, the legacy of corporate rivalry and pride, differences among economic systems ranging from the German commitment to *laissez-faire* to the French emphasis on planning and nationalized industries. At the same time, mergers taking place entirely within a nation, and especially the formation of an alliance with an American corporation, suffer no such inhibitions. "What happens," Raymond Aron has explained, "is that when a European firm is in trouble it always goes to an American firm to get out of trouble, because its European sister firms will not come forward and provide true security, size, technology, and financial means."

Embedded in all the technical factors involved in formulating a European corporate law or a common tax policy are profound political issues and conflicting national interests. Furthermore, given the French insistence that uniformity among national practices be achieved through the enactment of parallel national laws and policies ("parallelism") rather than through the emergence of a European legal structure, it will take a very long time to work out differences among the Six.

DISPERSION AND DUPLICATION

The formulation of a European science and technical policy requires not only the creation of a common institutional framework, but the elaboration as well of an extensive division of labor and concentration of resources. Given Europe's limited scientific resources, not every European country can have "centers of excellence" in every important and promising area of research and development. Unnecessary duplication must be avoided and priorities must be established within individual countries.

Unfortunately, the same fears and ambitions which cause Europeans to be wary of overdependence on the United States for science and technology operate also as barriers to effective intra-European cooperation. From basic research through technological development and production, each nation wants to maximize its own self-sufficiency and to minimize dependence on other nations. Few nations, for example, want to be dependent on another for basic research in potentially important areas; basic research is believed to be not only a source of useful inventions, but it also attracts the best scientific minds. Without a strong basic research program, a nation runs the risk of a "brain drain."

Similarly, with respect to collaboration in technological development the same tendency toward self-sufficiency obtains. In areas of considerable commercial or military importance, industries and nations are reluctant to collaborate. Even where equitable arrangements for the sharing of benefits can be worked out in advance, nations fear that their own industries will become atrophied. What one observes is that, rather than have its advanced technological industries link up with those of other European countries, each member of the Six—through research contracts, purchasing policies, and other inducements— is encouraging the merger of local companies into essentially nationalized industries in these areas.

This present tendency toward self-sufficiency tends to foreclose the possibility of large European firms and the creation of a guaranteed large European market with corresponding benefits of economies of scale. As *The Economist* has pointed out,

> the combined market for electronics capital goods in Britain, France, and
> West Germany was less than 20 per cent of the American market.

Divide that into three or less equal parts and you have indigenous firms based on national markets that are barely more than . . . twentieth the size of the American one. It is not surprising that American corporations have virtually taken over the computer industries of Germany, France, and Italy . . . and nearly knocked out the British industry in 1964.

The European response to the "technological gap," this article continues, "is that in a whole host of major industries, from coal and steel and aviation to nuclear energy and cars and computers, the trend is towards one or two national firms that are treated as national assets: they have become the chosen instruments of their governments." As a consequence commercial rivalries are being nationalized and a unified European response to the American industrial challenge cannot be articulated.

Just as France or Germany may worry about the gap between themselves and the United States, the lesser developed Western European countries such as Italy worry about the gap between themselves and the more developed of their partners. In Euratom, ELDO, and other organizations, the gap between the more developed and less developed nations makes cooperation and a "rational" division of labor extremely difficult. The arguments employed by both sides are reminiscent of those one encounters when Europeans and Americans talk about the Atlantic technological gap. In French eyes, intra-European cooperation should maximize Europe's (read France's) existing strengths; any other course is seen to be an ineffective use of Europe's scarce resources. The Italians, on the other hand, see this practice as a means to make the rich richer and the poor poorer. The purpose of European scientific and technical cooperation, according to the Italian Minister of State for Foreign Affairs, is not to enable France to compete better against America, but to close the intra-European science gap.

A similar tendency to subordinate community interest to national interest is seen with respect to the distribution of research and development contracts. In both Euratom and ELDO the policy is to distribute contracts among the participating states in proportion to their financial contribution, rather than on the basis of some more rational allocation criteria. As such it is impossible to concentrate resources on priority projects or to establish an effective division of labor.

INEFFECTUAL COLLABORATION

The several attempts of Europeans to collaborate in science and technology support these observations. Few of the cooperative efforts undertaken by Europeans in space, atomic energy, or electronics have been noteworthy for their success. On the contrary, the escalation of costs far beyond initial expectations, the unilateral decisions of one country or another to withdraw from projects, and the suspicions of certain countries that others see European collaboration solely as a means to enrich themselves have made further cooperation more difficult.

In one area, however, thoughtful Europeans see a hope for a breakthrough in scientific and technical cooperation—the area of military weaponry. Although Europeans, even the French, accept the necessity of dependence on the United States for their military security, Europeans have sought to maintain their own armaments industry. In part, this has been due to a desire not to become overly dependent on the United States. For France and Great Britain, in addition, the export of weaponry has long been an important means of foreign exchange; for this reason especially they have resisted a division of labor within the Atlantic Alliance which fosters "American domination of the new-weapons market." Lastly, the Europeans have been motivated by the belief that weapons research and development have an important spin-off for the civilian economy.

Collaboration in weapons research and development has also been forced on Europeans due to the fantastic escalation of costs. Whereas a Spitfire of World War II cost little more than £5,000 to produce, the Canberra fifteen years later cost £180,000 in its early version. The production cost of the TSR-2 would have been fifteen times as much as the Canberra; its research and development cost alone would have been £300 million.

Unfortunately, the experience of European collaboration in the development and production of weapons has not been a happy one. In the first place, the Europeans have not been able to supplant American domination of the advanced weapons market. All communal programs for the production of weapons as of 1964 had used weapons perfected in America which the Europeans have produced under license. The attempts of the Europeans to design and collaborate in the production of their own weapons such as a NATO tank and the VSTOL aircraft have met obstacles of conflicting national interests and an inability to agree on common military requirements. One expert reviewing this history concluded that "the prospects today for acceptable new projects are grim, partly because nations seem unable to work out an approach for items which would be appropriate for common production, and partly because many new weapons are either technically too intricate or politically too sensitive for pooled activity."

ABSENCE OF COMMON GOALS

Underlying this apparent inability of the Europeans to organize scientific and technical collaboration on a broad and continuing basis is the absence of common goals and purposes. The formulation of common objectives is the third requirement for effective European collaboration in science and technology. Unfortunately, Europeans are more divided among themselves in their interests and perspectives than they are united on the objectives to be achieved through cooperation. At the present time, only Great Britain and France have found a basis for extensive cooperation in a number of technical areas, but the obstacles to the ultimate success of even these projects remain very great because of the fundamental political questions which divide these two countries from each other and from the rest of Europe. The problem facing these two nations and the rest of Europe was well put by *The Economist*:

> In civilian as in military procurement, it is hard to agree on the goods or arms governments want if they do not subscribe to similar economic or defence strategies. This identity of view does not exist in piecemeal co-operation because this form of joint effort basically exists to shore up national industries, not to create a new structure. In fact, Anglo-French industrial co-operation is in many ways a form of the effort of the two countries to keep ahead of the non-nuclear rank and file in Europe.

The one significant effort of Europeans to frame common purposes and objectives as a basis for extensive collaboration in foreign policy, defense, science, and economics was the French-German Treaty of Cooperation of January 22, 1963. Negotiated by Charles de Gaulle and Konrad Adenauer, this treaty sought to create a Bonn-Paris axis around which European "unification" could form. To cement and further this alliance within an alliance, the two nations agreed to formulate common foreign and economic policies including, if de Gaulle had his way, a common policy toward American investments in Europe. In the military realm there was to be coordination of strategy and weapons development. In short, economic, scientific, and other types of collaboration were to be undertaken in order to serve a larger political purpose of French-German unity.

Perhaps this effort at close French-German cooperation was fated not to be a success regardless of American behavior toward it. French and German interests are not identical, and each wants something out of the treaty which the other is not prepared to give. For de Gaulle the purpose of the treaty is to forge a Franco-German nucleus around which could form a European community of sovereign nations independent of the United States. Germany, on the other hand, seeks to obtain greater French cooperation in support of its demands for reunification. Far from desiring the formation of a European bloc independent of the United States, the German Parliament (much to the annoyance of de Gaulle) in ratifying the treaty added a preamble that the treaty would also serve to reinforce the association between Europe and the United States as well as to strengthen NATO and to encourage British entry into Europe.

Even before the treaty was signed these differing German and French interests with respect to NATO and relations with Great Britain had come into open conflict, and the long-term prospects for the success of the treaty were dimmed. But whatever might have been or may yet be, the United States unintentionally or by design (as de Gaulle contends) destroyed the efficacy of the alliance through its subsequent actions. In the words of Henry Kissinger, the United States reacted to the treaty by undertaking

> an assiduous wooing of the Federal Republic. One motive behind the MLF was to prevent West Germany from accepting a possible French offer of nuclear cooperation. . . . In order to tie Germany to us, successful efforts were made to have German arms purchases funneled to the United States. The culmination of this process was an agreement between Secretary McNamara and Defense Minister von Hassel signed on November 14, 1964, which in effect made the German armed forces dependent on the United States for their military equipment.

Similarly, in other areas of advanced technology—aviation, computers, atomic energy—there has developed in effect an American-German alliance which in turn has limited close French-German collaboration. In aviation every German aviation company but one is linked with an American company; IBM dominates the German computer market; and, in atomic energy, Germany is developing her industry through purchasing American designs and licenses. Recent proposals of the American government for joint American-European space research cooperation, and the enthusiastic German response, impress Frenchmen as yet another example of American seduction of their German partner and a device calculated to destroy the budding joint European space effort.

THE PRIORITY OF POLITICS

Measured in terms of the past, progress in European scientific and technological cooperation since the end of World War II has been considerable. Twenty years ago one never would have thought that such developments as CERN and the Concorde were possible. Yet, cooperation on a scale which would enable Europe to balance the Great Powers in areas of advanced science and technology is severely limited by at least three factors. In the first place, bilateral cooperation will not take the European countries very far; it simply does not ensure a sufficient scale of resources or a guaranteed large market. Second, political agreement on diplomatic, strategic, and economic goals must precede successful scientific-technical cooperation; without such agreement on long-term goals the nations of Europe are unwilling to subordinate their immediate and parochial interests for the sake of a truly European effort in science and technology. And, third, in almost every area of science and technology, continental Europe—if it is to balance the United States—needs Great Britain; the entry of Great Britain into the European Economic Community could double its resources and also would do much to redress the Atlantic imbalance in science, technology, and economic power.

In the last analysis, therefore, one can only conclude that, without political unity, and unless the present course of developments is drastically altered, the Committee on Medium-Term Economic Policy of the Common Market is correct in its assertion that "if the six countries remain, as they probably have done for a generation, the main world importers of discoveries and exporters of brains, they will be condemning themselves to a cumulative underdevelopment which will soon render their decline irremediable." Perhaps, as de Gaulle would have it, European concern over American domination may yet generate common European policies toward science and technology. If not, Europe will become ever more irrelevant as an independent power in a world whose affairs are dominated by scientific societies of continental dimensions.

24 THEODORE LEVITT

The Gap is Not Technological

The curious thing about many discussions of the alleged technological gap between Europe and the United States is how little they actually say about technology. There is a sharp focus on science and the brain drain; technology gets only derivative attention. Nothing is more characteristic of this curious habit than Robert Gilpin's article. Its title was "European Disunion and the Technology Gap." The analysis dwelt almost entirely on science. The result was predictably and gravely incorrect conclusions.

Europe does indeed suffer from a technological gap. But it is not, as Professor Gilpin suggests, the result of a lack either of scientific brains or scientific accomplishments; nor is it the consequence of the fragmented character of European markets. It is the latter that Professor Gilpin holds most directly responsible for the trouble.

He asserts that the minuscule size of European national markets cannot support enterprises of sufficient scale to enable them to employ the brains which are needed for the basic research that produces the technology capable of competing with America's might. Cooperative efforts by European nations are not encouraging because of "the conflicts of interest and perspective which continue

Reprinted from *The Public Interest* No. 12 (Summer, 1968), pp. 119-124, by permission of the author and National Affairs, Inc., © 1968.

to divide the Europeans among themselves . . ." There is, in his words, no proper "institutional framework" for the kind of cooperation that can sponsor the kind of effective basic research necessary for Europe's economic survival. The result is a massive "brain drain" to the United States, which as a consequence vaults that much further ahead. If the brains could somehow be kept in Europe and profitably employed in basic research, the problem would disappear.

Professor Gilpin's argument is superficially plausible. But it is also very misleading.

Mr. Gilpin writes about R & D—research and development—as if the two were the same thing. They are not. And he writes about brains as if the mere production of knowledge were equivalent to its commercial implementation. It is not. People who have studied business enterprise from the inside—or indeed who have studied any kind of organization from the inside—know that things are much different. Research and development are not synonymous. Research deals with getting ideas and knowledge, development with their effective commercial utilization. The difference is similar and related to the difference between creativity and innovation. Creativity is thinking things up. Innovation is getting things done.

Europe's problem, and specifically the problem in France, England, and to a lesser extent Germany and Italy, is innovation, not creativity; it is translating scientific discoveries into market-oriented enterprises, not producing the discoveries themselves. For neither of these activities is the limited size of European markets disabling.

The logic is simple enough, and the facts support it. If we are talking about the production of useful new things, as Professor Gilpin clearly is, then the available markets are incontestably worldwide, not national or even European. If what has been discovered and produced is usefully new, the world is the producer's oyster, not Belgium or England or whatever the nationality of the discovering firm. If the market is worldwide, then the incentives are as adequate for a Swiss firm as for an American one. When Montecatini of Italy developed polypropylene in the late 1950's, it had not the slightest difficulty selling it in the United States. Indeed, it built a successful American plant right off. For it to have tried at that time to sell a mature product such as nylon in the United States would have been almost impossible. But polypropylene, being new, was easy. Montecatini held its position even after Phillips Petroleum, du Pont, Firestone, and others (often using Montecatini's patents) entered the race.

To suggest that European markets are too small to support the research which creates new knowledge is, furthermore, to ignore the remarkable example of Japan. Between 1951 and 1965, patents issued to their own nationals by Belgium, France, West Germany, the United Kingdom, and Sweden declined from 42,616 to 28,085 annually. At the same time, Japanese patents issued to

Japanese nationals rose from 4,350 to 17,797. Clearly, something more than size of nation or of domestic markets accounts for this difference. Professor Gilpin talks about the primal importance of military weapons in the science race, as if these automatically produce the big private-sector fallout that is said to keep America ahead. Yet Japan has no military establishment at all to speak of, while even Germany has a large and thriving one, not to speak of England and France. Moreover, it would be hard to attribute as much as 1 per cent of America's Gross National Product to the private-sector fallout of aerospace or military science.

Professor Gilpin refers in one fleeting sentence to arguments that Europe's gap is managerial, not technological. And that is all we hear of it. The remaining discussion builds on a deep prejudice in favor of the idea that scientific brains are central and that these require big companies with big markets.

Anyone who has looked carefully at European enterprise can recite horrendous tales suggesting the opposite. The basis of Japan's recent economic growth is its competitive international spirit. Japanese businessmen who visit America in such abundance visit, not its R & D departments, but its manufacturing plants and product development departments—not the managers of Huntsville's laboratories, but the managers of Huntington's shopping plazas. They seek not so much new scientific knowledge as commercial applications of knowledge; not newness as such, but commercial opportunity. Japan's thriving success, to the extent that it is based on technology, is heavily based on that country's commercial exploitation of scientific and technological knowledge spawned elsewhere. The Japanese have no hesitation about imitating others or improving on what others have done. It is not even innovation that characterizes their art, but inspired and commercially viable imitation.

The fact that the creation of new knowledge is not essential to, or a guarantee of, economic success can be demonstrated in Europe itself. In the aerospace and other high-technology areas, during recent years, Europe's record is far from the consistent lag that is so commonly depicted. The swing-wing plane and the hovercraft were initially developed in Europe. Laser technology and cryogenics came from Europe. Most of the underlying inventions for the office copying machine industry were European. The basic work in fluidics and holography was European.

Yet, in each of these it was in the United States that the translation of this creativity into commercially viable innovation occurred. Europe was the creator, America the innovator. It is not scientific brains that Europe lacks; it is entrepreneurial brawn. It is not an inability to support basic research; it is an inability to get moving. There is, moreover, the corrosive presence of an almost ideological antipathy to the commercialization of knowledge. It is okay and even prestigious to work at science and the creation of new scientific knowledge. To exploit it commercially is vulgar—perhaps okay only for the American barbarians.

In much of Europe, commerce is not a valued or even a fully respectable occupation. It is no accident that the public knows so little about who Europe's industrial leaders really are. In the United States, the leaders of industry make front-page news. In Europe, they hide almost pensively behind a carefully cultivated screen of anonymity. They do not hide because of any fear of verbal outpourings of socialists and reformers. They hide because business is still deemed to be somehow undignified. When they do talk in public, they take great pains to demonstrate their civility by talking about their enormous interest in art, music, and the ballet. Most American executives freely state that their work is their hobby.

This illegitimacy of commerce accounts for some spectacular failures in the recent annals of European enterprise. Several European firms pioneered in the development of ingenious magnetic-tape control devices for machine tools. They concentrated on developing and finally producing exceedingly high-precision products far superior to any available elsewhere. And, of course, high precision meant high cost. A United States firm came along later, doing from the beginning what the Europeans had not done at all. It made careful studies of the needs of the market and discovered that considerably larger tolerances were acceptable. It proceeded to produce lesser-precision control devices at lesser costs. Predictably, it has taken the bulk of the European market away from the original European producers.

It is the European executive's contempt for the realities of the market that accounts in large measure for Europe's problems. He does not study the market's needs in detail because the market is the rabble. The European executive operates on Ralph Waldo Emerson's immensely misleading advice to "make a better mousetrap, and the world will beat a path to your door." The advice is misleading because it focuses on the wrong issue. The issue is not to know that people will respond to a better product; it is to know what they define "better" to be.

One needs not only to do what the market requires, but also to do it well. This requires a kind of managerial dedication that often repels Europeans. Somehow, many European executives feel that business is simply not worthy of their best efforts, that business is simply not important enough to get all that excited about. You work at your job, but save your best energies for after work. Some years ago Britain developed the world's first fast all-weather military interceptor aircraft, the Javelin. The United States Department of Defense literally drooled. It would have bought all that Britain could produce. Even France stood in line. Britain was at least three years ahead of any other developer. But no benefit accrued to Britain—it was unable to manage the complex on-line production job to make adequate deliveries. The deficiency was not scientific brains; it was management talent and a proper sense of urgency.

There is no doubting the enormous importance in today's world of science. But whether modern science is all that important for economic growth and competitive strength is not so certain. A quick tour of any department store, any supermarket, any office, or any factory quickly shows that electronics, biophysics, cryogenics, and optics constitute a minuscule part of even America's vaunted economic power or resources. To say that there is a lag in these areas that accounts for European's problems is to focus on our own biases. We dismiss almost with contempt the vital importance to our economic vigor of the headache remedies and detergents whose advertisements we so much abhor. Yet the enormous, if seemingly obtrusive and vulgar, effort that sustains headache remedies, detergents, false eyelashes, bucket seats, and electric pencil sharpeners is central to America's success. It is great entrepreneurial energy, managerial effort, and involved preoccupation with the consumer's motivations and needs that distinguishes American from European business enterprise. Science is what makes news, especially among men who prefer brains to brawn. But science and advanced technology are not what primarily make the American economy run so fast and well.

An American company engaged in a joint venture with a French company in the production and delivery of ready-mix cement spent the greater part of its effort trying to persuade its partner of the importance of such seemingly trivial matters as making deliveries on time. Moreover, several months were consumed trying to persuade the French partner of the importance of planning truck routes carefully so as to increase the number of daily deliveries per vehicle, rather than trying to solve its cost-price squeeze by getting its competitors to agree to a price rise. A large German company in the ceramics business lost a lucrative American contract by its persistent failure to meet delivery dates, even after several German reassurances that it would not happen again. The Leica camera, for years the world's standard of quality, has fared badly, not because it has fallen behind scientifically, but because of the opposite. It refused to yield to the increasing convenience-orientation of the market place. Leica's self-assured and unbending attitudes defined a "better" camera differently from the way the market place defined it. Like the numerical control producer, it overengineered the product to the insular high-cost specifications of people accustomed to having their clothes tailor-made at the best shops.

This same distaste for the practical facts of the world to which they must address their efforts characterizes management methods in much of Europe. It is not enough to produce excellent products. One must produce the right products, at the right price, and engage in the right marketing efforts. But marketing is not a respectable word in many European companies. Employees engaged in marketing are viewed as a lesser breed—the chaps responsible for all that vulgar advertising and expense account wining. They give business a bad name. Marketing men are now grudgingly admitted into the enterprise, but are given little say and are seldom invited into the upper echelons or to the upper clubs. As a consequence, no really bright, promising, self-respecting young man willingly enters the marketing sector of a business. There is thus a selective breeding of mediocrity in the very sector of the business where brightness is, for European companies, most urgently needed. Hence, the solidly respectable men at the top who make vital decisions about product design, about market opportunities, about how much is to be spent for product and market development often make these decisions inside a sealed continuum. They get no reliable information from the market place or the people who are closest to it. Their companies are really organized *against* the market. They seal off from positions of influence the men who are likely to know most about the market.

The most frustrated and disillusioned men in Europe today are the able men who are aware of, and confined by, the artificial organizational barriers and practices that keep them from helping their companies be more successful. Britain has a particularly large and growing group of such men. To their enormous credit they are hanging on, sacrificing themselves to the day when the barriers will finally crumble. And they are crumbling, but not at a pace commensurate with the implacable demands of the competitive environment. This group is crumbling only as the men at the top literally die off.

A genuine European economic community will certainly help European firms compete, and for the reasons that Professor Gilpin in part mentions. But until we look at what actually happens inside the typical European enterprise, we cannot appreciate fully what is distinctive about America's success. Product planning is almost nonexistent in Europe. Hardly a company has anything such as profit planning, market plans, market research, formal capital budgeting or financial control systems. Manufacturing departments often operate like autonomous kingdoms, independent of, and sometimes at war with, their marketing departments. Owing in part to the double bookkeeping practices that systematic tax evasion has institutionalized in many European firms, and in part to ancient practices of secrecy designed to prevent even key employees from knowing how well their companies are doing, plant managers often have no idea what their real costs are, division managers have no idea of their profit contributions, and sales vice presidents cannot know which products to emphasize because they are not told of the profitability of their various products.

All this might have been very well thirty years ago. But American companies now plan, organize, control, budget, research the market, and work against profit and cost standards. There is a discipline and sense of purpose, an orientation to market opportunities that is alien in much of Europe. America's edge over Europe resides not in its possession of greater technical or scientific knowledge, but rather in its greater knowledge about the market and its greater commitment to the idea of a business system whose job is to serve the market.

The gap is not technological, not brains, and certainly not money. Europe does not need new scientific knowledge. It needs a new spirit, led by a new generation of business managers, to capitalize on the knowledge that is abundantly available.

25 KLAUS KNORR

Is NATO
Indispensable?

NATO, like all alliances and all instruments of foreign policy, is a
means to an end and should not be preserved if this end no
longer exists or if it can be served better by other means. Whatever
benefits it may confer on its members, NATO also imposes various
burdens on them. The key burden is, of course, the obligation to
come to the defense of any member subjected to military attack.
But there are many other costs: limitations on national freedom of
action in matters of foreign and defense policy; the possibility of
being drawn into a conflict by the imprudent, perhaps even aggressive, policy of an ally; allied pressure for more onerous defense
burdens than a member wants to assume; the presence of foreign
troops on national territory or, conversely, the maintenance of
one's own troops on foreign soil; the tensions and bickering that
interallied negotiation tends to generate. These and many other
costs—whether of a psychological, financial or political nature—
are real. To bear them makes sense only if the benefits, mostly in
terms of military security, are expected to yield greater value. As
estimated by each government, the balance between costs and
benefits may be large or small, positive or negative, clear or

Reprinted from Klaus Knorr, "NATO: Past, Present, Prospect,"
Headline Series No. 198 (December, 1969), pp. 23-31, 34-40, by
permission of the Foreign Policy Association, Inc.

uncertain. It may change over time as circumstances change; and at any one time it may differ for different allies.

It is therefore inevitable that an alliance stands in need of repeated review by its members. Such review, however, is very difficult, quite aside from the fact that once a major policy has been officially adopted, its change, let alone abandonment, is impeded by various resistances inherent in the operation of governments. A serious review does not involve a simple calculation of definitely known and measurable conditions. Past experience is a guide only to the extent that past conditions will continue into the future. But the future is hard to predict, indeed—so far as it involves the behavior of other nations, allied or potentially hostile—such prediction is impossible with any degree of confidence. Unavoidably, expectations regarding the future worth of an alliance are beset with uncertainties. Furthermore, the review process cannot content itself with the simple question of whether the existing alliance, as it operates, is worth maintaining in the future. To some extent, both the value and the costs of alliance are subject to control and manipulation. If an existing alliance is of small or dubious value in its present form of operation, it might be worth more if its operation were modified.

Therefore, when we consider the future of NATO, we must ask questions for which there are no certain answers at present. And we must also remember that we are concerned with an alliance and an organization which, as they have shown in the past, are to a degree adaptable to newly emerging circumstances.

PROBLEMS THAT ARISE

Let us now turn our attention to the main problems that have caused dissension among the allies in the past and are liable to do so in the future. We can be sure that NATO will undergo changes in response to permutations in the international environment and in response to political conditions within the allied nations themselves. As change is inevitable, it is also certain that the relations between the United States and Europe will be in motion, occasionally perhaps even in turbulent motion. We must note, further, that there is an interaction between NATO problem-solving and the cohesion of the alliance. When NATO cohesion is firm, for example, it is easier to solve NATO problems. Conversely, if old or newly emerging problems are solved satisfactorily, NATO cohesion stands to gain.

IS THERE A THREAT FROM THE SOVIET UNION?

Since NATO is primarily a defensive alliance, it presupposes the existence of an actual or potential military threat which its members feel must be met collectively. Assuming that the European members of the alliance will not revert to their former practice of carrying on war against one another, only the Soviet Union, with or without its Warsaw pact allies, can possibly pose such a threat. The key questions are: How real is such a threat? What forms can it take? Is NATO the only effective means of providing military security for Western Europe?

One relevant fact is absolutely beyond doubt. The Soviet Union has a military capability which dwarfs the forces of the European nations, singly and together. If NATO did not exist and American capabilities were uninvolved, the European countries alone could not prevent the occupation of the Continent by Soviet forces. And even if the U.S.S.R. chose not to attack or occupy Western Europe, it could subject this area to threats and military blackmail. This is so because the Soviet Union has an overwhelming superiority in troops, air power and nuclear forces. What is doubtful, given the assumption of no NATO or United States involvement, is that Soviet leaders nurse aggressive designs on Western European states. It can be argued that the awesome military posture of the U.S.S.R. serves merely its own need for security and that, without any American involvement in Europe, the Soviet Union would be freed from all threats to its security from that quarter. Yet we do not and cannot know that Soviet capabilities are wholly meant to satisfy defensive considerations.

It has been argued, especially in Europe, that even if the Soviet Union did constitute a serious threat in the past, it is no longer what it was under Stalin, that its dedication to the spread of communism has lost militancy, that Soviet leaders are in fact preoccupied with solving important domestic problems and that their key external problems are not in Europe but elsewhere, particularly in the Far East. All one can say about such speculations and beliefs is that they may be right even though the evidence of Soviet behavior is surely ambiguous, but that we do not know whether they are right, or, even if they are right at present, that they will be right next year or five years hence. Even though the Soviet invasion of Czechoslovakia was prompted by essentially defensive motives, it indicated Soviet willingness to use force if necessary for the achievement of vital objectives; and it surely cast doubts on assumptions about a "mellowing" of Soviet power.

As history has revealed again and again, the intentions of governments can change abruptly, and there is no dependable way of predicting these changes. In matters of security, it has therefore always been a rule of prudence not to rely mainly on intentions, but rather to relate security measures to the capabilities of states strong enough to constitute a threat should intentions turn hostile. This rule of caution does not mean that the intentions of such states should be disregarded. On the contrary, security considerations also demand that care be taken not to give cause for intentions to turn hostile. But a disregard of capabilities could be fatal.

From this point of view, there is not the slightest doubt in this author's mind that the Western nations should avoid all provocation of the Soviet Union and, as will be pointed out below, that they should strive to cooperate with the U.S.S.R. whenever doing so promises to minimize the chance of military conflict in Europe. But the author is also convinced that it would be foolhardy for the NATO countries to base their security wholly or mainly on trust in the peaceful nature of Soviet intentions. The actual record of Soviet behavior since World War II is perfectly compatible with the assumption that Soviet leaders have been interested in weakening the West, which to them is capitalist and hence, politically illegitimate; that they will not run dangerous risks in pursuing this interest but that they could be tempted to use force on behalf of their objectives when the risks are tolerable. In this view, the military deterrence power of the West effectively denies Soviet leaders any temptation to exert military pressure or commit aggression. Most American analysts agree with this premise and this conclusion. Though some Europeans may disagree, it is improbable that many would do so if the case were put to them in the blunt form adopted here. One suspects that much of the feeling of diminished insecurity in Western Europe rests on the absence of severe crises with Russia in recent years. But Western Europeans must also be aware of their inability to know whether crises were absent because the Soviet Union is a reliably peace-loving power or because, in some critical way, American involvement in NATO encourages peaceful Soviet behavior.

It is also important to remember that a prospective Soviet threat need not involve all of Western Europe at once or be motivated by a bold Kremlin plan to seize all the area in one fell swoop. It might only involve part of the area—Berlin, the Federal Republic of Germany, Norway or Turkey, for example—and it could be inadvertently generated by a sequence of events not deliberately planned by any government in advance. In such a localized crisis, the ally involved would be hopelessly outclassed militarily. It is precisely the rationale of a defensive alliance that it deter or cope with such contingencies by collective means.

SECURITY ALTERNATIVES TO NATO

Even if the existence of a possible security threat from the East to the NATO area in Europe is admitted, it may be asked if NATO is the best way to meet it. Several alternatives, mentioned from time to time, can be dismissed at this time: First, dreams of a politically united Atlantic community organized along confederate or federal lines and thus far more cohesive than NATO itself are unrealistic. They do not accord with the dominant preferences on either side of the Atlantic.

Second, effective international arms control and disarmament agreements could eventually free nations from the traditional necessity of seeking security primarily by military means for deterrence and defense. But such agreements, if they come at all, will come very slowly. Despite the strategic arms limitation talks currently under way between the United States and the Soviet Union in Helsinki, Finland, such an alternative has yet to be sufficiently developed. Third, the establishment of a comprehensive security pact covering all the nations of Europe, East and West, and featuring the dissolution of NATO and of the Warsaw pact and the exclusion of an American military presence in Europe, has been advocated by the Soviet Union for some years. There has been increasing European interest in this scheme. But most Europeans know that a mere treaty of this kind could scarcely guarantee their security. At least, such nonaggression pacts have failed to do so in the past.

Fourth, some or all Western European countries now in NATO could, perhaps in conjunction with a regional nonaggression pact, adopt a "neutralist" policy on the pattern of Sweden and Switzerland. However, it is interesting to observe that at present both the Swedes and Swiss appreciate and benefit from the existence of NATO which, as they see it, provides a European balance of power that makes the neutrality of a few European states feasible. Perhaps one or two more European countries could adopt a neutralist posture with fair prospects of success. However, if many states now committed to NATO withdrew from the alliance and embraced neutrality, and if the United States subsequently withdrew its commitment to Western Europe, or made it more conditional, the present balance of power would disappear and the integrity of all Western European nations would be subject to the mercy of the U.S.S.R.

INDEPENDENT EUROPEAN DEFENSE SYSTEM?

Fifth, there is the possibility that the Western European states, or some of them, could bolster and integrate their defense efforts and thereby make the security of the area independent of the United States. If feasible, this is certainly an alternative which most Americans would welcome. There is no doubt that all the Western European NATO countries together possess the manpower and other resources to develop military capabilities roughly equal to those of the Soviet Union and of the United States.

However, this alternative presupposes a political and military fusion of these countries, and, though such a development has supporters in many key countries, the overall structure of European politics does not at present favor it. And even if it came, many years would be needed for an integrated Western European power to transform economic and technological potential into sufficiently mobilized military strength for adequate deterrence and defense. A mere alliance among the Western European states would hardly be an effective substitute for NATO. Present British, French, German and Italian forces together would still fall far short of matching those of the Soviet Union. And since, singly or jointly, such a group of allies would be hopelessly outclassed, could any one of them, in the face of an intense security crisis involving the Soviet Union, really count on the unstinting support of the others? Suppose the Federal Republic of Germany were subjected to severe military pressure by the Soviet Union. Could it count on full backing by France and Britain? And even if it could, would the U.S.S.R. be deterred?

IS NATO INDISPENSABLE?

Yet even though these alternatives to NATO seem to be unpromising as protectors of European security, does this mean that NATO in its present shape is indispensable? This question must be faced if we want to understand the problems currently besetting the alliance. It could be said, if only for purposes of argument, that if it has been necessary to thwart the Soviet Union as a potential aggressor in Europe at any time since World War II, then Russia was not deterred by NATO but by the United States. In short, it can be argued that it was not what our European allies contributed to NATO forces, or what SHAPE planned, but American strategic power which guaranteed security in Europe. As far as it goes, this argument seems essentially correct to this author. If it is correct, then the question must be raised as to whether more than an American nuclear umbrella is necessary for the security of Europe in the future. As long as mutual nuclear deterrence prevails between the United States and the Soviet Union and as long as the United States attributes to the defense of Western Europe a value second only to the defense of itself, would not the Soviet Union stand deterred whether NATO existed or not?

If the above argument were fully realistic, the treaty commitment and the shield forces would be redundant, and the United States as well as its allies could save themselves a lot of unproductive expense and intramural bickering. There is, in fact, enough plausibility in this argument to permit some Western Europeans to assume that their military effort and cooperation is not required to secure the American guarantee, and that this guarantee is dependable because it is rooted in American self-interests. Some Frenchmen, for instance, feel that no matter how obnoxiously France behaves in American eyes the United States cannot afford to turn its back on France in the unlikely event that its security were endangered.

However, even if we assume that the United States has been the mainstay of deterrence in Europe, the inference that NATO is dispensable does not necessarily follow. Nuclear deterrence is effective only to the extent that the retaliatory threat is sufficiently credible to an opponent. The fact that the Soviet Union has very recently added greatly to its capacity to destroy the United States tends to diminish somewhat the credibility of the American deterrent threat. Vital as the interest of the United States is in the integrity of Western Europe, America's interest in saving itself from devastation comes first; and should strategic deterrence fail, the United States might be unable to protect Western Europe except by courses of action which would entail its own destruction.

Under these circumstances, it is clear that a solemn commitment adds to the credibility of deterrence. Hence, as an embodiment of this kind of commitment, the North Atlantic Treaty serves a purpose. Most Europeans understand this. But perhaps even more than the treaty, it is the presence of a sizable body of American troops in the heart of Europe which lends a great deal of credibility to American deterrence. No substantial aggression could take place in this crucial area without coming up physically against American forces. It is possible that these forces could remain on the Continent without a NATO treaty, within the framework of an American-German alliance, for example. But the presence of these forces is surely incomparably easier under the NATO arrangement. Whether SHAPE and its operations add to European security depends chiefly on the defense value of the shield forces—a subject discussed below.

There is, however, one additional function which SHAPE and its integrated military operations perform. When the allies discussed and finally agreed on the ending of West Germany's occupation and its inclusion as a NATO partner, there was a great deal of uneasiness about permitting the rearmament of the Federal Republic. These anxieties were mostly dispelled when agreement was reached that the new German forces would be directly under the command of SACEUR. All other allied forces come under his command only in an emergency and by an act of each government concerned. The West German forces have no general staff and no German supreme command. The integrated military structure which was developed under the North Atlantic Treaty has thus served the especially important purpose of integrating German military capabilities securely into a collective force. It is hard to say whether, in the eyes of the Germans or of their allies, this secondary function of NATO has become obsolete.

In any case, in terms of protecting Western European countries by the sole means of a strategic nuclear retaliatory threat, it cannot be concluded at this time that there is a viable alternative to NATO.

CHANCES OF A SECOND PILLAR

As noted earlier, one perennial problem of NATO has been the inequality of the allies in terms of their comparative military contributions. The United States is so overwhelmingly the strongest power that it has been easy, if not natural, for it to dominate in NATO councils. The frequent changes in NATO strategy have originated with the United States, sometimes to the bewilderment of its allies. Under these circumstances, it has been difficult to maintain the appearance and reality of a partnership of free nations.

Equal partnership happens to contradict the unequal facts of military life. It is understandable that American leaders have sometimes found it annoying to negotiate alliance business with a large number of countries. And it is even more understandable that Europeans, members of proud nations, many with glorious pasts, have found the role of junior partner demeaning, and that they have chafed under their inferior status. These resentments have deepened over time as the European nations have become more prosperous and as the security threat to Western Europe has seemed to diminish, if not completely pass away.

Proposals which would permit the European members to consolidate their capabilities and interests and deal collectively with the United States have been offered again and again as the proper remedy, for this would transform what is now a multilateral relationship into an essentially bilateral one. What is needed, it has often been pointed out, is a NATO resting on two equal pillars, one in Europe and one in the United States—an arrangement which looks like a "dumbbell." From the days of the Marshall Plan, the United States has in fact supported the idea of Western European integration. It favored the establishment of a European Defense Community to create unified European armed forces, but the idea was rejected by the French National Assembly in 1954. President Kennedy's call in July 1962 for a Grand Design expressed the same concern. Yet even though the members of the European Economic Community (EEC) have made a success of economic unification, the European forces aspiring toward political and military integration have been unable to overcome various resistances, among which General de Gaulle's policy has been the most insuperable.

The general's vision was a *Europe des patries* (a Europe of fatherlands) extending into Eastern Europe, perhaps as far as the Urals, but excluding the Anglo-Saxons, that is, Britain and the United States. This would apparently have been a Europe composed of sovereign states working in harmony by recognizing France as their leader and spokesman. While this vision had a utopian coloring, there was nothing unreal about the general's determination and ability, resulting from his veto power, to keep Britain from entering the EEC or—despite contrary desires by West Germany, Italy, the Netherlands and Belgium—to oppose any other arrangements designed to bring Britain into a common fold. Undaunted, Britain in 1968-69 pressed for a European caucus of NATO states to which France was invited but which might constitute itself even if France refused and which could integrate European defense policies within the NATO framework. But France's opposition kept the other partners in the EEC, especially the Federal Republic of Germany, from responding to the British initiative. In February 1969, when a meeting of the Western European Union (WEU) was called, France decided to boycott WEU meetings until further notice. The French government made it unmistakably clear that its boycott was intended to defeat Britain's design for a European defense caucus.

But something of this nature would make sense. It would give the Western European states a greater sense of responsibility for their own security and could restructure the entire complex of NATO relationships in a more egalitarian manner. If such a grouping could be organized and charged with important functions, such as coordinating European policies on military manpower, procurement, research and development, and finance, it could eventually establish some joint military forces. Then the European allies would speak with a single voice, and the role of the United States as the key strategic power would not be reduced. But first these countries must solve the issues and dispel the suspicions which now divide them on the political level. . . .

STRATEGIC NUCLEAR DETERRENCE

British and French strategic nuclear forces are clearly too small and vulnerable to deter the Soviet Union should Soviet leaders contemplate military pressure on one of the NATO states in Europe. Since this situation will not change in the foreseeable future, the United States remains the only power able to perform this protective function.

As mentioned above, however, this crucial role was more easily played by the United States in the past than it probably will be in the future. Although a state of mutual deterrence between the two superpowers prevailed in the late 1950's and throughout the 1960's, until very recently this deterrence was asymmetrical, with the United States enjoying a considerable superiority in strategic weaponry. Had a large-scale nuclear war broken out, the U.S.S.R. could have done nothing to avoid its own destruction. On the other hand, given some warning of an impending attack, the United States possessed the capability to destroy some Soviet missile launchers and airfields and, by thus blunting Soviet attack capabilities, to limit, perhaps very substantially, the damage which the Soviet Union could inflict on this country. By mid-1969, however, it was believed that the Soviet Union had advanced to rough parity with American deployment of intercontinental nuclear weapons. This passing of American preponderance does not mean that deterrence of Soviet aggression against Western Europe is no longer credible. Deterrence of any deliberate aggression works as long as Soviet leaders expect with some probability that any gains from aggression would be far exceeded by the losses Russia itself would suffer. The credibility of American deterrence rests primarily on Soviet estimates of how important a secure Western Europe is to the United States; and the effectiveness of American deterrence depends on the stake which the Soviet Union might have in producing a change in the European *status quo* by military might. But any possible gain would hardly be worth the destruction of Soviet cities. Even a possibility of such retaliation should suffice to produce restraint.

Lack of complete certainty in the continued readiness of the United States to deter the Soviet Union by a threat which, if it must be executed, endangers the lives of a large fraction of the American population, naturally engenders anxiety in European minds. In order to reduce this anxiety, which fluctuates with European perceptions of the Soviet Union as a potential source of danger, the United States is asked again and again to reaffirm its pledge; and any American talk about reducing American forces in Europe immediately touches off European anxieties lest the American commitment turn into a mere pledge on paper.

NUCLEAR SHARING STILL IMPRACTICAL

However, no matter how often and solemnly the United States renews its commitment, Europeans know that they are not integral parts of the United States. Only their effective control over the employment of the American retaliatory force could, therefore, remove their insecurity on this score. Yet such genuine nuclear sharing within the alliance is as impractical now as it was in the past. It is not only that the foreign-policy interests of the United States are not limited to maintaining European stability. The idea of many fingers on the safety-catch, let alone on the trigger, of the American nuclear capability is bizarre and completely unacceptable. To be effective the control of nuclear deterrence is indivisible and must remain subject to one directive center.

This dilemma of NATO could be resolved in principle only by the development of effective nuclear deterrent power under European control—collective or independently national. A case could be made that such a development would be in the American as well as in the European interest, and that, under certain circumstances, the United States should consider assisting in, rather than opposing it. From many points of view, it should appear desirable as well as natural for the inhabitants of Western Europe to provide for their own security. However, United States policy has been, and is, strictly opposed to nuclear proliferation, in Europe as well as elsewhere. As a party to the non-proliferation treaty of 1968, the United States is, in fact, obligated not to render such assistance. Even before this treaty was signed, the United States never considered aiding France in its effort to become an independent nuclear power. For one thing, such aid might have raised at some future time the question of helping other nations—notably the Federal Republic of Germany—to become independent nuclear powers.

On the other hand, the creation of a collective Western European deterrent capability, not subject, like the proposed MLF, to an American veto, remains as a possibility. If such a force were formed, initially from the independent nuclear forces of France or Britain or both, and if other NATO allies gained no independent access to nuclear weapons in the collective force, no technical violation of the nonproliferation treaty would occur. Yet ultimately such a capability would require a degree of interest-pooling by France and Britain which is, certainly at present, hard to imagine.

This absence of viable alternatives leaves the nuclear committees set up within the NATO framework as the only practicable way to mitigate the dilemma at the present time. What can be achieved in these committees is a sharing of information and a degree of consultation about possible responses to various hypothetical contingencies. This does not amount to much more than a palliative. Yet as recent experience has revealed, it is of some value to nonnuclear allies.

Before long the United States must decide on its future strategic nuclear posture, and these decisions will be followed attentively by NATO Europe. Any improvements designed to maintain the "assured destruction" capability on which stable deterrence must rest will unquestionably be welcomed. Two technological innovations—the antiballistic missile (ABM) and the Multiple Independently Targeted Re-entry Vehicle (MIRV)—could upset the present balance of terror with unforeseeable and perhaps injurious consequences.

BALANCE OF TERROR

If the United States and the U.S.S.R. negotiate an agreement to limit the deployment of ABM defenses, let alone all nuclear missiles, they will be co-operating toward stabilizing the existing balance of terror and, presumably, strengthening military stability in the heart of Europe. Should the superpowers fail to agree and proceed to the large-scale installation of defensive systems for the protection of cities, the consequences will depend on the technical effectiveness of these systems. If they are known on both sides to be incapable of preventing all hostile missiles from penetrating—a realistic estimate at present—then a great deal of money will have been spent but mutual nuclear deterrence will have been essentially preserved. If, on the other hand, ABM's on both sides should promise to limit the damage to an "acceptable" level, then mutual deterrence will have been weakened, perhaps decisively, especially as far as the protection of allies is concerned. Antimissile defenses for Western Europe would not only be enormously expensive but also technically less effective because of the greater proximity of the area to Soviet missile launchers.

The large-scale installation of MIRV's, that is, of missiles which, after launching, release several and perhaps as many as ten or twelve smaller missiles capable of hitting different targets, would tend to destabilize the balance of terror in a different way. MIRV's might raise the danger of preemptive nuclear attack. They could conceivably be used for a first nuclear strike designed to knock out as many of an opponent's missile launchers as possible. Of course, much will depend on the technical efficiency of MIRV's and on the vulnerability of an opponent's retaliatory forces. But if their efficiency is high, either super-power might be tempted to undertake a preemptive strike during an intense crisis with the other, fearing the adversary's decision to strike first. Once effective MIRV's were deployed, mutual deterrence would become highly unstable, and the allies of the two superpowers would be as much affected as the principal powers. It is to be hoped that this spiral in the nuclear arms race can be avoided or, at least, that the resulting instability can be moderated by appropriate controls on deployment.

26 PIERRE HASSNER

The Changing Context of European Security

Every period is by definition a time of transition. Some, however, tend to give an illusion of permanence; others an expectation of utopia or of doom. The remarkable feature of the present time is that it is almost impossible not to share the feeling that we are entering into a new period of international and European affairs— and almost as difficult to agree on where we go from here. Our feeling of change is based on our witnessing the decay of the old, rather than on fearing or hoping for the emergence of the new.

Somehow our belief in change is belied by a deeper feeling of security. Although the resources, the beliefs and the institutions on which the present European stability is based appear in danger of drying up, we somehow feel that the same stability will continue without a real upheaval, either by rejuvenating or somewhat re-freshing the solutions of today, or by reaching back to those of yesterday and the day before yesterday. The only brave new world we can imagine after the end of NATO or of the cold war bears the hardly very youthful face of the disengagement and denuclearization

Reprinted from the *Journal of Common Market Studies,* 7 No. 1 (September, 1968), pp. 1-2, 4-13, 17-21, by permission of Basil Blackwell, Publisher. Footnotes omitted by the editors.

plans of the fifties, of the projected peace treaties of the forties, of the collective security agreements of the twenties, or of the balance of power or the European concert of the nineteenth century. To look beyond the cold war means to look beyond the confrontation of the two alliances and this in turn is increasingly taken to mean a return to the task which was interrupted by the cold war or prevented by NATO—namely, a European settlement involving the signing of a German Peace Treaty, the acceptance of the results of World War II, and the organizing of collective security. An alternative to NATO and the Warsaw Pact would then mean a return either (1) to the situation immediately following the war (the two great powers stay on, but instead of facing each other they face Germany as occupying or supervising powers) or (2) to the situation preceding it (the two universal powers return to their domestic or extra-European concerns and play only a marginal role in a renewed European balance of power). To those who like their power-politics with collective security or international organization dressing, the formalized (and, thereby, hopefully, stabilized) equivalents of those patterns are (3) a mixture of Potsdam and San Francisco—with the great powers acting as the law enforcers, and (4) a mixture of Locarno and the Covenant of the League of Nations, with the great powers acting merely as guarantors in a reciprocal framework.

A common feature of these implicit or explicit models is that, on the one hand, they rely on East-West or multilateral and reciprocal cooperation, instead of East-West confrontation and intra-Western and intra-Eastern cooperation, and that, on the other hand, not being based on the great powers' perception of each other as the main threat, they tend in fact (even if they are reciprocal in scope) to be built around, about, or against Germany. As soon as one allows the European map, folded so far between the covers of the two blocs, to unfold, three concentric circles appear, with the two great powers and Germany providing the basic structure and the European states a more hazy and mobile intermediate zone. . . .

Today, however, neither Germany nor Russia can *really* be worried for their security in any immediate sense of aggression from the other side. Neither can have any real hopes or incentives to dramatically alter the status quo at the conference table. The military balance seems stabilized, the political status quo, in Germany at least, more and more consolidated. The question, then, must arise: if everybody's degree of dissatisfaction is so low, why start thinking up models for change? If the Soviet Union is so happy with the two alliances, why does she do her best to break the backbone of the Western one, the American-German relationship, and why does she call for their suppression by 1969? If Germany is so optimistic about her security and so pessimistic about her reunification, why does she need a new policy and dream of a new system?

A provisional and simplified answer would be: today, at any rate, the search for a European security system has nothing to do with any direct search for security. If one is concerned with maximizing security, surely the conservative answer: 'We have a pretty good security system right now, why tamper with it?' is glaringly true. He who wants to improve security will look for security measures, if he can still think of any, not to a new system involving a new set of political relationships. Surely, the answer has much more to do with these relationships themselves, that is with the exploitation, the formalization, the improvement or the erosion of the status quo, which in turn might, in the long run, raise the security problem again.

Perhaps the best way to gain a perspective on these two aspects of the European situation is to look back and ahead over the past and the next twenty years. If one looks back, one is impressed by how much security Europe has achieved. If one looks ahead, one is impressed by how little the status quo is likely to last. It is hard to find a time during the last twenty years when the situation in Europe was more secure than it is since 1963. It is hard to imagine this situation lasting for the next twenty years. Or, to focus on what symbolically and effectively is still the central factor characterizing the present security system, it is hard today to imagine a withdrawal of Soviet and American troops from Germany which would not lead to a situation less secure than the present one; it is no less hard to imagine that twenty years from now these troops will still be in Germany, unless it be in a completely different and unforeseeable (but not very likely) capacity and framework, either as occupying powers enforcing a Soviet-American condominium or as reciprocal hostages representing a multilateral security organization. In other words, the given 'mix' of confrontation and cooperation, of mutual balance between the two leaders and of control over their respective allies, constituted by the two alliances and constituting the present system, would probably be the safest one if it could last, but is likely to break down in one direction or another: even if—which is doubtful—the same components are still there and are not supplemented by others, the changes in their relative importance and their psychological meaning will be sufficient to amount to a new system.

The interaction of strategy, arms control and politics and the relative shift of gravity between them is illustrated by the successive meanings taken by the concern for security over the last twenty years.

Seen very broadly and from a Western point of view, one may distinguish three phases. In the late forties and the fifties, the concern was with security against aggression: the problem was essentially how to deter an attack and how to fight it by conceding as little territory as possible if it occurred. Hence, the rearmament and the setting up of the two defensive systems directed against each other.

In a second and relatively short-lived phase reflected by the discussions about disengagement and regional arms limitations in the late fifties, and by the theory and practice of arms control in the sixties, the concern for security became much more reciprocal. One may say that the problem was less security of the West against the East and vice versa than the security of both against the dangers from nuclear weapons themselves and from the presence of the two military establishments face to face.

Once very strong, the feeling of insecurity coming from these factors has now for all practical purposes disappeared. The balance has been stabilized. A great number of unilateral precautions to prevent the accidental or unauthorized firing of tactical nuclear weapons, and other measures of centralized control and arms restraint, have been taken. These efforts have been so successful that both the analysts or war gamers trying to devise scenarios for a war starting in Europe, and the arms controllers or diplomats trying to devise proposals for arms negotiations in Europe have more or less run out of ideas. They have been overtaken either by technical developments or by the change in political climate. In this respect, the effects of Kennedy's Cuba stand have been at least as important as those of his efforts on the military and arms control level in Europe. While by themselves many of the fears of American strategists about the low threshold for the use of nuclear weapons, or of the German Generals about the reinforcing capabilities of the Soviets, are, taken by themselves at least as justified as they were a few years ago, the fire has run out of the arguments of both because of the post-Cuban détente, and also of the apparent consolidation of the East German regime, which removes the fear of a new 1953. Arms control and strategy have gone out of fashion because nobody can bring himself to believe in a war in Europe. The victory of 'intentions' over 'capabilities' is complete.

The results are twofold. On the one hand, the security concerns of the great powers have been lifted from the regional level to those of bilateral strategic balance and arms race and to their bilateral concern with the universal problem of nuclear proliferation. On the other hand, in Europe, one is left with a huge and costly establishment which seems disproportionate given the general feeling of security; hence the temptation to dispense with, to discard part of it, or to exploit whatever modifications one can apply to political purposes. But here we are at the border between the problem of security proper and the problem of the status quo. On a first, simplest, and, in the short run, most powerful level, the feeling of security certainly reinforces the already heavily predominant weight of the status quo. In a direct or indirect way most of the hopes of changing the status quo were based on the fears of its dangers. These fears being removed, it would seem that for those predominant forces which have so far favoured and maintained the status quo, the logical conclusion of the process would be to remove, so to speak, the 'state of emergency' stamp from it, that is, to give it a formal sanction and hence de-emphasize its essentially military character. This first direction of legalizing or formalizing the status quo is expressed in the various Soviet proposals for a non-aggression pact between the two military organizations, for a peace treaty with the two German states, or even for the association of both organizations or of both states under an all-European or all-German roof or label.

In a way, this would appear as a logical and positive conclusion to the evolution we outlined. There would be a continuous progress from opposition through tacit cooperation to formal agreement and cooperation, and from preparation against deliberate war through avoidance of accidental war to keeping of agreed peace. But, again, the line between mere military peace-keeping and political peace-making would obviously be crossed: a formalization of the status quo is one type of political settlement, and, as all political settlements, it means reinforcing certain elements of the status quo, like the division of Germany into two states or its present borders, while weakening certain others (the ties between Germany and her Western allies, the psychological grounds for the American presence in Europe). There is then a case for handling political problems politically and for attempting to use the military stability in order to try and solve the open questions of political settlement instead of pre-empting them under the guise of normalization.

This, then, would be the second line, from political-military status quo to political settlement via military stabilization. In other words, military security should be the basis not of status quo, but of *status quo plus*. Precisely because we no longer fear war, we should start thinking about peace. The fulfilling of the negative task of avoiding war is only the basis for the political task of building the peace. As Willy Brandt has written: 'NATO will have fulfilled its military task only when we have fulfilled our political one'. Reversing the first line of reasoning, one can say that as long as the military situation was unstable, it made for political immobility, for any attempt at change was too dangerous. Conversely, military security could provide the basis for political expansion and flexibility.

This general line can lead to two different practical conclusions which diverge according to their evaluation of political trends. One can think that the time has now come for negotiating a settlement. But a more widespread and realistic line sees the European settlement not as the conclusion of the twenty years of cold war, but as the result of the new period which is just beginning. It will be the end of a process of an effort every bit as painstaking as the post-war reconstruction and stabilization of Europe. A settlement today could do little but formalize an unsatisfactory, hence unstable, hence insecure status quo—that of Europe's division. One should allow and encourage first the process of European reunification. It may be, however, that both the hopes of those who wish to remove the status quo and of those who wish to maintain it should be frustrated. Dreams of a future alternative order may not be able to bring it about, but may prevent the consolidation of the present one. Those who want to prevent change and those who want to plan it may be effectively neutralizing each other into promoting uncontrolled and unmanaged change. Instead of status quo or of status quo plus, what one would then have is a *status quo minus.*

Many signs seem to be pointing this way. Cold war alliances are less easily converted to détente-uses than war industries to civilian production. In both alliances, and especially, of course, in NATO, which relies on cooperation and cannot dispense with consent, unity is endangered by the feeling of the medium powers that only exceptional dangers justify relinquishing ultimate decisions to the leader, and by the latter's feeling that, again, only this danger justifies the extent of his commitment. To the weariness of public opinion in the West corresponds ideological erosion in the East. To the extent that, besides force, inertia and the self-preserving interests of ruling groups, the function of a real or imaginary German danger in keeping together the Eastern alliance is increasing, one wonders whether what the status quo needs most in order to be preserved is not precisely to be challenged. On both sides it may be most threatened by the lack of serious candidates for the status-quo preserving function of revisionism or of revanchism.

This problem, of course, arises in its most acute form when there is no lack of candidates for urgent attention and action in other fields. *The* basic question confronting the powers who have no desire for change in Europe is to what extent the conservation of the status quo can be assumed without having indefinitely to be given the first priority over more positive or more urgent tasks. It seems reasonable to assume that the same intensity of military and political effort is not required in times of calm as in times of crisis; it seems no less likely that neither the military balance nor political stability are automatic and self-sustaining.

The periodic and increasingly less symbolic quarrels over troop reductions are the most telling example of how the existing balance might be allowed to be frittered away.

Today, the storm arising from successive American and German intentions and suspicions has calmed down; but the result is more a provisional truce than a permanent solution. One can almost say that the main reason which prevents both the United States and the Federal Republic from operating the troop reductions they would like to achieve is the fear of encouraging the other to follow suit. The fear of being overcome by an enemy in an arms race is less important than that of being overcome by an ally in a disarmament race. But with the coming increase in America's air-lift capabilities and the likely persistence of her extra-European commitments, with, on the other hand, the growing cost for Germany of maintaining a big army and her growing interest in political exploration with the East, it is not unlikely, to say the least, that at some point a descending spiral should set in for good. As with European and NATO problems in general, it may be that the first disruptive element has been the French, the second (partly as a reaction) the Americans, but that the third and most decisive factor is yet to come, and that it will be the German one. In turn, of course, as a condition for each of these stages, one finds an evaluation of the threat or the promise emanating from Russia. Whether by mere passivity, making the military deployment appear less necessary, or by diplomatic initiatives holding out alternatively or simultaneously the perspective of an agreement with the United States on the status quo and of a dialogue with Germany on its modification, the Soviet Union is likely to contribute to a revision of the Western arrangements. She is not likely to oblige in maintaining Western cohesion by a military posture. It would seem, then, that the only way to avoid forcing the security issue on the basis of budgetary constraints and psychological fatigue is to look towards some kind of political progress. The only way of avoiding or limiting the destabilizing consequences of status quo *minus* is to accept some destabilizing risks in the direction of status quo *plus*.

Again, it is mainly to the German-Russian relationship that one has to look for the essential factor in these initiatives, the role of the other powers being mainly to provide the balance and the framework which could make all the difference between frustrating exercises in futility, dangerous adventures, and positive projects. Paradoxically, one may say that, being determined in the last instance by the American-Russian-German triangle, the future of European security will depend above all on the interaction between an extra-European development (the nature of the Soviet-German relationship, which is likely to be influenced by China and by the strategic arms race more than by European events) and a national domestic one (the evolution of German aspirations and frustrations). The other European powers will affect the European security situation in three possible ways.

First, they can contribute negatively to the collapse of the present system (via imitation or reaction through Germany, America or Russia)—by submitting it to the test of a major crisis. In the West the most likely example would be France's withdrawing from the alliance and adopting the ambitious neutralist military policy foreshadowed by General Ailleret's recent article. In the East, even more than a Russian withdrawal from the Warsaw Pact, a 1956-type situation in, for instance, Czechoslovakia, might force changes in the Soviet attitude.

Secondly, they could affect the situation in a direct and positive way by providing an alternative: this would be the case if the creation of a politically united Europe, eventually including a European deterrent, provided the conditions for a new system—since a new unit, large enough to provide a framework for Germany and a balance for Russia, might enable the United States, and perhaps the Soviet Union, to move towards a less direct and physical presence in Europe without endangering the stability of the continent.

Thirdly, in the short run, they can affect the existing system while remaining within it, by taking some steps in one of the first directions. Today, very few are the European powers who want directly to challenge the system as such: probably France and Rumania are the only ones. Those who are revisionist in the classical territorial sense are both more numerous (since, especially in Eastern Europe, there is no lack of minority and border issues) and less so (since they do not seem ready to challenge the system in order to act on their claims). But many states would like some limited transformation: they would like more flexibility, more détente, more cooperation, less risks, less arms and less expenses within the present system. However, within this general agreement, some interesting cleavages begin to appear. Medium powers like Britain and Italy increasingly look in the direction of a greater European role and of distinct European interests . . . as compared to the great powers, especially the United States. Conversely, many small powers, within or outside the two alliances, look to the continuation of the present system, including great-power leadership, as a guarantee against domination by this or that middle power. Besides the small-states solidarity, an increasing number of new alignments cut across the old ones without negating or opposing them. The most important ones are the birth of a certain common small-and-middle-state European consciousness as opposed to the great powers, which is, very timidly, spreading to the field of security . . . and of certain traditional geo-political alignments like 'the neighbours of Germany or of Russia'. But increasingly more limited groupings (within or across the two alliances, like the Balkan, the Danubian, the Northern or the Central European states) play a certain limited, psychological, cultural, economic role with political and military potentialities which could be activated in the framework of a solution to the German problem.

It is in Germany, however, that the crossroads of the status quo and of revisionist trends meet. There is no country which has better reasons for wanting to keep the status quo and for wanting to change it, which has more crucial cards and for whom it would be more dangerous to play them. From being the most predictable of countries, it slowly emerges into being again the most unpredictable. The old 'incertitudes allemandes' apply more acutely than ever both to her quest for identity and to her quest for a framework.

It has become a commonplace to assert that the post-war attempt at giving her both through integration in the West has proved too slow for the reawakening of nationalism by de Gaulle and for the opening of the horizon to the East. For the time being, nationalism is timid, peaceful and reasonable. The Eastern horizon offers no promise for any adventure. But this, in a way, only compounds the problem. Germany has lost a community, but has not found a role. Each of the possible roles and reactions is beginning to find its advocates, but on each no sooner does a way seem to open itself than a block appears further down the road. Her past and present revisionisms go in so many directions that they effectively balance each other out into the status quo. The only major country to be revisionist in the classical sense of the possession of goals, this revisionism, which has no thinkable way of being pursued by force, both encourages her to 'system revisionism' and prevents her from being accepted as a partner in this latter game. She shares with France, Britain or Italy the various frustrations of medium Eastern powers, and the wish to overcome them by some form of political Europe; but she is forbidden ever to entertain the thought of approaching her finger to the nuclear trigger—both by everyone else's distrust and by her imperative need to reassure the East if she is not to give up every hope of reunification. She shares with France an interest in exploration towards the East, but, unlike France, cannot afford seriously to alienate the United States. She is in the paradoxical situation that, while she is thus paralyzed and reduced to dreaming of movement, everyone else's policy is based on a calculation of her own future evolution. The great watershed of 1966 means that it is no longer Germany who has to wait on the decisions of the alliance; it is the future of the alliance which will be determined by Germany's orientation; it is France and the United States who will ask themselves about the meaning of German moves. For the time being, however, the scope of these moves is limited by the fact that neither the United States nor France are prepared to risk their ties with Russia to embark on any bold policy with Germany, and that in the East the total irresponsiveness of Moscow and Pankow leaves only a divided and mostly reluctant Eastern Europe as a largely symbolic field for détente activities. Hence Germany's predicament, which is the tantalizing one of becoming objectively a rebel without a cause, while subjectively having more than one cause, but being unable to see how her potential rebellion can bring her nearer to advancing them.

Just as good relations with Eastern Europe, détente with Moscow and Pankow may be the necessary precondition of a policy, it is not yet the policy itself, unless it be that of living with the status quo and trying to make it bearable. The two broad, long-range (perhaps contradictory, perhaps complementary goals of German policy—the uniting of Europe and the reunification of Germany have both receded at the same time into an indefinite and doubtful future. Just as the decline of faith in the first encourages Germany towards a more national policy, the decline of faith in the second deprives this national policy of her more natural goal. The first phenomenon creates a disposition towards challenging the status quo. The second one demonstrates the likely frustration of this disposition because of the solidarity of the status quo; Germany is then in danger of having a national policy without national goals, a recipe for instability if ever there was one.

It is very hard to tell if in front of this situation the policy of Germany is, or rather is going to be—since it is obviously in its very early formative stages—a policy of status quo disguised as revisionism or of revisionism disguised as status quo.

Certainly, the immediate aim of the policy is clear: to try and influence the East German regime in the direction of contacts and liberalization by holding out the promise of recognition and eventual confederation. The problem is how big a change is intended: whether one aims at some humanization of the Ulbricht regime or at the suppression of its communist character or at least of the features which distinguish it from, say, Yugoslavia. It becomes a semantic point to decide when the change is qualitative and the policy can be said to oppose the status quo, rather than to presuppose it. But the difference, in itself, is important.

In the first case, it would seem that the policy is primarily Pankow-oriented and that the international framework is much less important than the direct, tacit or explicit, dialogue between the two Germanys; in the second case, it is in fact a roundabout and much more clever isolation policy. It consists of giving Ulbricht enough rope to isolate himself. In the dialogue between the two Germanys, one always witnessed a 'case of the isolated isolator', the explicit announcement that one would isolate one's rival bringing in gradual isolation over its author—while the demonstration that Bonn wants only to be friends with everybody, including East Germany, may induce the Soviet Union and the communist states of Eastern Europe to put pressure on Ulbricht. In this case, the strategy is actually Moscow-oriented and the international framework (cooperation of Germany's allies and tolerance by Russia's) becomes much more important. For the ultimate result, too, the two emphases point to two different versions of the future European order.

The first one means acceptance of the division and is best conceivable in a framework of détente between the two existing alliances. The second one means, in fact, that the confederation between the two German states would be a real one. This would clearly be incompatible with each Germany remaining a member of its respective military alliances, unless the nature and role of these have undergone a fundamental transformation.

Whichever of these interpretations of the implicit emerging long-range goals of German policy is nearer the truth, the important point is that for quite some time neither is likely to carry the day, if only because of the divisions of the Germans themselves.

Germany is timidly feeling her way in every direction. Even while one begins to hear, in a distant background, the first notes of a *Germania Fara da Se,* she is for the time being extremely conscious of the limits and dangers posed by the environment. Whether she turns into an adventurous power will depend very much on the reaction of this environment. If she is met either with hostile immobility or with attempts at seduction, her evolution will not be the same as if the environment offers some genuine hope of progress in her uncertain quest for identity, for acceptance, and for some kind of fulfilment of her special responsibilities towards East Germany.

To provide a multilateral help and framework for this quest while respecting the necessity for Germany to reach her own decisions and her own answers, to ensure that a Germany which can no longer be taken for granted should not be condemned for this very reason to a lonely and resentful existence, is probably the greatest challenge to the European system. Its very emergence means that we have already left the status quo. . . .

THE FOUR PARADOXES OF THE EUROPEAN DISCUSSION ON EURO-PEAN SECURITY

If one accepts our appraisals both of the present situation of European security and of the various combinations of desires for conservation and for change in the policies of the various powers, one is, then, led to recognize a certain number of paradoxes.

The first paradox is that . . . the ambiguity of the various positions leads to the result that those who ask for the meeting of a security conference for the dissolution of the two alliances, for a Europe without military blocs and with a new European collective security system, are those who want to legitimize and to freeze the status quo. Conversely, those who want to keep the existing alliances and institutions do so by defining them as instruments for change, which either have been converted from defence to détente, from containment to negotiation, or have always had a built-in evolutionary purpose. The proposal for a radically new system may be an attempt to brutally stop or turn back the tide of change, the proposal for adapting the present one an attempt to cautiously ride the same wave. In fact, the paradox may be less great than it seems, if one reflects that, by a new dialectical reversal, the Soviet proposals, if they were actually implemented, would probably mean a destabilizing and revolutionary change, while the Western recipe for change by adapting existing institutions to the trends of the times may actually be little more than a dynamically passive acceptance of the status quo, cheerfully welcoming what it cannot prevent and hoping for what it cannot achieve.

There is, however, a lesson to the paradox, and it would seem to point towards the conception outlined among others by Willy Brandt, of evolutionary change within existing institutions leading to a qualitative change involving a new system. If the only way to maintain the status quo is to propose revolution, surely a better case can be made in favour of progress.

The second paradox is that, on specific security measures, most spectacularly and importantly on troop reductions, but perhaps increasingly so on measures like regional nuclear freezes or partial denuclearizations, the positions between West and East tend to be switched around. In the fifties and early sixties, it used to be the Soviet Union and Poland who asked for troop reductions and arms limitations in Europe. The Western answer was that they were militarily dangerous because they would unbalance the situation even further in favour of the East, or that they were politically unacceptable because they tended to single out Germany among Western countries and hence to suggest discrimination against her. But the most general answer was that there was no reason to change the military status quo if one did not also change the political one, that the West could live with the military situation and that if the East wanted to change it, it would have to pay by political concessions. Today, the position of the Soviets on European negotiations is still basically in security terms, and the West's in political ones. But on changes to the military posture, it is the West which is eager to achieve troop reductions; so eager, in fact, that it starts (as the Soviets did in the fifties) to apply them unilaterally and would be more than happy if the Soviets would reciprocate in kind, without dreaming of asking them, in addition, for any political concessions. The old 'dialogue of the deaf' between military and political considerations has been superseded by the verdict of a more decisive voice, the economic one. It seems that both military dangers and political hopes have faded away, that what is desired is a mutually advantageous economic deal in order to maintain the same political and military situation at reduced costs, and that in the bargain the position of the West is not the stronger one.

On the nuclear freeze issue and possibly, in the future, on the issue of nuclear means of delivery, it seems that it is the West Germans who, in their search for agreements with the East or at least for admission in the peace-lovers' club, are beginning to revive past Soviet demands in the security field and to express agreement or suggest negotiations on Rapacki-Gomulka types of proposals which have been rejected above all in the face of German opposition. There are several common items on the lists recently put forward by the Bucharest and Karlowy-Vary conferences on one side, by Willy Brandt and Helmut Schmidt on the other; but while in the Soviet lists they look rather like left-overs from past episodes, the emphasis being rather on the European framework, on the West German side there seems to be a genuine interest for new initiatives in this regional arms-control field. Again, the paradox may be reduced by this fact that, as for the European security system, this may be in great part the effect of SPD leaders, who have always been favourable to this type of measure, speaking for the first time from official positions; secondly, in this case the basic Western position of trying to link military or arms-control measures with political negotiations on evolution remains, since obviously it is these political considerations rather than concern with the dangers of the military balance which prompt this new German interest. Thirdly, it may well be that these proposals were militarily dangerous or unacceptable yesterday and are no longer so today in view of strategic changes, just as it may be that they could have been stabilizing from the point of view of accidental war and are no longer so: they may have lost both their dangers and their advantages by losing much of their relevance to the security situation. However, on the second point, it seems clear that while the West German government obviously would like, as everyone else would, to extract meaningful political concessions for meaningless military gestures, it is very likely that its purpose, while political, is an indirect one; it would be satisfied it if could negotiate on these arms control measures (which means, in fact, offering these military concessions) without any political *quid pro quo,* because first it would value having its credentials established and a dialogue with the Soviets started in the arms control field, and secondly, because once adopted, it may hope (rightly or wrongly) that these freezes of the running costs, reductions and renunciations may have an indirect impact on the political détente in central Europe and hence, ultimately, on the German problem.

But these two points taken together constitute a new paradox: on the one hand, the political status quo is accepted as a basis which it would be useless to try and renegotiate in an arms control context; but on the other hand classical arms-control measures (as distinct from a possible future new generation of arms-control discussions which would involve the possibility of a European BMD system versus the reality of Soviet MRBMs targeted on Western Europe, and would thus be directly relevant to the military balance) have no real security and military relevance any longer, and are proposed only for their symbolic meaning and political consequences. Each of the two aspects raises a paradox within a paradox—which constitute the third and the fourth on the list.

The third paradox is the constant progress of the Soviet position on every level of tacit or explicit bargaining connected with European security, whether on the German problem, on arms reduction and limitations in Europe, on the implications for Germany and Europe of non-proliferation negotiations. On each of these problems, the Soviet position has practically remained unchanged, whereas the Western approach (or rather approaches) have consistently moved towards accepting the Soviet terms at the expense of progress towards the positive goals of Western policy, such as German reunification, integration and Atlantic partnership. On the German problem, the trend is away from the goal of Germany reunified in freedom by four-power negotiations, away from the intermediary stage of isolating East Germany, towards direct contacts between the two Germanys, and towards an increasing degree of de facto recognition of East Germany and of acceptance of German division, with in-creasing odds of actual recognition in the future. On arms control, as we just saw, the problems of troop reduction and of measures affecting the level of the military balance on their own merits without worrying about their possible effects on consolidating or overcoming the political status quo. As for the non-proliferation treaty, André Fontaine has recently pointed out that, while the United States tended to congratulate herself on her global success or superiority over the Soviet Union, she tended to overlook the very important victory she had conceded to the Soviet Union in Europe at the expense of Germany and the prospects of any future Western collective nuclear enterprise.

Today, it remains true that in spite of both alliances having a mixed record of success and of troubles, basically the West has had a success story in Western Europe, while the Soviet attempt at building a unified communist society in Eastern Europe has broken down. But while this is still true economically, socially, ideologically, one must admit that politically the trend towards acceptance of the status quo and towards frustration of integrative hopes in the West has favoured more and more the Soviet Union. On the one hand, her preference for bilateralism seems satisfied as against Western hopes for common approaches; on the other hand, it is she who recently has been better able to check this bilateralism and to limit the damage caused by the Rumanian heresy. While fundamentally the communist world is more bitterly divided than the West, in Europe in the past two years the disintegration has been quicker in the West than in the East. This is due to the fact that the actual or potential challenges to the leader's authority have much greater weight and freedom in the West, and to the passivity of the United States.

The result is that the Soviet Union is not only more or less able to contain the effects of Western (French or German) initiatives, but, while feeling on the defensive in the world at large against what she chooses to interpret as an American offensive, she is able to recapture the initiative in Europe. It is not too far-fetched to fear that, as Raymond Aron said, after having won the cold war the West is handing back the spoils to the Soviet Union.

It is also possible, however, to acknowledge that, increasingly, the West is accepting the political framework favoured by the Soviet Union and yet to maintain that it can afford to do so precisely because it is winning. One may give the Soviet Union a pyrrhic political victory, based on and encouraging her historical defeat. Again, this would correspond to the interpretation of her political and propagandistic initiatives for a European security conference and system as being an attempt to compensate or reverse unfavourable long-range trends by short-term political victories.

This would also give a rationale to the prevailing American attitude of diplomatic passivity: the best chances for changing the status quo would be not in political, but in letting social and economic trends do their work, the role of the political and military factors being only to provide a stable environment for the process. Security problems and military alliances may have to be dealt with—but rather as one vehicle among others for East-West political contacts, manoeuvres, and cooperation.

This brings us to our fourth and last paradox. Just as détente and cooperation become a language on which everyone agrees (but through which, as has been the case for years for terms like 'peace', 'disarmament', or like 'Europe', everybody tries to foster his own political objectives and conceptions and to show that they are not only good *per se*, but also the right contribution to that particular value), so the debate on European security may turn not so much around the best way of achieving security but around *who* should achieve it against *whom* and in what framework. European Security discussions may be one language and one forum for discussing the political future of Europe, of the German nation, or of East-West relations. Even issues like the Soviet MRBMs or a European BMD system would probably take above all this symbolic meaning, in the context of which the debate on differences of interest or on continuity between Europe, the United States and Russia would be continued.

One may return then to the parallel between the non-proliferation treaty and the European Security System which we suggested earlier. In both cases there may be in the making a permanent very slightly veiled political discussion on the reordering of the international system and of the European one. It is only if and when a genuine political realignment is reached that the issue of security will be rediscovered in earnest and will become again the subject of a real, as opposed to a symbolic, debate.

27

ERNST B. HAAS

The Uniting of Europe Reconsidered

Let us summarize the structural homogeneities in Western Europe. All the West European countries were and are characterized by pluralistic social structure; all classes of the population may participate in many aspects of daily public decision-making, as suggested by the plethora of commissions and committees functioning at all levels of society and economy. Upward social mobility has steadily increased. The isolation of rural life has steadily declined. More and more people in all walks of life are somehow affiliated with voluntary groups which represent their interests in public policy-making. In politics, roughly similar political parties seek to represent these interests in parliament; with few exceptions, every national party can easily point to its counterpart in the other countries, ally with it, meet with it, and seek to make common policy. The same is true of the major economic and social interest groups.

This suggests a second major homogeneity, the similarity in feelings and expectations experienced by the major elite groups. A similarity in situation and the opportunity for getting together has triggered a commonality of outlook among socialists, as among

Reprinted from "The Uniting of Europe and the Uniting of Latin America," *Journal of Common Market Studies*, 5 No. 4 (June, 1967), pp. 320-331, by permission of Basil Blackwell, Publisher. Footnotes omitted by the editors.

christian democrats, among farmers, among miners, among insurance under-writers as among bottle manufacturers. Complementarity in expectations is furthered by a very high rate of trade, mail, visits, tourism which already existed in 1950 but which increased three- or four-fold since then. The picture may be more accurately summed up under the phrase 'symmetrical heterogeneity': each country is fragmented along the lines of pluralism; but each group or class has its counterpart in the neighbouring country. In other words, no country is internally homogeneous, but the lines of cleavage and interest are regionally homogeneous. . . .

A final homogeneity must be stressed: the bureaucratization of decision-making. European civil services are very similar to each other. Each stresses high professional competence and a certain peremptory style in the authority of administrative decisions. Each is accustomed to working with voluntary groups, to listen, to persuade, to combine the inducements of the carrot and the stick in obtaining public consent for public policy. No wonder, then, it proved relatively simple to arrive at regional administrative decisions through continuous bargaining and study among national civil servants, aided by supranational officials no different in training and outlook from their national colleagues.

These structural features, put into the context of the nationalism of the years following World War II, go a long way in explaining why supranational economic integration went as far as it did go. The explanation can be summed up in the phrase 'the expansive logic of functionalism'; it provided the bulk of my book *The Uniting of Europe*; it seemed to provide a complete explanation in 1958. Subject to the amendments to be introduced below it remains valid and useful to others who would use common markets and economic inter-dependence as a means to promote political unity.

The national situation in each West European country later involved in the European Community was such as to make people look for solutions to their problems in a framework larger than the discredited nation-state. The nation-state seemed unable to guarantee economic welfare, military security, or the enjoyment of democracy and human rights. Each nation possessed many groups which questioned the utility of national autarky, even if each group did so for its own reasons. However, the disenchantment was shared across the frontiers so that the lack of faith in the nation was expressed in the formation of a series of regional voluntary associations—of diverse ideological persuasions—each eager to safeguard the new lease gained on the democratic way of life as a result of the defeat of Fascism. Some wanted merely freer trade and investment; others wanted a full-fledged federation; all shared a sense of frustration. But far from wanting to create a new society, to innovate, to make a new kind of man, each merely sought to safeguard an *existing way of life* given a new birth through victory in World War II. . . . Regional unification was, in a sense, a conservative impulse: it sought to innovate in order to preserve something already existing.

Federalism was the initial watchword. European unity was hailed with glowing phrases by Winston Churchill, Léon Blum, Alcide de Gasperi, Salvador de Madariaga. A 'European Movement' was formed which sought to achieve federation by stressing the cultural unity of Western civilization and which drew heavily on the misery of Europe, overshadowed by the new giants of East and West. The pan-European ideal first enunciated by Count Coudenhove-Kalergi in 1923, extolling Europe to seek survival in a world increasingly dominated by the United States and the Soviet Union, was hailed once more. The result was failure: no federal institutions were created, no uniform enthusiasm for federation could be mobilized in equal measure on the continent, in Britain and in Scandinavia. The record of failure stretched from the creation of the far-from-federal Council of Europe, through the defeat of the European Defence Community treaty to the burial of the European Political Community project in 1954.

Something else happened instead which gave rise to the theory of gradual functional integration. Not cultural unity, but economic advantage proved to be an acceptable shared goal among the Six. The failure of the federalist European Movement saw the rise of the 'functionalist' school of technocrats led by Jean Monnet, the architect of France's post-war economic planning structure. Each of the Six, for individual national reasons, and *not* because of a clear common purpose, found it possible and desirable to embark on the road of economic integration using supranational institutions. Converging practical goals provided the leaven out of which the bread of European unity was baked. It was not the fear of the Soviet Union nor the envy of the United States which did the job. Slogans of the past glories of Charlemagne, of the popes, of western civilization were certainly heard; but they did not launch the Coal and Steel Community, the Atomic Energy Community, the European Parliament, the Court of Justice, or the Economic Community. Converging economic goals, embedded in the bureaucratic, pluralistic and industrial life of modern Europe provided the crucial impetus. The economic technician, the planner, the innovating industrialist and trade unionist advanced the movement, not the politician, the scholar, the poet or the writer.

Does the argument assert the victory of economics over politics, then? To do so would be to oversimplify unforgivably. Politicians *were* important in the process. Economic reasoning alone was not sufficient. When the Coal and Steel Community ran up against the limits of what integrative action it was permitted under its treaty, it could not simply expand its powers along the lines of economic needs. Unfulfilled economic promise could not simply and painlessly give rise to new supranational economic tasks, pushing the continent closer to political unity. Politics remained imbedded in the functional logic.

How? The decline of the old national consciousness in Europe brought with it the submerging of the traditional notion of 'high politics'. The new national situation changed the possibilities of strong and independent diplomatic moves on the world stage. Those who tried them—Britain in Greece, France in Indo-China—soon recognized their error. The sharp line between the politics of economic welfare at home and the politics of national self-assertion abroad simply disappeared. Men thought in terms of realizing the welfare state, of trimming world commitments and an independent foreign policy to the economic and fiscal demands of domestic welfare. Economics and politics became intermingled, and only a Churchill or a de Gaulle could keep the older vision of high politics alive. But, then, the Europe of the 1950's listened to neither. However, the decision to follow the gospel of Jean Monnet rather than that of the Federalists—which was 'political' in a pure sense—rested on a political commitment to realize peace and welfare by way of European unification. The statesmen who wrote the treaties of the European Communities, and who guided them through their national parliaments, were committed to the gradual, the indirect, the functional path towards political unity, They knew, or sensed, that the imperfections of one treaty and one policy would give rise to re-evaluations which would lead to new commitments and new policies moving farther along the road to unification. No federal utopia necessarily provided the guiding beacon. But an institutionally vague 'supranational' Europe did light the way. The logic of functional integration could move forward, then, because key politicians—Schuman, Adenauer, Spaak, Beyen, de Gasperi, Van Zeeland, Fanfani—had simply decided to leave the game of high politics and devote themselves to the building of Europe, to achieve more modest aims. And thus the economic technician could play his role within the shelter of the politicians' support.

In my book *The Uniting of Europe* the story stops in 1958. What have been the events in European integration since? Did the functional logic continue to work its way toward greater unity?

With the inauguration of the European Economic Community (EEC) the focus of integrative and disintegrative activity shifted from Luxembourg to Brussels, from coal and steel to tariff cutting, rules of competition and agriculture, from well-defined economic sectors to talk of political unity. The Coal and Steel Community continues to exist, but it is but a shadow of the vital institution described earlier. It has become a technical agency, concerned with improving the quality of steel and the demand for steel products, with negotiating a common European policy for oil, gas, nuclear energy and coal, with adapting a dying coal-mining industry to the demands of a different market for energy. It is no longer concerned with the more politically infused activities of regulating prices, eliminating subsidies and standardizing transport rates. The supreme effort at asserting its powers—in the effort to impose coal production quotas—was rebuffed by three of the six governments in 1959. The European Atomic Energy Community, by contrast, never attained the role played by the Coal and Steel Community. Despite the wide planning and control powers written into its treaty, Euratom has remained a technical and research agency.

The functional logic, however, was long carried further by EEC, whose leading official, President Walter Hallstein, even referred to his Commission as the engine of European integration. Until 1965 EEC seemed to bear out these brave words. Tariffs and quantitative restrictions in trade among the member states were progressively cut ahead of the schedule laid down in the Treaty, so that by mid-1968 they will be eliminated altogether. The common external tariff was negotiated. Commercial agreements were concluded, on behalf of the Community, with a half dozen foreign countries. The Commission negotiates on behalf of the six member states in GATT. Uniform rules of competition and industrial concentration were introduced in the six countries. A freer market for foreign labour was created. Agriculture, the stepchild of the modern industrial state, was subjected to common rules, pricing and protection—even though the financing of agricultural subsidies was the issue on which de Gaulle chose to fight his battle in 1965. More important still, the EEC Bank advances credit to industries in underdeveloped regions within Europe, and its Social Fund finances the retraining of displaced workers. Finally, EEC takes the initiative in regional economic forecasting and in seeking to approach a regional monetary policy by way of continuous discussion among central bankers. Some taxes have been unified and a common transport policy is being studied.

These activities come close to voiding the power of the national state in all realms other than defence, education and foreign policy. In the realm of methods of decision-making and institutions the work of EEC is equally striking. Most major economic decisions are made by the Council of Ministers on the basis of proposals by the Commission and, after negotiations conducted by the Commission, at the level of senior civil servants. While decisions required more and more prolonged 'marathon' negotiations after 1961, agreement was always eventually attained, usually resulting in increased powers for the Commission to make possible the implementation of what was decided. This is true particularly in the case of agriculture. In the process, the Commission established and cultivated direct relations with supranational interest groups of farmers, industrialists, merchants and workers; it cemented its relations with national officials; it gave the politicians and political parties represented in the European Parliament the opportunity to study, debate and criticize policy in considerable detail and on a continuing basis. Finally, it took the kinds of crucial decisions which prompted extensive and far-reaching litigation in the European Court of Justice, resulting in the definition, by that Court, of a European doctrine of individual rights *vis-à-vis* the actions of national courts and administrative agencies, as implied by the Treaty of Rome and enforceable by the Community.

The irony of the functional logic is underscored by the fact that these developments had not all been planned or approved by the governments. It is underscored further by the fact that the growth in the power of the Commission occurred in several instances as a result of bargains with the French government. For instance, the defeat of the British effort to scuttle the Common Market with the free trade area scheme discussed in 1958 and 1959 was due to an *ad hoc* alliance between France and the Commission. The victory of the French-flavoured policy for agriculture, prior to 1965, was mixed with the growing institutional authority of Commission-controlled marketing committees and a policy with respect to a lower external tariff favoured by the Commission. No single government or coalition controlled the decision-making process. The Commission, because of its power of initiative, was able to construct a different coalition of supporting governments on each major issue. In short, the functional logic which may lead, more or less automatically, from a common market to political unification, seemed to be neatly illustrated by the history of EEC.

How, then, could a single charismatic Frenchman stop the process? Word has it that not even the French negotiators in Brussels, in July of 1965, believed that the sessions then under way would lead to anything other than a last-minute comprehensive compromise agreement of real scope. But the General surprised his own staff, along with the rest of Europe. Has the pragmatic politics of regional negotiation for greater welfare benefits given way once more to high politics?

De Gaulle's sentiments toward supranational institutions—as distinguished from the policies they produce—was made perfectly plain in his statement to the press which we quoted above. In the grand style of high politics it is more important to resist the encroachment of supranational technocrats on the nation than it is to negotiate higher prices and subsidies, even if paid by Germans to the French farmer. We can only surmise the thoughts and calculations which passed through the General's oracular mind. But the results of our surmises add up to a rebirth of nationalism and anti-functional high politics as far as France is concerned. The Commission and the other five governments, while not sharing the sentiments leading to these results, in effect fell into a political trap set by de Gaulle and were thus forced to play politics once more.

De Gaulle had been perfectly willing to use the Common Market and the EEC apparatus in a larger game of welding Europe together under a French political umbrella, to make Europe 'truly independent' by dislodging the United States from the continent. The game proved a failure: his scheme for a political confederation which would absorb the economic communities was rejected by the other five; his bilateral alliance with Germany brought no results as the government of Ludwig Erhard embraced the American-sponsored

Multilateral Nuclear Force and attempted to achieve German security with American rather than French help; his attacks on NATO merely underscored his diplomatic isolation from his five economic partners. Continuation of the economic integration process thus seemed to make France more dependent on Europe without making Europe fall into line with French foreign policy. A common foreign and defence policy for Europe was de Gaulle's aim. The unwillingness of his partners to concede these items must have made de Gaulle wonder what the further advantages of economic unity might be if they entailed the loss of political sovereignty.

And French sovereignty was indeed threatened. According to the timetable of the Treaty of Rome, the Community was to pass into its third transitional stage on January 1, 1966. As of that date, positive decisions in the Council of Ministers could be made by majority vote; negative decisions overruling the Commission required unanimity. The powers of the Commission would increase finally and irrevocably. Progress toward ever more politically sensitive economic decisions, possibly over French dissent, would become automatic. De Gaulle struck while he could, sacrificing the benefits accruing to the French farmer. He did so by taking advantage of a political gambit launched by the Commission in the spring of 1965. The EEC technocrats, perhaps fearing that once France had obtained concessions on agricultural policy she would no longer have any interest in further integrative decisions, sought to pre-empt the political initiative. The Commission urged that the pro-French agricultural measures be accompanied by new powers for the Commission in the financial field. The yield of the common external tariff, up to four billion dollars per year, was to go to the Commission, the distribution of agricultural subsidies was to be handled by Brussels, and the European Parliament was to receive legislative powers in dealing with agriculture. In other words, the members of the Commission themselves may not have trusted to any indefinite automatic quality in the economic integration process.

And so the Commission fell into the General's trap. It violated its official technocratic style by making an open political bid. We know the results. The protests and frustrations of the other five governments availed them little. When forced by France to choose between the continued economic benefits of the Common Market and dedication to the supranational method of decision-making, they preferred the former. De Gaulle, apparently relying on the economic instincts of his partners, gave them a brutal choice by saying: 'France wants the Common Market as much as you; if you really want it, join me in preserving it, but restrain supranationality'. In January of 1966, the Council of Ministers voted to adhere indefinitely to a unanimous voting formula. High politics may not have taken the place of pragmatic economic calculation for all the players in the game; but if one of them so defines the situation, the others seem compelled to follow suit.

This sequence of events suggests that something is missing in the exploration of the integrative process presented in *The Uniting of Europe*. The phenomenon of a de Gaulle is omitted; the superiority of step-by-step economic decisions over crucial political choices is assumed as permanent; the determinism implicit in the picture of the European social and economic structure is almost absolute. Given all these conditions, we said, the progression from a politically inspired common market to an economic union, and finally to a political union among states, is automatic. The inherent logic of the functional process, in a setting such as Western Europe, can push no other way.

De Gaulle has proved us wrong. But how wrong? Is the theory beyond rescue? I suggest that the theory can be amended with the lessons de Gaulle has taught us and still tell us something about the logic of functional integration among nations. The chief item in this lesson is the recognition that pragmatic interest politics, concerned with economic welfare, has its own built-in-limits. Put differently, pragmatic interest politics is its own worst enemy. The politician and the businessman who has abandoned an interest in high politics and devotes himself only to the maximization of his daily welfare is compelled, by virtue of that very concern, to make concessions to another actor who forces him to choose so as to sacrifice welfare. Pragmatic interests, simply because they are pragmatic and not reinforced with deep ideological or philosophical commitment, are ephemeral. Just because they are weakly held they can be readily scrapped. And a political process which is built and projected from pragmatic interests, therefore, is bound to be a frail process, susceptible to reversal. And so integration can once more develop into disintegration.

With this amendment to our treatment of the logic of functionalism we can once more examine the character of political and economic decisions. Integrative decisions based on high politics and basic commitment are undoubtedly more durable than decisions based on converging pragmatic expectations. A process of integration spurred by the vision, the energy and force of a Bismarck, a Cavour or a Disraeli is clearly more productive of permanence than an indirect process fed by the slow fuel of economic expectations. On that type of scale, a Bismarck and a de Gaulle will always be more effective than a Monnet, a Hallstein, or an Erhard.

But the fact of the matter is that Europe did not have a Bismarck in 1948 or 1950. . . . In the absence of the statesman who can weld disparate publics together with the force of his vision, his commitment, and his physical power, we have no alternative, if we wish to integrate a region, but to resort to gradualism, to indirection, to functionalism. Pragmatic interests may be weak, but they are real nonetheless. The reliance on high politics demands either a statesman of this calibre or a widely shared normative consensus. In most actual situations in which regional integration is desired, neither ingredient is present in sufficient quantity.

Now the functionalist who relies on gradualism and indirection in achieving his goal must choose a strategy which will unite many people and alienate few. He can only move in small steps and without a clear logical plan because, if he moved in bold steps and in masterful fashion, he would lose the support of many supporters. He must make decisions 'incrementally', step by step, often in a very untidy fashion. The more pluralistic the society in which he labours, the more groups require satisfaction, the more disjointed and incremental the decision-making process will be. Everyone will receive a little, few groups will be deprived, few groups will receive a sudden large gift. If nothing happens to interfere with the incremental process the society or region in which this occurs will be transformed eventually into a larger entity. Incrementalism is the decision-making style of successful functionalism, if left undisturbed; in Europe, however, it was disturbed by de Gaulle.

And, true to our finding above, incremental processes, because they rest on pragmatic interests, are always subject to reversal. Just as pragmatic interest politics is its own worst enemy, so is the incremental decision-making style. While the Commission's policy, in the summer of 1965, remained within the incremental approach to political union, it began to stray far enough away from it to offer de Gaulle, given to a more heroic and direct approach, his excuse for bringing incrementalism to a halt.

This discussion of various decision-making styles brings us back to the distinction between frankly political choices and the more covert economic choices with hidden political implications, which stand at the heart of the politics of common markets. Regional integration can go forward smoothly if, as in the case of the heroic statesman-leader, there is a shared political commitment between him and the major elites in society in favour of union. This is precisely the condition that, in a pluralistic setting, cannot be expected to occur very often. Otherwise integration can go forward gradually and haltingly if both leaders and major elites share an incremental commitment to modest aims and pragmatic steps. The difficulty arises when the consensus between statesmen and major non-governmental elites is more elusive and temporary. An incremental commitment to economic aims among the leaders will not lead to smooth integration if the major elites are committed to dramatic political steps. More commonly, a political commitment to integration by the statesmen will rest on very shaky ground if the interests of the major elites are economic; they rest on an even weaker basis if the statesman's commitment is to national grandeur and the elites' to economic gradualism, as in the case of contemporary France. These relationships, then, amend our theses in the book. They can be represented in matrix form:

| | | Aims of Non-Governmental Elites | |
		Dramatic-Political	Incremental-Economic
Aims of Statesmen	Dramatic-Political	Integration either direct and smooth; or impossible	Integration erratic and reversible
	Incremental-Economic	Integration erratic and reversible	Integration gradual but automatic

This revision of the dynamics of supranational decision-making has a number of more specific implications. I have shown elsewhere how the incremental style of approaching the major policy choices involved in common markets and political unions depends on a certain pattern of pluralistic politics at the national level, as well as on a certain type of social and economic structure intimately related to industrialism and rational large-scale organizations. Political parties and interest groups avoiding sharp ideological conflict are essential; social units always able to unite and reunite in ever-changing coalitions are necessary at the national as well as the regional level. And the technical decisions always incorporated in the major choices must be made by technocrats; indeed, the leading role of the technocrat is indispensable in a process as close to the heart of the industrial economy as is the formation of common markets.

Hence integration is most nearly automatic when these forces are given maximal play, as is the case when both statesmen and elites entertain converging incremental-economic objectives. Until the French veto of 1963, with respect to the entry of Britain into EEC, the supranational European decision-making style was as described by Lindberg:

The members of the Community do not confront each other only or chiefly as diplomatic gladiators; they encounter each other at almost every level of organized society through constant interaction in the joint policy-making contexts of officials, parliamentarians, interest group leaders, businessmen, farmers, and trade unionists. Conflicts of interest and purpose are inevitable. There is no paradox between the progress of economic integration in the Community and sharpening political disagreement; indeed, the success of economic integration can be a cause of political disagreement. The member states are engaged in the enterprise for widely different reasons, and their actions have been supported or instigated by elites seeking their own particular goals. Therefore, conflicts would seem endemic as the results of joint activity come to be felt and as the pro-integration consensus shifts.

As more and more difficult choices become necessary, as the community moves from a mere customs union to an economic union and a political entity, the propensity for conflict increases. Hence it becomes imperative that the bargaining include the possibility of mutual concessions of roughly equal value, linked to a style of pragmatic moderation. Charisma and national self-assertion are clearly the worst enemies of this process. Benefits from concessions may have to involve calculated risks and gambles with respect to the future; a concession in the realm of agriculture may have to be reciprocated in the field of transport, or even in the form of a new institutional arrangement. The reintroduction of a dramatic political objective, even if only by one important member state, exposes the frailty of this process.

The strong political leader possesses an additional advantage over the functionalist when he can continue to hold out the possibility of rewards to non-government elites and the people at large while rejecting the supranational method of regional economic decision-making. This de Gaulle did in 1965 and 1966 when he gave his partners the choice between no common market and a common market without supranational powers. The very fact that the attachment of many elites to a United Europe is pragmatic and rests on incremental processes makes the supranational method dispensable. As long as the benefits of the common market are more important in people's minds than the means used to achieve these benefits, institutions and procedures can be sacrificed. The very success of the incremental method becomes self-defeating as important elites recognize that welfare can be safeguarded without a strong Commission and overt political unity. And the fact of the matter is that very few important European interest groups had embraced supranationality as a principle in itself, even though they had easily accommodated themselves to it in order to safeguard specific group aims. My book describes the process of accommodation, but it failed to spell out the limits here discovered.

This brings us back to the national situation. The functional logic which leads from national frustration to economic unity, and eventually, to political unification, presupposes that national consciousness is weak and that the national situation is perceived as gloomy. To be sure, the situation may improve. If integration has gone very far by then, no harm is done to the union; but in Europe it had not gone far enough before the national situation improved once more, before self-confidence rose, thus making the political healing power of union once more questionable. . . .

28

DAVID P. CALLEO

The Common Market and Federalist Europe

A great deal has been written about the unique organization of the European Communities. They are a blend of national and supranational elements which makes their structure unlike that of any national state. There is the Council of Ministers to represent the national governments, the Commission made up of supranational functionaries, the European Parliament with delegates chosen by the national parliaments, and the High Court of Justice. In classic terms, the Commission is the executive, the Council the legislature, and the Court the judiciary. The European Parliament serves as a forum to draw out and focus public opinion but has little role in legislation.

Policies result from a complex dialogue between the Council and the Commission. It is the Council which has the final say and, until 1966 at least, each member state has a veto. On the other hand, the Commission has substantial political powers of its own aside from its inevitable strength as the chief administrator of policies once they are made. The Commission, for example, has

Reprinted from *Europe's Future: The Grand Alternatives* by David P. Calleo, pp. 52-68, by permission of the publishers, Horizon Press, New York, copyright © 1965. Footnotes omitted by the editors.

great influence over the substance of Council debates. In most matters, only the Commission can initiate and formulate the actual proposals before the Council—a power which gives the Commission, among other things, a formal veto in the Council.

Furthermore, the Commission is reasonably independent. The Treaty insists that Commission members not be subject to instructions from their own governments and that they be appointed for long terms. Many are high civil servants of recognized ability and substance in their own countries. There is every indication that their personal independence has in fact been respected. They may not be in a position to take an intransigently hostile attitude towards the national governments—a determined government could probably destroy the position of any member of the Commission—but on the other hand, a Commissioner with such a provocative disposition would not contribute much to the Commission's work, for its chief role is that of an inspired mediator, coaxing the national states into agreement.

It is generally agreed that the extraordinary progress of the Common Market would have been impossible without the supranational Commission. As an institutionalized mediator with independent powers of initiative, it has often acted in Council debates as a catalyst, inspiring decisions that do in fact seem to represent a common European interest rather than an old-fashioned diplomatic compromise of separate and conflicting national aims. The Commission's role is self-consciously political rather than merely technical. It has actively sought to embody the "European" interest in the Council. Its identity with Europe makes it easier for the national governments to give in to the Commission than to one another. Altruism is more popular at home than appeasement. It is easier for Frenchmen to make sacrifices to Europe than to Germany.

The successes of the Commission, of course, are possible only because of the active cooperation of the national governments. Economic integration has not in reality come about through technocratic magic. A great many problems are completely insoluble on a technical level and in many issues diplomatic charm cannot mask the brutal truth that someone must lose. Agriculture is perhaps the most notable example. The best way to block agreement on such issues is to leave negotiations to technical experts alone. Solutions come only after politicians decide that the general advantages of agreement are worth the cost to their particular national interests. Only the states can make that decision. While the independent mediating role of the Commission has been a necessary condition of the success of the enterprise, it would not have been sufficient if the states had lost their fundamental will to pay the necessary costs to create a common European economy.

Writers on the Common Market have perhaps tended to place too much emphasis on the role of the Commission and not enough on that of the Council itself. The preoccupation is understandable. Among the Commission's skills, public relations is not the least. Furthermore, the Commission is a genuine institutional novelty and hence of great interest to the professional student. But it is at least as great a novelty that six European governments have sustained for so many years so constant a devotion to the success of an international institution which enters into a vital area of their national life. Given that will, it has been possible for the Commission to find a way.

Particularly striking is the degree to which, in a number of the most critical issues, the position of the French government has been close to that of the Commission. Indeed, it is quite possible to argue that, of all the national governments, it is de Gaulle's France which has supported most vigorously and constantly the first aim of the Rome Treaty, the creation of a genuinely integrated European economy. It is obvious that similar policies can have quite different ends in view. De Gaulle, in spite of his crucial and indeed indispensable aid to the specific goal of the Rome Treaty, economic integration, has a more dubious claim to being the chief supporter of the ultimate purpose of that treaty, political integration. He shares not at all the Commission's avowed aim of transforming the present supranational communities into a federal governing structure for Europe. Nevertheless, de Gaulle, in following his own purposes, has made it possible for the European Economic Community to advance far along the way towards the creation of a European economy. The question is whether in doing so he has unwittingly also advanced the cause of eventual political unity under the same supranational arrangements. That, of course, is the crucial question. Though the Commission's official view is perhaps more cautious, many who expect European union to grow out of the Common Market believe that economic integration will in itself almost inevitably lead to political union.

The basis for the confident hopes of the faithful is the so-called "spill-over effect" which has become the cherished theory—it might almost be said the ideology—of the avid partisans of the Common Market. Economic integration is believed to have an irresistible inner logic, as stated succinctly by the President of the Common Market Commission, Walter Hallstein: "Like the alphabet, all economic policy has an inner unity which is stronger than any arbitrary action of political powers." The federalizing tendencies of economic union will spill over into politics until national governments finally will have ceded so much of their power that European unity will have occurred in fact before it is conceded in principle. " 'Political' integration is not a condition of economic integration but its consequence." What are the basic tenets of this sanguine theory, the ideology of the Common Market?

The whole process by which the Common Market has worked towards integrating the Six into a common economy has been carefully studied with an eye to determining the inner logic of that process and the conditions that have helped or hindered it. There have been several attempts to formulate a general theory purporting to spell out the conditions which enable an international organization to become the nucleus for the eventual political integration of its members. Political integration is seen as the process by which member states give up making key public policies independently and instead make them jointly within a supranational cadre or pass them on to a new supranational administration.

Under the right conditions, it is said, the federalizing process of moving decisions to a new center accelerates from an inherent dynamism. As the new center gains importance, significant individuals and groups in society shift their attention and activities towards it. And with this shifting of attention and activity, new loyalties and allegiances are gradually developed. Up to a certain point, even conflicts among members are thought to hasten integration. Experience indicates that the most generally acceptable solution is that which can claim to be "in the Community interest." Such solutions generally result in a fresh delegation of power to the new center.

The whole integrating process, it is said, can take place quite apart from forces in the world of ideas and general public opinion. Thus, under the right conditions, there is felt to be in the process itself an internal dynamism which hurries it along faster the farther it has gone.

What are thought to be the right conditions? To begin with, the institutions which develop policies must actually exist. The importance of their tasks must be recognized if they are to stir up significant social and economic forces within the separate countries. The tasks, in addition, must be inherently expansive and thus tend to increase the role of the new central institutions. Finally, if the dynamism is to continue, the member states must continue to see their interests as consistent with the whole supranational enterprise. If these conditions exist, then it can be expected that there will be an inner push towards greater and greater concentration of power, attention, and loyalty towards the new center. Do these general theories of integration apply to the Common Market?

Obviously, and not surprisingly, they do. Elaborate and effective central institutions exist. Certainly, the task involved, to form a common European economy, is sufficiently interesting to arouse significant national, social, and economic forces within the member countries. But are the tasks of economic integration inherently expansive and, if so, will their expansiveness lead to a European government? The answer is believed to be tied to the fourth condition: will the member states continue to see their interests as consistent with the whole supranational enterprise?

For those involved with the Common Market, it seems an article of faith that the economic functions it performs are expansive, that a European federal government is only a logical development of the forces already set to work, and finally that the process has already gone so far as to be nearly irreversible by any member state.

As tariff barriers fall, the official argument runs, competition is increasingly between separate firms rather than whole national economies, and it becomes more and more essential that the conditions of competition be roughly the same throughout the whole market. Otherwise some individual firms are given special advantages. Where taxes, wages, laws and regulations, energy prices, or transportation costs are markedly different, those areas which impose unfavorable conditions will inevitably suffer. The natural tendency, then, is towards as much uniformity as possible.

Hence economic integration is expected to impose a great check on the freedom of action of the national governments. General laws and regulations that affect business will have to be harmonized, and wages, social security, and welfare costs equalized. The costs of raw materials cannot be allowed to differ markedly and so there must be a common external tariff. Taxes, or even the method of taxation, cannot vary too much without affecting competition, and therefore a limit is placed upon the ability of one government to follow unique policies that are extremely expensive. There might seem to be a limit, for example, on how much a government could spend on defense without cutting its other expenditures. A common economy would seem to imply a common trade or commercial policy towards the outside world. And it seems only reasonable, as in the present trade talks between the EEC and the United States, that the negotiations should be conducted by the Commission acting for the whole Community rather than by each member state separately. Since foreign policy is closely related to trade, economic integration can be expected to press towards a single foreign policy as well.

In a world where economic planning is commonplace, it is argued, progressive economic integration will lead to strong pressure for positive policies from a source that plans for the whole European economy. Fiscal policies will have to be in general harmony. It will not be reasonable to have a deflationary policy in one area and an inflationary one in another. As planning centers more and more around the supranational Community, its decisions will naturally have an increasing effect on the daily lives of the people of Europe. As present, the Community institutions are notable in that they appear so remote from popular control. In the democratic West, it is unacceptable that power should not be responsible to elected representatives of the people. Therefore, a popularly elected political body, a genuine European Parliament, can be expected to follow inevitably. Thus, according to the official ideology, the inexorable logic of economic integration is moving Europe slowly towards political union.

The Common Market argument is powerful and seductive. Does it accord with the facts? What are the real prospects for political unity to develop from economic integration alone? While the degree to which economic integration inhibits independent governmental policies may be exaggerated, there is no question but that continuing economic fusion calls for at least some increase in political unity. But will economic integration necessarily continue advancing? Can it be stopped or reversed?

At the present time, it is the national governments which hold the keys to the future. The progress of the Common Market depends upon their policies in the Council. It is almost axiomatic that the process of economic integration will continue as long as the member governments find its advance in their interest. It may also be true that the true economic interests of all Europe lie with economic and political union. But the crude Marxist premise that economic considerations determine political events is blatantly untrue.

Nations, communist nations above all, are constantly undertaking policies which are economically harmful if not ruinous in pursuit of goals which seem more important to them than the extra margin of economic well-being. Nations have been known to go to war and assume untold economic damage for the sake of honor, pride, grandeur, power, or faith. Economic growth does indeed have a logic of development, an idea of its own, but then so does nationalism. And time and time again in the past two centuries, the dynamics of nationalism have triumphed over the apparent logic of economics.

But although economic factors may not determine everything, they certainly pose a certain limit beyond which national policy cannot go without being self-destructive. The great question is whether a national government of the Six could now afford to pull out. Has it already become too costly to withdraw? When will the dynamic process have advanced so far that the Common Market can assume the continuing commitment of the national states?

At the present stage of unity, it is generally felt that a national government could withdraw, although the economic repercussions would be severe and therefore not lightly assumed by any popularly elected government in an opulent Western society. There are knowledgeable government officials who argue, at least privately, that the costs of withdrawing have been greatly exaggerated. They argue that although the increase in trade among the Six has been enormous, it is by no means clear that the increase which has taken place within the Common Market has taken place because of it. Some economists have maintained that the rapid increase of trade among developed countries is a universal phenomenon and would have happened in Europe with or without the Common Market. Furthermore, the whole general tendency towards an Atlantic market embodied in the Kennedy Round may change the particular relationship of the Six. Hence a state might withdraw without necessarily suffering a drastic cut, even in its European trade. And while formidable tariff barriers, should they exist, might close off foreign markets, they could also eliminate foreign competitors in the domestic market.

It is significant, however, that the big businessmen who weigh these gains and losses in their own affairs, are among the most vociferous supporters of the Common Market. Their support is a great source of comfort to the Communities. Especially enthusiastic are those giant industries which are too developed for their own national markets—such as Belgian steel or Dutch agriculture. But efficient or at least imaginative business everywhere seems to welcome the Continental market. French industrialists, once fearful and protectionist, are now among the strongest supporters of the EEC. Furthermore, with their strong national predilection for planning, they are among the most insistent advocates of more central power to assure the safeguards, control, and harmonization they believe necessary to make the European economy realize efficiently its potential. Hence, the Common Market can claim that there has been a fundamental change in the perspectives and habits of European businessmen. Business in Europe is committed to integration and it would be extremely difficult for a national government to reverse that commitment.

Skeptics argue that big business has always been internationalist. There have always been agreements and personal contact among European businessmen. The conditions for carrying on international business in Europe still have a long way to go before they reach the ease that was commonplace before the First World War. Even Hallstein admits that the Common Market is hoping to restore that freedom of trade which existed before war and economic crises caused "the old pattern of world trade" to disappear. And while there have been numerous agreements among similar industries, skeptics continue, there has in fact been remarkably little supranational merging among the Six themselves. Figures showing the relative degree of investment of the Six in each other are hard to come by, but some seasoned observers claim that as yet it is surprisingly slight. National firms have tended either to remain national or to merge with giant American companies. It seems as if American capital will be the federalizer of European business and not the Common Market. The tendency of European firms to go to the United States for capital is widely deplored, but as yet there is nothing like an adequate capital market within the Six.

Another factor cited by those who seek to minimize the permanence of integration is the supposed tendency of each national economy to move towards greater autarchy rather than towards a genuine Continental rationalization. Each nation, it is argued, instead of concentrating further on what it does best, has tended to develop its own full range of manufactures and thus in fact reduce its eventual dependence on its neighbors. Italy, for example, has developed a steel industry.

No doubt there is a good deal to some of these skeptical arguments. European economic integration must travel a long way before it is possible to speak of an indivisible Continental economy from which no sane government would possibly withdraw. But certainly important progress towards integration has been made. And however inconclusive previous moves may have been, the agricultural agreements of 1962 and 1964 are unquestionably a major if not irrevocable step. Ironically, it is the country ostensibly the most concerned with guarding its national independence, France, which would appear to be the most committed by the new agreements.

The net result of a common market in agriculture is that the French have succeeded in throwing the burden of their surplus on the rest of Europe. These arrangements are hardly natural. The Germans could buy food more cheaply outside Europe and by doing so help win markets for their manufactures. The French, through the politics of European integration, have solved a serious domestic situation. Any French government that renounced these new advantages would be taking grave political risks at home. On the other hand, the common market in agriculture would seem to imply or even to require further integration which cannot help but limit the political independence so cherished by Gaullist France.

The agricultural common market, because it requires so much conscious contrivance, illustrates to a heightened degree the dynamic tendency of economic integration to expand from one field to the next and to pass over into politics. To have a common market in agriculture, it is essential to have a common central regulatory organization which, among other things, sets common support prices for every commodity. The artificially controlled prices must be roughly the same throughout the Six. Since prices are expressed in terms of national currency, it is now argued that no European country can devalue its currency without raising its food prices. Otherwise food prices in one country would be lower than in the others, dumping would result, and the whole system would be deranged. On the other hand, if the devaluing country raised its domestic food prices, it would seriously undermine the effects of devaluation. The net result, the argument runs, is that it is no longer possible for one of the Six to devalue, not at any rate without destroying the Common Market, at least in agriculture. Since devaluation is generally seen as the ultimate weapon of a government which is following policies which make its industries noncompetitive—too high taxes for the soaring costs of a nuclear deterrent, for example—it is felt that the agricultural agreements in the Common Market will impose a strong monetary and fiscal discipline on all states and point towards a common fiscal policy.

Not only, however, does the supranational solution to France's agricultural problem lead to important new curbs on national independence, but it results in a major increase in power to the Community itself. It is the Commission which is to administer the complex program with the huge sums necessary to finance it. Not content with this substantial accretion of power to the Community, the Commission seized the occasion to propose that all tariff revenues should go to the Community and that the European Parliament should have a voice in the disposition of the huge sums that would be involved. Furthermore, the Commission has argued that since the Community pays to support Europe's farmers, it should have a veto over any export sales below the support price. Such power would be an important step towards a common commercial policy towards the outside world, and would, in turn, seriously impinge on national control over trade agreements, an important weapon of peaceful diplomacy. In short, there seem to be few limits to this imaginative train of logical extensions following from agricultural integration.

In summary, the technical arguments over how much integration has occurred are so complex and debatable that they seem beyond the power of laymen to understand or professionals to agree upon. There does appear, nevertheless, to be a logic to economic development which leads even the most recalcitrant governments into limitations on their independence from which they probably cannot escape without pulling out of the Common Market—a costly step. The Six could break up, but even if they continue to compose their differences, does that mean that the spill-over process of economic and political integration will necessarily go on until Europe has a federal government? Not necessarily.

To achieve a certain degree of integration is one thing, to go on with it is another. There is no mindless inevitable law of economics which compels the transition. States are free agents in the same sense that any conscious being is free. They are hedged in by circumstances, but they have a number of choices before them. If they cannot afford the increased independence that would come from pulling out of the Common Market, there is nothing which compels them to sacrifice further independence for further economic gains. Moreover, even assuming that integration does prevent governments from raising taxes beyond the general level, that may not be in itself a serious handicap to independence. Proponents of General de Gaulle's *force de frappe*, for example, argue that it costs less than an old-fashioned army. France, while building an atomic force, formally reduced her military budget by a great deal. An expanding economy offers any government the opportunity to increase substantially its expenditures in any one field without either raising taxes or cutting back in other fields. It can be argued perversely that the Common Market, by strengthening the economies of the members, has increased their means of political independence.

Even if it is true that more and more national decisions will have to be referred to the Community at Brussels, it would be unrealistic to equate growth in the importance of Community decisions with an increase of supranational at the expense of national power. The Community, after all, means the Council as well as the Commission. The success of the Community institutions has always depended upon the active political will of the member states. If the political will to integrate the European economy disappeared, the "miracle" in Brussels might continue, but would not progress. The death of

Europe would not necessarily be dramatic. Problems would simply be left to the experts and hence remain unsolved.

While the national veto is supposed to be replaced in 1966 by a qualified system of majority voting, any change is likely to be only a formality.[1] Almost any one of the Six, and certainly any of the major powers, will still be able to slow down the whole process of integration, stop it altogether, or even set it back. A state can follow an "empty-chair" policy, for example, and absent itself from the Council and various working committees. Since the whole spirit of the Council is necessarily cooperative rather than coercive, the threat of such a policy might well be enough in itself to constitute a *de facto* veto.

Furthermore, the much vaunted independence of the Commission and its admittedly indispensable role as catalyst for common policies depends finally on the indulgence of the national governments. Most of the members of the Commission and its staff are national civil servants on leave from their national governments. The French, in particular, have encouraged many of their finest civil servants to take posts in the Common Market administration. By taking severe retaliation on those functionaries who showed independence, or simply by not appointing men of ability and political initiative in the first place, it would be quite possible to reduce the quality of the European civil service and hence the now admirable effectiveness of the whole organization. Once the Common Market Commission really was made up of technicians without the extraordinary political skills of the present members, the whole push towards integration would slacken. It is said that the Coal and Steel Community has suffered from just such a decline.

In short the Common Market, for all the imaginative diplomatic skill of its executive and for all the administrative responsibility it has gradually gathered to itself, is still mainly dependent on the political will of the member states. Though there is clearly a logic of integration which, if allowed free rein, tends to accelerate the federalizing process towards political unification, it is doubtful if there is any inherent force in the process itself which compels the national states to follow along to the inherent conclusion.

Unless the states will otherwise, the Common Market can easily become not a federal government for Europe, but a sort of apolitical regulatory body, with real powers of its own, to be sure, but always subject ultimately to the political control of the states. The Common Market could thus become, not the nascent government of Europe, but a bureaucratic business manager for the economies of the Continent. It would remain an institutionalized monument to a dream from the past; it would survive only because it had found a way to be useful to its masters. The supranational community would become a sort of secular church, a church whose priests were rich and powerful but in whose religion no one really believed anymore.

In short, it is difficult to accept the thesis that the success of the Common Market as a federal government is assured by an inherent, autonomous logic of economic integration. If the Common Market is to unify Europe, it must expect to change the course of history, not float along placidly on the existing current of events. While spill-over may be useful as an ideology to warm the faithful, it would seem to offer in itself a meager basis for expecting a federal Europe to grow inevitably out of the Common Market.

It may be sad to realize that no impersonal economic law guarantees their success, but fortunately the supranational Communities enjoy other sources of power than the logic of economic integration. It is somewhat unreal to study European unity as if it owed its strength to a "process" rather than an idea. For there can be few movements which illustrate better the force of ideas or which depend more upon that force. Indeed, it is probably true that the major impulse behind European unity is less economic than psychological and political. According to the President of the Commission itself: "The reasons why European unity is useful, necessary, inevitable, are quickly enumerated. They are mainly psychological. . . ." The exhilarating sense of spaciousness, liberation, and renewed power that surrounds the dream of a united Europe may be more likely to create that Europe than calculations about the advantages of large-scale marketing.

Those calculations are, in any case, usually themselves part of the larger dream. In particular, the prospect of Europe's reviving into a great power is a strong force behind the European communities. A few minutes' conversation with an ardent partisan of supranational Europe usually provides ample evidence that his nationalism has not so much died as shifted to the new nation the Communities are believed to be creating. In Hallstein's words:

> We are trying to replace one political prejudice that has for centuries past swayed human beings in Europe, that has made the political map of Europe what it is today—the national prejudice—by a better attitude, a European attitude—provided you do not take it as a piece of cynicism, I would even say: by a better, a European, prejudice.

That European force should not be underestimated, no matter how inadequate the theories or institutions with which it momentarily seeks to express itself. The Common Market has attracted such extraordinary ardor and ability that it would be premature to write off the men of Brussels along with the theories of their partisans.

Whatever the power of the new European loyalties, the individual nations are far from dead. It may well be that nationalism is discredited among Italians and above all Germans who, for understandable reasons, are desperately seeking for a new political identity. But not everyone is as eager to escape from his national past. In France, after all, nationalism produced not Hitler but de Gaulle.

The French Resistance, unlike the Italian, was intensely nationalistic. In contrast to Altiero Spinelli, the chief theorist of the French was Michel Debré.

And while a few years ago it used to be taken for granted that we were in "an era of concentration," today there is some reason to think that the impulse to unify may have depended on economic and political pressures that are to some extent subsiding. Doubtless sentiment for unity is still very strong among Europeans. But it is hardly so strong that unity can be treated as a foregone conclusion, dictated by inexorable automatic processes. For the real power of the national states remains virtually untouched. It is they alone who command the organized political loyalties of their peoples. Even in the citadel of supranational Europe, it is the states who hold the determining power.

Under the circumstances, it would not seem unreasonable to predict that the drive for a federal Europe will take its decisive step only when the supranational institutions find some way to escape from their complete dependence on the cooperation of the national governments. In a democratic world where legitimacy comes from the people, supranational Europe must ultimately find the means for a direct, organized, political relationship with the peoples it hopes to govern. Otherwise, it will never be able to challenge the national governments in the ultimately decisive arena, that is, before their own people. Until then the functionaries of Brussels may prove to be what some nationalists call them—flies of the summer, likely to be blown away by the first big storm.

FOOTNOTES

1.   In January 1966 the Council of Ministers voted to retain the unanimity requirement—Eds.

Selected Bibliography

I Western Europe in Transition

For additional discussions of the topics treated in this section, the following works are suggested:

Raymond Aron, *France: Steadfast and Changing* (Harvard University Press: Cambridge, 1960).

Ralf Dahrendorf, *Society and Democracy in Germany* (Wiedenfeld and Nicholson: London, 1968).

Stephen Graubard, ed., *A New Europe?* (Houghton Mifflin: Boston, 1964).

Stanley Hoffmann, ed., *In Search of France* (Harvard University Press: Cambridge, 1963).

Samuel P. Huntington, "Political Modernization: America vs. Europe," *World Politics*, **28**(3), pages 378-414, April 1966.

Peter Merkl, *Germany, Yesterday and Tomorrow* (Oxford University Press: London, 1965).

_____, *The Origins of the West German Republic* (Oxford University Press: New York, 1965).

John Ney, *The European Surrender; A Descriptive Study of the American Social and Economic Conquest* (Little, Brown: Boston, 1970).

Richard Rose, *Studies in British Politics* (St. Martin's Press: New York, 1968).

Anthony Sampson, *Anatomy of Europe* (Harper: New York, 1968).

Jean-Jacques Servan-Schreiber, *The American Challenge* (Atheneum: New York, 1968).

Harvey Waterman, *Political Change in Contemporary France: The Politics of an Industrial Democracy* (Charles E. Merrill: Columbus, Ohio, 1969).

II Western European Publics in a Changing Environment: Integration and Alienation

For additional discussions of the topics treated in this section, the following works are suggested:

Gabriel Almond and Sidney Verba, *The Civic Culture: Political Attitudes and Democracy in Five Nations* (Princeton University Press: Princeton, 1963).

Edward Banfield, *The Moral Basis of a Backward Society* (The Free Press: Glencoe, 1958).

Jack Dennis, Leon Lindberg, Donald McCrone, and Rodney Stiefbold, "Political Socialization to Democratic Orientations in Four Western Systems," *Comparative Political Studies*, **1**(1), 1968.

Harry Eckstein, *Pressure Group Politics: The Case of the British Medical Association* (Stanford University Press: Stanford, 1960).

Henry W. Ehrmann, ed., *Interest Groups on Four Continents* (Pittsburgh University Press: Pittsburgh, 1958).

W. Feld, "National Economic Interest Groups and Policy Formation in EEC," *Political Science Quarterly*, **81**(3), September 1966.

R. C. Fried, "Urbanization and Italian Politics," *Journal of Politics*, **29**(3), August 1967.

Fred. I. Greenstein and Sidney G. Tarrow, "The Study of French Political Socialization: Toward the Revocation of Paradox," *World Politics*, **XXII**, October 1969.

Richard Hamilton, *Affluence and the French Worker* (Princeton University Press: Princeton, 1967).

Timothy M. Hennessey, "Democratic Attitudinal Configurations Among Italian Youth," *Midwest Journal of Political Science*, **13**(2), May 1969.

Norman Kogan, "Italian Communism, the Working Class, and Organized Catholicism," *Journal of Politics*, **28**(3), August 1966.

Joseph LaPalombara, *The Italian Labor Movement: Problems and Prospects* (Cornell University Press: Ithica, 1957).

Seymour Martin Lipset, "The Changing Class Structure and Contemporary European Politics," *Daedalus*, **93**(1), Winter 1964.

Roy Macridis, "Interest Groups in Comparative Analysis," *Journal of Politics*, **23**(1), 1961.

Richard L. Merritt, "The Student Protest Movement in West Berlin," *Comparative Politics*, **1**(4), July 1969.

Eric A. Nordlinger, *The Working-Class Tories* (MacGibbon and Kee: London, 1967).

Gianfranco Poggi, *Catholic Action in Italy* (Stanford University Press: Stanford, 1967).

William Safran, *Veto-Group Politics; The Case of Health Insurance Reform in West Germany* (Chandler Publishing Company: San Francisco, 1967).

Ronald J. Stupak, "The Military's Ideological Challenge to Civilian Authority in Post-World War II France," *Orbis*, **12**(2), Summer 1968.

Sidney Tarrow, *Peasant Communism in Southern Italy* (Yale University Press: New Haven, 1967).

Laurence William Wylie, ed., *Chanzeaux, A Village in Anjou* (Harvard University Press: Cambridge, 1966).

_____, *Village in the Vaucluse* (Harvard University Press: Cambridge, 1964).

III Political Parties in the New Europe: Adaptation and Resistance

For additional discussions of the topics treated in this section, the following works are suggested:

E. Allardt and Y. Littunen, *Cleavages, Ideologies and Party Systems* (Academic Bookstore: Helsinki, 1964).

Samuel H. Barnes, *Party Democracy: Politics in an Italian Socialist Federation* (Yale University Press: New Haven,(1967).

L. Barzini, "Italy: The Fragile State," *Foreign Affairs*, **46**(3), April 1968.

Donald Blackmer, *Unity and Diversity: Italian Communism and the Communist World* (MIT Press: Cambridge, 1967).

Jean Blondel, "Party Systems and Patterns of Government in Western Democracies," *Canadian Journal of Political Science*, **1**, 1968.

David Butler and Donald Stokes, *Political Change in Britain* (St. Martin's Press: New York, 1969).

John M. Cammet, *Antonio Gramsci and the Origins of the Italian Communist Party* (Stanford University Press: Stanford, 1967).

Douglas Chalmers, *The Social Democratic Party of Germany* (Yale University Press: New Haven, 1964).

Hans Daadler, "Parties, Elites and Political Developments in Western Europe" in Joseph LaPalombara and Myron Weiner, eds., *Political Parties and Political Development* (Princeton University Press: Princeton, 1966).

Robert Dahl, *Political Oppositions in Western Democracies* (Yale University Press: New Haven, 1966).

Maurice Duverger, *Political Parties* (2nd rev. ed., North trans., Science Editions: New York, 1965).

L. D. Epstein, *Political Parties in Western Democracies* (Praeger: New York, 1967).

Stanley Henig, ed., *European Political Parties: A Handbook* (Praeger: New York, 1970).

Stanley Henig and John Pinder, eds., *European Political Parties* (Allen and Unwin: London, 1969).

Seymour Martin Lipset and Stein Rokkan, eds., *Party Systems and Voter Alignments* (The Free Press of Glencoe: New York, 1967).

Gerhard Lowenberg, "The Remaking of the German Party System," *Polity*, **1**(1), Fall 1968.

Giovanni Sartori, *Parties and Party Systems* (Harper and Row: New York, 1971). (Tentative title and publication date.)

Sidney Tarrow, "Economic Development and the Transformation of the Italian Party System," *Comparative Politics*, **1**(2), January 1969.

Philip Williams, *Crisis and Compromise: Politics in the Fourth Republic* (Anchor: New York, 1964).

Frank Wilson, *The Attempted Unification of the French Democratic Left, 1963-1969* (Stanford University Press: Stanford, 1971). (Tentative title and publication date.)

IV The Governmental Response

For additional discussions of the topics treated in this section, the following works are suggested:

Pierre Bauchet, *Economic Planning: The French Experience* (Praeger: New York, 1964).

Samuel Brittain, *Steering the Economy* (Martin Secker and Warburg, Ltd.: London, 1969).

A. H. Brown, "Prime Ministerial Power, Parts I and II," *Public Law*, Spring 1968 and Summer 1968.

Michel Crozier, *The Bureaucratic Phenomenon* (University of Chicago Press: Chicago, 1965).

Gordon J. Di Renzo, *Personality, Power and Politics* (Notre Dame University Press: Notre Dame, 1967).

Alex N. Dragnich, *Major European Governments* (Dorsey Press: Homewood, Ill., 1970).

Lewis Edinger, ed., *Political Leadership in Industrialized Societies* (Wiley: New York, 1967).

Lewis J. Edinger and Donald D. Searing, "Social Background in Elite Analysis," *American Political Science Review*, **21**(2), 1967.

Arrigo Levi, "Italy, The Crisis of Governing," *Foreign Affairs*, **49**(1), October 1970.

Gerhard Loewenberg, *Parliament in the German Political System* (Cornell University Press: Cornell, 1967).

Austin Ranney, *Pathways to Parliament: Candidate Selection in Britain* (Macmillan: London, 1965).

Richard Rose, *People in Politics: Observations Across the Atlantic* (Basic Books: New York, 1970).

_____, *Policy-Making in Britain* (The Free Press: New York, 1969).

V The Challenge of the Future: Some Problems and Prospects

For additional discussions of the topics treated in this section, the following works are suggested:

Louis Armand and Michel Drancourt, *The European Challenge* (Patrick Evans trans., Atheneum: New York, 1970).

Richard J. Barnet and Marcus G. Raskin, *After Twenty Years—The Decline of NATO and the Search for a New Policy in Europe* (Vintage Books: New York, 1966).

Carol Edler Baumann, *Western Europe: What Path to Integration?* (D. C. Heath and Company: Boston, 1967).

Andre Beufre, "Security and Defense in Western Europe," *Orbis*, **13**(1), Spring 1969.

Alastair Buchan, *Europe's Futures, Europe's Choices: Models of Western Europe in the 1970's* (University Press for the Institute for Strategic Studies: New York, 1969).

P. Calvocoressi, "Europe's Alliance Blues," *Political Quarterly*, **37**(4), October-December 1966.

W. Hartley Clark, *The Politics of the Common Market* (Prentice-Hall: Englewood Cliffs, 1967).

Harold van B. Cleveland, "The Common Market After de Gaulle," *Foreign Affairs*, **47**(4), July 1969.

E. Combaux, "French Military Policy and European Federalism," *Orbis*, **13**(1), Spring 1969. Special NATO issue.

Karl W. Deutsch, Lewis J. Edinger, Roy C. Macridis and Richard L. Merritt, *France, Germany and the Western Alliance* (Charles Scribner's Sons: New York, 1967).

Werner Feld, *The European Common Market and the World* (Prentice-Hall: Englewood Cliffs, 1967).

Carl J. Friedrich, *Europe: An Emergent Nation?* (Harper and Row: New York, 1969).

Ernst B. Haas, *The Uniting of Europe; Political, Social and Economic Forces, 1950-1957* (Stanford University Press: Stanford, 1958).

Ronald Inglehart, "An End to European Integration?" *American Political Science Review*, **61**(1), March 1967.

U. W. Kitzinger, *The Politics and Economics of European Integration* (Praeger: New York, 1963).

Christopher Layton, *European Advanced Technology. A Programme for Integration* (George Allen and Unwin, Ltd.: London, 1969).

Leon N. Lindberg, *The Political Dynamics of European Economic Integration* (Stanford University Press: Stanford, 1963).

Leon N. Lindberg and Stuart A. Scheingold, *Europe's Would-be Polity; Patterns of Change in the European Community* (Prentice-Hall: Englewood Cliffs, 1970).

Richard Mayne, *The Community of Europe* (Norton: New York, 1963).

—————, "Economic Integration in the New Europe," *Daedalus*, Vol 93, pp. 109-133, Winter 1964.

John H. Sloane, "Political Integration in the European Community," *Canadian Journal of Political Science*, **1**(4), December 1968.

Hans A. Schmitt, *European Union: From Hitler to de Gaulle* (Van Nostrand Reinhold: New York, 1969).

Franz Josef Strauss, *Challenge and Response; A Programme for Europe* (Henry Fox trans., Atheneum: New York, 1970).

Paul Taylor, "The Concept of Community and the European Integration Process," *Journal of Common Market Studies*, **7**(2), December 1968.

Index